Critiques of
GOD

Critiques of

GOD

KURT BAIER

JOHN DEWEY

PAUL EDWARDS

ANTONY FLEW

SIGMUND FREUD

ERICH FROMM

SIDNEY HOOK

WALTER KAUFMANN

CORLISS LAMONT

WALLACE I. MATSON

H. J. McCLOSKEY

ERNEST NAGEL

KAI NIELSEN

RICHARD ROBINSON

BERTRAND RUSSELL

MICHAEL SCRIVEN

Making the case against belief in God

Edited by
PETER A. ANGELES

Prometheus Books

59 John Glenn Drive
Amherst, New York 14228-2197

Published 1997 by Prometheus Books

Inquiries should be addressed to
Prometheus Books
59 John Glenn Drive
Amherst, New York 14228–2197
VOICE: 716–691–0133, ext. 207
FAX: 716–564–2711
WWW.PROMETHEUSBOOKS.COM

05 04 03 02 01   7 6 5 4 3

Library of Congress Cataloging-in-Publication Data

Critiques of God / edited by Peter Angeles.
     p. cm.
    Originally published: Buffalo, N.Y. : Prometheus Books, 1976.
    Includes bibliographical references.
    ISBN 1–57392–123–8 (pbk. : alk. paper)
    1. God. 2. Atheism. 3. Religion—Philosophy. I. Angeles, Peter Adam,
1931–   .

BT102.C74   1997
211—dc21   96–40053
                                               CIP

Printed in the United States of America on acid-free paper

DEDICATED

to

DALLAS POTTINGER

and

ADAM SEBESTYEN

Contents

III. ARGUMENTS FOR GOD'S EXISTENCE

IV. FAITH AND REASON

V. MYSTICISM

VI. RELIGION AND THE RELIGIOUS

XII. SCIENCE AND THE RELIGIOUS IMPULSE

Preface

There is no anthology in the philosophy of religion that exclusively presents the case against God. This one does. Anthologies have favored religious beliefs or they have presented a mixture of arguments, pro and con, usually favoring the former. The selections here make explicit the basic criticisms of the God concept and some of its related paraphernalia. They reveal the many modes of reasoning involved in theorizing about God. The authors are all well known in philosophy. They write sincerely, candidly and honestly about the issues in a straightforward, "no-holds-barred" fashion. They were chosen for these qualities.

The themes being criticized throughout this anthology are:

1. The universe owes its original and continued existence to an immaterial, omnipotent, omniscient, omnipresent and omnibenevolent God.

2. The God concept answers the questions "Why is there a universe at all?" and "Why should things be this way rather than some other way?"

3. This God can be known by some specific means or a variety of means: reason, faith, revelation, the mystical experience, biblical authority and tradition.

4. Scientific knowledge is limited knowledge that gives only a partial view (only the mechanical activities) of reality. Scientific knowledge does not give us an adequate and total explanation of the universe. The God concept is required to end the infinite search for a completed system of explanation for the universe.

5. God is a cosmic mind as evidenced in the design and purposiveness of all things.

6. This God created the universe for a particular purpose.

7. God's purpose is to create in His own image a creature who will glorify and stand in awe of Him as a sacred and mysterious object and will, only with His assistance, become a moral creature capable of receiving the gift of eternal immortality bestowed by His grace.

8. God is the source of all good that exists.

9. Morality can only be what is sanctioned and wished by God.

10. Man's fate ultimately is related to (regulated by) the omniscience and omnipotence of an omnibenevolent and omnipresent God.

2

If there is a desire to validate specific religious claims, that desire must rest on the justification given to the concept of a God. So it is, especially in our Judeo-Christian tradition. When asked why he goes to Mass as opposed to, say, the theater, a Roman Catholic at some point will have to appeal for justification to his belief in God: all things owe their being to God; God took human form in Jesus, who was born of a virgin; Jesus was crucified so that man could be saved from his sinfulness inherited from Adam; man can redeem himself by taking holy communion, whereby he absorbs, physically and spiritually, the body and the blood of Jesus; and so it goes. All of his beliefs (miracles, the existence of angels, creation, immortality, purpose) eventually will be seen to be justifiable only on the grounds of a God.

The concept of a God as a causal agent has been taken less and less seriously during the past two hundred years. The movement of the "heavenly" bodies, diseases, the ebb and flow of the oceans, earthquakes, famines, floods, wars, the origin of the universe and life, the course of history, the subconscious—these and many more natural events have been related at one time or another to the deliberate activity of God. As our knowledge of the universe increases, we recognize that all forms of phenomena can be explained in terms of the interrelatedness of natural processes without reference to a God.

Beliefs in supernatural beings have vanished from our culture. Any general serious belief in God is fading in our culture. God has lost his spatial location as a monarch in heaven. He has lost his temporal precedence to the universe as its Creator ex nihilo. It is not that God is being relegated to a remote region. It is not that God has become a bodiless abstraction (a sexless It). It is the realization that there is *no* God left to which to relate.

Without God, what is left? Man and the universe. That should be enough. That *has* to be enough because that is all there is. Our morals, our emotional reactions, our purpose in life and the universe have been explained as originating in God. A message as old as the expression of human thought, and which is gaining ascendancy, tells us that man's motivation and orientation must be found—and can only be found— within his individual and social structures and ideals that must encompass mankind as a whole. The ardor men once held for God must be ardor showered upon man and mankind's potential for good and for survival.

It has been argued in many diverse quarters that human beings have a fundamental and deep-seated philosophic need to view the universe as a whole and to relate in a meaningful way to that whole. In metaphysics and theology there is a persistent desire to present a coherent and comprehensive picture of the universe as an interrelated whole in which man has a place—or can find his place. Without this general outlook, it is believed, man's life is insignificant and impoverished.

This desire reflects a primal urge in man as a symbol-relating and symbol-creating organism to relate meaningfully to his surroundings as far as thoughts of those surroundings can be extended. It may even be acknowledged that a satisfactory definition of religion is "the attempt of man to relate in a meaningful way to other humans, to himself and to the universe around him." Nevertheless, reference to God is not an integral part of the fulfillment of this desire. A meaningful relationship of man with things around him and within him can be accomplished without the superfluity of God. Religion has to do with man, not God. For my part, I have no desire to relate my fragmentary life to the universe as a whole in order to find significance. And I find my life not in the slightest impoverished because of this supposed lack. I do not believe that man "has" a place in the universe. Nor do I believe that man can "find" *his place* in the universe. But I believe that man can find *a* place—if *he* cares to—in the universe, and—if *he* cares to—he can find a rather noble and relatively significant one at that.

I am. I am in many respects an insignificant part of the universe. I accept that. I acccept that without remorse or sadness because there are many things about living that I enjoy and cherish and love whether I am the center of the universe or not, whether I am a significant aspect of the universe or not, whether I "have" a purpose in the universe assigned by God or not. Any significance to be found in life will *not* be found, except illusorily, in relating myself to the universe as a whole—to the imagined grand design of the universe—but in making the best I can with what I have and with what I can develop cooperatively with others who love man and mankind. My life feels impoverished and insignificant not when I cannot relate it meaningfully to the universe as a whole but when I cannot take some of my life, and some of the universe, into my hands and make art out of them.

I am. But I don't believe that the universe particularly cares for me as an individual. Again, that doesn't bother me. Why should the universe care? The universe will "care" only if *I* care. The universe will care for us only if we each take care of ourselves and others. How can the universe care when it is not a personality but an existentiality? Nor does the universe care for species. (I have often heard it said that nature does not concern itself with the preservation of individuals but that it does concern itself with the preservation of the species.) Given enough time, all things as they stand are dispensable, and we must accept this courageously. All we can do is, with our efforts, extend that time period by evolving to meet the challenges in that inexorable movement toward dispensability.

I am. And in existing I must create meaning from my own depths and with my own resources in conjunction with others who also seek to act and create humane meaning. There are no alternatives to this other than ennui and the eventual destruction of mankind.

3

The selections of this anthology are not snippets. They are either chapters from books or articles from journals, and they have been kept intact to convey the author's style as well as the mood that permeates the original work. With the exception of four essays, all the readings have been selected from books that are easily accessible for further, more complete perusal and which can be used as supplements to this volume. There are many excellent authors whom I agonizingly could not include, such as Raziel Abelson, A. J. Ayer, Paul Blanshard, Arthur C. Danto, Clarence Darrow, William Dennes, J. N. Findlay, Hector Hawton, Ronald Hepburn, Robert Ingersoll, Paul Kurtz, Alasdair MacIntyre, C. B. Martin, H. L. Mencken, George Nakhnikian, Max Otto, Mark Twain, and Marvin Zimmerman.

Reference has been made to many of them in the selective bibliography at the end of the text. Originally the thrust of this anthology was to present choice articles hidden in philosophy journals and not readily available. Readers of this volume may want to pursue this approach, so I include below a short bibliography to indicate in a general way some of the articles I would have selected. Sometime in the future there may be an opportunity to edit an anthology that solely presents some of the unique critiques of God found in the journals. The decision for the present approach was based on the wish to present essays by authors of known stature that would be of value to undergraduate philosophy classes as well as to the general public.

Alston, William P. "Ineffability," *Philosophical Review* 65 (1956): 506-22.
————. "The Ontological Argument Revisited," *Philosophical Review* 69 (1960): 452-74.
Ayer, A. J. "The Fallacies of Deism," *Polemic*, no. 1.
Dodds, E. R. "Why I Do Not Believe in Survival," *Proceedings of the Society for Psychical Research*, 1934.
Findlay, J. N. "Can God's Existence Be Disproved?" *Mind* 57 (1948): 176-83.
Haight, David F., and Haight, Marjorie A. "An Ontological Argument for the Devil," *The Monist* 54, no. 2 (April 1970): 606-8.
Henle, Paul. "Mysticism and Semantics," *Philosophy and Phenomenological Research* 9, no. 3 (March 1949): 416-22.
Hoffman, B. "Logic, Meaning and Mystical Intuition," *Philosophical Studies* 11, no. 5 (October 1960): 65-70.
Kennick, W. E. "A New Way with the Five Ways," *Australasian Journal of Psychology and Philosophy* 38, no. 3 (December 1960): 225-33.
Kretzmann, Norman. "Omniscience and Immutability," *Journal of Philosophy* 63, no. 14 (July 14, 1966): 409-21.
MacIntyre, A. C. "God and the Theologians," *Encounter* 21, no. 3 (September 1963): 3-10.
Mackie, John. "Evil and Omnipotence," *Mind* 64, no. 254 (April 1955): 200-12.
————. "Omnipotence," *Sophia* (1963).

McPherson, T. "The Argument from Design," *Philosophy* 32, no. 122 (July 1957): 219-28.

Puccetti, R. "The Concept of God," *Philosophical Quarterly* 14 (1964): 237-45.

———. "Omniscient God," *Australasian Journal of Philosophy* 41 (1963): 92-3.

Shaffer, Jerome. "Existence, Predication, and the Ontological Argument," *Mind* 71 (1962): 307-25.

Smart, J. J. C. "The Existence of God," *Church Quarterly Review* 156 (1955): 178-94. (Based on a public lecture given at the University of Adelaide in 1951.)

Smith, Norman Kemp. "Is Divine Existence Credible?" *Proceedings of the British Academy* 17 (1931): 209-34. (The Annual Philosophical Lecture, the Henriette Hertz Trust, read July 15, 1931.)

Watts, G. Stuart. "The Thomist Proofs of Theism," *Australasian Journal of Philosophy* 35, no. 1 (May 1957): 30-46.

4

I wish to express my thanks to Paul Kurtz, editor of Prometheus Books, who gave me encouragement for this project and made valuable suggestions about its organization, to Lee Nisbet, assistant editor, and to Richard Hagle and Cynthia Dwyer, copy editors, who assisted in getting this through the mill. My gratitude to all the members of my family, my wife Elizabeth and my children, Beth, Jane and Adam, who have all patiently, though sometimes reluctantly, excused my absences from our family activities in order to work on this volume. There were many achievements by them during this time in spite of (perhaps because of) my absence. I am inestimably grateful to my colleagues Dallas Pottinger and Adam Sebestyen—Dallas for his invaluable typing and clerical assistance and Adam for his vast library knowledge and research abilities. I cannot thank them enough for the help they have given me on my previous books as well as on manuscripts on which I am presently working. This book is dedicated to them both in friendship, for we did this as a team. Without their conversations and help I might have lost interest. They illustrate to me the value and importance of people working harmoniously together and interrelating humanely. I especially would like to express my gratitude to Professor Ernest Nagel, whose essays open and close this book. As my former undergraduate and graduate teacher at Columbia University, he has continually served as an example and as an inspiration to me and has taught me the worth of good teaching done with patience, kindness and a love of humans. My thanks also extend to Santa Barbara City College students, faculty, staff and administrators who have contributed to an environment conducive to good teaching and the encouragement of works such as this one.

I. Introduction and a General Critique

Ernest Nagel

Philosophical Concepts of Atheism

Ernest Nagel, university professor emeritus of philosophy at Columbia University, was educated at the City College of New York and at Columbia University. He has served as editor of the *Journal of Philosophy* (1938-56), the *Journal of Symbolic Logic* (1940-46), and *Philosophy of Science* (1956-59). He is the author of several books including: *An Introduction to Logic and Scientific Method* (1934, with Morris Cohen); *Principles of the Theory of Probability* (1939); *Sovereign Reason* (1954); *Logic Without Metaphysics* (1957); *The Structure of Science* (1961); and *Godel's Proof* (1958, with J. R. Neuman). He has published extensively in philosophical journals. The following essay is one he wrote for an anthology on comparative religions.

3

... This ... paper ... will show how atheism belongs to the great tradition of religious thought. ... Bertrand Russell reports [an anecdote] in his ... book *Portraits from Memory*. Russell was imprisoned during the First World War for pacifistic activities. On entering the prison he was asked a number of customary questions about himself for the prison records. One question was about his religion. Russell explained that he was an agnostic. "Never heard of it," the warden declared. "How do you spell it?" When Russell told him, the warden observed, "Well, there are many religions, but I suppose they all worship the same God." Russell adds that this remark kept him cheerful for about a week. Perhaps philosophical atheism also is a religion.

1

I must begin by stating what sense I am attaching to the word "atheism," and how I am construing the theme of this paper. I shall understand by "atheism" a critique and a denial of the major claims of all varieties of theism. And by theism I shall mean the view which holds, as one writer has expressed it, "that the heavens and the earth and all that they contain owe their existence and continuance in existence to the wisdom and will of a supreme, self-consistent, omnipotent, omniscient, righteous, and benevolent being, who is distinct from, and independent of, what he has created." Several things immediately follow from these definitions.

In the first place, atheism is not necessarily an irreligious concept, for theism is just one among many views concerning the nature and origin of the world. The denial of theism is logically compatible with a religious outlook upon life, and is in fact characteristic of some of the great historical religions. For as readers of this volume will know, early Buddhism is a religion which does not subscribe to any doctrine about a god; and there are pantheistic religions and philosophies which, because they deny that God is a being separate from and independent of the world, are not theistic in the sense of the word explained above.

The second point to note is that atheism is not to be identified with sheer unbelief, or with disbelief in some particular creed of a religious group. Thus, a child who has received no religious instruction and has never heard about God, is not an atheist—for he is not denying any

From Ernest Nagel, Basic Beliefs: The Religious Philosophies of Mankind *(New York: Sheridan House, 1959), pp. 173-92. Reprinted by permission of Sheridan House Publishers, New York.*

theistic claims. Similarly in the case of an adult who, if he has withdrawn from the faith of his fathers without reflection or because of frank indifference to any theological issue, is also not an atheist—for such an adult is not challenging theism and is not professing any views on the subject. Moreover, though the term "atheist" has been used historically as an abusive label for those who do not happen to subscribe to some regnant orthodoxy (for example, the ancient Romans called the early Christians atheists, because the latter denied the Roman divinities), or for those who engage in conduct regarded as immoral, it is not in this sense that I am discussing atheism.

One final word of preliminary explanation. I propose to examine some *philosophic* concepts of atheism, and I am not interested in the slightest in the many considerations atheists have advanced against the evidences for some particular religious and theological doctrine—for example, against the truth of the Christian story. What I mean by "philosophical" in the present context is that the views I shall consider are directed against any form of theism, and have their origin and basis in a logical analysis of the theistic position, and in a comprehensive account of the world believed to be wholly intelligible without the adoption of a theistic hypothesis.

Theism as I conceive it is a theological proposition, not a statement of a position that belongs primarily to religion. On my view, religion as a historical and social phenomenon is primarily an institutionalized *cultus* or practice, which possesses identifiable social functions and which expresses certain attitudes men take toward their world. Although it is doubtful whether men ever engage in religious practices or assume religious attitudes without some more or less explicit interpretation of their ritual or some rationale for their attitude, it is still the case that it is possible to distinguish religion as a social and personal phenomenon from the theological doctrines which may be developed as justifications for religious practices. Indeed, in some of the great religions of the world the profession of a creed plays a relatively minor role. In short, religion is a form of social communion, a participation in certain kinds of ritual (whether it be a dance, worship, prayer, or the like), and a form of experience (sometimes, though not invariably, directed to a personal confrontation with divine and holy things). Theology is an articulated and, at its best, a rational attempt at understanding these feelings and practices, in the light of their relation to other parts of human experience, and in terms of some hypothesis concerning the nature of things entire.

2

As I see it, atheistic philosophies fall into two major groups: (1) those which hold that the theistic doctrine is meaningful, but reject it either on the ground that (a) the positive evidence for it is insufficient, or (b) the negative evidence is quite overwhelming; and (2) those who hold that the theistic thesis is not even meaningful, and reject it (a) as just nonsense or (b) as literally meaningless but interpreting it as a symbolic rendering of human ideals, thus reading the theistic thesis in a sense that most believers in theism would disavow. It will not be possible in the limited space at my disposal to discuss the second category of atheistic critiques; and in any event, most of the traditional atheistic critiques of theism belong to the first group.

But before turning to the philosophical examination of the major classical arguments for theism, it is well to note that such philosophical critiques do not quite convey the passion with which atheists have often carried on their analyses of theistic views. For historically, atheism has been, and indeed continues to be, a form of social and political protest, directed as much against institutionalized religion as against theistic doctrine. Atheism has been, in effect, a moral revulsion against the undoubted abuses of the secular power exercised by religious leaders and religious institutions.

Religious authorities have opposed the correction of glaring injustices, and encouraged politically and socially reactionary policies. Religious institutions have been havens of obscurantist thought and centers for the dissemination of intolerance. Religious creeds have been used to set limits to free inquiry, to perpetuate inhumane treatment of the ill and the under-privileged, and to support moral doctrines insensitive to human suffering.

These indictments may not tell the whole story about the historical significance of religion; but they are at least an important part of the story. The refutation of theism has thus seemed to many as an indispensable step not only towards liberating men's minds from superstition, but also towards achieving a more equitable reordering of society. And no account of even the more philosophical aspects of atheistic thought is adequate which does not give proper recognition to the powerful social motives that actuate many atheistic arguments.

But however this may be, I want now to discuss three classical arguments for the existence of God, arguments which have constituted at least a partial basis for theistic commitments. As long as theism is defended simply as a dogma, asserted as a matter of direct revelation or as the deliverance of authority, belief in the dogma is impregnable to rational argument. In fact, however, reasons are frequently advanced in support of the theistic creed, and these reasons have been the subject of acute philosophical critiques.

One of the oldest intellectual defenses of theism is the cosmological argument, also known as the argument from a first cause. Briefly put, the argument runs as follows. Every event must have a cause. Hence an event A must have as cause some event B, which in turn must have a cause C, and so on. But if there is no end to this backward progression of causes, the progression will be infinite; and in the opinion of those who use this argument, an infinite series of actual events is unintelligible and absurd. Hence there must be a first cause, and this first cause is God, the initiator of all change in the universe.

The argument is an ancient one, and is especially effective when stated within the framework of assumptions of Aristotelian physics; and it has impressed many generations of exceptionally keen minds. The argument is nonetheless a weak reed on which to rest the theistic thesis. Let us waive any question concerning the validity of the principle that every event has a cause, for though the question is important its discussion would lead us far afield. However, if the principle is assumed, it is surely incongruous to postulate a first cause as a way of escaping from the coils of an infinite series. For if everything must have a cause, why does not God require one for His own existence? The standard answer is that He does not need any, because He is self-caused. But if God can be self-caused, why cannot the world itself be self-caused? Why do we require a God transcending the world to bring the world into existence and to initiate changes in it? On the other hand, the supposed inconceivability and absurdity of an infinite series of regressive causes will be admitted by no one who has competent familiarity with the modern mathematical analysis of infinity. The cosmological argument does not stand up under scrutiny.

The second "proof" of God's existence is usually called the ontological argument. It too has a long history going back to early Christian days, though it acquired great prominence only in medieval times. The argument can be stated in several ways, one of which is the following. Since God is conceived to be omnipotent, he is a perfect being. A perfect being is defined as one whose essence or nature lacks no attributes (or properties) whatsoever, one whose nature is complete in every respect. But it is evident that we have an idea of a perfect being, for we have just defined the idea; and since this is so, the argument continues, God who is the perfect being must exist. Why must he? Because his existence follows from his defined nature. For if God lacked the attribute of existence, he would be lacking at least one attribute, and would therefore not be perfect. To sum up, since we have an idea of God as a perfect being, God must exist.

There are several ways of approaching this argument, but I shall consider only one. The argument was exploded by the 18th-century philosopher Immanuel Kant. The substance of Kant's criticism is that it is just a confusion to say that existence is an attribute, and that though the *word* "existence" may occur as the grammatical predicate in the sentence, no attribute is being predicated of a thing when we say that the thing exists or has existence. Thus, to use Kant's example, when we think of $100 we are thinking of the nature of this sum of money; but the nature of $100 remains the same whether we have $100 in our pockets or not. Accordingly, we are confounding grammar with logic if we suppose that some characteristic is being attributed to the nature of $100 when we say that a hundred-dollar bill exists in someone's pocket.

To make the point clearer, consider another example. When we say that a lion has a tawny color, we are predicating a certain attribute of the animal, and similarly when we say that the lion is fierce or is hungry. But when we say the lion exists, all that we are saying is that something is (or has the nature of) a lion; we are not specifying an attribute which belongs to the nature of anything that is a lion. In short, the word "existence" does not signify any attribute, and in consequence no attribute that belongs to the nature of anything. Accordingly, it does not follow from the assumption that we have an idea of a perfect being that such a being exists. For the idea of a perfect being does not involve the attribute of existence as a constituent of that idea, since there is no such attribute. The ontological argument thus has a serious leak, and it can hold no water.

3

The two arguments discussed thus far are purely dialectical, and attempt to establish God's existence without any appeal to empirical data. The next argument, called the argument from design, is different in character, for it is based on what purports to be empirical evidence. I wish to examine two forms of this argument.

One variant of it calls attention to the remarkable way in which different things and processes in the world are integrated with each other, and concludes that this mutual "fitness" of things can be explained only by the assumption of a divine architect who planned the world and everything in it. For example, living organisms can maintain themselves in a variety of environments, and do so in virtue of their delicate mechanisms which adapt the organisms to all sorts of environmental changes. There is thus an intricate pattern of means and ends throughout the animate world. But the existence of this pattern is unintelligible, so the argument runs, except on the hypothesis that the pattern has been deliberately instituted by a supreme designer. If we find a watch in some deserted spot, we do not think it came into existence by chance, and we do not hesitate to conclude that an intelligent creature designed and made it. But the world and all its contents exhibit mechanisms and mutual adjustments that are far more complicated and subtle than are those of a watch. Must we not therefore conclude that these things too have a Creator?

The conclusion of this argument is based on an inference from analogy: the watch and the world are alike in possessing a congruence of parts and an adjustment of means to ends; the watch has a watchmaker; hence the world has a worldmaker. But is the analogy a good one? Let us once more waive some important issues, in particular the issue whether the universe is the unified system such as the watch admittedly is. And let us concentrate on the question, What is the ground for our assurance that watches do not come into existence except through the operations of intelligent manufacturers? The answer is plain. We have never run across a watch which has not been deliberately made by someone. But the situation is nothing like this in the case of the innumerable animate and inanimate systems with which we are familiar. Even in the case of living organisms, though they are generated by their parent organisms, the parents do not "make" their progeny in the same sense in which watchmakers make watches. And once this point is clear, the inference from the existence of living organisms to the existence of a supreme designer no longer appears credible.

Moreover, the argument loses all its force if the facts which the hypothesis of a divine designer is supposed to explain can be understood on the basis of a better supported assumption. And indeed, such an alternative explanation is one of the achievements of Darwinian biology. For

Darwin showed that one can account for the variety of biological species, as well as for their adaptations to their environments, without invoking a divine creator and acts of special creation. The Darwinian theory explains the diversity of biological species in terms of chance variations in the structure of organisms, and of a mechanism of selection which retains those variant forms that possess some advantages for survival. The evidence for these assumptions is considerable; and developments subsequent to Darwin have only strengthened the case for a thoroughly naturalistic explanation of the facts of biological adaptation. In any event, this version of the argument from design has nothing to recommend it.

A second form of this argument has been recently revived in the speculations of some modern physicists. No one who is familiar with the facts can fail to be impressed by the success with which the use of mathematical methods has enabled us to obtain intellectual mastery of many parts of nature. But some thinkers have therefore concluded that since the book of nature is ostensibly written in mathematical language, nature must be the creation of a divine mathematician. However, the argument is most dubious. For it rests, among other things, on the assumption that mathematical tools can be successfully used only if the events of nature exhibit some *special* kind of order, and on the further assumption that if the structure of things were different from what they are mathematical language would be inadequate for describing such structure. But it can be shown that no matter what the world were like—even if it impressed us as being utterly chaotic—it would still possess some order, and would in principle be amenable to a mathematical description. In point of fact, it makes no sense to say that there is absolutely *no* pattern in any conceivable subject matter. To be sure, there are differences in complexities of structure, and if the patterns of events were sufficiently complex we might not be able to unravel them. But however that may be, the success of mathematical physics in giving us some understanding of the world around us does not yield the conclusion that only a mathematician could have devised the patterns of order we have discovered in nature.

4

The inconclusiveness of the three classical arguments for the existence of God was already made evident by Kant, in a manner substantially no different from the above discussion. There are, however, other types of arguments for theism that have been influential in the history of thought, two of which I wish to consider, even if only briefly.

Indeed, though Kant destroyed the classical intellectual foundations for theism, he himself invented a fresh argument for it. Kant's attempted proof is not intended to be a purely theoretical demonstration, and is based on the supposed facts of our moral nature. It has exerted an enormous influence on subsequent theological speculation. In barest outline, the argument is as follows. According to Kant, we are subject not only to physical laws like the rest of nature, but also to moral ones. These moral laws are categorical imperatives, which we must heed not because of their utilitarian consequences, but simply because as autonomous moral agents it is our duty to accept them as binding. However, Kant was keenly aware that though virtue may be its reward, the virtuous man (that is, the man who acts out of a sense of duty and in conformity with the moral law) does not always receive his just deserts in this world; nor did he shut his eyes to the fact that evil men frequently enjoy the best things this world has to offer. In short, virtue does not always reap happiness. Nevertheless, the highest human good is the realization of happiness commensurate with one's virtue; and Kant believed that it is a practical postulate of the moral life to promote this good. But what can guarantee that the highest good is realizable? Such a guarantee can be found only in God, who must therefore exist if the highest good is not to be a fatuous ideal. The existence of an omnipotent, omniscient, and omnibenevolent God is thus postulated as a necessary condition for the possibility of a moral life.

Despite the prestige this argument has acquired, it is difficult to grant it any force. It is easy enough to postulate God's existence. But as Bertrand Russell observed in another connection, postulation has all the advantages of theft over honest toil. No postulation carries with it any assurance that what is postulated is actually the case. And though we may postulate God's existence as a means to guaranteeing the possibility of realizing happiness together with virtue, the postulation establishes neither the actual realizability of this ideal nor the fact of His existence. Moreover, the argument is not made more cogent when we recognize that it is based squarely on the highly dubious conception that considerations of utility and human happiness must not enter into the determination of what is morally obligatory. Having built his moral theory on a radical separation of means from ends, Kant was driven to the desperate postulation of God's existence in order to relate them again. The argument is thus at best a tour de force, contrived to remedy a fatal flaw in Kant's initial moral assumptions. It carries no conviction to anyone who does not commit Kant's initial blunder.

One further type of argument, pervasive in much Protestant theological literature, deserves brief mention. Arguments of this type take their point of departure from the psychology of religious and mystical experience. Those who have undergone such experiences often report that during the experience they feel themselves to be in the presence of the divine and holy, that they lose their sense of self-identity and become merged with some fundamental reality, or that they enjoy a feeling of total dependence upon some ultimate power. The overwhelming sense of transcending one's finitude which characterizes such vivid periods of life, and of coalescing with some ultimate source of all existence, is then taken to be compelling evidence for the existence of a supreme being. In a variant form of this argument, other theologians have identified God as the object which satisfies the commonly experienced need for integrating one's scattered and conflicting impulses into a coherent unity, or as the subject which is of ultimate concern to us. In short, a proof of God's existence is found in the occurrence of certain distinctive experiences.

It would be flying in the face of well-attested facts were one to deny that such experiences frequently occur. But do these facts constitute evidence for the conclusion based on them? Does the fact, for example, that an individual experiences a profound sense of direct contact with an alleged transcendent ground of all reality constitute competent evidence for the claim that there is such a ground and that it is the immediate cause of the experience? If well-established canons for evaluating evidence are accepted, the answer is surely negative. No one will dispute that many men do have vivid experiences in which such things as ghosts or pink elephants appear before them; but only the hopelessly credulous will without further ado count such experiences as establishing the existence of ghosts and pink elephants. To establish the existence of such things, evidence is required that is obtained under controlled conditions and that can be confirmed by independent inquirers. Again, though a man's report that he is suffering pain may be taken at face value, one cannot take at face value the claim, were he to make it, that it is the food he ate which is the cause (or a contributory cause) of his felt pain—not even if the man were to report a vivid feeling of abdominal disturbance. And similarly, an overwhelming feeling of being in the presence of the Divine is evidence enough for admitting the genuineness of such feeling; it is no evidence for the claim that a supreme being with a substantial existence independent of the experience is the cause of the experience.

5

Thus far the discussion has been concerned with noting inadequacies in various arguments widely used to support theism. However, much atheistic criticism is also directed toward exposing incoherencies in the very thesis of theism. I want therefore to consider this aspect of the atheistic critique, though I will restrict myself to the central difficulty in the theistic position which arises from the simultaneous attribution of omnipotence, omniscience, and omnibenevolence to the Deity. The difficulty is that of reconciling these attributes with the occurrence of evil in the world. Accordingly, the question to which I now turn is whether, despite the existence of evil, it is possible to construct a theodicy which will justify the ways of an infinitely powerful and just God to man.

Two main types of solutions have been proposed for this problem. One way that is frequently used is to maintain that what is commonly called evil is only an illusion, or at worst only the "privation" or absence of good. Accordingly, evil is not "really real," it is only the "negative" side of God's beneficence, it is only the product of our limited intelligence which fails to plumb the true character of God's creative bounty. A sufficient comment on this proposed solution is that facts are not altered or abolished by rebaptizing them. Evil may indeed be only an appearance and not genuine. But this does not eliminate from the realm of appearance the tragedies, the sufferings, and the iniquities which men so frequently endure. And it raises once more, though on another level, the problem of reconciling the fact that there is evil in the realm of appearance with God's alleged omnibenevolence. In any event, it is small comfort to anyone suffering a cruel misfortune for which he is in no way responsible to be told that what he is undergoing is only the absence of good. It is a gratuitous insult to mankind, a symptom of insensitivity and indifference to human suffering, to be assured that all the miseries and agonies men experience are only illusory.

Another gambit often played in attempting to justify the ways of God to man is to argue that the things called evil are evil only because they are viewed in isolation; they are not evil when viewed in proper perspective and in relation to the rest of creation. Thus, if one attends to but a single instrument in an orchestra, the sounds issuing from it may indeed be harsh and discordant. But if one is placed at a proper distance from the whole orchestra, the sounds of that single instrument will mingle with the sounds issuing from the other players to produce a marvelous bit of symphonic music. Analogously, experiences we call painful undoubtedly occur and are real enough. But the pain is judged to be an evil only because it is experienced in a limited perspective—the pain is there for the sake of a more inclusive good, whose reality eludes us because our intelligences are too weak to apprehend things in their entirety.

It is an appropriate retort to this argument that of course we judge things to be evil in a human perspective, but that since we are not God this is the only proper perspective in which to judge them. It may indeed be the case that what is evil for us is not evil for some other part of creation. However, we are not this other part of creation, and it is irrelevant to argue that were we something other than what we are, our evaluations of what is good and bad would be different. Moreover, the worthlessness of the argument becomes even more evident if we remind ourselves that it is unsupported speculation to suppose that whatever is evil in a finite perspective is good from the purported perspective of the totality of things. For the argument can be turned around: what we judge to be a good is a good only because it is viewed in isolation; when it is viewed in proper perspective, and in relation to the entire scheme of things, it is an evil. This is in fact a standard form of the argument for a universal pessimism. Is it any worse than the similar argument for a universal optimism? The very raising of this question is a *reductio ad absurdum* of the proposed solution to the ancient problem of evil.

I do not believe it is possible to reconcile the alleged omnipotence and omnibenevolence of God with the unvarnished facts of human existence. In point of fact, many theologians have concurred in this conclusion; for in order to escape from the difficulty which the traditional attributes of God present, they have assumed that God is not all-powerful, and that there are limits as to what He can do in his efforts to establish a righteous order in the universe. But whether such a modified theology is better off, is doubtful; and in any event, the question still remains whether the facts of human life support the claim that an omnibenevolent deity, though limited in power, is revealed in the ordering of human history. It is pertinent to note in this connection that though there have been many historians who have made the effort, no historian has yet succeeded in showing to the satisfaction of his professional colleagues that the hypothesis of a divine providence is capable of explaining anything which cannot be explained just as well without this hypothesis.

6

This last remark naturally leads to the question whether, apart from their polemics against theism, philosophical atheists have not shared a common set of positive views, a common set of philosophical convictions which set them off from other groups of thinkers. In one very clear sense of this query the answer is indubitably negative. For there never has been what one might call a "school of atheism," in the way in which there has been a Platonic school or even a Kantian school. In point of fact, atheistic critics of theism can be found among many of the conventional groupings of philosophical thinkers—even, I venture to add, among professional theologians in recent years who in effect preach atheism in the guise of language taken bodily from the Christian tradition.

Nevertheless, despite the variety of philosophical positions to which at one time or another in the history of thought atheists have subscribed, it seems to me that atheism is not simply a negative standpoint. At any rate, there is a certain quality of intellectual temper that has characterized, and continues to characterize, many philosophical atheists. (I am excluding from consideration the so-called "village atheist," whose primary concern is to twit and ridicule those who accept some form of theism, or for that matter those who have any religious convictions.) Moreover, their rejection of theism is based not only on the inadequacies they have found in the arguments for theism, but often also on the positive ground that atheism is a corollary to a better supported general outlook upon the nature of things. I want therefore to conclude this discussion with a brief enumeration of some points of positive doctrine to which, by and large, philosophical atheists seem to me to subscribe. These points fall into three major groups.

In the first place, philosophical atheists reject the assumption that there are disembodied spirits, or that incorporeal entities of any sort can exercise a causal agency. On the contrary, atheists are generally agreed that if we wish to achieve any understanding of what takes place in the universe, we must look to the operations of organized bodies. Accordingly, the various processes taking place in nature, whether animate or inanimate, are to be explained in terms of the properties and structures of identifiable and spatio-temporally located objects. Moreover, the present variety of systems and activities found in the universe is to be accounted for on the basis of the transformations things undergo when they enter into different relations with one another—transformations which often result in the emergence of novel kinds of objects. On the other hand, though things are in flux and undergo alteration, there is no all-encompassing unitary pattern of change. Nature is ineradicably plural, both in respect to the individuals occurring in it as well as in respect to the processes in which things become involved. Accordingly, the human scene and the human perspective are not illusory; and man and his works are no less and no more "real" than are other parts or phases of the cosmos. At the risk of using a possibly misleading characterization, all of this can be summarized by saying that an atheistic view of things is a form of materialism.

In the second place, atheists generally manifest a marked empirical temper, and often take as their ideal the intellectual methods employed in the contemporaneous empirical sciences. Philosophical atheists differ considerably on important points of detail in their accounts of how responsible claims to knowledge are to be established. But there is substantial agreement among them that controlled sensory observation is the court of final appeal in issues concerning matters of fact. It is indeed this commitment to the use of an empirical method which is the final basis of the atheistic critique of theism. For at bottom this critique seeks to show that we can understand whatever a theistic assumption is alleged to explain, through the use of the proved methods of the positive sciences and without the introduction of empirically unsupported ad hoc hypotheses about a deity. It is pertinent in this connection to recall a familiar legend about the French mathematical physicist Laplace. According to the story, Laplace made a personal presentation of a copy of his now famous book on celestial mechanics to Napoleon. Napoleon glanced through the volume, and finding no reference to the Deity asked Laplace whether God's existence played any role in the analysis. "Sire, I have no need for that hypothesis," Laplace is reported to have replied. The dismissal of sterile hypothesis characterizes not only the work of Laplace; it is the uniform rule in scientific inquiry. The sterility of the theistic assumption is one of the main burdens of the literature of atheism, both ancient and modern.

And finally, atheistic thinkers have generally accepted a utilitarian basis for judging moral issues, and they have exhibited a libertarian attitude toward human needs and impulses. The conceptions of the human good they have advocated are conceptions which are commensurate with the actual capacities of mortal men, so that it is the satisfaction of the complex needs of the human creature which is the final standard for evaluating the validity of a moral ideal or moral prescription.

In consequence, the emphasis of atheistic moral reflection has been this-worldly rather than other-worldly, individualistic rather than authoritarian. The stress upon a good life that must be consummated in this world has made atheists vigorous opponents of moral codes which seek to repress human impulses in the name of some unrealizable other-worldly ideal. The individualism that is so pronounced a strain in many philosophical atheists has made them tolerant of human limitations and sensitive to the plurality of legitimate moral goals. On the other hand, this individualism has certainly not prevented many of them from recognizing the crucial role which institutional arrangements can play in achieving desirable patterns of human living. In consequence, atheists have made important contributions to the development of a climate of opinion favorable to pursuing the values of a liberal civilization and they have played effective roles in attempts to rectify social injustices.

Atheists cannot build their moral outlook on foundations upon which so many men conduct their lives. In particular, atheism cannot offer the incentives to conduct and the consolations for misfortune which theistic religions supply to their adherents. It can offer no hope of personal immortality, no threats of divine chastisement, no promise of eventual recompense for injustices suffered, no blueprints to sure salvation. For on its view of the place of man in nature, human excellence and human dignity must be achieved within a finite life-span, or not at all, so that the rewards of moral endeavor must come from the quality of civilized living, and not from some source of disbursement that dwells outside of time. Accordingly, atheistic moral reflection at its best does not culminate in a quiescent ideal of human perfection, but is a vigorous call to intelligent activity—activity for the sake of realizing human potentialities and for eliminating whatever stands in the way of such realization. Nevertheless, though slavish resignation to remediable ills is not characteristic of atheistic thought, responsible atheists have never pretended that human effort can invariably achieve the heart's every legitimate desire. A tragic view of life is thus an uneliminable ingredient in atheistic thought. This ingredient does not invite or generally produce lugubrious lamentation. But it does touch the atheist's view of man and his place in nature with an emotion that makes the philosophical atheist a kindred spirit to those who, within the frameworks of various religious traditions, have developed a serenely resigned attitude toward the inevitable tragedies of the human estate.

II. The God Concept

Sidney Hook

Modern Knowledge and the Concept of God

Sidney Hook, professor of philosophy at New York University, was educated at the City College of New York and at Columbia University. He is the author of many books on a variety of subjects, some of which include: *Towards the Understanding of Karl Marx* (1933); *The Quest for Being* (1934); *From Hegel to Marx* (1936); *Planned Society—Yesterday, Today and Tomorrow* (1937); *John Dewey: An Intellectual Portrait* (1939); *Reason, Social Myths and Democracy* (1940); *The Hero in History* (1943); and *Education for Modern Man* (1946). He has contributed articles to a wide range of professional journals in philosophy, ethics, sociology, political science and education. He has organized a number of conferences on political and philosophical themes.

1

Many years ago when I was in a discussion with Jacques Maritain he remarked that anyone who was as keenly interested in arguments for the existence of God as I seemed to be was not beyond hope of redemption. One can with equal justification observe that strong concern with the validity of the arguments for God's existence threatens the integrity of belief in him. Some believers have become agnostic when they discovered that the chain of argument which was the anchor of their faith had defective links.

I owe it to the reader to indicate that the point of view from which I shall develop my position is that of a still unredeemed, "skeptical God-seeker." I call myself a "God-seeker" because I am willing to go a long way, to the very ends of reason itself, to track down every last semblance of evidence or argument which promises fulfillment of the quest. I call myself a "skeptical God-seeker" because I have so far returned from previous expeditions empty-handed. Since I am prepared to undertake the quest anew, I have not embraced any of the final negations of traditional disbelief which would forever close off further objective inquiry by metaphysical fiat.

This freedom from question-begging commitment is all the more appropriate because I am primarily concerned with "the concept of God" and only secondarily concerned with the question whether that of which we form or have the concept exists. It is of the utmost importance that we abide by this distinction. Who would dispute for long about whether "snow men" exist or whether a "hippogriff" exists without first defining or indicating in a rough way what the meaning of these terms is? Such definitions or concepts do not have to be very precise, but they cannot be so vague that we are unable to distinguish them from definitions and concepts of quite different terms altogether. The least we must know is what we are to count as "snow man" or "hippogriff" before looking for it.

Although this initial demand for clarity is regarded as legitimate in the analysis of most concepts, there is an extraordinary resistance to following the same procedure in connection with the term "God." Many people will heatedly discuss the question whether God exists—without displaying any concern over the fact that they are encompassing the most heterogeneous notions in the use they make of the word "God." After such

From Sidney Hook, Quest for Being (New York: St. Martin's Press, 1961), pp. 115-35. Copyright Sidney Hook. Reprinted by permission of Sidney Hook.

discussions, one is tempted to say, "God only knows what 'God' means."

Now this expression "God only knows what 'God' means" is perfectly good theology, for it can be taken as a way of saying that "Only God has complete or perfect knowledge of God." Unfortunately, however, not only "complete or perfect knowledge" of the meaning of God is denied us by some theologians, but even *adequate* knowledge. According to these theologians, the concept of God refers to something "unique," and therefore it is impossible to describe him in terms which are applicable to other things. Otherwise God would merely be another item in the catalogue of common things. But he is *sui generis*. Father Copleston, the able Jesuit philosopher, puts the point explicitly: "God by hypothesis is unique; and it is quite impossible to describe Him adequately by using concepts which normally apply to ordinary objects of experience. If it were possible, He would not be God . . . this must be so, owing to the finitude of the human intellect. . . . "

Now I believe it can be shown that this conclusion is false. The finitude of the human intellect is no bar to adequate knowledge of other things, even of things which are not finite; for example, we can give an adequate account of an infinite series of integers. Nor can our inability to describe God adequately flow from the presumed uniqueness of God because there are unique things in the world which we can describe adequately in terms that apply to other things. If there was a first man in the world, then by definition he is or was certainly unique. There couldn't be two first men. Nevertheless, we have a rather adequate understanding of what it would mean for anything to be the first man.

What must be intended by Father Copleston and those who share his views is that God is uniquely unique. In order to understand why God is considered uniquely unique, we must recognize the second of the difficulties that are said to be involved in getting an adequate knowledge of God. This is that the concept of God refers to something or someone that *necessarily* exists. What does it mean to say that something necessarily exists? It means that our knowledge of its existence cannot be the conclusion of an empirical or inductive argument, for such can only lead to a probability judgment. Nor can our knowledge be the conclusion of a formal deductive argument—unless the premises are taken as absolutely or necessarily true, which is never the case even with propositions in geometry. The only test which is at all plausible of the necessary truth of an assertion concerning the existence of anything is that the denial of this assertion is self-contradictory. There are enormous difficulties here, the upshot of which is that at most and at best the only assertions which fulfill this requirement are the laws of logic. Everything else which is given or discovered in the world can be otherwise. Now if the laws of logic are taken as formal conditions of discourse, they cannot establish the existence of anything (including God) as necessary. If they are taken as statements about things, then they produce an embarrassing richness of necessary existences. Those who accepted them would be under the intellectual compulsion of finding a way to distinguish between God and other necessary existences. This makes it impossible for believers to use the laws of logic alone, for since they generally assume that the existence of other things *depends* upon God, they cannot accept any method of argument which leads to the conclusion that there are other necessary existences as well. Such a conclusion would entail that God's power is limited. If, for example, we assert that the world necessarily exists, it would be self-contradictory to bring in God as its necessary creator or sustainer.

It should now be clear why those who talk about the concept of God, especially in traditional terms, have such difficulties, and why their arguments keep breaking down. In intellectual fairness we must recognize that they have embarked upon a project of belief which forces them to use the language of paradox and analogy. What exacerbates their difficulty is that the language of paradox and analogy cannot be the same as the ordinary models of paradoxical or analogical discourse. To do injustice to the theologians, imagination must give wings to our understanding and broaden the perspective of our vision. But we must also remain within the horizon of intelligibility or of what makes sense.

If the term "God" has meaning, we must be able to say what it is. If we say what God is, we must be able to describe him in certain distinct combinations of words and sentences, and therefore we must find some principle which controls our statements. No one who regards the term "God" as meaningful will admit the propriety of *any* statement about God, but at the very least he must recognize *degrees* of appropriateness with respect to language. And the problem with which we are wrestling breaks out all over again when we ask: what principle determines the *appropriateness* of the language? For example, the reflective believer in God knows that the epithet "person" or "father" cannot be literally applied to God, that God isn't a person like other persons or a father like other fathers. Nonetheless he finds no difficulty in praying to "Our Father in Heaven." He would, however, deem it singularly inappropriate for anyone to refer to God in prayer as "Our Nephew in Heaven." Why?

The most plausible answer, based upon a study of the names of God and the attributes predicated of him, suggests that the principle which controls the appropriateness of our utterances is derived from the language of human ideals, in their anthropological and ethical dimensions. The conclusion is incontestable that in some sense every intellectual construction of man will reflect his nature. Nor does this fact necessarily entail subjectivity. For even science (which next to mathematics is most frequently taken as a paradigm of objectivity) can be considered a human enterprise whose propositions are constructions of, or inferences from, the data of ordinary experience, and describable in language either continuous with ordinary language or constructed from terms which are ultimately so derived, no matter how technical. But the great difference between God as an object of religious belief, and the objects of scientific belief, is that assertions about the latter are controlled by familiar rules of discourse, understood by all other investigators, that they are related by logical steps to certain experimental consequences, and that these consequences can be described in such a way that we know roughly what counts as evidence for or against the truth of the assertions in question. Now this is not the case with respect to those statements which affirm the existence of God. Certain observable phenomena will sometimes be cited as evidence *for* the truth of the assertion, but it will not be shown how this evidence follows from God's existence; nor will there ever be any indication of what would constitute evidence *against* its truth.

This is what militates against the so-called experimental arguments for the existence of God, as distinguished from the traditional or rationalistic arguments. It must be acknowledged that there is wisdom in the refusal of the traditional position (except for certain aspects of the argument from design) to *risk* the belief in God's existence on any experimental findings. For if it is the case that God's existence is to be inferred from, or confirmed by, the *presence* of certain experimental findings, then the absence of these findings must be taken insofar forth as evidence against the hypothesis. But in fact, those who talk about experimental evidence for the existence of God are obviously prepared to believe in Him no matter what the evidence discloses. It is considered blasphemous in many quarters to put God to any kind of test. Truth or falsity, as we use the terms in ordinary discourse about matters of fact or as synonyms for warranted or unwarranted assertions in science, are not really intended to apply in the same way to religious assertions.

This brings us back to a consideration of the principle which controls the *appropriateness of our utterances* about God. The most fruitful hypothesis about this principle seems to me to have been formulated by Ludwig Feuerbach, that greatly neglected figure of the nineteenth century, who declared after a study of the predicates attributed to God that they were projections of human needs—not the needs of the understanding but the needs of the heart, not of the human mind but of human feeling: emotions, hopes, and longings. What Feuerbach is saying, as I interpret him, is that the principle which controls the appropriateness of our utterances about God is man's idealized conception of himself, and that the predicates of God, particularly those which make him an object of reverence, worship, and aspiration are objectifications of man's highest ethical ideals.

What I propose to do briefly is to show that certain modern conceptions of knowledge tend to confirm the Feuerbachian hypothesis, both negatively and positively. Negatively, I wish to indicate some reasons why the idea of a transcendent God and the idea of an immanent God are intellectually unacceptable, that is, they cannot give an intelligible account of the concept of God, and a fortiori, of his existence. Positively, I shall try to suggest the way in which the concept of God has functioned as a moral ideal without supernaturalism.

2

The idea of God as a transcendent power, independent of the world of nature and man, is perhaps the oldest of the concepts of a divine and supreme being. Certainly it is the most traditional in the West. It views God as a creator but in such a way as to make an inexplicable mystery of creation. In this connection, it should be pointed out that the argument from the first cause, even if it were valid, which it obviously is not, would by itself be insufficient to establish the existence of God as a creator. Aristotle's God is a first cause, too, and is introduced as a support, so to speak, for Aristotle's physics—an Unmoved Mover toward which everything aspires. But Aristotle's God does not create the world which exists with him from eternity. It was none other than Aquinas who taught that on grounds of reason alone we could not tell whether the world had existed from eternity or had been created by God: only revelation or faith could be the source of our knowledge that God created the world. Aquinas, however, also assumed that although the truths of revelation are not the same as the truths of reason, the two must nevertheless be logically compatible.

Yet the concept of a creative God has always been a stone of stumbling to the human mind—and with good cause.

"Creation" ordinarily presupposes three things: (a) a plan or purpose; (b) a method and instrument of execution; and (c) an antecedently existing subject matter or material which is reshaped or reworked by the instrument in the light of the design or plan. When we speak of God as "creating" the world, there is no difficulty with the notion of plan or purpose. But there is a grave difficulty with the notions of the instrument and subject matter. For God is supposed to have created the world out of nothing—*ex nihilo*. Now in our experience nothing is or can be created out of nothing. There is always some subject matter, some instrument. How, then, is creation *ex nihilo* to be understood? The common reply is that God creates "analogically" not literally. But analogical creation is like analogical fatherhood. It doesn't explain why one kind of analogical expression is used rather than another. Why can't we say that God coexists with the world—"coexists analogically," of course? The reason, Feuerbach would say, is not to be found in God but in man. He worships in idealized form the fulfillment of conscious or unconscious need, especially his needs as a person threatened in a world of impersonal things. He expresses this in the analogical transfiguration of the concept Creator and in its analogical predication of God.

Does modern knowledge in any way help to explain the notion of a "creative God" or *creatio ex nihilo*? Some have thought that this concept of a creative God can be clarified by suggestions from modern cosmology and modern depth psychology. I should like to say a word about each.

According to the so-called cosmology of "continuous creation" developed by Fred Hoyle, Herman Bondi, and others, new matter is continuously being generated out of nothing and in this way the universe (which is continuously expanding) remains "in a steady-state and at an over-all constant density." As Hoyle puts it, "Matter simply appears—it is created. At one time the various atoms composing the material do not exist *and at a later time they do.*"[1] What is true now is presumably true for original matter—for the very first speck of matter that ever appeared. But it should be pointed out that this theory says nothing about the *process* by which matter comes into existence. The expression "appearing suddenly" is certainly not synonymous with "creating." One can speak of "life" spontaneously "appearing" or "emerging" in the past or present without implying that it was "created" or that it is necessarily beyond scientific explanation. Matter is "found" to appear at certain times and under certain conditions. That it is "created" is something to be established only after the expression "creation" is given some determinate meaning. But without reference to plan or purpose, act or instrument, the term "creation" is a misnomer. At any rate, whatever the chaotic state of affairs which is described by the new cosmology as having existed in the universe about five billion years ago when matter was born, it came into being at time t, and therefore *in principle* is open to a scientific explanation in terms of the state of affairs at time, $t\text{-}I$. If it is objected that there was no time before matter came into existence and that therefore $t\text{-}I$ is ruled out, then the objection equally applies to any creative act as well. Hoyle, too, speaks of time *before* and after matter appears. Creation becomes just as mysterious in the new cosmology as in the old theology.

It is a far cry from scientific cosmology to depth psychology. I must content myself with only a passing reference to an effort by Professor William Poteat[2] to elucidate the expression "creation out of nothing." He admits that any aspect or piece of behavior of the human body—physical, biological, psychological—can be explained in terms of events which precede it of the same logical order, and that these events constitute a theoretically infinite series without any first term. But, he says, when we speak of the human body or being as a "person," when we add to the language of impersonal behavior the personal pronouns "I" and "my," something radically discontinuous with the rest of the nonpersonal world comes into the picture. The world which is "mine" is altogether different from a world in which "mine" refers to nothing. Now the act of suicide is an act of radical destruction, which destroys at one stroke the possibility of any kind of personal experience. "I am not destroying something or other *in* the world (by my act of suicide), I am destroying the world as a whole." This is the exact opposite of the process of radical creation. God creates the world out of nothing in an analogously opposite way to our making nothing out of the existing or created world. Granted, then, that "creation out of nothing" is a queer sort of thing, inexplicable in terms of ordinary language. So is suicide. A similar analysis of the notion "I was born"—a phrase I may use when I become aware of the world as related to myself, a person at whose center is the personal pronoun "I"—reveals that this notion is no less queer than suicide. In one case "I make nothing out of something"; in the other "I make something out of nothing." Both escape explanation by ordinary and scientific modes of speech: both provide the analogy for God as "maker of heaven and earth."

All this seems to me more ingenious than persuasive. The psychological phenomena of suicide and "becoming aware" can be given quite different explanations which make them less mysterious than "creation out of nothing." About the causes, motives, conditions, and consequences of suicide we know quite a little. Suicide phenomenologically blots out the world—but so does sleep and unconsciousness. A man may commit suicide not because he wants to destroy the world but because others have destroyed it for him. And since a man who firmly believes in immortality can commit suicide, Professor Poteat's analysis must be revised. "Becoming aware" or "being born" to myself as a first-person singular does not so much create a world as light up an antecedently existing one. I undergo the experience of being-in-the-world, of being treated as object or person, long before I become aware of the world as distinct from myself or of myself as counterposed to the world. The discovery of myself is not primary to everything else in the way in which creation out of nothing must be.

These makeshift attempts to demystify the mystery of *creatio ex nihilo* either call our attention to something which is unusual in speech or action but which is otherwise intelligible, or generate mysteries as dark as the one they would illumine. The concept of a transcendent God, who creates the world *ex nihilo,* in time or out of time, can no more be clearly thought than the concept of the last number in a series in which every number has a successor. There is a sort of brutal honesty in Karl Barth's contention that God is "altogether Other" from man and the world, and that philosophic reason is unable to grasp what is "ineffable," "unfathomable," and "inconceivable."

What Barth does not understand, however, is that in applying the axe to human reason, he destroys the possibility of any solid ground for faith or revelation. If the concept of God defies adequate grasp by human reason, then what can it mean to say that belief in him rests on faith or revelation? Men thirst to know what they have faith in "as the hart pants for water." Man's reason will not be denied, despite the pronouncements of Luther and Barth. It makes sense to say, "My belief that X is my friend is based on faith, not evidence or reason," but only because I know what the phrases "X is a friend" and "X is *my* friend" mean. Similarly the statement "Belief in God's existence is based on faith, not rational evidence or argument" takes on meaning only if I am able to describe what it is I have faith in. But how can anyone who eschews intelligence or reason know or describe what he has faith in? How can he distinguish between the assertion, "I have faith in God" and the assertion "I have faith in Mumbo Jumbo"? Whether we approach divinity by reason or by faith, we cannot escape wrestling with the concept of God, even if we are unsure thereby to win Jacob's blessing.

If the foregoing analysis is sound, then the idea of a transcendent God has certain root logical and linguistic difficulties which are not likely to be affected by the progress of modern knowledge—unless the latter leads to a shift in the basic categories of our understanding. If the concept of a transcendent God is incomprehensible, it is difficult to see what difference it makes whether we declare that he created the earth in six days or six million years, whether he created man in one operation out of dust or through a long series of evolutionary changes. At the Darwin Centennial celebration at the University of Chicago, Sir Julian Huxley denied that our earth and its inhabitants were created, and he presented anew the evidence for believing that both evolved out of earlier forms. To which Father J. Franklin Ewing, professor of anthropology at Fordham University, replied in somewhat the same way as other distinguished theologians replied to Huxley's grandfather: "God is the creator of man—body and soul. Whether he used the method of evolution for the preparation of the human body or created it from unorganized matter is not of primary importance. In either case he is the Creator. . . . God created not only all beings but also all potentialities for evolution."

In short, no matter what the findings of science are, they cannot affect the truths of religion. And it is significant that in his address to the Vatican Academy of Sciences on November 22, 1951, Pope Pius XII without any embarrassment accepted the findings of modern astronomy about the age and evolution of the universe. This withdrawal in advance from any possible conflict with the claims of science to true knowledge of the physical universe makes it difficult to understand the intense warfare waged by religion and theology against science in the past. If it really is the case that the domains of scientific inquiry and religious beliefs do not touch at any point, and therefore cannot conflict, then it becomes hard to explain why the advance of science should in fact have weakened religious belief and produced periodic crises of faith. Whatever the present situation may be, science was not in the past given such autonomy either by religion or theology.

Feuerbach's interpretation of these periodic crises of belief is that they are nodal points in human consciousness, when men become dimly aware that their statements about God are not the same kind of thing as their statements about ordinary matters, but are expressions of need and hope for an absolutely secure source, a power or an Ideal, beyond Nature, yet not foreign to human nature, on which to rely for protection against all the evils that beset them in their precarious careers on earth. "The Creation, like the idea of a personal God in general, is not a scientific, but a personal matter," he writes, "not an object of the free intelligence but of the feelings. . . . " If God is awesome and tremendous and mysterious it is because he has unlimited power over nature—and therefore unlimited Will which is related to human will. God defies rational analysis because his "existence" is postulated not by any imperative of thought but by the anguished feelings of finite, suffering man, who wishes to preserve his "personality or subjectivity" against the forces which reduce him to the level of matter. For him "the belief in God is nothing but the belief in human dignity . . . and the true principle of creation the self-affirmation of subjectivity in distinction from Nature." Religion must find a form in which the dignity of men cannot be destroyed by discoveries about nature, whose creatures men are.

3

So far I have been discussing the concept of a transcendent God and the insuperable intellectual difficulties attached to it—difficulties experienced by reflective religious individuals (among whom even Wittgenstein is to be numbered, according to Professor Malcolm's memoir on him). The concept of an immanent God is much easier to understand, particularly since it contains no reference to personality. In the history of Western religious thought there has always been among the orthodox a deep suspicion of concepts of an immanent God, which are often regarded as sophisticated expressions of religious unbelief masquerading in the language of piety. We may take the God of Spinoza and Hegel as examples. Novalis once referred to Spinoza as a God-intoxicated man, but in his own time Spinoza was denounced as an atheist, for his God was neither the God of Abraham, Isaac, and Jacob, nor the God of Maimonides or Aquinas. Spinoza's God is Substance or Structure conceived as a self sufficient network of timeless logical relations. This God is one to whom man cannot pray, and who cannot be loved as one loves a father or friend. So, too, with Hegel's God. Hegel gladdened the hearts of the pietists when he declared that "the world cannot exist without God," but he brought down an excommunicatory wrath on his head when he added: "God cannot exist without the world." Hegel's God is the God of Spinoza, except that Substance has been replaced by a timeless process, a dynamic system of evolving logical relations which constitute a great Self. In its strict form the concept of an immanent God (which must not be confused with the idea of an Incarnate God) leads to pantheism, but almost all believers in an immanent God have shrunk from this consequence. They have been reluctant to see Divinity in everything because the feeling of cosmic piety, or what Einstein calls "cosmic religious feeling," cannot be sustained for very long against a close-up view of each and every item in the world: there is too much that is ugly, disordered, and painful. Consequently some selection must be made. God may be *in* the world, but even to a believer in immanence not everything in the world is equally divine, or even divine at all.

Two features of experience have been most commonly identified with God. The first is Reason or Order, or the pattern of rationality in things without which, it has been said (by Einstein, among others), the success of human thought in charting the ways of things would be a matter of luck or miracle. Not surprisingly, the scientists who hold to this conviction invariably turn out to be the most religious of men. The God of the scientist is not the God of the prophet, priest, or moralist. "His religious feeling takes the form of rapturous amazement at the harmony of natural law which reveals an intelligence of such superiority that, compared with it, all the systematic thinking and acting of human beings is an utterly insignificant reflection."[3] Helmholz, however, was amazed that the eye should be so defective an organ of vision, while Heisenberg and Bohr are not prepared to give the universe high marks for the order of rationality found in nuclear behavior.

Some thinkers, however, find their God not in the rationality of the natural order but in its thrust of creativity. A merely rational world to them seems dead—not the ever fresh and blooming world of our experience with its surprises and novelties. Bergson's identification of God with the principle of *élan vital*, Whitehead's identification of God with "the principle of concretion" are strong cases in point. In Whitehead's philosophy, God is introduced to account for the fact that not all eternal objects are found in actuality or experience. Out of the realm of infinite possibilities of what might logically be, we must find some principle of limitation to account for the fact that this possibility comes into being and not that, that this "process of actual occasions" is realized here and now and not then and there. Whitehead admits that no logical reason can be adduced for the givenness, the facticity, the just-so-ness of things. His God is the polar opposition of Einstein's. "God is the ultimate limitation, and his existence is the ultimate irrationality. For no reason can be given for just that limitation which stands in His nature to impose."[4] And lest there is any doubt that he is speaking of an immanent God, he adds in his *Process and Reality:* "In this aspect, He [God] is not *before* all creation but *with* all creation."[5]

An immanent God cannot be plausibly conceived as a personal God, and it is not surprising that so many immanentists wage a fierce polemic against the conception of God as a transcendent person. The boundaries between the natural and supernatural tend to be blurred by this immanentism, and a certain irresolution and ambiguity is introduced into traditional religious faith. For a genuine religious function to be served, it is not sufficient to identify God with logical structure or process or any other generic feature of existence. What must be shown is that the world or cosmos, in virtue of the principle of Incarnate Divinity, has an objective purpose or plan which in some way explains or justifies human suffering. Evil, natural and human, must in the religious perspective appear meaningful and, in some fashion, acceptable. That is why in order to warrant the appellation of "God" or "Divinity," in order to be distinguished from a merely natural force or a purely logical pattern, the immanent Principle must be thought of as working itself out in nature, society, and history in such a way that evil loses its sting. As a rule, the evil of the part is represented as necessary to the good of the whole; God, as it were, uses the Devil for His own purposes.

With respect to the problem of evil, the immanence of God is manifestly superior as a conception to the transcendent God. A transcendent God, no matter how analogically conceived, must be endowed with will or intent. Since his power is such that he can intervene in the order of nature (a small feat to one who is the author of nature), anyone who feels himself an innocent suffering victim of the order of nature is psychologically hopeful that by prayer or petition or sacrifice, he can influence the Divine Will or Intent. But if the all-powerful Divine Will refuses to prevent unjust suffering, he becomes to some extent responsible for that suffering—all the more so since he is also omniscient and cannot, like the Epicurean God, plead business elsewhere. The agony of the problem of evil consists in not understanding how an all-powerful, all-loving Father can permit his innocent children to be tortured in a world he has created. And although every honest theologian must in the end declare that the existence of evil is a Divine Mystery, the agony is not therewith dispelled. It may be attenuated by a temporary mood, but it keeps breaking through in every human being who has sensed in his own life and on his own skin something like the afflictions of Job.

One cannot in the same way question, blame, or complain to an immanent God. If "evil" is represented as a *necessary* element in the cosmic order, one may have difficulty in *comprehending* its necessity, but the premise itself commits one to the belief that it could not be otherwise, and that if we persisted and were keen enough, we would finally understand why it couldn't be otherwise. Consequently the alleged mystery of evil finally dissolves in the blinding vision of its necessity. The psychological ground for this is obvious: for example, we can resign ourselves without defiance or resentment to the weather because we assume that no one controls it. When the weather becomes controllable, the weatherman will have hard questions to answer.

Although the concept of an immanent God does not carry in its train such a cluster of theoretical difficulties as the idea of a transcendent God, its practical availability for the most religious purposes, especially in the Western tradition, is highly limited. Its own theoretical difficulties are grave enough, and its moral consequences are confusing. To interpret the natural cosmos as a moral cosmos is, in effect, to identify physics with ethics, and the laws of nature with the laws and judgments of morality. This tends to paralyze the nerve of morality, sometimes by identifying the actual with the ideal, the "what is" with the "what should be," and sometimes by suggesting that human judgments of better or worse are altogether irrelevant to the course of affairs—both the course of nature and of history. The pattern of Divinity is to be understood without laughter and without tears, unmoved and immovable by the petty concerns of our petty lives.

4

There is another, modern view of God which is intermediate between the transcendent and immanent conceptions, and perhaps ultimately unclassifiable in terms of the customary distinction—the idea that God is identical with mystical experience itself. The element of transcendence in this view is that it sees God as beyond ordinary temporal experience—he can only be reached by a *break* in the natural jointures and continuities of things. The element of immanence is that once the breakthrough has been achieved, the experience itself is defined as a manifestation of Divinity.

Thus Professor Walter Stace, who is the most gifted expositor of this conception, writes: "Just as Nirvana simply is the supreme experience of the Buddhist saint, so God simply is the supreme experience of the Christian mystic." And "the mystic experience of the Christian, as well as of the Hindus, is itself identical with God." This experience can be described only in paradoxical terms. It is the experience of "an undifferentiated unity," of the merging of self and nonself, object and subject, an eloquent stillness, a rapturous peace, an awesome joy. No language can be adequate to it, not even the language of oxymoron.

But three important questions must be asked. First, is this a genuine experience, in the sense that if one has not been seized or blessed by it oneself, one can still find good reasons for believing that others have? Second, if this experience *is* genuine, is it only a psychological event in a particular individual's biography or does it testify to a cosmological or ontological fact? Third, do any ethical consequences for human life follow from the fact of the experience and/or its variant interpretations?

Short of an entire volume, I must content myself with apparently dogmatic answers, but I believe they can be rationally grounded. On the first question: there is little reason to doubt that this experience occurs and that the descriptions of it are authentic. Personally I think that the experience is quite widespread and that anyone suffering an intense emotion in extreme situations may undergo it. It is felt in moments of great danger, great love, great beauty, great joy—and, I am prepared to believe, even at the height of raging hate and the depths of total despair. The nearest I myself have come to it is when getting an anaesthetic, just before going under, and once when I almost drowned. The answer to the second question is that no experience can itself be conclusive evidence for the truth of an assertion about matters independent of that experience. An overwhelming conviction that an oasis which we see on top of a sand dune will be there when we reach it may be the result of a mirage. Even if several people report seeing the oasis, we are still not justified in assuming its existence, for they may all be common victims of the heat and thirst. The testimony of one man who had followed certain canons and methods of scientific inquiry would count far more, even if we grant that it would not be conclusive. Not everyone has experienced seasickness. Yet it is an authentic experience. But not all the unanimous testimony of the seasick can prove that the terrible vision of a nauseated reality experienced at the time gives an *objective* glimpse of those dread abysses of being by which according to the existentialists, all of us, seasick or not, are surrounded.

As for the third question, whatever consequences for human life follow from the mystic vision must be justified, if they are valid, by their observable effects on ordinary human experience. Whether an actual angel speaks to me in my beatific vision or whether I only dreamed he spoke, the *truth* of what he says can only be tested in the same way as I test what my neighbor says to me. For even my neighbor may claim to be a messenger of the Lord.

5

This brings me to the third main conception of God, according to which God is neither a supernatural power nor a principle of immanent structure, but a symbolic term of our most inclusive moral ideals. The "divine" refers to that dimension in human life which is not reducible *merely* to the physical, the social, and the psychological, although it emerges from and affects them. It is a dimension which is experienced whenever ideal ends, justice, compassion for all suffering creatures, dedication to truth and integrity move men to change the world and themselves. This is the humanist conception of God. It is what Feuerbach's God becomes when men grow aware of the mechanisms of transference and projection by which their needs create the objects of ideal allegiance.

The humanist conception of God, which is suggested by John Dewey's phrase, "the effective union of the ideal and actual," is fundamentally opposed to any notion of a supernatural power as the *source* of human morality or even as the *justification* of morality, although it admits that belief in such a power can serve as a *support* of human morality. This entire problem of the relation between religion and morality, between God and the Good, is extremely complex. The history of the traditional religions of transcendence reveals a profound ambiguity in the way God is conceived to be related to the Good—an ambiguity on which I have dwelt elsewhere, and here briefly mention.

On the one hand, God appears in the traditional religions as the source and inspirer of the moral ideals which separate men from beasts of prey. He is the lawgiver, from whom Moses received the tablets at Sinai; the fountain of righteousness, from which the Prophets drank; the infinite sea of mercy and love, which Jesus invoked to dissolve human sinfulness. Religion so conceived is the shield of morality—so much so that any doubt or disbelief powerful enough to pierce it strikes down at the same time any possibility of a good life or a good society.

On the other hand, since God is by definition altogether different from man, he cannot be bound by man's understanding nor can his ways be judged by human ideas of justice. It is an act of impiety to apply to God and his works the same standards which men apply to each other, even if these standards are derived from Him. It would be monstrous on the part of a man to punish an innocent child for a misdeed committed by its grandfather. But when the Lord proclaims, "I shall visit the sins of the fathers upon the heads of the children unto the third and fourth generation," the pious man must murmur with a full and loving heart, "Thy will be done."

Social Christianity (like prophetic Judaism before it) is a conspicuous illustration of the first strain of thought—the idea of God as the source of ethical ideals. It leads to a withering away of strictly theological issues, tends to define the religious man not in terms of belief but in terms of action or good works, and interprets the religious consciousness as "a participation in the ideal values of the social consciousness." It is, therefore, always suspect of Pelagianism.

The second strain—which stresses the impiety of applying human standards to God—is exemplified in existentialist theology, whose roots go back to Paul, Augustine, Pascal, and Calvin, but which has put forth its finest modern flower in Kierkegaard. In his commentary on the Abraham-Isaac story in the essay *Fear and Trembling*, . . . Kierkegaard praises Abraham as the most pious of men, greater in his religious heroism than all the tragic figures of history because Abraham was prepared to carry out his absolute duty to God—a duty which as a merely finite creature he could not possibly understand but one which cut sharply across his ethical responsibilities. Kierkegaard calls this "the teleological suspension of the ethical," which means that in serving God, one is beyond all considerations of good and evil. One "acts by virtue of the absurd." In the strongest contrast between the ethical and the religious mode of feeling and conduct that has ever been drawn, Kierkegaard says that Abraham must be regarded either as a "murderer" (the term is his) from the ethical standpoint, or a "true believer" from the standpoint of absolute religion. The truly pious man is prepared to accept any command whatever as a test of his faith.

The position of the religious humanist, whether that of Ludwig Feuerbach or John Dewey, reverses this appraisal in a most dramatic way. Its principle must be called "the ethical suspension of the theological."

Religious humanism analyzes the parable of Abraham and Isaac quite differently in order to show that a new moral insight was born when Abraham identified the voice which bade him stay his hand as the voice of God. Thus the parable illustrates the Feuerbachian contention that men create and worship gods in their own moral image and confirms the Kantian principle of the autonomy of moral reason with respect to traditional conceptions of religion and God.

Feuerbach's insight is sometimes recognized by existentialist theologians, but they then compromise it by bringing in some obscure—and irrelevant—metaphysical or ontological conception. For example, Paul Tillich interprets religion as an expression of man's ultimate concern. God, therefore, can be defined as the object of man's ultimate concern. This means that there are as many gods as there are objects of ultimate concern, and their existence can be established, not in the way we establish the existence of atoms or stars or genes or anything else in nature, but only in the way we determine what a man's overriding concern may be. So we say, "He is a worshipper of Mammon" or Venus, or Minerva, or Mars, or Apollo, depending upon whether a man makes a fetish of money, love, knowledge, war, or art. Tillich thus reduces the conflict of gods to the conflict of moral ideals. This is good as far as it goes, especially because it contains a suggestion of moral pluralism and religious polytheism, and because it is coupled with the explicit denial of God's existence as a supernatural power. Indeed, in this respect Tillich seems to go even further than avowed atheists. Literally construed, he is saying that it is simply meaningless, a confusion of dimensions (or what Ryle calls a category mistake), to affirm that God is an entity among, but greater than, other entities. Such extremism, in my opinion, would make almost all the historical religions irreligious and many forms of irreligion profoundly religious. Moreover, since all human beings are passionately concerned about something— unless they are already half-dead—we must call them all "religious." Because the objects of their ultimate concern are what they are, many people are characterized as "godless," in accordance with proper English usage. Why, then, give the term "God" to their object of concern, and convert "erring souls" by arbitary definition? This is not the only difficulty. Matters become even more obscure when God is also identified by Tillich as "the Unconditioned," as "beyond finitude and infinity," as "the ground of Being," as "Being-itself" which "includes both rest and becoming." These terms . . . defy logical analysis and require some kind of Feuerbachian resolution to become intelligible.

6

I wish to conclude with a few observations about the humanist conception of God. The great problem which humanism as a religion must face is not so much the validity of its conception of God but how to justify its use of the term "God." The defense can be made briefly. All large terms in human discourse are historically variable in meaning or actually ambiguous in use: "atom," "substance," "experience," "reason," "love," even "man"—all show this variation in meaning. Each term stands for a family of meanings (like the term "game" in Wittgenstein's analysis) which resemble one other but are nevertheless not completely consonant. Consequently, it is argued that if the same penumbral complex of attitudes (intellectual humility, piety, reverence, wonder, awe, and concern) are manifest in a use of the term "God" which designates no thing or person but our highest ethical commitment, no legitimate objection can be raised —providing, of course, we make it clear that the new use or meaning is different from the old.

The criticism can be made just as briefly. The new use always invites confusion with the old use, and there is, after all, such a thing as the ethics of words. By taking over the word "God" as the religious humanists do, the waters of thought, feeling, and faith are muddied, the issues blurred, the "word" itself becomes the object of interest, and not what it signifies. When Marguerite in her simple faith asks Faust whether he believes in God, Faust replies with a kind of pantheistic, pre-Whiteheadian doubletalk about luck, heart, love, and God, call it what you will!

> *Ich habe keinen Namen*
> *Dafur! Gefuhl ist alles;*
> *Name ist Schall und Rauch*
> *Umnebelnd Himmelsglut.*

To which Marguerite makes reply:

> *Das ist alles recht schon und gut;*
> *Ungefahr sagt das der Pfarrer auch;*
> *Nur mit ein bischen andern Worten.*

This may be called a paradigm case of religious misunderstanding.

Is, then, the religion of humanism justified in using the term "God" for its conception of the moral enterprise? John Dewey answered the question affirmatively. I answer it negatively. Each one of my readers must answer it for himself.

NOTES

1. My italics. I am drawing here on the illuminating account of my colleague's exposition and criticism, Milton Munitz, *Space, Time and Creation* (1957). Cf. also for analysis of the concept of creation, the chapter on "The Metaphysics of the Instrument," in my *The Metaphysics of Pragmatism* (1927).

2. *Mind,* July, 1959.

3. Albert Einstein, *The World As I See It* (New York, 1949), p. 29.

4. A. N. Whitehead, *Science and the Modern World* (New York, Macmillan, 1925), p. 249.

5. A. N. Whitehead, *Process and Reality* (New York, 1929), p. 486.

III. Arguments for God's Existence

Paul Edwards

L The Cosmological Argument

Paul Edwards, professor of philosophy at Brooklyn College, was educated at the University of Melbourne and at Columbia University. He is the editor-in-chief of the eight-volume *Encyclopedia of Philosophy* (1967), the author of *The Logic of Moral Discourse* (1965), and the author of articles on a variety of subjects in philosophical journals. His anthology, *A Modern Introduction to Philosophy* (1957), has gone through several editions. The following article has been reprinted in many anthologies in philosophy and the philosophy of religion.

1

The so-called "cosmological proof" is one of the oldest and most popular arguments for the existence of God. It was forcibly criticized by Hume,[1] Kant,[2] and Mill,[3] but it would be inaccurate to consider the argument dead or even moribund. Catholic philosophers, with hardly any exception,

From The Rationalist Annual *for the year 1969* (*since 1968,* Question)*, pp. 63-77. Reprinted with permission of the author and of the Rationalist Press Association, London.*

appear to believe that it is as solid and conclusive as ever. Thus Father Copleston confidently championed it in his Third Programme debate with Bertrand Russell;[4] and in America, where Catholic writers are more sanguine, we are told by a Jesuit professor of physics that "the existence of an intelligent being as the First Cause of the universe can be established by *rational scientific inference.*"[5]

"I am absolutely convinced [the same writer continues] that any one who would give the same consideration to that proof (the cosmological argument), as outlined for example in William Brosnan's *God and Reason,* as he would give to a line of argumentation found in the *Physical Review* or the *Proceedings of the Royal Society* would be forced to admit that the cogency of this argument for the existence of God far outstrips that which is found in the reasoning which Chadwick uses to prove the existence of the neutron, which today is accepted as certain as any conclusion in the physical sciences."[6]

Mild theists like the late Professor Dawes Hicks[7] and Dr. Ewing,[8] who concede many of Hume's and Kant's criticisms, nevertheless contend that the argument possesses a certain core of truth. In popular discussions it also crops up again and again—for example, when believers address atheists with such questions as "You tell me where the universe came from!" Even philosophers who reject the cosmological proof sometimes embody certain of its confusions in the formulation of their own position. In the light of all this, it may be worthwhile to undertake a fresh examination of the argument, with special attention to the fallacies that were not emphasized by the older critics.

2

The cosmological proof has taken a number of forms, the most important of which are known as the causal argument and the argument from contingency, respectively. In some writers, in Samuel Clarke for example, they are combined, but it is best to keep them apart as far as possible. The causal argument is the second of the "five ways" of Aquinas and proceeds roughly as follows: we find that the things around us come into being as the result of the activity of other things. These causes are themselves the result of the activity of other things. But such a causal series cannot "go back to infinity." Hence there must be a first member, a member which is not itself caused by any preceding member—an uncaused or "first" cause.

It has frequently been pointed out that even if this argument were sound it would not establish the existence of God. It would not show that the first cause is all-powerful or all-good or that it is in any sense personal. Somebody believing in the eternity of atoms, or of matter generally, could quite consistently accept the conclusion. Defenders of the causal argument usually concede this and insist that the argument is not in itself meant to prove the existence of God. Supplementary arguments are required to show that the first cause must have the attributes assigned to the Deity. They claim, however, that the argument, if valid, would at least be an important step towards a complete proof of the existence of God.

Does the argument succeed in proving so much as a first cause? This will depend mainly on the soundness of the premise that an infinite series of causes is impossible. Aquinas supports this premise by maintaining that the opposite belief involves a plain absurdity. To suppose that there is an infinite series of causes logically implies that nothing exists now; but we know that plenty of things do exist now; and hence any theory which implies that nothing exists now must be wrong. Let us take some causal series and refer to its members by the letters of the alphabet:

$$A \longrightarrow B \ldots W \longrightarrow X \longrightarrow Y \longrightarrow Z$$

Z stands here for something presently existing, e.g. Margaret Truman. Y represents the cause or part of the cause of Z, say Harry Truman. X designates the cause or part of the cause of Y, say Harry Truman's father, etc. Now, Aquinas reasons, whenever we take away the cause, we also take away the effect: if Harry Truman had never lived, Margaret Truman would never have been born. If Harry Truman's father had never lived, Harry Truman and Margaret Truman would never have been born. If A had never existed, none of the subsequent members of the series would have come into existence. But it is precisely A that the believers in the infinite series is "taking away." For in maintaining that the series is infinite he is denying that it has a first member; he is denying that there is such a thing as a first cause; he is, in other words, denying the existence of A. Since without A, Z could not have existed, his position implies that Z does not exist now; and that is plainly false.

This argument fails to do justice to the supporter of the infinite series of causes. Aquinas has failed to distinguish between the two statements:

(1) A did not exist, and
(2) A is not uncaused.

To say that the series is infinite implies (2), but it does not imply (1). The following parallel may be helpful here: Suppose Captain Spaulding had said, "I am the greatest explorer who ever lived," and somebody replied, "No, you are not." This answer would be denying that the Captain possessed the exalted attribute he had claimed for himself, but it would not be denying his existence. It would not be "taking him away." Similarly, the believer in the infinite series is not "taking A away." He is taking away the privileged status of A; he is taking away its "first causeness." He does not deny the *existence* of A or of any particular member of the series. He denies that A or anything else *is the first member* of the series. Since he is not taking A away, he is not taking B away, and thus he is also not taking X, Y, or Z away. His view, then, does not commit him to the absurdity that nothing exists now, or more specifically, that Margaret Truman does not exist now. It may be noted in this connection that a believer in the infinite series is not necessarily denying the existence of supernatural beings. He is merely committed to denying that such a being, if it exists, is uncaused. He is committed to holding that whatever other impressive attributes a supernatural being might possess, the attribute of being a first cause is not among them.

The causal argument is open to several other objections. Thus, even if otherwise valid, the argument would not prove a *single* first cause. For there does not seem to be any good ground for supposing that all the various causal series in the universe ultimately merge. Hence, even if it is granted that no series of causes can be infinite, the possibility of a plurality of first members has not been ruled out. Nor does the argument establish the *present* existence of the first cause. It does not prove this, since experience clearly shows that an effect may exist long after its cause has been destroyed.

3

Many defenders of the causal argument would contend that at least some of these criticisms rest on a misunderstanding. They would probably go further and contend that the argument was not quite fairly stated in the first place—or at any rate that if it was fair to some of its adherents it was not fair to others. They would in this connection distinguish between two types of causes—what they call "causes *in fieri*" and what they call "causes *in esse*." A cause *in fieri* is a factor which brought or helped to bring an effect into existence. A cause *in esse* is a factor which "sustains" or helps to sustain the effect "in being." The parents of a human being would be an example of a cause *in fieri*. If somebody puts a book in my hand and I keep holding it up, his putting it there would be the cause *in fieri*, and my holding it would be the cause *in esse* of the book's position. To quote Father Joyce:

> If a smith forges a horse-shoe, he is only a cause *in fieri* of the shape given to the iron. That shape persists after his action has ceased. So, too, a builder is a cause *in fieri* of the house which he builds. In both these cases the substances employed act as causes *in esse* as regards the continued existence of the effect produced. Iron, in virtue of its natural rigidity, retains in being the shape which it has once received; and, similarly, the materials employed in building retain in being the order and arrangement which constitute them into a house.[9]

Using this distinction, a defender of the argument now reasons in the following way. To say that there is an infinite series of causes *in fieri* does not lead to any absurd conclusions. But Aquinas is concerned only with causes *in esse* and an infinite series of *such* causes is impossible. In the words of the contemporary American Thomist, R. P. Phillips:

> Each member of the series of causes possess being solely by virtue of the actual present operation of a superior cause. . . . Life is dependent, *inter alia*, on a certain atmospheric pressure, this again on the continual operation of physical forces, whose being and operation depends on the position of the earth in the solar system, which itself must endure relatively unchanged, a state of being which can only be continuously produced by a definite—if unknown—constitution of the material universe. This constitution, however, cannot be its own cause. That a thing should cause itself is impossible: for in order that it may cause it is necessary for it to exist, which it cannot do, on the hypothesis, until it has been caused. So it must *be* in order to cause itself. Thus, not being uncaused nor yet its own cause, it must be caused by another, which produces and preserves it. It is plain, then, that as no member of this series possesses being except in virtue of the actual present operation of a superior cause, if there be no first cause actually operating none of the dependent causes could operate either. We are thus irresistibly led to posit a first efficient cause which, while itself uncaused, shall impart causality to a whole series. . . .
>
> The series of causes which we are considering is not one which stretches back into the past; so that we are not demanding a beginning of the world at some definite moment reckoning back from the present, but an actual cause now operating, to account for the present being of things.[10]

Professor Phillips offers the following parallel to bring out his point:

> In a goods train each truck is moved and moves by the action of the one immediately in front of it. If then we suppose the train to be infinite, i.e. that there is no end to it, and so no engine which starts the motion, it is plain that no truck will move. To lengthen it out to infinity will not give it what no member of it possesses of itself, viz. the power of drawing the truck behind it. If then we see any truck in motion we know there must be an end to the series of trucks which gives causality to the whole.[11]

Father Joyce introduces an illustration from Aquinas to explain how the present existence of things may be compatible with an infinite series of causes *in fieri* but not with an infinite series of causes *in esse.*

> When a carpenter is at work, the series of efficient causes on which his work depends is necessarily limited. The final effect, e.g. the fastening of a nail, is caused by a hammer: the hammer is moved by the arm: and the motion of his arm is determined by the motor-impulses communicated from the nerve centres of the brain. Unless the subordinate causes were limited in number, and were connected with a starting-point of motion, the hammer must remain inert; and the nail will never be driven in. If the series be supposed infinite, no work will ever take place. But if there is question of causes on which the work is not essentially dependent, we cannot draw the same conclusion. We may suppose the carpenter to have broken an infinite number of hammers, and as often to have replaced the broken tool by a fresh one. There is nothing in such a supposition which excludes the driving home of the nail.[12]

The supporter of the infinite series of causes, Joyce also remarks, is "asking us to believe that although each link in a suspended chain is prevented from falling simply because it is attached to the one above it, yet if only the chain be long enough, it will, taken as a whole, need no support, but will hang loose in the air suspended from nothing."[13]

This formulation of the causal argument unquestionably circumvents one of the objections mentioned previously. If Y is the cause *in esse* of an effect, Z, then it must exist as long as Z exists. If the argument were valid in this form it would therefore prove the present and not merely the past existence of a first cause. In this form the argument is, however, less convincing in another respect. To maintain that all "natural" or "phenomenal" objects—things like tables and mountains and human beings—require a cause *in fieri* is not implausible, though even here Mill and others have argued that, strictly speaking, only *changes* require a causal explanation.

It is far from plausible, on the other hand, to claim that all natural objects require a cause *in esse*. It may be granted that the air around us is a cause *in esse* of human life and further that certain gravitational forces are among the causes *in esse* of the air being where it is. But when we come to gravitational forces or, at any rate, to material particles like atoms or electrons it is difficult to see what cause *in esse* they require. To those not already convinced of the need for a supernatural First Cause, some of the remarks by Professor Phillips in this connection appear merely dogmatic and question-begging. Most people would grant that such particles as atoms did not cause themselves, since, as Professor Phillips observes, they would in that event have had to exist before they began existing. It is not at all evident, however, that these particles cannot be uncaused. Professor Phillips and all other supporters of the causal argument immediately proceed to claim that there is something else which needs no cause *in esse*. They themselves admit thus, that there is nothing self-evident about the proposition that everything must have a cause *in esse*. Their entire procedure here lends substance to Schopenhauer's gibe that supporters of the cosmological argument treat the law of universal causation like "a hired cab which we dismiss when we have reached our destination."[14]

But waiving this and all similar objections, the restatement of the argument in terms of causes *in esse* in no way avoids the main difficulty which was previously mentioned. A believer in the infinite series would insist that his position was just as much misrepresented now as before. He is no more removing the member of the series which is supposed to be the first cause *in esse* than he was removing the member which had been declared to be the first cause *in fieri*. He is again merely denying a privileged status to it. He is not denying the reality of the cause *in esse* labelled A. He is not even necessarily denying that it possesses supernatural attributes. He is again merely taking away its "first causeness."

The advocates of the causal argument in either form seem to confuse an infinite series with one which is long but finite. If a book, Z, is to remain in its position, say 100 miles up in the air, there must be another object, say another book, Y, underneath it to serve as its support. If Y is to remain where it is, it will need another support, X, beneath it. Suppose that this series of supports, one below the other, continues for a long time, but eventually, say after 100,000 members, comes to a first book which is not resting on any other book or indeed on any other support. In that event the whole collection would come crashing down. What we seem to need is a first member of the series, a first support (such as the earth) which does not need another member as *its* support, which in other words is "self-supporting."

This is evidently the sort of picture that supporters of the First Cause argument have before their minds when they rule out the possibility of an infinite series. But such a picture is not a fair representation of the theory of the infinite series. A *finite* series of books would indeed come crashing down, since the first or lowest member would not have a predecessor on which it could be supported. If the series, however, were infinite this would not be the case. In that event every member *would* have a predecessor to support itself on and there would be no crash. That is to say: a crash can be avoided either by a finite series with a first self-supporting member or by an infinite series. Similarly, the present existence of motion is equally compatible with the theory of a first unmoved mover and with the theory of an infinite series of moving objects; and the present existence of causal activity is compatible with the theory of a first cause *in esse* as much as with the theory of an infinite series of such causes.

The illustrations given by Joyce and Phillips are hardly to the point. It is true that a carpenter would not, *in a finite time-span*, succeed in driving in a nail if he had to carry out an infinite number of movements. For that matter, he would not accomplish this goal in a finite time if he broke an infinite number of hammers. However, to make the illustrations relevant we must suppose that he has infinite time at his disposal. In that case he would succeed in driving in the nail even if he required an infinite number of movements for this purpose. As for the goods train, it may be granted that the trucks do not move unless the train has an engine. But this illustration is totally irrelevant as it stands. A relevant illustration would be that of engines, each moved by the one in front of it. Such a train would move if it were infinite. For every member of this series there would be one in front capable of drawing it along. The advocate of the infinite series of whose members are not really causally connected with one another. In the series he believes in, every member is genuinely the cause of the one that follows it.

4

No staunch defender of the cosmological argument would give up at this stage. Even if there were an infinite series of causes *in fieri* or *in esse*, he would contend, this still would not do away with the need for an ultimate, a first cause. As Father Copleston put it in his debate with Bertrand Russell:

> Every object has a phenomenal cause, if you insist on the infinity of the series. But the series of phenomenal causes is an insufficient explanation of the series. Therefore, the series has not a phenomenal cause, but a transcendent cause.[15]
>
> An infinite series of contingent beings will be, to my way of thinking, as unable to cause itself as one contingent being.[16]

The demand to find the cause of the series as a whole rests on the erroneous assumption that the series is something over and above the members of which it is composed. It is tempting to suppose this, at least by implication, because the word *series* is a noun like *dog* or *man*. Like the expression "this dog" or "this man," the phrase "this series" is easily taken to designate an individual object. But reflection shows this to be an error. If we have explained the individual members there is nothing additional left to be explained. Suppose I see a group of five Eskimos standing on the corner of Sixth Avenue and 50th Street and I wish to explain why the group came to New York. Investigation reveals the following stories:

Eskimo No. 1 did not enjoy the extreme cold in the polar region and decided to move to a warmer climate.

No. 2 is the husband of Eskimo No. 1. He loves her dearly and did not wish to live without her.

No. 3 is the son of Eskimos 1 and 2. He is too small and too weak to oppose his parents.

No. 4 saw an advertisement in the *New York Times* for an Eskimo to appear on television.

No. 5 is a private detective engaged by the Pinkerton Agency to keep an eye on Eskimo No. 4.

Let us assume that we have now explained in the case of each of the five Eskimos why he or she is in New York. Somebody then asks: "All right, but what about the group as a whole; why is *it* in New York?" This would plainly be an absurd question. There is no group over and above the five members, and if we have explained why each of the five members is in New York we have ipso facto explained why the group is there. It is just as absurd to ask for the cause of the series as a whole, as distinct from asking for the causes of individual members.

5

It is most unlikely that a determined defender of the cosmological line of reasoning would surrender even here. He would probably admit that the series is not a thing over and above its members and that it does not make sense to ask for the cause of the series if the cause of each member has already been found. He would insist, however, that when he asked for the explanation of the entire series, he was not asking for its *cause*. He was really saying that a series, finite or infinite, is not "intelligible" or "explained" if it consists of nothing but "contingent" members. To quote Father Copleston once more:

> What we call the world is intrinsically unintelligible apart from the existence of God. The infinity of the series of events, if such an infinity could be proved, would not be in the slightest degree relevant to the situation. If you add up chocolates, you get chocolates, after all, and not sheep. If you add up chocolates to infinity, you presumably get an infinite number of chocolates. So, if you add up contingent beings to infinity, you still get contingent beings, not a necessary being.[17]

This last quotation is really a summary of the "contingency argument," the other main form of the cosmological proof and the third of the five ways of Aquinas. It may be stated more fully in these words: All around us we perceive contingent beings. This includes all physical objects and also all human minds. In calling them "contingent" we mean that they might not have existed. We mean that the universe can be *conceived* without this or that physical object, without this or that human being, however certain their actual existence may be. These contingent beings we can trace back to other contingent beings—for example, a human being to his parents. However, since these other beings are also contingent, they do not provide a real or full explanation. The contingent beings we originally wanted explained have not yet become intelligible, since the beings to which they have been traced are no more necessary than they were. It is just as true of our parents, for example, as it is of ourselves, that they might not have existed. We can then properly explain the contingent beings around us only by tracing them ultimately to some necessary being, to something which exists necessarily, which has "the reason for its existence within itself." The existence of contingent beings, in other words, implies the existence of a necessary being.

This form of the cosmological argument is even more beset with difficulties than the causal variety. In the first place, there is the objection, stated with great force by Kant, that it really commits the same error as the ontological argument, in tacitly regarding existence as an attribute or characteristic. To say that there is a necessary being is to say that it would be a self-contradiction to deny its existence. This would mean that at least one existential statement is a necessary truth; and this in turn presupposes that in at least one case existence is contained in a concept. But only a characteristic can be contained in a concept and it has seemed plain to most philosophers since Kant that existence is not a characteristic, that it can hence never be contained in a concept, and that hence no existential statement can ever be a necessary truth. To talk about anything "existing necessarily" is, in their view, about as sensible as to talk about round squares, and they have concluded that the contingency-argument is quite absurd.

It would lead too far to discuss here the reasons for denying that existence is a characteristic. I will assume that this difficulty can somehow be surmounted and that the expression "necessary being," as it is intended by the champions of the contingency argument, might conceivably apply to something. There remain other objections which are of great weight. I shall try to state these by first quoting again from the debate between Bertrand Russell and Father Copleston:

RUSSELL: ... It all turns on this question of sufficient reason, and I must say you haven't defined "sufficient reason" in a way that I can understand—what do you mean by sufficient reason? You don't mean cause?

COPLESTON: Not necessarily. Cause is a kind of sufficient reason. Only contingent being can have a cause. God is his own sufficient reason; and he is not cause of himself. By sufficient reason in the full sense I mean an explanation adequate for the existence of some particular being.

RUSSELL: But when is an explanation adequate? Suppose I am about to make a flame with a match. You may say that the adequate explanation of that is that I rub it on the box.

COPLESTON: Well for practical purposes—but theoretically, that is only a partial explanation. An adequate explanation must ultimately be a total explanation, to which nothing further can be added.

RUSSELL: Then I can only say that you're looking for something which can't be got, and which one ought not to expect to get.

COPLESTON: To say that one has found it is one thing; to say that one should not look for it seems to me rather dogmatic.

RUSSELL: Well, I don't know. I mean, the explanation of one thing is another thing which makes the other thing dependent on yet another, and you have to grasp this sorry scheme of things entire to do what you want, and that we can't do.'[18]

Russell's main point here may be expanded in the following way. The contingency argument rests on a misconception of what an explanation is and does, and similarly on what it is that makes phenomena "intelligible." Or else it involves an obscure and arbitrary redefinition of "explanation," "intelligible," and related terms. Normally, we are satisfied that we have explained a phenomenon if we have found its cause or if we have exhibited some other uniform or near-uniform connection between it and something else. Confining ourselves to the former case, which is probably the most common, we might say that a phenomenon, Z, has been explained if it has been traced back to a group of factors, a, b, c, d, etc., which are its cause. These factors are the full and real explanation of Z, quite regardless of whether they are pleasing or displeasing, admirable or contempible, necessary or contingent. The explanation would not be adequate only if the factors listed are not really the cause of Z. If they are the cause of Z, the explanation would be adequate, even though each of the factors is merely a "contingent" being.

Let us suppose that we have been asked to explain why General Eisenhower won the elections of 1952. "He was an extremely popular general," we might answer, "while Stevenson was relatively little known; moreover there was a great deal of resentment over the scandals in the Truman Adminstration." If somebody complained that this was only a partial explanation we might mention additional antecedents, such as the widespread belief that the Democrats had allowed communist agents to infiltrate the State Department, [the fact] that Eisenhower was a man with a winning smile, and [the fact] that unlike Stevenson he had shown the good sense to say one thing on race relations in the North and quite another in the South. Theoretically, we might go further and list the motives of all American voters during the weeks or months preceding the election. If we could do this we would have explained Eisenhower's victory. We would have made it intelligible. We would "understand" why he won and why Stevenson lost. Perhaps there is a sense in which we might make Eisenhower's victory even more intelligible if we went further back and discussed such matters as the origin of American views on Communism or of racial attitudes in the North and South. However, to explain the outcome of the election in any ordinary sense, loose or strict, it would not be necessary to go back to prehistoric days or to the amoeba or to a first cause, if such a first cause exists. Nor would our explanation be considered in any way defective because each of the factors mentioned was a "contingent" and not a necessary being. The only thing that matters is whether the factors were really the cause of Eisenhower's election. If they were, then it has been explained although they are contingent beings. If they were not the cause of Eisenhower's victory, we would have failed to explain it even if each of the factors were a necessary being.

If it is granted that, in order to explain a phenomenon or to make it intelligible, we need not bring in a necessary being, then the contingency argument breaks down. For a series, as was already pointed out, is not something over and above its members; and every contingent member of it could in that case be explained by reference to other contingent beings. But I should wish to go further than this, and it is evident from Russell's remarks that he would do so also. Even if it were granted, both that the phrase "necessary being" is meaningful and that all explanations are defective unless the phenomena to be explained are traced back to a necessary being, the conclusion would still not have been established. The conclusion follows from this premise together with the additional premise that *there are* explanations of phenomena in the special sense just mentioned. It is this further premise which Russell (and many other philosophers) would question. They do not merely question, as Copleston implies, whether human beings can ever obtain explanations in this sense, but whether they *exist*. To assume without further ado that phenomena have explanations, or an explanation in this sense, is to beg the very point at issue. The use of the same word, *explanation*, in two crucially different ways lends the additional premise a plausibility it does not really possess. It may indeed be highly plausible to assert that phenomena have explanations, whether we have found them or not, in the ordinary sense in which this usually means that they have causes. It is then tempting to suppose, because of the use of the same word, that they also have explanations in a sense in which this implies dependence on a necessary being. But this is a gross non sequitur.

6

It is necessary to add a few words about the proper way of formula-
ting the position of those who reject the main premise of the cosmological
argument, in either of the forms we have considered. It is sometimes maintained in this connection that in order to reach a "self-existing" entity it is
not necessary to go beyond the universe: the universe itself (or "Nature") is
"self-existing." And this in turn is sometimes expanded into the statement
that while all individual things "within" the universe are caused, the universe itself is uncaused. Statements of this kind are found in Büchner,
Bradlaugh, Haeckel, and other freethinkers of the nineteenth and early
twentieth century. Sometimes the assertion that the universe is "self-
existing" is elaborated to mean that *it* is the "necessary being." Some
eighteenth-century unbelievers, apparently accepting the view that there is
a necessary being, asked why Nature or the material universe could not fill
the bill as well as or better than God.

"Why," asks one of the characters in Hume's *Dialogues,* "may not the
material universe be the necessarily existent Being? . . . We dare not
affirm that we know all the qualities of matter; and for aught we can
determine, it may contain some qualities, which, were they known, would
make its non-existence appear as great a contradiction as that twice two is
five." [19] Similar remarks can be found in Holbach and in several of the
Encyclopedists.

The former of these formulations immediately invites the question
why the universe, alone of all "things," is exempted from the universal
sway of causation. "The strong point of the cosmological argument,"
writes Dr. Ewing, "is that after all it does remain incredible that the physical universe should just have happened. . . . It calls out for some further
explanation of some kind." [20] The latter formulation is exposed to the
criticism that there is nothing any more "necessary" about the existence of
the universe or Nature as a whole than about any particular thing within
the universe.

I hope some of the earlier discussions in this article have made it clear
that in rejecting the cosmological argument one is not committed to either
of these propositions. If I reject the view that there is a supernatural first
cause, I am not thereby committed to the proposition that there is a
natural first cause, and even less to the proposition that a mysterious
thing called the universe qualifies for this title. I may hold that there is no
universe over and above individual things of various sorts; and, accepting

the causal principle, I may proceed to assert that all these things are caused by other things, and these other things by yet other things, and so on, ad infinitum. In this way no arbitrary exception is made to the principle of causation. Similarly, if I reject the assertion that God is a "necessary being," I am not committed to the view that the universe is such an entity. I may hold that it does not make sense to speak of anything as a "necessary being" and that even if there were such a thing as the universe it could not be properly considered a necessary being.

However, in saying that nothing is uncaused or that there is no necessary being, one is not committed to the view that everything, or for that matter anything, is merely a "brute fact." Dr. Ewing laments that "the usual modern philosophical views opposed to theism do not try to give any rational explanation of the world at all, but just take it as a brute fact not to be explained." They thus fail to rationalize the universe. Theism, he concedes, cannot completely rationalize things either since it does not show "how God can be his own cause or how it is that he does not need a cause." [21] Now, if one means by "brute fact" something for which there *exists* no explanation (as distinct from something for which no explanation is in our possession), then the theists have at least one brute fact on their hands, namely God. Those who adopt Buchner's foundation also have one brute fact on their hands, namely the universe. Only the position I have been supporting dispenses with brute facts altogether. I don't know if this is any special virtue, but the defenders of the cosmological argument seem to think so.

NOTES

1. *Dialogues Concerning Natural Religion,* Part IX.
2. *The Critique of Pure Reason,* Transcendental Dialectic, Book II, Ch III.
3. "Theism," Part I, in *Three Essays on Religion.*
4. Reprinted in Russell's *Why I Am Not a Christian* (London: Allen and Unwin, 1957).
5. J. S. O'Connor, "A Scientific Approach to Religion," *The Scientific Monthly,* 1940, p. 369; my italics.
6. Ibid., pp. 369-70.
7. *The Philosophical Bases of Theism,* Lecture V.
8. *The Fundamental Questions of Philosophy,* Ch XI.
9. *The Principles of Natural Theology,* p. 58.
10. *Modern Thomistic Philosophy,* Vol. II, pp. 284-85.
11. Ibid., p. 278.

12. Joyce, *Principles of Natural Theology,* pp. 67-8.

13. Ibid., p. 82.

14. *The Fourfold Root of the Principle of Sufficient Reason,* pp. 42-3. My attention to this passage was drawn by Professor C. J. Ducasse. See his excellent discussion of the arguments for the existence of God in *A Philosophical Scrutiny of Religion,* Ch 15.

15. *Why I Am Not a Christian,* pp. 152-53.

16. Ibid., p. 151.

17. Ibid.

18. Ibid., p. 150.

19. Hume, *Dialogues,* Part IX.

20. Ewing, *Fundamental Questions of Philosophy,* p. 225.

21. Ibid.

Wallace I. Matson

L_ The Argument From Design

Wallace I. Matson, professor of philosophy, was educated at the University of California at Berkeley, where he presently teaches. His books include *The Existence of God* (1965) and *A History of Philosophy* (1968).

Unlike the ontological and cosmological arguments, which are mostly the preserves of theologians and philosophers, the third member of the traditional triad is of great popular appeal. In skeleton outline it is this:

 1. Nature everywhere exhibits orderly structures and processes.

 2. Orderly structures and processes are always the work of an intelligent personality.

Reprinted from Wallace I. Matson, The Existence of God *(Ithaca, N.Y.: Cornell University Press, 1965). Copyright 1965 by Cornell University. Used by permission of Cornell University Press.*

3. Therefore nature is the work of an intelligent personality, i.e., of a god.

The Psalmist sang: "The heavens declare the glory of God; and the firmament sheweth his handywork."[1] This, the central thought of the design argument, is virtually as old as humanity. Naturally the argument has been stated in numerous forms, which differ among themselves according to what orderly structures and processes are regarded as especially significant, and with respect to the means adopted for proving the second premise, that order presupposes intelligence.

The evidences for order in the world are derived from our experience of nature; and in general the argumentation in support of the second premise (which I shall refer to hereafter as "the design axiom") purports to show that it too is a generalization warranted by experience. Thus the argument, it is claimed, has the same form as scientific argument or as inference from circumstantial evidence in judicial proceedings: "Here is the evidence, visible to everyone; we need to account for it; and the only hypothesis, or at least the most plausible one, that will account for it is that of a god. Nature is orderly; but if there were no god, nature (if there were any) would in all likelihood be a mere chaos; therefore there is a god."

I say "a god," not "God," conceding at the outset the objection that our experience of the causes of order at best can never show that any organization whatsoever has to be the production of a single and infinite personal intelligence. The argument from design cannot prove, by itself, monotheism as against polytheism; nor can our finite experience of finite kinds and amounts of orderliness, however vast in scale, establish the infinity of its cause. Moreover, our experience of order is always of the imposition of organization on pre-existing materials; thus the argument from design cannot by itself prove, or render probable, the creation of the world out of nothing. This is not to say that the argument disproves, or tends to disprove, the existence of God. The argument is neutral on this point: God's existence is compatible with it, but not necessitated by it. (This seems so prima facie. However, we shall have to consider later, in connection with the problem of evil, an argument which professes to show that the existence of God is in fact incompatible with the existence of nature as we know it.)

The argument from design thus differs from the other two traditional arguments in being an induction from factual evidence, whereas the ontological argument wholly, and the cosmological argument almost wholly, are products of "pure reason." Unlike the latter two, it aims to show only that there is at least one small-g god; and it can do no more than demonstrate this conclusion to be highly probable, not logically necessary. It does not follow, however, that the design argument is the weakest of the three, only that it is more modest in its pretensions. It purports to offer us the kind of evidence that would be accepted in a physical laboratory, or in a court of law. Surely it would be finicky to reject as of no account argumentation for the existence of a god that establishes that inference as firmly as the physicist proves the existence of electrons, or as the prosecuting attorney showed that Bruno Hauptmann murdered the Lindbergh baby. And this is the kind and degree of proof that supporters of the design argument claim for it.

Moreover, if there is a god—and the argument, if it proves anything, proves the existence of a rather august deity—then the further step to the existence of God is in practice a short one, even though one might say that theoretically it is infinite. If there exists an intelligence so stupendous as to be the effective source of the whole organization and harmony of the universe, it would be overly nice to grumble that monotheism remains to be proved.

SKETCH OF THE HISTORY OF THE ARGUMENT

At least four stages can be distinguished in the development of the design argument. I shall call these the primitive, the teleological, the clockwork, and the entropy stages.

1. *The Primitive Stage.* Here the argument is not yet explicitly formulated, for the good reason that arguments are not constructed to prove beliefs that no one conceives of doubting. When primitive man, "having dined" (Rousseau[2]), begins to think about the origins and guiding forces of nature conceived more or less as a whole, he does not "reach the conclusion" that nature is the product of manlike beings; he does not, that is, consider various alternatives and hit on this one as the most likely. Rather, the conception of an impersonal force or agency does not occur to him—not because he is obtuse, but because, first, there are only a few cause-effect relationships known to him in which his experience encompasses both the cause and the effect: hunting, canoe making, pottery, sorcery, etc.; all or nearly all of these involve personal agency. Second, primitive thinking is conducted in social terms, for the idea of the individual contrasted and possibly opposed to the social unit has scarcely

arisen—and in social terms, the question that is asked about any event that needs accounting for is not "What caused it?" but "Who is guilty?" It would be misleading to describe primitive thought as conceiving of all causes as personal, for our notion of cause is simply not present. It is better to say that all primitive explanations consist in imputing guilt or responsibility.[3]

Since, furthermore, primitive man recognizes no sharp boundaries between himself, his tribe, and nature, it is inevitable that his thinking about nature will be in social terms. Thus the question "Is nature ordered and controlled by persons?" is not asked; one only asks specific questions about the identities and characteristics of the controllers. To these questions mythologies provide the answers. Primitive man, we may note, does not seem much concerned with problems of the literal truth of his myths. Nor need we concern ourselves with the matter. What we must emphasize is that the framework of primitive thought excludes from consideration any interpretation of nature other than a personal one. To primitive mentality, the questions "But really, *is* there a being—a being with thoughts, loves, hates, and power—who hurls the lightning? Might not the lightning 'just happen'?"—these questions would be very strange, perhaps incomprehensible; just as physicists early in this century found strange the suggestion that perhaps they could not find the cause of the disintegration of a radium atom because that event had no cause.

2. *The Teleological Stage.* In the primitive stage, there is no design argument, because there is no occasion for it. There is a world outlook that finds verbal expression in mythology, and that goes beyond particular myths to dominate the whole mode of thinking. This world outlook is personal, animistic. No one bothers to set it out, so to speak, in a textbook; there is no need to do so. Probably the textbook could not be written in any case, for one could not say intelligibly to one's audience that "the world is the abode of personal forces" unless the contrary of the statement would make some sense to them.

Only in response to the challenges of objectors, innovators, and subverters does the textbook get written. The Psalmist, besides assuring us that the heavens declare the glory of God, also complains, most significantly, "The fool hath said in his heart, There is no God."[4] In Western thought, the doubts and alternative hypotheses—of the world being as it is because of the operations of impersonal fate or chance or "fortuitous concourse of atoms"—were put forward by the Ionian Greek philosophers of nature, beginning with Thales and culminating with Democritus. The response, the reintroduction into serious and advanced thought of the notion of cosmic purpose and personality, was the work of Anaxagoras, Socrates, Plato, Aristotle, and the Stoics. The philosophies of these men comprise sophisticated world outlooks in which teleology is central: one's understanding of the world, or indeed of anything in it, is declared to be incomplete unless one grasps the relevant purpose or goal. The claim of the nature philosophers, that understanding consists in knowledge of causes (in the modern sense of the word), is not rejected, but held to be incomplete. Thus according to Aristotle's celebrated doctrine of "four causes" we understand a thing only if we know what it is made of: the material cause; who or what made it, and how: the efficient cause (roughly, "cause" in the modern sense); its form (shape or activity): the formal cause; and its end, that which it naturally tends to become, its raison d'être: the final cause, its *telos*. Of these four, all but the first, according to Aristotle, are really aspects of a single notion, the essence of the thing, its purpose and the fulfillment of that purpose.[5]

All this is a far cry from wood nymphs, thunder gods, and Marduk and Osiris making their mud pies. And in fact, belief in a superhuman organizer who conceives the cosmic project and carries it out by forming the originally chaotic matter of the world, as a potter moulds his clay— this belief was held only halfheartedly or perhaps in a figurative sense by Plato,[6] and not considered at all by Aristotle and the Stoics. Stoicism is pantheistic in holding that God is the soul of the world, an aspect of it, not outside it, and not personal, except in a very attenuated sense. Aristotle's god moves the world through the intricate evolutions of the spheres only "as the beloved moves the lover,"[7] or as the goal posts move the football players; though his pure activity is thought and he is a personal god in the sense of being a unitary intelligence, he makes nothing, nor is he even aware of the world.[8]

In consequence, the argument from design had no place in Aristotle's theology, which was based instead on the cosmological argument.[9] And while the Stoics expatiated upon the orderliness of the cosmos, their inference was that since the universe, like the human body, is organized, so also it must have a soul; but this doctrine is pantheism, not personal theism. Thus in antiquity, the design argument declined in relative importance. It is instructive to consider why the decline was only temporary.

Philosophically, what had happened was that these thinkers had tried to retain the notion of purpose while doing away with the proposer. What remained was a sort of grin without a cat, which could not long endure.

Theologically, or rather religiously, the excogitated deities (or divine aspects) were of no use, because of their depersonalization and consequent lack of interest in and responsibility for the affairs of men. Hence it is not surprising that the general run of even cultured men came to prefer the grossest superstitions to the abstractions served up by the philosophers.

Christianity asserts the existence of a personal creator and designer. But original Christianity was not a philosophical system at all, and propounded no arguments. Thus Aristotelian metaphysics and Christian religion each lacked what the other could provide. We see through hindsight that it was inevitable for the two to unite; though the union had to wait until the twelfth century for its consummation. Aristotle's cosmological argument supplied, for St. Thomas Aquinas, the principal rational means for demonstrating the existence of God; but since the Christian God, not the Aristotelian *theos,* was shown to exist, it was appropriate for St. Thomas to reintroduce the design argument:

> The *fifth way* is taken from the governance of the world. For we see that certain things which lack consciousness, such as natural bodies, act for an end; this is evident from their acting always, or rather often, in the same way, so as to obtain the best result. Hence it is plain that not by chance, but by intention, do they achieve their end. Now whatever has not consciousness does not move toward an end unless directed by some being endowed with consciousness and intelligence; as the arrow is shot by the archer. Therefore some intelligent being exists by whom all natural things are directed to their end; and this being we call God. [10]

The Aristotelian contribution to this version of the argument is the premise that all things "act for an end," and the support of this premise, "this is evident from their acting . . . in the same way, so as to obtain the best result." St. Thomas departs from the Philosopher in arguing further that the movement toward an end must be the result of direction by "some being endowed with consciousness and intelligence, as the arrow is shot by the archer"—in Aristotelian words, there must be an intelligent efficient cause, applied *ab extra,* to account for orderly processes. This is not to say that the regulators (Aristotelian "entelechies") of orderly action—the nesting instinct of birds, the gravitation ("seeking its natural place") of stones, the perfect circular motions of celestial spheres—may not be, so to speak, "built in"; however, the Saint insists that if they are built in, some intelligent being must have built them in. Everything orderly must have an intelligent efficient cause—our design axiom. St. Thomas does not argue in support of this axiom; it is self-evident for him.

3. *The Clockwork Stage.* The Aristotelian system was based on animism, but the edifice was so elaborate that the foundations were hardly visible; and in fact the principle support, the design axiom, was removed altogether. St. Thomas strengthened the whole by putting this pillar back; nevertheless, other weaknesses eventuated in collapse, in the seventeenth century.

I shall not relate the story of this debacle. For our purposes it is sufficient to note that Galileo and Newton did away with the idea that motion (and consequently other kinds of change, if there are any) required some explanation of its persistence; in Newton's system only changes in the direction or speed of motion need be accounted for. Second, change of motion was to be accounted for, and accounted for completely, in terms of force, two varieties of which were recognized: impact of one body on another, and gravitational attraction. Both of these were measurable and impersonal; description of events in these terms rendered superfluous the notion of Aristotelian final causes. That is, final causes disappear because their principal function, in the Aristotelian system, was to explain why things left to themselves do not come to a dead halt; while in the new science uniform motion was as "natural" as rest. Nor could the Aristotelian system be patched up by invoking final causes to explain nonuniform motion. In the Newtonian system acceleration was fully explicable in terms of the interactions of forces communicated from one body to another by impact or gravitation. The latter force had been purged of the connotation of "seeking natural place," for Copernicus, Kepler, and Bruno had abolished the absolute center of the universe.

We must emphasize, however, that only strictly Aristotelian final causes—internal sources of motion and change, built-in purposes not entailing a planner—were excluded from the new mechanical philosophy. Final causes, in the wider sense of purposes *ab extra*, were not eliminated from scientific thinking in one fell swoop. It was then, and perhaps still is, rather audacious to speculate that every kind of event, including the phenomena of life and consciousness, is amenable to mechanical explanation. The more advanced thinkers admitted that final causes had no place in explaining any change that could be analyzed without remainder into a complex motion of particles; but they by no means regarded it as certain that every event was of this kind.

But although final causes and purposes are easily confused, they are really distinct notions; hence the abolition of the former did not entail the extinction of the latter from the world outlook. Final causes are at the heart of the cosmological argument; cosmic purposes are of the essence of the argument from design. The principal effects of the scientific revolution on natural theology were as might have been expected: de-emphasis of the cosmological argument, with a tendency to revert from the subtle to the crude form, the elevation of the relative importance of the argument from design. Less was heard of immediate providence (it became incredible, for instance, that comets, whose orbits had been calculated, should be divine portents), and compensatingly more of the necessity of a god as original designer of the harmonious universe.

For, it was thought, there are two kinds of order, and the mechanical philosophy can explain only one of them. There are aggregates, and there are organizations. When a volcano erupts, boulders of various sizes and shapes are strewn about the landscape—all in strict accordance with the laws of motion and of gravitation. Some peasants come along, select stones of the right size, dress them, and make a wall of them. The muscular forces that they have to apply to lift, transport, and chip the stones are also mechanically explainable. None of the laws of motion would have been violated if the forces in the volcanic eruption had been just right to deposit the whole collection of boulders, not as a heap, but as a wall in the first place. Nevertheless, volcanic forces are "blind"—they might produce an organization, but they seldom do. On the other hand, the forces exerted by the peasants' muscles are purposefully directed; they ordinarily produce organizations rather than aggregates.

Now if nature were nothing but the playground of blind forces, nature should be (so the argument goes) wholly, or almost wholly, composed of aggregates. But in fact it is full of organizations, very many of which exceed in fineness, intricacy, and ingenuity any production of human purposiveness. Here is where mechanical explanation shows itself incomplete: not that anything in nature is necessarily incompatible with, a "violation" of, the laws of motion; but these laws of themselves cannot account for the amount and kind of organization that is to be found. Nature is a cosmos, not a chaos; but it is so probable as to amount almost to certainty that a nature that was the product only of the forces inherent in matter would be a chaos. Hence nature must have been organized from outside, by the only kind of force we know to be capable of producing organization: purposive intelligence.

Newton himself wrote in this vein:

> The six primary planets are revolved about the sun in circles concentric with the sun, and with motions directed towards the same parts, and almost in

the same plane. Ten moons are revolved about the earth, Jupiter and Saturn, in circles concentric with them, with the same direction of motion, and nearly in the planes of the orbits of those planets; but it is not to be conceived that mere mechanical causes could give birth to so many regular motions, since the comets range over all parts of the heavens in very eccentric orbits. . . . This most beautiful system of the sun, planets, and comets, could only proceed from the counsel and dominion of an intelligent and powerful Being. . . . [Though we have no adequate idea of God's attributes,] we know him by his most wise and excellent contrivances of things, and final causes. . . . Blind metaphysical necessity, which is certainly the same always and everywhere, could produce no variety of things. All that diversity of natural things which we find suited to different times and places could arise from nothing but the ideas and will of a Being necessarily existing. . . . And thus much concerning God; to discourse of whom from the appearances of things, does certainly belong to Natural Philosophy.[11]

The perfect example of a mechanical system is, of course, a machine; and to the eighteenth century the most fascinating kind of machine[12] —the only one, besides the harpsichord, allowed in the drawing room—was the clock. Here is a complicated assemblage of parts, each interacting with all the others, directly or remotely, not capriciously or confusedly but with the regularity for which the word "clockwork" has become a synonym. The whole concerted action serves a purpose, the purpose envisaged by the clockmaker; the organization would not exist but for that purpose, and for the intelligence that designed and made that elegant instrument out of aggregates of raw materials. The classical statement of the argument from design, by "Cleanthes" in Part II of Hume's *Dialogues Concerning Natural Religion*, draws an analogy between the universe and a machine:

Look round the world, contemplate the whole and every part of it: you will find it to be nothing but one great machine, subdivided into an infinite number of lesser machines, which again admit of subdivisions to a degree beyond what human senses and faculties can trace and explain. All these various machines, and even their most minute parts, are adjusted to each other with an accuracy which ravishes into admiration all men who have ever contemplated them. The curious adapting of means to ends, throughout all nature, resembles exactly, though it much exceeds, the productions of human contrivance—of human design, thought, wisdom, and intelligence. Since therefore the effects resemble each other, we are led to infer, by all the rules of analogy, that the causes also resemble, and that the Author of nature is somewhat similar to the mind of man, though possessed of much larger faculties, proportioned to the grandeur of the work which he has executed. By this argument a posteriori, and by this argument alone, do we prove at once the existence of a Deity and his similarity to human mind and intelligence.

In its cultural context, this formulation of the argument was a very strong one, appealing even—or especially—to men who rejected most of the tenets of orthodox religion. It was the crushing retort to atheists: in Coleridge's famous lines,

> *Forth from his dark and lonely hiding-place*
> *(Portentous sight!) the owlet Atheism*
> *Sailing on obscene wings athwart the noon,*
> *Drops his blue-fringèd lids, and holds them close,*
> *And hooting at the glorious sun in Heaven,*
> *Cries out, "Where is it?"* [13]

Hume's trenchant criticism of the argument, usually considered definitive, was in fact limited in its scope. He concerned himself principally with showing that the analogy on which the argument rests (or appears to rest) is weak—for the universe is not very much like a machine; that the argument generates a vicious regress—for we are entitled to ask after the material basis of the cosmic intelligence; that the argument at best cannot prove the unity, infinity, benevolence, or even continued existence of a deity; and that it "affords no inference that affects human life, or can be the source of any action or forbearance." [14] The design axiom itself, however, was still left standing, though wobbling, at the end of the *Dialogues:* "the cause or causes of order in the universe probably bear some remote analogy to human intelligence." [15]

4. *The Entropy Stage.* Hume could not demolish the design axiom, for want of an alternative hypothesis to account for cosmic order. Not quite seriously he suggested "generation" as an alternative principle of ordering, revealed in experience; and he speculated that the universe might be as well compared to an animal, or even a vegetable, as to a machine. That would not do, of course, since "generation"—a process the mechanisms of which were entirely unknown in Hume's day—was precisely the principal fact that design was invoked to explain.

In the middle of the nineteenth century, Darwin and Lyell provided the alternative hypothesis that would account mechanistically for biological order. While the Ionian Greeks had developed evolutionary speculations to an astonishing extent, Aristotle had rejected their conclusions, and on this subject his authority, later reinforced by Genesis, stood unchallenged for more than two millennia. This fact should be borne in mind when assessing the plausibility of the design argument before Darwin: even Hume was obliged to assume that either the present array of living things had eternally existed in all its complex variegation, or else everything had come into being all at once and together.

After 1859, it was possible to regard the curious adapting of means to ends in nature as the outcome of a long process of development, in which, beginning with the simplest kinds of proto-organisms, those varieties that just happened to possess some slightly superior adaptation to their environment—some little added fillip of complexity—would survive and reproduce themselves, passing on their advantage to their descendants, while their inferior rivals became extinct. Darwin in biology, like Laplace in celestial mechanics half a century earlier, "had no need of the hypothesis" of God.[16]

The furious attacks on Darwinism in the nineteenth century were motivated chiefly by desire to preserve the literal interpretation of the Scriptures. In the long run, however, the danger posed to traditional theism by Darwinism was more fundamental: it lay in the undermining of the design axiom. In our own day the new science of genetics has shown how both slight individual differences and major mutations come about, while Darwin's principles still suffice to account for the change in character, over a long period, of a population in which variations occur—the "origin of species."

It should not, however, be concluded too hastily that 1859 marked the demise of the argument from design. Recently, attempts have been made to rehabilitate this argument by showing that the process of evolution itself, being progressive in character, is inexplicable unless a guiding intelligence is postulated. Two related inferences are urged in support of this conclusion. One purports to be derived from the statistical theory of probability: the universe, big as it is and old as it is, is still not big enough or old enough for there to be a significant probability of organizations as complex as those found in living things being formed by mere planless mixing. The other comes from the second law of thermodynamics (law of increase of entropy), according to which (so it is argued) all merely mechanical processes move in the direction of greater disorganization, whereas evolutionary processes, which show the opposite tendency, must in consequence be other than merely mechanical.

At the present time, the question whether the argument from design offers a reasonable basis for belief in the existence of a god is very much the same as the question whether the probability and entropy considerations lend any support to the design axiom. I shall therefore examine these arguments in greater detail.

THE PROBABILITY ARGUMENT

Human Destiny (1947), the last work of the French physiologist Pierre Lecomte du Noüy, contains the best-known recent presentation of the probability argument. In summary it is as follows:

Life has not always existed on this planet. The origin of life was either the result of the working of intelligence in some sense, or it was not. If it was not, then it happened "by chance alone," that is, as the result of fortuitous concourse of atoms moving randomly.

Now one essential constituent of all living things is protein. The simplest protein molecule contains about 2,000 atoms of five different kinds; and it is not just an aggregate of these atoms, but an intricate organization of them.

For the sake of simplicity, assume that a simple protein molecule consists of 2,000 atoms, and of two kinds only, not five. Assume further that the structural complexity of the molecule can be represented by degree of dissymmetry 0.9. ("Dissymmetry" is a measure of separation of distinct constituents. Thus a bottle of milk in which all the cream is at the top exhibits the maximum degree of dissymmetry, that is, 1; while homogenized milk has 0 dissymmetry.) Professor Charles-Eugene Guye has calculated the probability of a chance occurrence of a configuration of these specifications. It is 2.02×10^{-321}, that is, two chances out of a total number that would be represented by 1 followed by about six lines of zeros on this page. The volume of substance necessary for such a probability to take place is beyond all imagination. It would be that of a sphere with a radius so great that light would take 10^{82} years to cover this distance. The volume is incomparably greater than that of the whole universe including the farthest galaxies, whose light takes only two million years to reach us. In brief, we would have to imagine a volume more than one sextillion, sextillion, sextillion times greater than the Einsteinian universe.

> The probability for a *single* molecule of high dissymmetry to be formed by the action of chance and normal thermic agitation remains practically nil. Indeed, if we suppose 500 trillion shakings per second, which corre-

sponds to the order of magnitude of light frequencies. . . , we find that the time needed to form, on an average, one such molecule . . . in a material volume equal to that of our terrestrial globe is about 10^{234} billions of years.

BUT WE MUST NOT FORGET THAT THE EARTH HAS ONLY EXISTED FOR TWO BILLION YEARS AND THAT LIFE APPEARED ABOUT ONE BIL-LION YEARS AGO, AS SOON AS THE EARTH HAD COOLED.

Life itself is not even in question but merely one of the substances which constitute living beings. Now, one molecule is of no use. Hundreds of millions of *identical* ones are necessary. . . .

We are brought to the conclusion that, actually, it is *totally impossible* to account scientifically for all phenomena pertaining to Life, its development and progressive evolution, and that, unless the foundations of modern science are overthrown, they are unexplainable.[17]

Du Noüy was not so incautious as to conclude at once that since it is totally impossible to account scientifically (i.e. mechanically) for life, therefore the existence of God is proved. More modestly, he contented himself with the inference of "telefinalism," that an "anti-chance factor" must be at work in the universe. Quite understandably, nevertheless, apologists for theism greeted Du Nouy's book as a vindication of their position, a turning of the tables on "materialists," who were thus shown to be the real believers in miracles. As our author permitted himself to remark: "The writer is not naive enough to think that this discussion will convince any materialist. People who have a faith cannot be convinced by mere words and logic. Men with an irrational faith—and we hope that we have made it clear that such is their case—do not yield to rational arguments."[18]

CRITICISM OF THE PROBABILITY ARGUMENT

It is not wise, however, to believe that an argument is irrefutable just because its author says so. In the present instance the "rational argument" rests on an untenable assumption, and the "logic" leads to an unwarranted conclusion. For the only thing really proved, granting the calculations, is the fantastic improbability of any protein molecule ever having come into existence all at once as the result of the simultaneous combination of its simple atomic constituents. But no "materialist"—at least, none since the fifth century B.C.—ever dreamed of anything of this sort.

Let us make a further simplifying assumption and talk not of protein molecules but of adult human beings. We are justified in doing so, because while a human body is more complicated than a protein molecule, the latter is already so incredibly complex that the future for the improbability of the "chance" production of a human body is scarcely more staggering than the protein figure given us by Guye and Du Noüy.

In these terms, which may be pictorially somewhat more vivid, the alternative posed by Du Noüy becomes this: either human bodies are the products of intelligent design, or else they are the results of atoms somehow coming together, in their haphazard motions, in just the right way.

About 440 B.C., the physician-philosopher Empedocles accepted this dilemma; and since he believed that everything came about by "mixture and separation," he took the second horn. His speculation about the origin of life was that the earth, at a certain period, spontaneously produced all kinds of monsters and *disjecta membra:* "Where many heads grew up without necks, and arms were wandering about naked, bereft of shoulders, and eyes roamed about alone in need for foreheads."[19] "Many creatures arose with faces and breasts on both sides, offspring of cattle with human faces, and again there sprang up children of men with cattle's heads; creatures, too, in which were mixed some parts from men and some of the nature of women, furnished with sterile members."[20]
Of these chance productions the only ones to survive were the very few that were so organized as to be able to live and reproduce.

The principle of Empedocles' reasoning—"survival of the fittest"—is that of modern evolutionary theory; but his detail is fantastic. We may say that Du Noüy has thoroughly refuted him—but him only. For it is another principle of evolutionary thought, equal in importance to the survival of the fittest, that nature makes no leaps. The chance agglutination of atoms into fully formed men, or protein molecules, would not be evolution but its antithesis. The evolutionary concept is that just as man is the last stage reached to date of an immensely slow and complicated process of successive modifications in less complex creatures, so also the protein molecule itself is the resultant of a very large number of successive stages of synthesis, beginning with quite simple compounds.

Chemists have long been able to synthesize very complex compounds in the laboratory. The first synthesis of proteins has recently been announced. To be sure, laboratory procedures are instances of "telefinalism," the chemist's manipulations being the "anti-chance factor." It is more relevant, however, to observe that the synthesis of a complicated compound always proceeds in the laboratory in steps. One does not make even so simple and common a compound as acetic acid just by mixing up its constituent carbon, hydrogen, and oxygen. We must leave it to the French to calculate how many sextillions of sextillions of sextillions of years that would take. Instead, one takes some lime (calcium oxide) and heats it with carbon to produce calcium carbide, which then reacts with water to yield acetylene. This can be oxidized to produce acetaldehyde, and further oxidation of the latter compound yields acetic acid. But every step in this process consists in bringing certain ingredients together at certain pressures and temperatures, whereupon the desired reaction occurs spontaneously.

The acetic acid that occurs in nature is the product of a far more complicated process—involving, as a matter of fact, the action of proteins. But the same considerations apply. We may, if we like, stupefy ourselves at the fantastic improbability of the "chance" occurrence of acetic acid out of its atomic constituents, *tout court*. But that would be nothing to the point. The "probability" of acetic acid being formed in nature is not this probability, but the product of the probabilities of conditions permitting the steps of the synthesis to be realized in succession.

But is it meaningful at all to speak of probabilities in such contexts? This brings us to the unwarranted assumption of Du Noüy's argument. He states it in this way: "Let us define what is understood by the *probability* of an event: it is the ratio of the number of cases favorable to the event, to the total number of possibilities, *all possible cases being considered as equally probable.*"[21]

This amounts to what statisticians call the "principle of indifference" or the "principle of insufficient reason": if there are n possibilities, and we know of no reason why one should be more likely to occur than another, then the probability of each is $1/n$. It is sometimes said that we assume this principle when we declare the probability of throwing double six to be $1/36$; for there are thirty-six ways in which two dice can fall, only one of which is "favorable to the event," and we know no reason why any one of the thirty-six possibilities should be more likely than any other. Even here, though, the application of the so-called principle is dubious. Is it not, rather, that all those who concern themselves with the probabilities of dice have at hand a great deal of antecedent knowledge about the behavior of symmetrical objects? And what if nonloaded dice inexplicably kept falling double six—would we go on saying that the probability was still just $1/36$? In any case, the general application of the principle would yield some very curious results. For instance, we know nothing of the causes of baldness. We know, then, of no reason why any person should, or should not, be bald; consequently the probability that any person—young or old, male or female—is bald is the same as the probability that he is not bald. Therefore it is a matter of astonishment that only a small fraction of human beings are bald (and there must be a cosmic hairdresser at work?). And we know of no reason why the star Sirius should have, or should not have, a planet. Therefore, the probability that Sirius has a planet is 1/2. Moreover, we know of no reason why it should, or should not, have a hundred planets. Therefore the probability that Sirius has a hundred planets is 1/2, and identical with the probability that it has just one planet. The principle of insufficient reason is only one more fairly ingenious attempt to distill knowledge out of ignorance.

The conception of probability employed by most statisticians is that of relative frequency in the long run. The probability that a given individual will be bald is just the number of bald persons, divided by the total number of persons, bald and hairy. If our livelihood depends on probabilities (if we are insurance actuaries, say), we shall choose the best-defined reference class we can in making our estimate: if we have to make a bet on whether Jones will die in the next ten years, we shall not content ourselves with using the mortality rate for the general population, but will want to know the age, sex, race, personal habits, medical history, etc., of Jones; and we shall make our estimate on the basis of the class containing individuals who approximate Jones in these characteristics, which are antecedently known, by experience, to be relevant to longevity. If we cannot get the information about Jones, then the best we can do is calculate the probability relative to the whole population; if we happen to have no statistics about that, then we can assign no probability at all. We may make a random guess; but that is not the same thing.

How probable is it that Sirius has at least one planet? Many, perhaps most, statisticians would refuse to speak of such a "probability"; but if there is one, it is equal to the number of stars, in a significantly large random sample of stars, which have each at least one planet, divided by the total number of stars in the sample. Since we have no adequate sample of stars to go by, we do not know at all what the probability is. Indirectly, we may approach the problem by finding out something about cosmic evolution; but that is another matter, though it may still involve probabilities, in relation to another kind of reference class. The principle of insufficient reason, however, is not to be invoked.

The question "What is the probability of proteins developing 'by chance'?" is an extremely complicated one—supposing it to make any sense at all. To answer the question adequately, we would need to know in the first place what the successive steps are in the natural synthesis of proteins out of basic constituents. But after leaping that formidable hurdle, we would still need a lot of other information hard to come by, such as the value of the probability that a given planetary atmosphere will at some time be composed principally of ammonia and methane. (The formula "Number of planetary atmospheres containing ammonia and methane, divided by total number of planetary atmospheres," though correct, is no help.) Indirectly, statistics which astrophysicists can obtain about the relative abundances of carbon, hydrogen, and nitrogen in the universe provide some very slight basis for estimating this probability; but in general we may say that we have no data at all on which to base an estimate of the probability of "chance" occurrence of protein.

If we did have the answer, it would be of no interest to us. We would merely know, then, that we live on a rare planet, or on a common one, as the case might be. Knowledge of the statistical probability would not of itself entail any knowledge of the causes.

It should not be supposed that if Du Noüy's version of the probability argument fails, some other such argument might succeed. If in the present state of our cosmic knowledge there is no way of selecting a reference class so as to make a meaningful estimate of the probability of life beginning "by chance," then it is not possible even to state any version of the probability argument without assuming the principle of insufficient reason. Or in other words, every such argument must be vitiated by the initial fallacy of deciding a priori what is probable and improbable, or (what amounts to the same thing) of confusing the wonderful with the improbable. Of course, the origin and development of life on this planet is an awe-inspiring theme. By no means does it follow that the process cannot have an explanation of the usual scientific sort.

Since the actuarial concept of probability is of no help in estimating the chance of protein, or men, occurring from "random shuffling of atoms," we may choose to invoke some other notion of probability: for instance, we may define probability as the measure of rational expectation. But if we do, then we should remember that it is reasonable to expect things to happen as they do happen; and that is all there is to say about the matter.

The arguments based on "the fitness of the environment"[22] resemble the probability argument in dwelling on the complex concatenation of "improbable" characteristics that matter in general, and the earth in particular, must have in order to render life possible. If the earth were only a few million miles closer to the sun, or farther away from it, the climate would be too hot or too cold; or if the earth did not revolve as it does, with the angle between the polar axis and the ecliptic being just what it is, the climate would be extremely unpropitious; or if water did not exhibit the anomalous behavior of expanding upon freezing, the oceans would all be frozen, and so forth. Such arguments, however, amount to regarding this world, with the laws of nature operative in it, as only one of the infinite "possible worlds." In effect, they bid farewell to the argument from design and return us to the cosmological argument.

THE ENTROPY ARGUMENT

There is another modern form of the argument from design which, while it has much in common with Du Noüy's, appeals not primarily to the mathematical calculus of probabilities in order to make its point, but to a well-established generalization of physics: the second law of thermodynamics (law of increase of entropy).

The law can be stated in various ways. Perhaps the most common statement is this: in any isolated system, entropy tends to a maximum. Now entropy is not a concept that is easy to grasp intuitively. It can be defined precisely only in terms of the integral calculus. Very roughly,[23] the entropy of a region (spatial volume) is the amount of heat energy in the region divided by the temperature of the hottest object in the region. If the region is isolated, that is, if no energy flows into it or out of it (a tightly stoppered themos bottle approximates this), the second law of thermodynamics states that the entropy cannot decrease; it must either remain the same or grow larger. This does not mean that the temperature of the hottest body in the isolated region, or indeed of the whole region, may not increase: for example, a fire may break out in it. According to the law, however, even in that case the increase of energy in the form of heat must outstrip the rise in temperature.

All this may seem remote from natural theology. The connection will begin to be visible when we observe that what the law states, abstractly and precisely, is that all things left to themselves tend to "run down." For the entropy of a system is a measure of the amount of energy in the system that is unavailable to do work. By the law of conservation of energy, the total energy in an isolated system remains constant. Energy may exist in various forms, however: coiled springs, electric cells, gunpowder, fire, etc.

Suppose an ice chest contains initially air and a battery-operated electric fan. This array will run for a while, then stop. But there is still as much energy in the chest as at the beginning. What has happened to it? It existed at first as chemical potential energy in the cells of the battery; this was converted into electrical energy, the directed flow of electrons in a wire; the motor converted it into mechanical energy, rotation of the armature and fan blades—and finally the fan blades stirred up the air, that is, imparted additional *random* motion to the air molecules, this random motion constituting an increase in the amount of heat in the air. But that is the end of the line. There is no way of reversing the process and using the random motion of the air molecules to turn the fan blades, to operate the motor as a generator and recharge the battery. The energy which at the beginning was available to do work (turn the fan) has now been rendered unavailable, dissipated, "degraded." The entropy has reached a maximum, and nothing further can happen as long as the chest is closed.

The only way to extract work from heat energy is to have two bodies at different temperatures and utilize the flow of energy from the hotter to the colder. But the process entails the heating of the colder and the cooling of the hotter. If left to itself, the system must reach thermal equilibrium, the point at which the two bodies are at the same temperature and no more work can be done. The molecules are still moving, but moving at random —as many, on the average, in one direction as in another. Their motion, at first organized and hence available to do work, is now disorganized. When a wind is blowing, i.e., when most of the air molecules are moving in the same direction, a windmill can be operated; when the air is still, the molecules are still moving, nearly as fast individually as in the wind, but their motion will not now actuate any mechanical device.

From this we may conclude (but with a caution to be emphasized later) that the entropy of a system is a measure of its disorganization, and we may rephrase the second law to read: any isolated system tends to become more and more disorganized.

The application to the design argument should now be apparent: nature, left to its own devices, runs down. Two inferences are drawn: first, nature must have been "wound up" in the first place by some outside force; second, those processes within nature that show increase of organization cannot be "merely natural," but must be somehow under the guidance of an extranatural organizing force. Now the only such organizing force we know is mind; therefore we must postulate a cosmic mind as director of the evolutionary, that is, progressive, processes in the universe.

In his book *Belief Unbound* William Pepperell Montague defended theism by a combination of the probability and entropy arguments. Montague's version of the latter runs this way: The law of increase of entropy holds universally, "in any world in which there is random motion alone, or random motion supplemented by such reciprocal *ab extra* determinations as are formulated in the laws of physics."

> And yet within this world that is forever dying, there have been born or somehow come to be, protons, and electrons, atoms of hydrogen and helium, and the whole series of increasingly complex chemical elements culminating in radium and uranium. And these atoms not only gather loosely into nebulae, but in the course of time combine tightly into molecules, which in turn combine into the various complicated crystals and colloids that our senses can perceive. And on the only planet we really know, certain of the compounds of carbon gain the power of building themselves up by assimilation, and so growing and reproducing. Life thus started "evolves," as we say, into higher and higher forms, such as fishes, reptiles, and birds, mammals, primates, men, and, among men, sages and heroes.[24]

This tendency to organization, contrary to the otherwise universal entropic degeneration, is not plausibly to be explained "with only the types of mechanistic causality ... that are recognized in physics."

> But what is the alternative ... ? Nothing so very terrible; merely the hypothesis that the kind of causality that we know best, the kind that we find directly and from within, the causality, in short, that operates in our lives and minds, is not an alien accident but an essential ingredient of the world that spawns us. ... We merely suggest that the kind of anabolic and antientropic factor of whose existence we are certain in ourselves, is present and operative in varying degree in all nature. If we are right, we escape the universe of perpetual miracle, on which the atheist sets his heart.[25]

In summary:

1. All merely physical processes are entropic.

2. All entropic processes tend to dissolution and disorganization.

3. Therefore all merely physical processes tend to dissolution and disorganization.

4. But some processes—namely, evolutionary ones—tend to synthesis and organization.

5. Therefore some processes are antientropic and not merely physical.

6. Now we know that mind is an antientropic factor; and mind is the

only antientropic factor we know.

7. Therefore evolutionary processes are probably mind-directed.

The main things wrong with this argument are that the sixth premise is dubious and the second is certainly false. Let us begin by discussing the sixth premise.

A common example of increase of entropy is the diffusion of liquids. Half fill a beaker with water and then very carefully pour red wine into the upper half. There will then be two layers, the bottom one colorless and the top one red. If the beaker is left undisturbed, in time the differentiation will vanish; a uniformly pink fluid will be found in it. This is because the molecules of water and wine [26] at the boundary are in constant random motion, some up, some down. The molecules of wine will pass into the water, and vice versa. The process is not reversible; separate layers of wine and water will mix themselves up, but no mixture of wine and water will separate itself.

Strictly speaking, the latter eventuality is not impossible, only highly improbable. For the second law is a law of statistically average behavior. At some time all the wine molecules just might happen to be moving upward, while simultaneously all the water molecules happened to be moving downward. The chance of such an occurrence, however, is represented by the rather French number of one in 1,550 sextillions, if the beaker holds one quart.

But suppose now that a solid disc is placed horizontally in the middle of the beaker. There is a hole in it just big enough to allow a single molecule to pass; and the hole is provided with a cover. This cover is held by an infinitesimal but intelligent being ("Maxwell's demon") who is able to distinguish water molecules from wine molecules, as in their random motion they approach the hole. Whenever he sees a wine molecule approaching from below, or a water molecule from above, he opens the hole and lets the molecule pass through; otherwise he keeps it shut. In this way the mixture might separate itself (for the demon does not *shove* any of the molecules; he does no work on this isolated system), and its entropy might decrease under the guidance but not added physical energy of an intelligence.

What this hypothetical case shows is that a pure, i.e. disembodied, intelligence could conceivably be an antientropic factor. But it is a dizzy leap from this to the conclusion that the intelligence we have is antientropic. Sorting, to be sure, is a typical intelligent activity. The oranges come down the chute; the sorter (a man or a machine) causes the good ones to roll to the right, the culls to the left. However, if the sorter is a machine, it is constantly degrading electrical and mechanical energy into heat; if a man, he is doing the same with carbohydrates and proteins. The "isolated system" here cannot exclude the sorter and its energy needs. A machine sorter that would degrade no energy is impossible. I shall not dogmatize that a mind independent of a material and entropic structure is out of the question, but it cannot be seriously maintained that we know of the existence of any such entity. There is no "anabolic and antientropic factor of whose existence we are certain in ourselves."

Montague seems to overlook the fact that the second law applies only to real entropy in an isolated system. There is nothing to forbid the entropy of some part of a system being decreased, and in fact this is very common. A steam generator, burning coal and producing electricity, is upgrading energy. A man lifting a rock onto an elevated platform is doing the same. All that the law requires is that the amount of energy degraded in the whole process should exceed the amount upgraded; and there is no reason to believe that this requirement is not satisfied in both cases—not to mention more spectacular examples such as the synthesis of proteins by plants, in which the "isolated system" must be regarded as including not only the plant and its immediate environment, but the sun also.

However that may be, the argument is certainly vitiated by its second premise, that all entropic processes tend to dissolution and disorganization. "Disorganization" is a vague term; nevertheless, most people would presumably regard H_2O as more "organized" than H_2 and O_2, cream-on-top-and-milk-below as more organized than mixed cream and milk, stars as more organized than clouds of cosmic dust. Yet the processes whereby these "organizations" come into being exhibit increase in entropy no whit less than "levelling, scattering, and disorganization." From the standpoint of thermodynamics it is as Heraclitus said: the way up and the way down are one and the same.

If this were not so, the second law would be a scientific monstrosity. The laws of science have no exceptions—not because of the strictness of their enforcement, or the wisdom of scientists, but just because if a real contrary instance to an alleged law is discovered, the law ceases to be a law (more exactly: "We thought it was a law, but we were mistaken"). If evolutionary and other anabolic processes—of which physicists are hardly unaware—were antientropic, the second law of thermodynamics would long since have been discarded or explicitly limited in its scope. It would have to read, in effect: all processes occurring in an isolated system are such as to increase the total entropy of the system, except for those that decrease it. To put it another way: Montague, in effect, has claimed to have discovered that the second law of thermodynamics is false. And the fact that the literature of physics contains no discussion of this claim should hardly be taken as indicating a cowardly conspiracy of silence.

There is one plausible though not certain inference to be drawn from the second law, which may have some bearing on the question of the existence of God. If the universe can be considered as an isolated system (this is questioned by Hoyle and other "steady-state" cosmologists), and its entropy is constantly increasing, then, extrapolating backwards, there must have been a time in the remote past when that entropy was zero, or at least very small. And several independent lines of evidence converge in pointing to something extraordinary having taken place about eleven billion years ago. A creation out of nothing, by an infinite Being if you like, is a hypothesis that cannot be ruled out by the physical evidence presently available. But neither is it in any degree confirmed by that evidence, nor is it the only possible hypothesis.

THE DESIGN AXIOM CONSIDERED FURTHER

It would be a mistake to think that Du Noüy and Montague have bungled jobs that others might do more skillfully. For any attempt to show that the basis on which probabilities are to be calculated is improbable, or that nature is unnatural, is bound to fail.

While the fallaciousness of an argument does not entail the falsity of its conclusion, it ought to be admitted that repeated failures to offer any sound reasons for a belief create some presumption that the belief is false. Nothing more than a presumption can thus arise, however; in the case of the design axiom, there are counterpresumptions in its favor, which are perhaps so strong that even the complete destruction of all forms of the design argument could not offset them. But before continuing our discussion, let us see where we now stand with respect to the design axiom.

The universe is full of complex organizations exhibiting "curious adapting of means to ends." Our question is, how are these to be accounted for?

There are three (and, as far as I can see, only three) abstractly tenable hypotheses: Aristotelian, mechanistic, and teleological.

1. The order in the world might have existed eternally. Particular

instances of order in the present would be the outcomes of pre-existing equivalent orders, and so on back ad infinitum. If we held this view, and also allowed that the cosmological argument is fallacious, there would be no need to account further for order at all. However, facts available to us are incompatible with this hypothesis, which we therefore can omit from consideration.

2. Complex organisms—we can restrict our survey to living beings without loss of generality—might be the outcome of a progressive development from simpler organisms; and the simplest organisms might themselves have developed gradually from even simpler combinations of material constitutents, so that in the whole procession from the atom to the theologian there is nowhere any gap. Scientists, not philosophers, must decide whether this is in outline the picture of what has in fact happened; but at any rate I shall assume that it is correct.

The philosophical question does not concern the facts. It is this: Is evolution able to account for itself in its own terms? The mechanistic answer is affirmative. Given some initial distribution of matter in the universe (and we need not raise the question where that came from), the inherent properties—essentially, the energy distribution patterns—of the elementary particles are sufficient to account for their building up into all the complexes presently encountered, including living and conscious ones. Thus organisms would be "chance" products of the shifting distribution of energy in the universe—"chance" in the sense of not being directed by intelligent foresight, though not chance in the sense of being lawless. Leucippus, the first great Greek mechanist, expressed this in the only words of his that have survived: "Nothing happens at random, but everything for a reason and from necessity." [27]

It is essential to the mechanistic view that although a complex can arise only from pre-existing parts, the parts can and sometimes do pre-exist dissociated from each other, and can and sometimes do unite spontaneously—that is, complex effect does not always require an equally complex cause. There is occasionally something new under the sun, though what is new is made from what is old.

3. The teleological hypothesis, while admitting the facts of evolution, insists that these facts are not self-explanatory. The effect cannot exceed the cause; in particular, organisms must be, ultimately, the effects of causes at least as complex and ordered as they themselves; and those organisms possessing consciousness could not exist unless their pre-existing cause were itself conscious and purposive. This is not to deny that

the particular material configurations may have been produced out of simpler constituents, but it is to deny that the union could be merely spontaneous and inherent in the parts. "Dead matter" could no more form itself into an amoeba or a theologian than lumber, nails, and wire could, without the activity of a carpenter, form themselves into a chicken coop.

But the theologist, in admitting the facts of evolution, really abandons his case. He has admitted that as far as immediate causes are concerned it is possible—since it is actual—that highly organized structures can evolve "naturally" out of relatively unorganized materials. If he insists that the remote, unobserved, and unobservable causes of order must be intelligent, what possible justification for this view can he put forward? Is this not just the final retreat, to the limits of the universe, of the animism that once triumphantly occupied the whole of it? If you ask, soberly and seriously, for an explanation of the order in the universe (says the mechanist to the teleologist), you are asking for an account of the causes of that order. Well, here is the outline of that explanation; here are some of the details that go to fill it out; and if you want more, scientists are uncovering them faster than you can assimilate them. What more can you ask for? To go on saying: but the ultimate cause of order must be orderly, the ultimate cause of adaptation must be purposive, the ultimate cause of consciousness must be conscious—to go on saying this is simply to betray the fact, suspected all along, that nothing will satisfy you but an animistic explanation; and this is a fact about your psychology, not a certain or probable inference about the nature of things.

SOME AFTERTHOUGHTS

Yet after the fallacies of the probability and entropy arguments have been exposed, and after the propensity to accept the design axiom has been ascribed to natural animism, the argument from design is but scotched. Its extraordinarily tough core continues to pulsate with life. That core is the impressive analogy between the universe and the products of intelligent foresight.

> You will find [the world] to be nothing but one great machine, subdivided into an infinite number of lesser machines. . . . All these various machines, and even their most minute parts, are adjusted to each other with an accuracy which ravishes into admiration all men who have ever contemplated them. The curious adapting of means to ends, throughout all nature, resembles exactly, though it much exceeds, the productions of human contrivance.

... Since therefore the effects resemble each other, we are led to infer, by all the rules of analogy, that the causes also resemble.[28]

Hume himself, after he had done all he could to expose the weakness of the analogy, grudgingly admitted that it has sufficient force to justify the conclusion that "the cause or causes of order in the universe probably bear some remote analogy to human intelligence." May we not still say that this is a matter of opinion, and that it is reasonable for us to hold the analogy to be really strong and sufficient to validate the reasonableness of theism?

Perhaps we may, if the argument really establishes an analogy. But does it?

Stripped of rhetoric, the argument as presented by Hume (and accepted as a fair statement of it, by advocates and critics alike) is this:

Premise I. Natural objects share with artifacts the common characteristics of adjustment of parts and curious adapting of means to ends.

Premise II. Artifacts have these characteristics because they are products of design.

Conclusion. Therefore natural objects are probably products of a great designer.

In form this is an argument by analogy. The proponents of the argument maintain that the analogy is a strong one; the detractors judge it weak; all agree that the argument is an analogy.

Two curious circumstances, however, lead to the suspicion that this form misrepresents the gist of the argument. The first of these is that the dispute about this argument does not conform to the usual pattern of discussion of analogies in other contexts. Two examples will show what I understand to be the "usual pattern."

Are Australoids akin to Negroids? On the positive side are similarities in nose, lips, chin, leg-to-trunk ratio, pigmentation. Against the hypothesis are differences in hair, in brow, jaw, and forehead structures, and in predominant blood types. Anthropologists are agreed about the facts; although they may differ as to how much weight to assign to the inference, their differences are not very great. Anyone who thought the facts either prove or disprove the hypothesis conclusively would be regarded as a crank by his colleagues. All are agreed, furthermore, that if there were exact similarity in nearly all physical respects, if the two peoples told similar legends in languages of the same family, then there could be no reasonable doubt about it.

Was early Greek philosophy influenced by Indian thought? There is the featureless One of Parmenides, the metempsychosis of Pythagoras, Empedocles, and Plato, both of which conceptions are commonplaces of the "gymnosophists." On the other hand, there is a concern with nature, even in these putative Orientalizers, that is lacking or less emphasized in the East; it is plausible to suppose that ideas of these sorts are likely to crop up almost anywhere, etc. If the opposing viewpoints on the question have their devoted partisans, this may show only that philosophers are crankier than anthropologists. Here again, at any rate, it is agreed that if old Indian texts were discovered containing argumentation exactly parallel to that of Parmenides, if Greek inscriptions of the fifth century B.C. were shown to contain translation from the Rig Veda, and so on, then a point would be reached at which the matter would be settled.

Controversy about design is conducted quite differently, as we have seen. Although there may be a fair amount of agreement about the particular facts of "adjustment of parts" and "curious adapting of means to ends," there is nevertheless violent partisanship in respect to the inferences to be drawn from these facts. The design proponents collect the evidences, and proclaim that any fool can plainly see what conclusion they inevitably lead to; the critics yawn and say it is no use going on like this, that no matter how many such curiosities are piled up, the inference is still inadmissible and must remain so. The analogy is weak, and no conceivable amount of further evidence of the same kind could strengthen it appreciably.

This is a curious circumstance. But since it may be explained away by reference to the importance of the subject, or to the pecularities of philosophers and theologians, I do not lay great stress on it in isolation.

The second reason for doubting whether the design argument is an analogy is a weightier one. If the argument is an analogy, then it is an extremely weak one—much weaker even than Hume judged, so weak that we must be amazed that anyone could have thought it to have any force whatsoever. For it is in fact at least as weak as the following argument:

Premise I. Natural objects share with artifacts the common characteristic of being colored.

Premise II. Artifacts are colored by being painted or dyed.

Conclusion. Therefore natural objects are probably colored by a great painter-dyer.

I take it as self-evident that this is an extremely weak argument, to which no one would assent. Yet it cannot be weaker than the design analogy, because it is of the same form and its premises are obviously true. (It may be objected that the second premise is not true, since some artifacts retain their "natural" colors. I mean, though, that when we know how they got their colors, we know that they got them by being painted or dyed. And besides, some artifacts retain as components, "natural" adaptation of means to ends: for example, squirrel cages.) How so weak an argument could seem strong needs accounting for; and I doubt whether cynical references to the unbounded credulity of *homo religiosus* will suffice.

I shall try to explain these anomalies by suggesting that the paint argument is less convicing than the design argument precisely because its premises are more obviously true. From this I shall conclude that the analogical form disguises the real form of the design argument.

If it were quite obvious—as obvious as that everything (not transparent) is colored—that everything has the property of curious adapting of means to ends, would there then be any temptation to argue that the cause of adaptation in natural objects must be like that in artifacts? I do not think so; but perhaps the thought-experiment is difficult and inconclusive. Let us go at it indirectly.

Suppose someone wanted seriously to urge the paint argument. One thing we can be sure of is that he would waste no effort on proving the first premise. It is obvious that everything, artificial and natural objects alike, is colored. No one would say: "Look here. Automobiles and billboards and books and wigs and so forth are colored, as you can plainly see. But look again and you will discern, on close inspection, that not only these but also peaches and strawberries and snow and the sky and natural hair and so forth are colored. Now, having established that beyond reasonable doubt, we can go on."

But this sort of thing is just what advocates of the design argument do at the greatest possible length. They take it for granted only that the curious adapting of means to ends is obvious where artifacts are concerned; they judge that the thesis they must devote their eloquence to convincing people of is the existence of adaptation in nature. In the heyday of the argument from design, books such as the eight volumes of the *Bridgewater Treatises* [29] were almost wholly devoted to establishing this fact. Their authors assumed, correctly, that they were presenting the public with information not otherwise available, and with inferences such as would not occur to just anyone.

Let us rewrite the argument in a way that will bring out this insistence on the nonobviousness of adaptation:

1. You can distinguish artifacts from natural objects; and you know two things about artifacts: first, that they exhibit curious adapting of means to ends; second, that they do so because they are consciously designed to do so. This you have learned from the experience of seeing them made.

2. If, then, you were to discover some object the origin of which was unknown to you, but which obviously resembled something else known to be an artifact, you would immediately, and correctly, infer that it too was an artifact and was the product of conscious design.

3. Now it is granted that natural objects, such as eyeballs and lizards, do not obviously resemble artifacts. But on closer inspection, they are seen to possess the essential characteristic of artifacts, that characteristic which when obviously present warrants an inference to design, namely, curious adapting of means to ends.

4. Therefore by parity of reasoning you should come to realize that natural objects too are products of conscious design.

This, I think, is a fair summary of the argument from design as it is actually argued (for example, by Paley[30]). Adverbs are often dispensable parts of speech, but not here. The gist of the argument comes in the third paragraph, and its force lies in the contrast between inspecting things superficially and inspecting them carefully.

There is nothing inherently illegitimate about argumentation of this form. It often happens that we divide a large class of things into two subclasses, those that have the property P and those that lack it—or so it seems; and then later we discover that really all the members of the class have P after all. Thus well into the nineteenth century biologists commonly divided living things into those that were generated from seed and those that were spontaneously generated. Then Pasteur showed conclusively that there is no such thing as spontaneous generation—all living things are generated from seed.

Reasoning of this kind is valid only when a division is made between two species on the basis of some clear and relevant criterion, such that things of one kind are found, on the evidence available, to satisfy it, and others are not; and subsequently it is discovered that the things thought not to satisfy the criterion really do. In the example, the criterion was a clear one: reproduction from germ cells provided by parent organisms. No one had discovered any bodies, produced by flies, mosquitoes, molds, etc., such that from them, and from them only, other organisms of the same kind would develop. All that was known was that in certain conditions (decaying vegetation, and so forth) those flora and fauna seemed inevitably to develop. The criterion was clear, and the division in accordance with it was justified on the evidence available. It took ingenious investigation to demonstrate that in these cases too seeds were present.

Does the reformulated argument from design conform to these requirements? Perhaps it satisfies the second. It is not obvious that very many natural objects, and features of nature, show fine adjustment of parts and curious adapting of means to ends; but closer scrutiny may establish this. And the criterion itself, though not so clear and easy to apply as that of presence or absence of seeds, may be conceded to be sufficiently definite.

The criterion assumed is the wrong one, however. Proponents of the design argument take it for granted that the properties according to which we judge whether or not some object is an artifact, are accurate adjustment of parts and curious adapting of means to ends. But that is not the way we judge, even provisionally, whether something is an artifact or not. This is clear from our being able to tell whether something is an artifact without knowing what is it for or whether its parts are accurately adjusted.

Suppose someone is given a heap of miscellaneous objects: watches, leaves, eyeballs, pistols, lizards, stone axes, sealing wax, abstract paintings, etc.; then suppose he is required to separate them into two piles, the one containing only artifacts, the other only "natural" objects. Anyone can easily do this. The reason why one can accomplish the task so easily, though, is perhaps just that one knows in advance which are man-made and which are not. So let us make the task more difficult. Let us put in the heap a number of "gismos"—objects especially constructed for the test by common methods of manufacture, i.e., metallic, plastic, painted, machined, welded, but such that the subject of the test has never seen such things before, and they do not in fact display any "accurate adjustments of parts" or "curious adapting of means to ends." Put into the heap also a number of natural objects which the subject has never seen. Will he have any more difficulty? He will not. The gismos go into one pile, the platypuses and tektites into the other, quite automatically.

Of course one might conceivably make mistakes in this sorting procedure. And it is perhaps hazardous to predict that human visitors to another planet would be entirely and immediately successful in determining, from an inventory of random objects found on its surface, whether it was or had been the abode of intelligent beings. But space explorers would not be at a loss as to how to proceed in the investigation. They would look for evidences of machining, materials that do not exist in nature, regular markings, and the like. Presence of some of these would be taken as evidence, though perhaps not conclusive, of artifice.

This is how archaeologists decide hard cases. Is this object just a rock, or is it a hand ax? The scientist's inspection is not directed toward determining whether the object can serve a purpose; he looks instead for those peculiar marks left by flaking tools and not produced by weathering. Again: there is no question at all that Stonehenge is a human contrivance, though there is much controversy about its purpose.

We are now in a position to understand why the friends of design go to so much trouble to show design in nature, and why the critics, blandly conceding all their opponents put forth, attack the argument at another point. Both accept the Humean formulation. For the advocate, the main job is to establish the first premise; once this is done, he thinks, the assimilation of natural objects to the category of machines follows immediately. The critic, on the other hand, goes to great lengths to resist this coalescence. His usual strategy is to show that the analogy—though proper in that natural objects and machines do both exhibit curious adapting of means to ends—is "weak," on the ground that the total disanalogy is great. But in taking this line the critic falls into the snare set by the advocate. Thus even such astute and skeptical inquirers as Hume and J. S. Mill [31] conceded some force to the design argument. They need not have done so; for properly considered, the argument is not really an argument by analogy, strong or weak. It is just another argument with a false premise, and therefore of no force at all.

NOTES

1. Psalms 19:1.
2. Jean-Jacques Rousseau, *A Discourse of the Origin of Inequality,* Appendix.
3. This account of primitive thinking, which is perhaps obvious a priori, is abundantly confirmed by anthropological investigations. See, e.g., the summaries and references in Hans Kelsen, *Society and Nature* (Chicago: University of Chicago Press, 1943).
4. Psalms 14:1; also 53:1.
5. *Metaphysics* V, 2.
6. *Timaeus, passim.*

7. *Metaphysics* XII, 7.

8. *Ibid.*, 9.

9. *Ibid.*, 6; *Physics* VII-VIII.

10. *Summa Theologiae*, Pt. I, Ques. II, Art. 3; tr. by the author.

11. *Principia* (1687), tr. Motte, Bk. III, General Scholium; quoted in T. V. Smith and M. G. Grene, eds., *From Descartes to Kant* (Chicago: University of Chicago Press, 1940), pp. 375-378.

12. It is odd in English, though not in French, to call clocks "machines." They are, rather, mechanisms. However, the classic statements of the argument ignore this fact, and no harm seems to come of it.

13. "Fears in Solitude" (1798).

14. *Dialogues*, Pt. XII.

15. *Ibid.*

16. Laplace's reply when asked by Napoleon why there was no mention of God in his *Mécanique Céleste*.

17. Pierre Lecomte du Noüy, *Human Destiny* (New York: Longmans, Green, 1947; Signet ed., 1949), Bk. I, Pt. 3, Signet ed., pp. 35-37; quoted by courtesy of David McKay Co., Inc.

18. *Ibid.*, conclusion of Bk. I, p. 46.

19. Fragment 57 (Diel's numbering).

20. Fragment 61.

21. Du Noüy, *Human Destiny*, p. 31.

22. For exhaustive examples see the publications listed in note 29.

23. A little less roughly: for a given spatial region, if Q is the quantity of heat measured in calories, T the temperature of the hottest body measured in degrees Kelvin, and S the entropy,

$$S = \frac{Q}{T}$$

If S_i is the entropy of the initial state of some isolated system, and S_f the entropy of the final (or any later) state of the same system, then the second law of thermodynamics is: the quantity of $S_f - S_i$ is always either zero or positive,

$$S_f - S_i = Q_f \div T_f - P_i \div Q_i \geq 0$$

For a precise statement, see any textbook of physics.

24. William Pepperell Montague, *Belief Unbound* (New Haven: Yale University Press, 1930), pp. 70 f.

25. *Ibid.*, p. 73.

26. I need hardly say that "molecule of wine" is a *façon de parler*.

27. Fragment 2.

28. Hume, *Dialogues*, Pt. II (see text, p. 67).

29. Eight books published 1833-1840 under the auspices of the Royal Society. The authors shared a legacy of £8,000 from the eighth Earl of Bridgewater. In order of publication, they are: Thomas Chalmers, *The Adaptation of External Nature to the Moral and Intellectual Constitution of Man;* William Prout, *Chemistry,*

Meteorology, and the Function of Digestion, Considered with Reference to Natural Theology; William Kirby, *The History, Habits, and Instincts of Animals with Reference to Natural Theology;* William Buckland, *Geology and Mineralogy Considered with Reference to Natural Theology;* Sir Charles Bell, *The Hand: Its Mechanism and Vital Endowments, as Evincing Design;* John Kidd, *On the Adaptation of External Nature to the Physical Condition of Man;* William Whewell, *Astronomy and General Physics Considered with Reference to Natural Theology;* and Peter Mark Roget, *Animal and Vegetable Physiology Considered with Reference to Natural Theology.*

30. William Paley, *Natural Theology, or Evidences of the Existence and Attributes of the Deity* (1802).

31. John Stuart Mill, *Theism* (1874), "The Argument from Marks of Design in Nature."

IV. Faith and Reason

Michael Scriven

God and Reason

Michael Scriven, professor of philosophy at the University of California at Berkeley, was educated at the University of Melbourne and at Oxford University. His books include: *Applied Logic* (1964) and *Primary Philosophy* (1966). He has edited with Herbert Feigl the *Minnesota Studies in the Philosophy of Science, Volume I, Foundations of Science and the Concepts of Psychology and Psychoanalysis* (1956), and with W. J. Moore and Eugene P. Wigner *Symmetries and Reflections* (1967). He has contributed more than one hundred fifty articles and reviews to professional journals.

1

THE RELEVANCE OF REASON

Does it matter whether the arguments are sound? Indeed, should we be trying to reason about God at all? It is often said that such an attempt is hopelessly inappropriate, and indeed it is sometimes said to be sacrilegious. By His very nature God transcends merely human categories of thought, and to attempt to imprison Him in them is a simple fallacy. The attempt, in fact, demonstrates that some other, limited being is under discussion, not God Himself. Our enterprise and, indeed, our very definition of "God" in terms of human concepts are thus doomed from the start.

But a mountain that is infinitely tall does not thereby cease to be a mountain; those who lived in its shadow would not lack good reason for saying that there was a mountain near them just because none could determine where the end of the shadow was to be found. A God that exists everywhere is nonetheless present here and now. A God that is perfectly loving is at least as loving as a human being who loves with all his human heart. An omnipotent God is at least as powerful as you and I; indeed He is certainly more powerful than any human being. So we *can* legitimately begin by looking into the question whether there is any reason for thinking that this world is inhabited (or permeated) by a Being who is superhuman in respect of His knowledge, power, and love to the extent set out in our definition.

If such a Being exists, then we might or might not be able to go on to argue that It is *infinitely* powerful, and so forth, or the grounds we uncover may immediately lead to that conclusion. Despite a common belief to the contrary, this task is obviously possible in principle. We have already learned, from the fossils and footprints of the dinosaurs, that there were once beings on the Earth's surface with greater physical power than human beings. There is nothing in the least self-contradictory about a human being reasoning to the conclusion that there are beings with *more-than-human* power, just as the big-game hunter frequently reasons to the presence of elephants. One might as well argue that it is impossible to reason about the existence of beings with *less*-than-human power—after all, they are just as different from us. Indeed we can go further; the whole of modern particle physics involves reasoning about the existence of beings with properties that are so fundamentally different from the ones with which we are familiar that comprehension in the sense of simple analogy with the familiar is almost completely lacking, but the success of applied physics shows that such inferences are not only possible but very effective. And mathematics readily demonstrates the possibility of reasoning to the existence of infinite entities and properties.

So there is a clear possibility of direct proof of the existence of a Being with wholly unfamiliar powers, and there is nothing inappropriate about approaching that possibility via the simpler stratagem of discussing the finite and more comprehensible Basic God, however different this may be in itself from the mighty God of our fathers. It is different but not irrelevant. After all, if someone can show there is nothing on the Earth's surface stronger than a man, then there are no elephants; and if his first claim is true, he need not go into detail about the other properties of elephants. This is likely to seem very irreverent to elephant lovers, but it is an exceptionally powerful procedure, because it also shows there are no gorillas, dinosaurs, or tigers around. And on the theist's side, the Basic God step has advantages, too. Some of the worst difficulties with the claim that there is a God around arise over the particular properties that are ascribed to the particular version of God favored by, for example, Christianity. Although we shall later discuss some of these, the first part of the argument will not require us to look into any details about such questions as whether God is a Trinity or a Unity. So an approach via the existence of Basic God makes it possible to show there is a God that many would consider worthy of awe, reverence, and prayer even if the difficulties about the more complicated entities of certain religions are insuperable.

But surely there could be arguments which would show that a Being with truly immense powers exists, even though they would not in any way show that a lesser Being existed; and by showing that no such lesser Being exists (if indeed that can be done) would one not in fact only be showing something which many theists would grant anyway? The mightiest arguments of the theologians are aimed higher, it might be said, and for better or for worse they bear on a different question. God is not just *more* of everything or even the *most*. He is different in kind from other things: He is the *Creator* and not just a jumbo-sized friendly handyman, and so on with the other properties.

These points are good but irrelevant. Direct proofs of a More-than-Basic God will certainly be considered; but theism does not depend on their success, since a Basic God might be all there is. So their role is limited. Conversely, grounds for believing that there is nothing *as or more powerful* than Basic God eliminate both kinds of God. There can be a God even if He is not Basic, but there cannot be a God that is not at least Basic.

In a somewhat desperate move, some theologians have argued that the words we use to describe God do not have their ordinary use at all. All religious language is symbolic and not to be taken literally, they say. This move throws out the baby of belief with the bath water of mythology; it is too sophisticated for its own good. In the first place, almost all believers and potential believers, past and present, take the usual claims about

God's nature to be something like the truth, even if not quite literally true; and it is to them we are addressing these discussions. The points made will not be vulnerable to the possibility that analogical or symbolic reference is the best we can do (in any comprehensible sense of "analogical" or "symbolic"). In the second place, if we try to take the sophisticated position seriously and ask what it is about religious belief, interpreted in this way, that distinguishes it from the beliefs of a pagan or an avowed atheist, we find that either there is no agreement on the answer or the answer is that no such distinction exists. The latter comment has been taken to be the profound discovery that everyone is "really" religious or even theistic (for example, because everyone has some "ultimate concern" about something or believes in the existence of substance). But, of course, it equally well proves that everyone is "really" irreligious or atheistic; if there is no difference between chalk and cheese, you can just as well call the stuff on the supermarket's cold shelves chalk as call the stuff on the blackboard cheese. There is a real difference between almost everyone who believes in the existence of God and everyone who does not; the difference is that the two groups disagree about what a thorough census of all existing entities would show and only one of them thinks it would include an intelligent Being with supernatural powers, concerned with our welfare. Attempts to eliminate this residual content in theism, common in recent "liberal" Protestant theology, are the survival attempts of a system of belief that sees its only salvation in camouflage but fails to see that what is indistinguishable cannot be indispensable.

Someone who wanted to adopt a really disproof-proof position here (many have been tempted, and at least one Indian philosopher has succumbed) could *define* God as the Unknowable; or he could say that whatever else God is, He is certainly unknowable. The only trouble with this position is that you really cannot eat your cake and worship it too; there cannot be any reason for worshiping, or respecting, or loving, or praying to, or believing in such a God. The Unknowable may be evil, stupid, inanimate, or nonexistent; a religion dedicated to such a pig in a poke would be for the feeble-minded. If religious belief means anything at all, it means belief in something whose properties may not be entirely clear but which are at least worthy of respect (most have said, humble adoration). Such a Being is not wholly unknowable, since we know some very important things about Him, such as His goodness. We may certainly say that He is not fully knowable, and the ensuing discussion does not assume that God is fully knowable. The theist's claim is that there is a good supernatural force, perhaps with many mysterious properties. And the atheist's claim is simply that the God of the great religions has quite enough properties to make him, on the one hand, worthy of respect and, on the other, non-existent.

The extreme form of the defense against the relevance of reason is therefore itself indefensible. There are no obvious mistakes in the attempt to reason about God. One can all too easily get carried away by catchy little slogans like "The finite cannot comprehend the infinite," "Man cannot presume to judge God," "God takes up where Reason gives out," and so on. Their merits, if any, lie in their potential use as tricky titles for sermons in fashionable surburban churches. They have no force as a defense against skepticism or as a support for belief. We can be quite sure there *is* an infinite sequence of digits after 1, 2, and 3, and we can be quite sure there *is not* an infinitely long ribbon in our typewriter or an infinitely heavy nuthatch sitting on the bird feeder; so the preacher just has to get down from the pulpit and do some hard, logical work to show that there is some special reason why an infinite God cannot be reasoned about in the same way. Why should the human mind be incapable of dealing with the infinite in theology but not in mathematics or cosmology, where it is a commonplace and well-defined part of the subject?

Yet, a more profound point is involved behind the scenes here. There is a nagging nervousness about talking as if there were no limitations on the power of the human reason. After all, there *must* be a certain parochialism about our present views and a certain poverty about our capacity for analyzing the evidence. We have only been thinking systematically for a few millenniums (some would say, centuries), and in that short span we have constantly found ourselves abandoning the absolute convictions of previous generations. How then can one have any degree of certainty about the existence or nonexistence of a Being so different from the beings of our immediate experience and so vastly superior to ourselves in thought?

The point is very weighty, but it is not decisive here. In the first place, the very nature of the Being we are now undertaking to discuss makes Him approachable by reason. For God, Who is often said to be ever present, is at the very least *able* to be present almost anywhere at almost any time— He is ever accessible. If He lacked this power, He would be of little concern to us. We cannot be certain about the existence of beings on other planets just because they are on other planets and not here, and thus far we have not been close enough to see if they do, in fact, exist. But a Being that is here, indeed often said to have been here since Creation—such a Being, with the opportunity and the power and the interest in doing something that would prevent or improve an imperfect work, would surely have to leave some traces in *this* world. Indeed, whether He created the world or merely had the chance to change it, the world itself must to some extent be a reflection of His character. If we can show that the world is best explicable in terms of a divine plan, we have the best reasons for theism. If the world is simply a natural phenomenon, whose natural properties are grossly imperfect for our needs and not improved by any unseen force, it seems at first sight as if we would have some kind of reason for thinking Him less than good, powerful, and wise. So reason can in principle both prove and disprove the existence of God.

Second, even if it were in His nature to be anonymous, the nature of our basic question still makes an answer possible. For we are not discussing the question whether the existence of God is possible but the question whether it is likely. And, as we shall see, the absence of all evidence for God's existence would make it most unlikely that He exists.

We are ignorant of many things that exist in the Universe, of course, and we always shall be; but the whole reason for concern about God is His immense importance for our affairs here and now, and we are not blind about the here and now.

2

FAITH AND REASON

We must now contend with the suggestion that reason is irrelevant to the commitment to theism because this territory is the domain of another faculty: the faculty of faith. It is sometimes even hinted that it is morally wrong and certainly foolish to suggest we should be reasoning about God. For this is the domain of faith or of the "venture of faith," of the "knowledge that passeth understanding," of religious experience and mystic insight.

Now the normal meaning of *faith* is simply "confidence"; we say that we have great faith in someone or in some claim or product, meaning that we believe and act as if they were very reliable. Of such faith we can properly say that it is well founded or not, depending on the evidence for whatever it is in which we have faith.[1] So there is no incompatibility between this kind of faith and reason; the two are from different families and can make a very good marriage. Indeed if they do not join forces, then the resulting ill-based or inadequate confidence will probably lead to disaster. So faith, in this sense, means only a high degree of belief and may be reasonable or unreasonable.

But the term is sometimes used to mean an *alternative to reason* instead of something that should be founded on reason. Unfortunately, the mere use of the term in this way does not demonstrate that faith is a possible route to truth. It is like using the term "winning" as a synonym for "playing" instead of one possible outcome of playing. This is quaint, but it could hardly be called a satisfactory way of proving that we are winning; any time we "win" by changing the meaning of winning, the victory is merely illusory. And so it proves in this case. To use "faith" *as if* it were an alternative way to the truth cannot by-pass the crucial question whether such results really have any likelihood of being true. A rose by any other name will smell the same, and the inescapable facts about "faith" in the new sense are that it is still *applied* to a belief and is still supposed to imply *confidence in* that belief: the belief in the existence and goodness of God. So we can still ask the same old question about that belief: Is the confidence justified or misplaced? To say we "take it on faith" does not get it off parole.

Suppose someone replies that theism is a kind of belief that does not need justification by evidence. This means either that no one cares whether it is correct or not or that there is some other way of checking that it is correct besides looking at the evidence for it, that is, giving reasons for believing it. But the first alternative is false since very many people care whether there is a God or not; and the second alternative is false because any method of showing that belief is likely to be true is, by definition, a justification of that belief, that is, an appeal to reason. You certainly cannot show that a belief in God is likely to be true just by having confidence in it and by saying this is a case of knowledge "based on" faith, any more than you can win a game just by playing it and by calling that winning.

It is psychologically possible to have faith in something without any basis in fact, and once in a while you will turn out to be lucky and to have backed the right belief. This does not show you "really knew all along"; it only shows you cannot be unlucky all the time. But, in general, beliefs without foundations lead to an early grave or to an accumulation of superstitions, which are usually troublesome and always false beliefs. It is hardly possible to defend this approach just by *saying* that you have decided that in this area confidence is its own justification.

Of course, you might try to *prove* that a feeling of great confidence about certain types of propositions is a reliable indication of their truth. If you succeeded, you would indeed have shown that the belief was justified; you would have done this by justifying it. To do this you would have to show what the real facts were and show that when someone had the kind of faith we are now talking about, it usually turned out that the facts were as he believed, just as we might justify the claims of the telepath. The catch in all this is simply that you have got to show what the real facts are in some way *other* than by appealing to faith, since that would simply be assuming what you are trying to prove. And if you can show what the facts are in this other way, you do not need faith in any new sense at all; you are already perfectly entitled to confidence in any belief that you have shown to be well supported.

How are you going to show what the real facts are? You show this by any method of investigation that has itself been tested, the testing being done by still another tested method, etc., through a series of tested connections that eventually terminates in our ordinary everyday reasoning and testing procedures of logic and observation.

Is it not prejudiced to require that the validation of beliefs always involves ultimate reference to our ordinary logic and everyday-plus-scientific knowledge? May not faith (religious experience, mystic insight) give us access to some new domain of truth? It is certainly possible that it does this. But, of course, it is also possible that it lies. One can hardly accept the reports of those with faith or, indeed, the apparent revelations of one's own religious experiences on the ground that they *might* be right. So *might* be a fervent materialist who saw his interpretation as a revelation. Possibility is not veracity. Is it not of the very greatest importance that we should try to find out whether we really can justify the use of the term "truth" or "knowledge" in describing the content of faith? If it is, then we must find something in that content that is known to be true in some other way, because to get off the ground we must first push off against the ground—we cannot lift ourselves by our shoelaces. If the new realm of knowledge is to be a realm of knowledge and not mythology, then it must tell us something which relates it to the kind of case that gives meaning to the term "truth." If you want to use the old word for the new events, you must show that it is applicable.

Could not the validating experience, which religious experience must have if it is to be called true, be the experience of others who also have or have had religious experiences? The religious community could, surely, provide a basis of agreement analogous to that which ultimately underlies scientific truth. Unfortunately, agreement is not the only requirement for avoiding error, for all may be in error. The difficulty for the religious community is to show that its agreement is not simply agreement about a shared mistake. If agreement were the only criterion of truth, there could never be a shared mistake; but clearly either the atheist group or the theist group shares a mistake. To decide which is wrong must involve appeal to something other than mere agreement. And, of course, it is clear that particular religious beliefs are mistaken, since religious groups do not all agree and they cannot all be right.

Might not some or all scientific beliefs be wrong too? This is conceivable, but there are crucial differences between the two kinds of belief. In the first place, any commonly agreed religious beliefs concern only one or a few entities and their properties and histories. What for convenience we are here calling "scientific belief" is actually the sum total of all conventionally founded human knowledge, much of it not part of any science, and it embraces billions upon billions of facts, each of them perpetually or frequently subject to checking by independent means, each connected with a million others. The success of *this* system of knowledge shows up every day in everything we do: we eat, and the food is not poison; we read, and the pages do not turn to dust; we slip, and the gravity does not fail to pull us down. We are not just relying on the existence of agreement about the interpretation of a certain experience among a small part of the population. We are relying directly on our extremely reliable, nearly universal, and independently tested senses, and each of us is constantly obtaining independent confirmation for claims based on these, many of these confirmations being obtained for many claims, independently of each other. It is the wildest flight of fancy to suppose that there is a body of common religious beliefs which can be set out to exhibit this degree of repeated checking by religious experiences. In fact, there is not only gross disagreement on even the most fundamental claims in the creeds of different churches, each of which is supported by appeal to religious experience or faith, but where there is agreement by many people, it is all too easily open to the criticism that it arises from the common cultural exposure of the child or the adult convert and hence is not independent in the required way.

This claim that the agreement between judges is spurious in a particular case because it only reflects previous common indoctrination of those in agreement is a serious one. It must always be met by direct disproof whenever agreement is appealed to in science, and it is. The claim that the food is not poison cannot be explained away as a myth of some subculture, for anyone, even if told nothing about the eaters in advance, will judge that the people who ate it are still well. The whole methodology of testing is committed to the doctrine that any judges who could have learned what they are expected to say about the matter they are judging are completely valueless.[2] Now anyone exposed to religious teaching, whether a believer or not, has long known the standard for such experiences, the usual symbols, the appropriate circumstances, and so on. These suggestions are usually very deeply implanted, so that they cannot be avoided by good intentions, and consequently members of our culture are rendered entirely incapable of being independent observers. Whenever observers are not free from previous contamination in this manner, the only way to support their claims is to examine independently testable *consequences* of the novel claims, such as predictions about the future. In the absence of these, the religious-experience gambit, whether involving literal or analogical claims, is wholly abortive.

A still more fundamental point counts against the idea that agreement among the religious can help support the idea of faith as an alternative path to truth. It is that every sane theist also believes in the claims of ordinary experience, while the reverse is not the case. Hence, the burden of proof is on the theist to show that the *further step* he wishes to take will not take him beyond the realm of truth. The two positions, of science and religion, are not symmetrical; the adherent of one of them suggests that we extend the range of allowable beliefs and yet is unable to produce the same degree of acceptance or "proving out" in the ordinary field of human activities that he insists on before believing in a new instrument or source of information. The atheist obviously cannot be shown his error in the way someone who thinks that there are no electrons can be shown his, *unless some of the arguments for the existence of God are sound*. Once again, we come back to these. If some of them work, the position of religious knowledge is secure; if they do not, nothing else will make it secure.

In sum, the idea of separating religious from scientific knowledge and making each an independent realm with its own basis in experience of quite different kinds is a counsel of despair and not a product of true sophistication, for one cannot break the connection between everyday experience and religious claims, for purposes of defending the latter, without eliminating the consequences of religion for everyday life. There is no way out of this inexorable contract: if you want to support your beliefs, you must produce some experience which can be shown to be a reliable indicator of truth, and that can be done only by showing a connection between the experience and what we know to be true in a previously established way.

So, if the criteria of religious truth are not connected with the criteria of everyday truth, then they are not criteria of truth at all and the beliefs they "establish" have no essential bearing on our lives, constitute no explanation of what we see around us, and provide no guidance for our course through time.

THE CONSEQUENCES IF THE ARGUMENTS FAIL

The arguments are the only way to establish theism, and they must be judged by the usual standards of evidence—this we have argued. It will now be shown that if they fail, there is no alternative to atheism.

Against this it has commonly been held that the absence of arguments *for* the existence of something is not the same as the presence of arguments *against* its existence; so agnosticism or an option remains when the arguments fail. But insofar as this is true, it is irrelevant. It is true only if we restrict "arguments for the existence of something" to highly specific demonstrations which attempt to establish their conclusion as beyond all reasonable doubt. The absence of these is indeed compatible with the conclusion's being quite likely, which would make denial of its existence unjustified. But if we take arguments for the existence of something to include all the evidence which supports the existence claim to any significant degree, i.e., makes it at all probable, then the evidence means there is no likelihood of the existence of the entity. And this, of course, is a complete justification for the claim that the entity does not exist, provided that the entity is not one which might leave no traces (a God who is impotent or who does not care for us), and provided that we have comprehensively examined the area where such evidence would appear if there were any.[3] Now justifying the claim that something does not exist is not quite the same as proving or having arguments that it doesn't, but it is what we are talking about. That is, we need not have a proof that God does not exist in order to justify atheism. Atheism is obligatory in the absence of any evidence for God's existence.

Why do adults not believe in Santa Claus? Simply because they can now explain the phenomena for which Santa Claus's existence is invoked without any need for introducing a novel entity. When we were very young and naively believed our parents' stories, it was hard to see how the presents could get there on Christmas morning since the doors were locked and our parents were asleep in bed. Someone *must* have brought them down the chimney. And how could that person get to the roof without a ladder and with all those presents? Surely only by flying. And then there is a great traditional literature of stories and songs which immortalize the entity and his (horned) attendents; surely these cannot all be just products of imagination? Where there is smoke, there must be fire.

Santa Claus is not a bad hypothesis at all for six-year-olds. As we grow up, no one comes forward to *prove* that such an entity does not exist. We just come to see that there is not the least reason to think he *does* exist. And so it would be entirely foolish to assert that he does, or believe that he does, or even think it likely that he does. Santa Claus is in just the same position as fairy godmothers, wicked witches, the devil, and the ether. Each of these entities has some supernatural powers, i.e., powers which contravene or go far beyond the powers that we know exist, whether it be the power to levitate a sled and reindeer or the power to cast a spell. Now even belief in something for which there is no evidence, i.e., a belief which goes *beyond* the evidence, although a lesser sin than belief in something which is *contrary* to well-established laws, is plainly irrational in that it simply amounts to attaching belief where it is not justified. So the proper alternative, when there is no evidence, is not mere suspension of belief, for example, about Santa Claus, it is *disbelief*. It most certainly is not faith.

The situation is slightly different with the Abominable Snowman, sea serpents, or even the Loch Ness monster. No "supernatural" (by which, in this context, we only mean wholly unprecedented) kinds of powers are involved. Previous discoveries have been made of creatures which had long seemed extinct, and from these we can immediately derive some likelihood of further discoveries.[4] Footprints or disturbances for which no fully satisfactory alternative explanation has yet been discovered (although such an explanation is by no means impossible) have been seen in the Himalayan snow and the Scottish lochs. It would be credulous for the layman to believe firmly in the existence of these entities. Yet it would be equally inappropriate to say it is certain they do not exist. Here is a domain for agnosticism (though perhaps an agnosticism inclined toward skepticism). For the agnostic does not believe that a commitment either way is justified, and he is surely right about strange creatures which, while of a new *appearance*, have powers that are mere extensions, proportional to size, of those with which we are already familiar on this earth. There is some suggestive, if by no means conclusive, evidence for such entities; and the balance of general considerations is not heavily against them.

But when the assertion is made that something exists with powers that strikingly transcend the well-established generalizations we have formulated about animal capacities or reasonable extrapolations from them, then we naturally expect correspondingly better evidence before we concede that there is a serious likelihood of having to abandon those generalizations. It is entirely appropriate to demand much stronger support for claims of telepathy or levitation or miraculous cures than for new sports records or feats of memory in which previous levels of performance are merely bettered to some degree, in a way that is almost predictable. On the other hand, it is entirely prejudiced to reject all such evidence on the ground that it *must* be deceptive because it contravenes previously established generalizations. This is simply to deify the present state of science; it is the precise opposite of the experimental attitude. It is right to demand a stronger case to overthrow a strong case and to demand very strong evidence to demonstrate unprecedented powers. It is irrational to require that the evidence of these powers be just as commonplace and compelling as for the previously known powers of man or beast: one cannot legislate the exceptional into the commonplace.

We can now use a set of distinctions that would previously have seemed very abstract. First, let us distinguish a belief which is wholly without general or particular evidential support from one which can be directly disproved. The claim that a race of men lives on the moons of Jupiter or that a certain cola causes cancer of the colon is entirely unfounded but not totally impossible. The view that the ratio of a circle's circumference to its diameter can be expressed as a fraction is demonstrably untenable, as is the view that some living men are infinitely strong, or that any man is or has been unbeatable at chess, or that the FBI has wiped out the Mafia. We normally say that a claim is *well founded* if there is evidence which is best explained by this claim. We may say it is *provable* if the evidence is indubitable and the claim is very clearly required. If there is no evidence which points to this particular claim, although some general background considerations make it not too unlikely that something like this should be true (Loch Ness monster, mile record broken twice in 1980), we would say there is *some general support* for the claim. We shall say it is *wholly unfounded* (or *wholly unsupported*) if there is no evidence, for it in particular and no general considerations in its favor, and *disprovable* if it implies that something would be the case that definitely is not the case.

Of course it is foolish to believe a claim that is disproved, but it is also foolish to believe a wholly unsupported claim, and it is still foolish even to treat such a claim as if it were worth serious consideration. A claim for which there is some general or some particular support cannot be dismissed, but neither can it be treated as established. The connection between evidential support and the appropriate degree of belief can be demonstrated as shown in the diagram on page 109, which is quite unlike the oversimplified idea that the arrangement should be:

Provable	Theism
Disprovable	Atheism
Neither	Agnosticism

The crucial difference is that both "unfounded" and "disprovable" correlate with atheism, just as the two corresponding types of provability correlate with theism; hence the agnostic's territory is smaller than he often supposes.

Recalling that to get even a little evidential support for the existence of a Being with supernatural powers will require that the little be of very high quality (*little* does not mean "dubious"), we see that the failure of all the arguments, that is, of all the evidence, will make even agnosticism in the wide sense an indefensible exaggeration of the evidential support.[5] And agnosticism in the narrow sense will be an exaggeration unless the arguments are strong enough to establish about a 50 per cent probability for the claim of theism. Apart from the wide and narrow senses of agnosticism there is also a distinction between a positive agnostic and a negative agnostic.

A *positive agnostic* maintains that the evidence is such as to make his position the correct one and those of the theist and atheist incorrect. *Negative agnosticism* is simply the position of not accepting either theism or atheism; it does not suggest that they are both wrong—it may be just an expression of felt indecision or ignorance. The difference between negative and positive agnosticism is like the difference between a *neutral* who says, "I don't know who's right—maybe one of the disputants, or maybe neither," and a *third force* who says, "Neither is right, and I have a third alternative which *is* right." Obviously, the negative agnostic has not progressed as far in his thinking as the positive agnostic, in one sense, because he has not been able to decide which of the three possible positions is correct. The view of the negative agnostic cannot be right, but his position may be the right position for someone who has not thought the matter

EVIDENTIAL SITUATION	APPROPRIATE ATTITUDE	NAME FOR APPROPRIATE ATTITUDE IN THEISM CASE
1. Strictly disprovable, i.e., demonstrably incompatible with the evidence.	Rejection	Atheism
2. Wholly unfounded, i.e., wholly lacking in general or particular support.		
3. Possessing some general or particular support; still improbable.	Skepticism but recognition as a real *possibility*; not to be wholly disregarded in comprehensive planning out to be bet *against*.	Skepticism
4. Possessing substantial support but with substantial alternatives still open; a balance of evidence for and against; about 50 per cent probable.	Suspension of judgment. Make no commitment either way; treat each alternative as approximately equally serious.	Agnosticism (narrow sense)
5. Possessing powerful evidential support; some difficulties of inadequacies or significant alternatives remaining; probable.	Treat as probably true; be *on*.	Pragmatic theism
6. Possessing overwhelming particular support and no basis for alternative views; beyond reasonable doubt; provable in the usual sense.	Acceptance	Theism
7. Strictly provable, i.e., as a demonstrably necessary result of indubitable facts.		

Agnosticism (wide sense) [brackets grouping rows 3–5]

through or who lacks the capacity to do so.

In practice, an agnostic's position is often the product of an untidy mixture of factors. He may never have happened to come across an argument for either theism or atheism which struck him as compelling; a rough head counting has revealed intelligent people on either side; his nose for social stigmas indicates a slight odor of intellectual deficiency attached to theism by contemporary intellectuals and a suggestion of unnecessary boat rocking or perhaps rabid subversion attached to atheism. This makes the agnostic fence look pretty attractive; so up he climbs, to sit on top. But now we put the challenge to him. Is he incapable of thinking out an answer for himself? If so, he is intellectually inferior to those below; if not, he must descend and demonstrate the failings of the contestants before he is entitled to his perch. Agnosticism as a position is interesting and debatable; agnosticism as the absence of a position is simply a sign of the absence of intellectual activity or capacity.

COMBINING AND SEPARATING ARGUMENTS AND EVIDENCE

There used to be a standing joke in the Rationalist Club at Melbourne University about the theologian who said: "None of the arguments is any good by itself, but taken together they constitute an overwhelming proof." Alas for the simple approach; the instinct of the theologian was better than the formal training of the rationalists, although the error is not easily stated. There used to be a small book on the market which contained 200 "proofs" that $-1 = +1$; entertaining though these are, they do not make it one bit more likely that -1 really does equal $+1$, for they are all invalid. If you knew nothing about mathematics, even about elementary arithmetic, and the only way you could find out whether $+1$ equaled -1 was by counting the number of alleged proofs in each direction, you might reasonably conclude that it did. But if you were seriously concerned with the truth of the matter, you would want to investigate the validity of the proofs for yourself; and you would find that they were all unsound. So there is no advantage in numbers, *as far as mathematical proofs go*. They either do the whole trick or nothing at all.[6]

The situation is different with scientific proofs, whereby we hope to do no more than show that one conclusion is so probable as to be beyond reasonable doubt. Let us suppose you are investigating a murder case. There are three clues. The first one points most strongly at North as the suspect; the second, at East; the third, at West. Obviously, you could not argue that South had been shown to be the culprit from a consideration of any one of these clues by itself. Yet there are circumstances in which you can put them all together and conclude that South was, *without any doubt*, the murderer. Here we have a number of "proofs" (items of evidence) which separately do nothing to establish a particular conclusion but which add up to a good proof of that conclusion. How is this possible? The point about probability proofs is that they do not make the alternative explanations completely impossible and may indicate a second-best hypothesis. So, although the first clue is North's handkerchief at the scene of the crime, you also know that South is North's roommate and may have borrowed his handkerchief, while no one else could have done so without considerable difficulty. And although the second clue is that East very frequently had violent arguments with the victim and had been heard to threaten him with injury, it was also true that South stood to gain by the victim's death since he inherited his job in a public relations firm. And West's professional skill at judo, which ties in well with the victim's curiously broken neck, is not such as to make South's army training in basic karate blows an irrelevant consideration. So South is by a long way the most likely murderer. In the same way, with respect to those arguments for the existence of God which are of the probability-increasing kind, we shall have to consider not only whether they make God's existence likely on their own but whether some of them make it a sufficiently good alternative explanation so that when we take all the arguments together it is the best overall explanation.

Obviously this can happen only if the *same hypothesis* receives support as an alternative in each case, for example, the hypothesis that South is the murderer. It would not work at all if the first clue made a secondary suspect of one man called South and the next of a cousin of the first suspect, also called South. After looking at all the arguments in this kind of situation, we would not have any one candidate who was better qualified than any other; we could not even say that it was probably someone from the family of South, for as a matter of fact this is less likely than that it was one of the other three, North, East, and West.

It could be argued that the greatest confidence trick in the history of philosophy is the attempt to make the various arguments for the existence of God support each other by using the same term for the entity whose existence each is supposed to establish. In fact, almost all of them bear on entities of apparently quite different kinds, ranging from a Creator to a moral Lawgiver. The proofs must, therefore, be supplemented with a further proof or set of proofs that shows these apparently different entities to be the same if the combination trick is to work. Otherwise the arguments must be taken separately, in which case they either establish or fail to establish the existence of a number of remarkable but unrelated entities.

It can sometimes be argued that considerations of simplicity require one to adopt the hypothesis that only a single entity is involved, when the alternative is to introduce several special entities. But the circumstances in which this is legitimate are quite limited; we do not, for example, argue that simplicity requires us to assume that the murderer South is also the unknown person who stole some bonds from a bank the day before the murder. We would have to show some connection through means, opportunity, motive, or *modus operandi*, before the identification could be made at all plausible. Simplicity is a fine guide to the best hypothesis if one can only decide which hypothesis is the simpler. Although there is a greater simplicity in terms of the number of entities involved if we say, for example, that the Creator is the moral Lawgiver, there is a greater complexity in terms of the number of explanations required, since now we must explain why and how one entity could perform these two functions. In short, we have really got to give a plausible specific reason before we can identify the two criminals or the two theological entities, since simplicity is now clearly gained by either alternative, and until we do so, any commitment to such an identification is wholly unfounded.

If only a very weak case can be made for the claim that the same entity is involved in the different arguments, the "linkage proof," it will mean that the separate arguments must be much stronger (though they need not be individually adequate) for the conclusion that God exists.[7]

Instead of attempting to establish monotheism, one can, of course, frankly accept the arguments as separate proofs of the existence of separate beings. Roughly speaking, such a polytheist loses one god for each argument that fails and in this sense has a more vulnerable position. But the monotheist may still lose one property or power of his God for each argument that fails and thus fail altogether to establish the existence of the Being he has defined as God, Who has *all* these properties.

It is possible that monotheism owes some of its current support to the feeling that few if any of the separate arguments are without defect and hence *must* be combined for strength. But if this is so, it is surprising that more attention has not been paid to the linkage arguments, which then become crucial.

Another factor acting in favor of monotheism is the feeling that it is less difficult, in the face of the increasing success of naturalistic science, to postulate one supernatural being than several. (But it may be that only the *combination* of properties is supernatural.) To this extent there is a kind of negative justification for the widespread and curious claim that Christianity was in some sense the precursor of modern science with its allegedly unifying theories, but the causal relation is reversed. Christian theology may have been fleeing into monotheism from the shadow cast ahead of the development of Babylonian and Greek science.

NOTES

1. For faith to be well founded, especially faith in a person, it is not required that the evidence available at a particular moment justify exactly the degree of confidence one exhibits. There may be overriding reasons for retaining trust beyond the first point of rationally defensible doubt. But this minor divergence does not seriously affect the discussion here.

2. More precisely, a judge is said to be "contaminated" if he could know which way his judgment will count insofar as the issue at stake is concerned. The famous double-blind experimental design, keystone of drug research, achieves reliability by making it impossible for either patient or nurse to know when the real drug, rather than the dummy drug or placebo, is being judged.

3. This last proviso is really superfluous since it is built into the phrase "the absence of such evidence," which is not the same as "ignorance of such evidence"; but it is included for the sake of clarity. When we are investigating the existence of God, we naturally attempt to discuss all the evidence, conclusive or not; so if this comes to naught, we would be left with no alternative to atheism. Fence-sitting with the agnostic is not only uncomfortable; it is even indefensible.

4. We would not normally say this general consideration is "*evidence* for the existence of the Loch Ness monster"; evidence, like proof, must be rather specifically tied to a claim. But these general background considerations set the stage for proofs, and they directly determine the legitimacy of total skepticism or complete confidence. We regard them as relevant considerations, and the present claim is that without even these no option but atheism is possible.

5. Technical note: Attempts to formulate the general principle of evidence involved have usually run into difficulties related to those made familiar in the discussion of the paradoxes of confirmation. For example, negative existential hypotheses in natural language can be supported by the failure of proofs of their contradictories, but positive existential hypotheses are not made plausible by the failure of disproofs of their denials.

6. On the frontiers, this is not quite true. There is a large realm of mathematical inference which is very like ordinary scientific inference, especially in prime-number theory and in foundational work. Reasoning from examination of samples, from analogy, and from the preponderance of expert opinion is here not with-

out weight; but these are not the procedures of mathematical proof.

7. A formal statement of the probability inequality is surprisingly complex, but easily developed.

Richard Robinson

Religion and Reason

Richard Robinson is a fellow of Oriel College, Oxford. He was educated at Oxford and at Cornell. His books include: *The Province of Logic* (1931); a translation of Werner Jaeger's *Aristotle* (1947); *Definition* (1950); *Plato's Earlier Dialectic* (1953); a translation of *Aristotle's Politics: Books III and IV* (1962); and *An Atheist's Values* (1964).

1

I . . . [shall take up] something commonly accepted as a great good which I reject, namely religion.

Religion has held a big place in the thoughts and feelings of most of the human beings who have yet lived; and, though some have found it an inescapable evil, most have found it a great good. The founder of the Gifford Lectures said that "religion is of all things the most excellent and

From Richard Robinson, An Atheist's Values *(Oxford: Basil Blackwell, 1964), pp. 113-23. Reprinted by permission of Basil Blackwell, Publisher, Oxford.*

precious" (according to Sherrington, *Man on His Nature*, p. 360).

The religious man feels that his god is the supreme good, and the worship of him is the supreme good for man; and he obtains an immense satisfaction in worship and obedience. His creed gives him the feeling that the universe is important and that he has his own humble but important part in it. "God is working his purpose out, as year succeeds to year"; and in this august enterprise the believer has an assured place. When he says that "man cannot be at ease in the world unless he has a faith to sustain him," the faith he is thinking of is in part that there is something extremely important to do. Thus his religion lays that specter of futility and meaninglessness, which man's self-consciousness and thoughtfulness are always liable to raise. The convert says to himself, in the words at the end of Tolstoy's *Anna Karenina:* "My whole life, every moment of my life, will be, not meaningless as before, but full of deep meaning, which I shall have power to impress on every action." The great comfort of such a belief is obvious.

But this is still less than half of the comfort religion can give. For it is not yet an answer to man's greatest horror, the death of his loved ones and himself. If his religion also makes him believe that death is not the end of life, that on the contrary he and his loved ones will live for ever in perfect justice and happiness, this more than doubles his feeling of comfort and security. This doctrine of the happy survival of death is the chief attraction of the Christian religion to most of its adherents; and their first profound religious belief comes to them as a reassurance after their first realization that they are going to die. It is an easy defensive reaction against this terrible discovery. (This point is well put by Bergson in *Les Deux Sources,* for example, p. 137.)

Such is the enormous comfort that religion can give. Because of it a man who deprives the people of the comfort of believing "in the final proportions of eternal justice" is often regarded as a "cruel oppressor, the merciless enemy of the poor and wretched" (Edmund Burke, "Reflections on the French Revolution," *Works,* v. 432.)

But is it a cruel oppression to preach atheism? There is a sinister suggestion in this idea, namely the suggestion that we ought to preach religion whether or not it is true, and that we ought not to estimate rationally whether it is true, which implies that truth is below comfort in value.

It seems to me that religion buys its benefits at too high a price, namely at the price of abandoning the ideal of truth and shackling and perverting man's reason. The religious man refuses to be guided by reason and evidence in a certain field, the theory of the gods, theology. He does not say: "I believe that there is a god, but I am willing to listen to arguments that I am mistaken, and I shall be glad to learn better." He does not seek to find and adopt the more probable of the two contradictories, "there is a god" and "there is no god." On the contrary, he makes his choice between those two propositions once for all. He is determined never to revise his choice, but to believe that there is a god no matter what the evidence. The secretary of the Christian Evidence Society wrote to *The Times* (19 March 1953) and said: "When demand is made upon devout Christians to produce evidence in justification of their intense faith in God they are apt to feel surprised, pained, and even disgusted that any such evidence should be considered necessary." That is true. Christians do not take the attitude of reasonable inquiry towards the proposition that there is a god. If they engage in discussion on the matter at all, they seek more often to intimidate their opponent by expressing shock or disgust at his opinion, or disapproval of his character. They take the view that to hold the negative one of these two contradictories is a moral crime. They make certain beliefs wicked as such, without reference to the question whether the man has reached them sincerely and responsibly. This view, that certain beliefs are as such wicked, is implied in these two sentences in John's gospel (16: 8-9 and 20:29): "He will reprove the world of sin . . . because they believe not on me," and "Blessed are they that have not seen, and yet have believed." There is an extensive example of this attitude in Newman's fifteenth sermon.

Along with the view that certain beliefs are as such wicked there often goes, naturally, the view that it is wicked to try to persuade a person to hold certain beliefs. The believer's complaint, "you are undermining my faith," implies that it is wrong as such to try to convince a man that there is no god. It implies that whether one believes the proposition or not, and whether one has a good reason to believe it or not, are irrelevant, because it is just wrong in itself to recommend this proposition. This view is contrary to the search for truth and the reasonable attitude of listening to argument and guiding oneself thereby.

If theology were a part of reasonable inquiry, there would be no objection to an atheist's being a professor of theology. That a man's being an atheist is an absolute bar to his occupying a chair of theology proves that theology is not an open-minded and reasonable inquiry. Someone may object that a professor should be interested in his subject and an atheist cannot be interested in theology. But a man who maintains that there is no god must think it a sensible and interesting question to ask whether there is a god; and in fact we find that many atheists are interested in theology. Professor H. D. Lewis tells (*Philosophy,* 1952, p. 347) that an old lady asked him what philosophy is, and, when he had given an answer, she said: "O, I see, theology." She was nearly right, for theology and philosophy have the same subject-matter. The difference is that in philosophy you are allowed to come out with whichever answer seems to you the more likely.

In most universities the title of theology includes a lot of perfectly good science which is not theory of god, and which I do not reject, I mean the scientific study of the history of the Jews and their languages and their religious books. All that can be reasonable study, and usually is so. But it is a hindrance to the progress of knowledge that we are largely organized for research in such a way that a man cannot be officially paid to engage in these branches of research unless he officially maintains that there is a god. It is as if a man could not be a professor of Greek unless he believed in Zeus and Apollo.

Religious persons often consider gambling to be a bad thing. It certainly causes a great deal of misery. But much of the badness of gambling consists in its refusal to face the probabilities and be guided by them; and in the matter of refusing to face the probabilities religion is a worse offender than gambling, and does more harm to the habits of reason. Religious belief is, in fact, a form of gambling, as Pascal saw. It does more harm to reason than ordinary gambling does, however, because it is more in earnest.

It has been said that the physicist has just as closed a mind about cause as the Christian has about god. The physicist assumes through thick and thin that everything happens according to causal laws. He presupposes cause, just as the Christian presupposes god.

But the physicist does not *assume* that there is a reign of law; he *hopes* that there is. He looks for laws; but, whenever a possible law occurs to him, he conscientiously tries to disprove it by all reasonable tests. He asserts at any time only such laws as seem at that time to have passed all reasonable tests, and he remains always prepared to hear of new evidence throwing doubt on those laws. This is far from the Christian attitude about god. The Christian does not merely hope that there is a god and maintain only such gods as the best tests have shown to be more probable than improbable.

The main irrationality of religion is preferring comfort to truth; and it is this that makes religion a very harmful thing on balance, a sort of endemic disease that has so far prevented human life from reaching its full stature. . . . For the sake of comfort and security there pours out daily, from pulpit and press, a sort of propaganda which, if it were put out for a nonreligious purpose, would be seen by everyone to be cynical and immoral. We are perpetually being urged to adopt the Christian creed not because it is true but because it is beneficial, or to hold that it must be true just because belief in it is beneficial. "The Christian faith," we are assured, "is a necessity for a fully adjusted personality" (a psychiatrist in the *Radio Times* for 20 March 1953, p. 33). Hardly a week passes without someone recommending theism on the ground that if it were believed there would be much less crime; and this is a grossly immoral argument. Hardly a week passes without someone recommending theism on the ground that unless it is believed the free nations will succumb to the Communists; and that is the same grossly immoral argument. It is always wicked to recommend anybody to believe anything on the ground that he or anybody else will feel better or be more moral or successful for doing so, or on any ground whatever except that the available considerations indicate that it is probably true. The pragmatic suggestion, that we had better teach the Christian religion whether it is true or not, because people will be much less criminal if they believe it, is disgusting and degrading; but it is being made to us all the time, and it is a natural consequence of the fundamental religious attitude that comfort and security must always pervail over rational inquiry.

This pragmatic fallacy is not the only fallacy into which religion is frequently led by preferring comfortingness to truth, though it is the main one. The religious impulse encourages all the fallacies. It encourages the argument ad hominem, that is, the argument that my adversary's view must be false because he is a wicked man: the atheist is impious, therefore he is wicked, therefore his view is false. Religion encourages also the argument from ignorance: instead of rejecting a proposition if it is probably false, the religious man thinks himself entitled to accept it because it is not certainly false. Biased selection of the instances is also very common in religious language. Any case of a man getting his wish after praying for it, or being struck by lightning after doing something mean, is taken as good evidence that there is a god who gives and punishes. Contrary cases are not looked for; and if they obtrude themselves they are dealt with by the further hypothesis that "God's ways are inscrutable." Religious arguments even exhibit, very often, what seems the most fallacious possible fallacy, namely inferring a theory from something that contradicts the theory. Thus we often find: "since no explanation is final, God is the final explanation"; and "since everybody believes in God, you are wrong not to believe in God."

I have been saying that religion is gravely infected with intellectual dishonesty. You may find this very unlikely for a general reason. You may think it very unlikely that such widespread dishonesty would go unnoticed. I do not think so. I think, on the contrary, that it is quite common for a moral defect to pervade a certain sphere and yet escape notice in that sphere, although the people concerned are wide awake to its presence in other places. I think there are plenty of other cases of this. One of them is that the English, who are greater haters of the bully and the might-is-right man, nevertheless bully and intimidate each other when driving a motor-car. They know that power does not confer any right, but they assume that horsepower does. Life is full of such inconsistencies, because we can never see all the implications and applications of our principles. In religion it is particularly easy for intellectual dishonesty to escape notice, because of the common assumption that all honesty flows from religion and religion is necessarily honest whatever it does.

FAITH

According to Christianity one of the great virtues is faith. Paul gave faith a commanding position in the Christian scheme of values, along with hope and love, in the famous thirteenth chapter of his first letter to the Corinthians. Thomas Aquinas held that infidelity is a very great sin, that infidels should be compelled to believe, that heretics should not be toler-ated, and that heretics who revert to the true doctrine and then relapse again should be received into penitence, but killed (*Summa Theologica*, 2-2, 11, 4).

According to me this is a terrible mistake, and faith is not a virtue but a positive vice. More precisely, there is, indeed, a virtue often called faith, but that is not the faith which the Christians make much of. The true virtue of faith is faith as opposed to faithlessness, that is, keeping faith and promises and being loyal. Christian faith, however, is not opposed to faithlessness but to unbelief. It is faith as some opposite of unbelief that I declare to be a vice.

When we investigate what Christians mean by their peculiar use of the word *faith*, I think we come to the remarkable conclusion that all their accounts of it are either unintelligible or false. Their most famous account is that in Hebrews 11:1: "Faith is the substance of things hoped for, the evidence of things not seen." This is obviously unintelligible. In any case, it does not make faith a virtue, since neither a substance nor an evidence can be a virtue. A virtue is a praiseworthy habit of choice, and neither a substance nor an evidence can be a habit of choice. When a Christian gives an intelligible account of faith, I think you will find that it is false. I mean that it is not a true dictionary report of how he and other Christians actually use the word. For example, Augustine asked: "What is faith but believing what you do not see?" (*Joannis Evang. Tract.,* c. 40, 8). But Christians do not use the word *faith* in the sense of believing what you do not see. You do not see thunder; but you cannot say in the Christian sense "have faith that it is thundering," or "I have faith that it has thundered in the past and will again in the future." You do not see mathematical truths; but you cannot say in the Christian sense "have faith that there is no greatest number." If we take Augustine's *see* to stand here for *know,* still it is false that Christians use the word *faith* to mean "believing what you do not know," for they would never call it faith if anyone believed that the sun converts hydrogen into helium, although he did not know it.

A good hint of what Christians really mean by their word *faith* can be got by considering the proposition: "Tom Paine had faith that there is no god." Is this a possible remark, in the Christian sense of the word *faith?* No, it is an impossible remark, because it is self-contradictory, because part of what Christians mean by *faith* is belief that there is a god.

There is more to it than this. Christian faith is not merely believing that there is a god. It is believing that there is a god no matter what the evidence on the question may be. "Have faith," in the Christian sense, means "make yourself believe that there is a god without regard to evidence." Christian faith is a habit of flouting reason in forming and maintaining one's answer to the question whether there is a god. Its essence is the determination to believe that there is a god no matter what the evidence may be.

No wonder that there is no true and intelligible account of faith in Christian literature. What they mean is too shocking to survive exposure. Faith is a great vice, an example of obstinately refusing to listen to reason, something irrational and undesirable, a form of self-hypnotism. Newman wrote that "if we but obey God strictly, in time (through His blessing) faith will become like sight" (Sermon XV). This is no better than if he said: "Keep on telling yourself that there is a god until you believe it. Hypnotize yourself into this belief."

It follows that, far from its being wicked to undermine faith, it is a duty to do so. We ought to do what we can towards eradicating the evil habit of believing without regard to evidence.

The usual way of recommending faith is to point out that belief and trust are often rational or necessary attitudes. Here is an example of this from Newman: "To hear some men speak, (I mean men who scoff at religion), it might be thought we never acted on Faith or Trust, except in religious matters; whereas we are acting on trust every hour of our lives. . . . We trust our *memory* . . . the general soundness of our reasoning powers. . . . Faith in [the] sense of *reliance on the words of another* as opposed to trust in oneself . . . is the common meaning of the word" (Sermon XV).

The value of this sort of argument is as follows. It is certainly true that belief and trust are often rational. But it is also certainly true that belief and trust are often irrational. We have to decide in each case by rational considerations whether to believe and trust or not. Sometimes we correctly decide *not* to trust our memory on some point, but to look the matter up in a book. Sometimes even we correctly decide not to trust our own reason, like poor Canning deciding he was mad because the Duke of Wellington told him he was. But Christian faith is essentially a case of irrational belief and trust and decision, because it consists in deciding to believe and trust the proposition that there is a god no matter what the evidence may be.

Another common way to defend Christian faith is to point out that we are often obliged to act on something less than knowledge and proof. For example, Newman writes: "Life is not long enough for a religion of inferences; we shall never have done beginning if we determine to begin with proof. Life is for action. If we insist on proof for everything, we shall never come to action; to act you must assume, and that assumption is faith" (*Assent*, p. 92).

The value of this argument is as follows. It is true that we are often unable to obtain knowledge and proof. But it does not follow that we must act on faith, for faith is belief reckless of evidence and probability. It follows only that we must act on some belief that does not amount to knowledge. This being so, we ought to assume, as our basis for action, those beliefs which are more probable than their contradictories in the light of the available evidence. We ought not to act on faith, for faith is assuming a certain belief without reference to its probability.

There is an ambiguity in the phrase "have faith in" that helps to make faith look respectable. When a man says that he has faith in the president he is assuming that it is obvious and known to everybody that there is a president, that the president exists, and he is asserting his confidence that the president will do good work on the whole. But, if a man says he has faith in telepathy, he does not mean that he is confident that telepathy will do good work on the whole, but that he believes that telepathy really occurs sometimes, that telepathy exists. Thus the phrase "to have faith in *x*" sometimes means to be confident that good work will be done by *x*, who is assumed or known to exist, but at other times means to believe that *x* exists. Which does it mean in the phrase "have faith in God"? It means ambiguously both; and the self-evidence of what it means in the one sense recommends what it means in the other sense. If there is a perfectly powerful and good god it is self-evidently reasonable to believe that he will do good. In this sense "have faith in God" is a reasonable exhortation. But it insinuates the other sense, namely "believe that there is a perfectly powerful and good god, no matter what the evidence." Thus the reasonableness of trusting God if he exists is used to make it seem also reasonable to believe that he exists.

It is well to remark here that a god who wished us to decide certain questions without regard to the evidence would definitely *not* be a perfectly good god.

Even when a person is aware that faith is belief without regard to evidence, he may be led to hold faith respectable by the consideration that we sometimes think it good for a man to believe in his friend's honesty in spite of strong evidence to the contrary, or for a woman to believe in her son's innocence in spite of strong evidence to the contrary. But, while we admire and love the love that leads the friend or parent to this view, we do not adopt or admire his conclusion unless we believe that he has private evidence of his own, gained by his long and intimate association, to outweigh the public evidence on the other side. Usually we suppose that his love has led him into an error of judgment, which both love and hate are prone to do.

This does not imply that we should never act on a man's word if we think he is deceiving us. Sometimes we ought to act on a man's word although we privately think he is probably lying. For the act required may be unimportant, whereas accusing a man of lying is always important. But there is no argument from this to faith. We cannot say that sometimes we ought to believe a proposition although we think it is false!

So I conclude that faith is a vice and to be condemned. As Plato said, "It is unholy to abandon the probably true" (*Republic* 607 C). Out of Paul's "faith, hope, and love" I emphatically accept love and reject faith. As to hope, it is more respectable than faith. While we ought not to believe against the probabilities, we are permitted to hope against them. But still the Christian overtones of hope are otherworldly and unrealistic. It is better to take a virtue that avoids that. Instead of faith, hope, and love, let us hymn reason, love, and joy.

What is the application of this to the common phrase "a faith to live by"? A faith to live by is not necessarily a set of beliefs or valuations maintained without regard to evidence in an irrational way. The phrase can well cover also a criticized and rational choice of values. To decide, for example, that the pursuit of love is better than the pursuit of power, in view of the probable effects of each on human happiness and misery, and to guide one's actions accordingly, is a rational procedure, and is sometimes called and may well be called "a faith to live by." In this case a faith to live by is a choice of values, a decision as to great goods and evils, and is what I am doing in these lectures. On the other hand, many "faiths to live by" are irrational and bad. Some people will not count anything as a faith to live by unless it deliberately ignores rational considerations; so that what they will consent to call a faith to live by must always be something that is bad according to me. Other people refuse to count anything as a faith to live by unless it includes a belief that the big battalions are on their side, so that according to them a man who rationally concludes that he is not the darling of any god by definition has no faith to live by.

V. Mysticism

Walter Kaufmann

The Core of Religion

Walter Kaufmann, professor of philosophy at Princeton University, received his degrees from Williams College and from Harvard University. His books include: *The Portable Nietzsche* (1954), selections from Nietzsche's works that he translated; *Existentialism from Dostoevsky to Sartre* (1956); *Critique of Religion and Philosophy* (1958); *From Shakespeare to Existentialism* (1959); *Goethe's Faust: A New Verse Translation* (1961); *The Faith of a Heretic* (1961); *Cain and other Poems* (1962); translator and editor of *Twenty German Poets* (1962); *Hegel* (1965); *The Will to Power* (1967); *Tragedy and Philosophy* (1968); a translation and edition of *Basic Writings of Nietzsche* (1968); *Hegel's Political Philosophy* (1970); a translation and edition of *Martin Buber, I and Thou* (1970); and *Nietzsche, The Gay Science* (1974). He has edited a series of biographies on such writers as Sartre, Wittgenstein, Luther, and Lenin and has published articles in many books, encyclopedias, and journals.

CLAIMS FOR MYSTICISM

Many writers find the core of religion in mysticism. This provides an experiential basis for religion and an excuse for the conflicts between religion and common sense, faith and reason. Religion, it is said, represents an attempt to do injustice to a singular kind of experience which is ignored by common sense and by the sciences; at the very least, religion supplements the partial world views that are based on sense and reason; and some writers even claim that the world of sense and reason is a phantom while mysticism affords us a glimpse of ultimate reality.

It would follow that there are two kinds of religion: the genuine religion of the mystics, and the secondhand religion of the rest of mankind. The mystics are said to have experienced something to which religious scriptures, dogmas, rites and propositions try to give form, however inadequately. The mystic himself does not need these aids: they are for the rest of us who must, alas, get our religion secondhand.

Some think that all the mystics agree on essentials, which is, on the face of it, patently false; but the term can be defined so narrowly that it insures uniformity: those who do not agree are not called real mystics. Even to the extent to which there is agreement, there is doubt about its significance. Against those who assume that, if the mystics agree, they must be right, Bertrand Russell has argued in his essay "Mysticism": "From a scientific point of view we can make no distinction between the man who eats little and sees heaven and the man who drinks much and sees snakes. Each is an abnormal physical condition, and therefore has abnormal perceptions."[1]

In a similar vein, Santayana has repeatedly called mysticism "a religious disease." Although Santayana and Russell, usually poles apart, are in partial agreement on this point, their view is decidedly a minority view. Catholics think of some mystics as saints, while most Protestants are thrilled by the individualism of so many mystics. Those who are not religious often feel that for the mystic it is reasonable to be religious, because he is after all a kind of empiricist.

There is more agreement among authors who have written on the subject that mysticism is admirable than there is about what precisely it is. In 1899, Dean Inge selected for critical discussion twenty-six definitions of mysticism, and since then many further suggestions have been made. The

From Walter Kaufmann, Critique of Religion and Philosophy (*New York: Doubleday, 1958*), *pp. 314-29. Reprinted by permission of Walter Kaufmann.*

difficulty here is not merely one of definition, on the same plane with the problem of defining religion or philosophy. In the latter case, we might agree that Plato, Aristotle, Descartes, Hume, Hegel, and Mill have all been notable philosophers, but we might be perplexed if asked to state briefly what they had in common. It is similar with religion, where we can agree that Buddhism, Christianity, Judaism, Hinduism, and Islam, for example, are religions. In both cases, there are borderline phenomena, but we have no doubt about the chief representatives. In the case of mysticism it will not do to speak of Elijah and the prophets, or of Jesus and St. Paul, as borderline phenomena; but according to some writers they were mystics, and according to others, not. There is no agreement what is meant by mysticism. There are a few clear-cut cases, like Meister Eckhart and Plotinus; and many more, from the Buddha to Buber, who present a problem.

INEFFABILITY

In his chapter "Mysticism" in *The Varieties of Religious Experience,* William James proposed "four marks which, when an experience has them, may justify us in calling it mystical."[2] These four criteria were: ineffability, noetic quality, transiency, and passivity. After briefly discussing each, James reiterated: "These four characteristics are sufficient to mark out a group of states of consciousness peculiar enough to deserve a special name."[3] Yet the last three criteria afford us no grounds whatever for distinguishing the mystic experience: sense experiences also yield knowledge, do not last, and find us receptive rather than active. It would seem therefore that it must be ineffability that sets apart mystic experiences.

In his emphasis on ineffability, James is far from alone. On the basis of many assertions in this vein by mystics themselves, other writers have stressed this point, too; most emphatically, perhaps, Walter Stace in his attempt to show that mysticism is the core of all religion. This claim of a unique ineffability deserves closer scrutiny.

The first objection that comes to mind is that so many mystics have been downright garrulous. A sympathetic immersion in the texts, however, suggests that their effusions often issued from dissatisfaction with any single statement they could make.

The second objection is that this criterion might exclude the major figures of the Bible from Moses to St. Paul: they did not take refuge in any claim of ineffability, and their own statements apparently struck them as adequate and clear. This objection may be answered by saying that these men were indeed no mystics.

The third objection is more detailed and involves some analysis of the assertion that the mystic experience is distinguished by its ineffability. What is supposed to be ineffable? Is it the experience or its object? Let us begin by supposing that it is the *experience*.

There are two aspects of an experience that might well lead a person to call it ineffable: first, direct acquaintance; secondly, emotion. Suppose you have long known a description or even a picture of the temple of Poseidon at Paestum in southern Italy; and then you see the temple for the first time. This experience might well be ineffable in a sense. What you can say about the temple after this experience might be nothing new at all. What you now describe, you could have described before, too. But the difference between reading a description or even seeing a picture and seeing the temple itself may be overwhelming. If it is, the second element comes into play, too: you have an emotional experience; and emotional experiences are extremely difficult to describe.

James cites many analogous examples from the mystics. Saint Ignatius Loyola suddenly understood "the deep mystery of the holy Trinity" without being able to say anything about it that he could not have said before. But according to a life of the saint which James quotes, "This last vision flooded his heart with such sweetness, that the mere memory of it in after times made him shed abundant tears."[4] In a similar vein, James cites Santa Teresa: "On another day, she relates, while she was reciting the Athanasian Creed—'Our Lord made me comprehend in what way it is that one God can be in three persons. He made me see it so clearly that I remained as extremely surprised as I was comforted, . . . and now, when I think of the holy Trinity, or hear It spoken of, I understand how the three adorable persons form only one God and I experience an unspeakable happiness.' On still another occasion, it was given to Saint Teresa to see and understand in what wise the Mother of God had been assumed into her place in Heaven."[5]

Pratt is surely right: "the mystics are by no means always unable to communicate the truths which they have intuitively perceived during their ecstasy, although it must be noted that the 'revealed' truths which they can communicate are always old truths which they knew (though in a much less living form) before."[6] And two pages later Pratt adds: "Possibly *all* the mystical 'revelations' may be accounted for as being carried into the ecstasy by the mystic, and derived originally from social education, and all except this sense of presence may possibly be mere conclusions which the mystic comes to after reflecting upon his experience by a process of ordinary discursive thought; a number of mystics will be found to admit this. . . ."[7]Later on, Pratt cites Coe's critique of James in which this point is briefly epitomized: "The mystic brings his theological beliefs to the mystical experience; he does not derive them from it."[8]And elsewhere Pratt himself argues that "The visions of the mystics are determined in content by their belief, and are due to the dream imagination working upon the mass of theological material which fills the mind."[9]A fundamentally similar view was developed by J. H. Leuba, who was much less sympathetic toward mysticism than Pratt.

Both the element of acquaintance and that of emotion are present in all of our experiences, and neither is entirely ineffable. The element of acquaintance can be communicated, and usually is, simply by the statement that we saw something, or heard, or smelled, or felt something with our own eyes, ears, nose, or body. The element of emotion is generally communicated by means of an approximate label: I was thrilled, excited, disappointed, desperate, or possibly dumfounded. To achieve greater precision requires art. If utterly unimaginative declaratory sentences would do full justice to all our nonmystic experiences, there would be no need for poetry and painting, for the subtle prose of Joyce and Faulkner, or for music.

The frequent claim in discussions of mysticism that language is adapted only to the realm of subject-object experiences, while the mystical experience transcends this realm uniquely, overlooks that even the simplest subject-object experience involves an element of acquaintance which is not fully describable. The claim further ignores emotional experience.

All experience has a trans-scientific dimension which it takes art to communicate. The inadequacy of ordinary propositions to the mystic's experience does not set his experience apart. Some mystics are unpoetic souls who require special exercises and an eventual trance to see anything but the everyday world.

The mystic's insistence on the unique ineffability of his experience may prove no more than that he has never known any other intense experience. He may even have gone into a monastery to make sure of that.

Now it may be claimed that the mystic differs from other men by having a kind of second sight which enables him to perceive an ineffable *object*. Where the mystic himself claims something of this sort, we must consider three possibilities.

First, his experience may actually have no object at all: it may be intransitive like the experience of hunger, bliss, despair, or ecstasy. If we realize that we are hungry and that some food would allay our discomfort, we are not likely to be very puzzled by our experience or to think of it as ineffable, though, if we concentrated on what we actually feel, we should find that it was exceedingly hard to describe. But if we are hungry, as occasionally happens, without realizing that we are hungry, we are quite apt to consider our experience ineffable. It is similar with homesickness when a child does not diagnose its own condition. It cannot rightly say what it feels. Words fail the child: it must depend on the intuitive understanding of a person who has had the same experience and knows how it feels.

Bliss, despair, and ecstasy present fundamentally the same picture. They are all ineffable in a sense but amenable to an imaginative attempt at communication. When we know what prompted the experience, we are less apt to emphasize its ineffability; when we feel elated or dreadfully depressed without quite understanding our own condition, we are more apt to stress the inadequacy of words.

Secondly, it is possible that an experience has a definite object which *is* describable, and that it is only the element of acquaintance or the emotional aspect which all but defies description. In that case, my description will sound like the descriptions I used to read; it will miss what I had always missed—and what my audience will miss until and unless they have the experience themselves. As in all of the preceding cases, there is no essential difference between mystic and nonmystic experience.

Thirdly, let us imagine a case in which a person desires to have a particular experience of which he has some preconception. He may, for example, crave a vision of the Virgin Mary. He may go into seclusion, forgo sleep, fast, practice austerities, pray and meditate, and hope for his vision all the time. When the moment of his vision comes, we should hardly expect him to see Shiva in his glory, dancing. Lutherans do not usually see the Virgin Mary, and Catholics do not see Martin Luther, unless it were in hell. On the nonreligious level, a man who desires passionately to evoke the vivid picture of a loved one who is either dead or distant will usually find, if he succeeds, that the image conforms, at least in important respects, to the image he expected.

Now, if a man desires the experience of an ineffable object, whether Brahma or the One or God, then any experience that is not ineffable will be ruled out as not yet the ultimate experience. If, on the other hand, the man has an experience which is in important respects indescribable, he will be inclined to insist that it was ineffable even if it belonged in one of the categories considered above. If he was determined all along to experience something timeless and eternal, he will construe his oblivion of time during his experience as an indication that he has experienced something timeless. If he wished for the experience of the One, he will take the absence of plurality in his experience for a proof that its object was the One.

... [In Zen Buddhism] the ineffability of experience is stressed from generation unto generation, and any attempt to describe it is, to put it mildly, discouraged from the outset. Yet the Zen Buddhist admits that *all* experience has a trans-scientific dimension; and on this he concentrates. Those modern writers who insist that the religious experience differs from the so-called aesthetic experience posit a distinction which the great mystics would have failed to understand.

Many modern writers banish religion to some special province of experience. But the concept of religion is lacking in the great religions to begin with: it appears only as religion becomes problematic.

If those who decided what books to include in the Hebrew canon had accepted the modern distinction between the religious and the aesthetic, or if they had assumed, as so many writers do today, that the religious experience is *sui generis*, they would not only have omitted the Song of Songs—which later exerted a greater influence on Christian mysticism than any other book of the Bible—but more than half of the Scriptures. And if the early Christians or the Reformers had accepted these false modern ideas, they would have thrown out of the Bible most of the Old Testament.

Some people think that the Old Testament *is* a medley of religious books, secular history, love songs, laws, and all kinds of things that have little or nothing to do with religion. But all of it has a great deal to do with religion and actually *was* religion not only for the ancient Hebrews but also for millions of Jews and Christians down to our time.

Defenders of religion who, never having had a mystical experience, would identify religion with the experience of the great mystics would save it by placing it in protective custody: in a reservation, museum, or grave.

The eulogists of mysticism may reply that some of the mystics have emphatically insisted that the mystical experience is ineffable in a way in which no other experience is ineffable; and that any attempt to assimilate mysticism to other experiences disregards this testimony. To this a threefold answer may be made.

First: for every mystic who insisted on the apartness of the mystical experience one could probably cite two who did not.

Second: mysticism is a name for a vast variety of phenomena. William James follows a personal preference in concentrating disproportionately on eccentrics and downright crackpots. Meister Eckhart presents a very different picture; and the serene sages of the Upanishads have little in common with Santa Teresa.

Third: mysticism, though encountered in all religions, is not encountered in all religions at all times; it is a historical phenomenon which belongs to a particular stage in the development of a religion. This last point deserves special emphasis and needs to be developed further.

MYSTICISM AS A HISTORICAL PHENOMENON

If the plea of ineffability is considered a definitive criterion of mysticism, the religion of the Old Testament was nonmystical, and prophetic religion represents a powerful alternative to mysticism. By the same token, there would be little mysticism in the New Testament. The prime example of mysticism would have to be found in the Upanishads. The Buddha, on the other hand, would have to be considered the leader of an antimystic movement. In the West, the great age of mysticism would have to be found in the late Middle Ages, carrying over into the seventeenth century. In short, mysticism that claims ineffability is a phenomenon confined to rationalistic ages, and its plea is meant as a defense against rationalistic attacks or as a protest against theology, or both.

The Hebrew prophets were not subjected to critical questioning about the nature of their experience; the sages of the Upanishads were. Upanishads means something like "seminars"; and the typical situation is that a teacher answers the questions of a student. The plea of ineffability is a last resort. The student asks whether the experience was like this? Like this? Like this? He always misunderstands. The situation invites comparison with an older brother telling his younger brother that he has fallen in love for the first time. What is it like?—I am excited.—Oh, the way one feels during an examination?—No, very happy.—Oh, the way one feels at the circus.—Not at all; I am upset and do not feel like eating.—Oh, I had an upset stomach once not long ago.—Not like that; and I can't sleep at night either.—Oh, you have insomnia like Uncle Wilbur.—No, no, no; I could sing all the time, but when I see her I suddenly can't get out a word.—Oh, like Aunt Prudence the night when she had stage fright and suddenly could not sing.—No, not this, not that.

This is the schema of many an interrogation in the Upanishads. An older man tries to describe an experience to a younger man who has not had the experience and who keeps asking bright questions which are over-literal and show no imaginative understanding whatsoever until the teacher finally exclaims *"neti! neti!"* Not this, not that.

What is decisive is not that the experience is mystical but that it is subjected to persistent unsympathetic questions. Where that condition is met, the concluding line can always be: not this! not that! And the modern writer concludes: the experience is clearly ineffable.

In the late Middle Ages, systematic questioning was the order of the day. The man who wanted to make a point of his religious experience could not speak the language of the prophets; he spoke that of the mystics.

The mystic feels that the theologian's descriptions miss the crucial element of acquaintance which in many cases did not come to the mystic easily but only as the result of much effort. Also, the theologians's intellectualism misses the element of emotion which means so much to the mystic. And so he insists that what matters most is left out: it is ineffable.

The Buddha's experience of enlightenment was no less ineffable than that of the sages of the Upanishads; but since he was protesting against their esoteric coterie and wished to emphasize four truths that could be rather baldly stated, he did not stress the ineffability of his experience. Amos' experience of God's call had its ineffable aspect, but he was more concerned to state unequivocally what he thought of the morals of his contemporaries than to be coy about his experience.

The plea of ineffability, far from being proof of singular profundity, is a plea of impotence, if it is not a polemic as in Zen. The poet who can communicate his experience need not plead that it is indescribable; that is the poor poet's excuse. Shakespeare finds words where lesser poets would not.

The claim of ineffability expresses a negation—sometimes of one's own power to communicate; sometimes of the questioner's power to understand; and sometimes of the profundity of theology. The claim is essentially critical and belongs to critical ages.

To say it once more: great art and philosophy begin on the other side of ineffability.

CRITERIA OF MYSTICAL EXPERIENCE

We have found William James' set of four criteria utterly inadequate: what sets apart mystical experiences is not that they are, unlike other experiences, ineffable, noetic, transient, and passive. Other similar attempts are little better; and many are a great deal worse.

Evelyn Underhill, for example, in one of the best-known studies of mysticism, offers an effusive tribute rather than objective criteria when she stipulates five points in Chapter IV, following up each with a little paean. In the original, all five sentences are italicized. "(1) Mysticism is practical, not theoretical. . . . (2) Mysticism is an entirely spiritual activity. . . . (3) The business and method of Mysticism is Love. . . . (4) Mysticism entails a definite Psychological Experience. . . . (5) True Mysticism is never self-seeking." [10]

These suggestions came out of years of study which issued in other books, too, and they have some evocative power; but they do not offer adequate criteria. In fact, Miss Underhill seems to imply that the experience itself has no distinctive criteria and can be judged to have been an instance of "True Mysticism" only in the light of its fruits: mysticism—that appears to be the implication—is a psychological experience which affects a person's life and leads him to engage in "entirely spiritual activity" which is marked by the prominence of "love" and the absence of "self-seeking." The emphasis on love excludes the sages of the Upanishads and the Zen Buddhists. Nor did Miss Underhill realize that her five points fit the Hebrew prophets rather better than many of the most-renowned mystics, for example, Plotinus. Clearly, she was thinking of certain Christian mystics whom she admired especially.

Miss Underhill was perhaps the best-known English writer on mysticism. Her American counterpart was Rufus Jones. He defined mysticism as "other type of religion which puts the emphasis on immediate awareness of relation with God, on direct and intimate consciousness of the Divine Presence." [11] But this definition would restrict mysticism to theistic religions, which is hardly reasonable. Again, the Zen Buddhists would be left out.

What James and Jones and Underhill, among others, overlook is this: what sets apart the mystic experience is not anything given, but the interpretation and evaluation which the person who has the experience accords to it. And this interpretation need not be theistic.

To be considered mystical, an experience must, first, be considered different from everyday perception. It stands out, it is uncommon, it marks a break in the everyday world. James' four criteria take no note of this. It may seem to be a highly elusive criterion, but it is not. Two men may have two very similar experiences: if one of them feels that it was part of the everyday world and really not at all extraordinary, he rules out the suggestion that it might have been a mystical experience; while the other man, if he feels that it was an uncommon experience, leaves open the possibility that it might have been mystical.

The second criterion is that the experience is considered much more important than our everyday perceptions. If a man says that while crossing the street and being narrowly missed by a car he had an uncommon experience, but that he attaches no importance to it, then he is implying that it was not a mystical experience.

The third criterion is that the person who has the experience finds no objective correlative for it in nature. The conception of the objective correlative was popularized by T. S. Eliot, who took the idea—and not only this idea—from Santayana's *Interpretations of Poetry and Religion,*[12] and Eliot's use of it was anything but propitious. He argued that Shakespeare's *Hamlet* "is most certainly an artistic failure" and then tried to back up this extraordinary judgment by finding "the grounds of *Hamlet's* failure" in the lack of an objective correlative. It will be best to quote Eliot's own explanation of his term from "Hamlet and His Problems" (1919): "The only way of expressing emotion in the form of art is by finding an 'objective correlative'; in other words, a set of objects, a situation, a chain of events which shall be in the formula of that *particular* emotion; such that when the external facts, which must terminate in sensory experience, are given, the emotion is immediately evoked." To give an example, Eliot claims that "the words of Macbeth on hearing of his wife's death strike us as if, given the sequence of events, these words were automatically released by the last event in the series. The artistic 'inevitability' lies in the complete adequacy of the external to the emotion; and this is precisely what is deficient in *Hamlet*. Hamlet (the man) is dominated by an emotion which is inexpressible, because it is in excess of the facts as they appear."[13]

A short critique of Eliot will provide a helpful perspective for our third criterion of the mystical experience. In the first place, there is a very important sense in which Hamlet's emotions are fully warranted by the facts. His father, whom he worshiped, has been murdered. If Hamlet's feelings toward his father were deeply ambivalent, this would complicate his emotion and make it harder for him to express it. His mother, whom he loves, has remarried almost immediately—a man whom Hamlet loathes, and of whom he suddenly hears that he was the murderer. Moreover, his murdered father was king, he himself is the heir, and his loathsome uncle is now the head of the state: even without going into Hamlet's relation to

Ophelia, it should be clear that Hamlet's emotions are *not* "in excess of the facts as they appear." And yet there is a sense in which they *are*: a less sensitive person would feel less emotion even under such extraordinary provocation; it is only in conjunction with Hamlet's sensibility that the objective correlative is adequate for his emotions.

It is a commonplace that Hamlet is highly sensitive; and highly sensitive people, by definition, feel emotions which are, if one insists on putting it that way, "in excess of the facts"—from the point of view of less sensitive people. The average person would not have broken out into the words of Macbeth either, even if he had heard of his wife's death under the very same circumstances; and one might with more justice question the unity of Shakespeare's conception of Macbeth—even though Eliot considers *Macbeth* one "of Shakespeare's more successful tragedies"—than the emotion of Hamlet.

There is, in sum, no objective correlation of fact and emotion in such a way that one could say generally that certain facts warrant a certain amount of emotion, unless we include among the facts of the case the sensibility of the person who has the experience. If we apply this result to experiences which may or may not be mystical, it appears that a highly emotional experience in a situation in which most men would not feel nearly so much emotion does not establish the absence of an objective correlative: if the person who has the experience is extremely high-strung and excitable and has possibly even worked himself into a state of hypersensitivity by fasting, going without sleep, and praying fervently, then there is an objective correlative even for an enormous amount of emotion. Our criterion, however, is that the person who *has* the experience finds no objective correlative for it in nature; that he himself feels that his experience is in excess of what is warranted by the naturalistic facts. If he does find an objective correlative for it in nature, then he rules out the suggestion that it might be a mystical experience.

The fourth criterion is that the person who has the experience finds the objective correlative either beyond nature or in nature as a whole, as opposed to any conjunction of things *in* nature. Which of these two alternatives he embraces and what name he gives to the objective correlative will generally depend on the religious tradition in which he stands. The man of the Upanishads will speak of Brahma; the Taoist of the Tao; some Buddhists of Nirvana; some Christians of God, others of the Trinity, and still others of the Virgin; and some who stand outside all denominations may speak of nature or the cosmos.

These four criteria are meant to be taken in conjunction: where all four are satisfied we are confronted with what is usually called a mystical experience. It does not at all follow from all this that mystical experiences must be particularly hard to explain: the Society for Psychical Research keeps records of experiences which few, if any, would call mystical, but which are far harder to explain in terms of modern science than most of the experiences of the great mystics.

If the fourth criterion were qualified further to demand that the person who had the experience must feel afterward that he was altogether one with the non-naturalistic objective correlative we mentioned—if, in short, we should restrict mysticism to experiences of a so-called *unio mystica*— we should exclude altogether too much that is generally included in discussions of mysticism. "Numerous mystics, Jews as well as non-Jews, have by no means represented the essence of their ecstatic experience, the tremendous uprush and soaring of the soul to its highest plane, as a union with God."[14] Scholem has shown this in considerable detail as far as Jewish mysticism is concerned; but there can be no doubt that he is right about non-Jewish mystics, too.

Mystical experiences are by no means all the same, and the differences are not reducible to the interpretations which the mystics offer afterward. The experiences themselves are molded by the personality and the prior beliefs and expectations of the mystic. Suzuki does not have the same experience as Santa Teresa.

In one way, however, the mystic experience might well be narrowed down further. There is an experience which might be called mystical in accordance with the four criteria offered but which in fact we generally do not call mystical and which I should prefer to distinguish from the mystical experience. The Hebrew prophets are among the most outstanding representatives of this other type of experience and one might therefore call it prophetic. Against this term one may urge at least three objections.

First, it is apt to suggest falsely that the experience usually issues in some forecast of the future. Secondly, it may be better not to associate this experience primarily with the prophets. Else, the question arises immediately whether all the prophets had essentially the same experience. Perhaps the experiences of Amos and most of the earlier prophets, but also the Second Isaiah, were very different from those of Ezekiel, Zachariah, and other visionaries. Also, some might feel that the Hebrew prophets represent a unique phenomenon rather than a typical experience. Therefore, a more neutral term seems preferable. Thirdly, Fried-

rich Heiler has contrasted mysticism and prophetic religion along somewhat different lines in his book *Prayer*[15] and use of the same terms for a
similar contrast might lead to confusion. Let us therefore call the other
type an experience of inspiration.

NOTES

1. Bertrand Russell, "Mysticism," in *Religion and Science,* Home University
Library (Oxford: Oxford University Press, 1935, 1947), p. 188.

2. William James, *The Varieties of Religious Experience, Gifford Lectures,
1901-02* (New York: The Modern Library), p. 371.

3. Ibid., p. 372.

4. Ibid., p. 401.

5. Ibid., p. 403.

6. James Bisset Pratt, *The Religious Consciousness* (New York: Macmillan,
1940), p. 410.

7. Ibid., p. 412.

8. Ibid., p. 450.

9. Ibid., p. 403.

10. Evelyn Underhill, *Mysticism* (New York: Meridan Books, 1954), pp. 82-92.

11. Rufus M. Jones, *Studies in Mystical Religion* (London: Macmillan, 1923),
p. xv.

12. George Santayana, *Interpretations of Poetry and Religion* (New York: Harper and Brothers, 1957), p. 277.

13. T. S. Eliot, "Hamlet and His Problems," in *Selected Essays, 1917-1932*
(New York: Harcourt, Brace, 1932), pp. 124-25.

14. Gershom G. Scholem, *Major Trends in Jewish Mysticism* (Jerusalem:
Schocken Publishing House, 1941), p. 5.

15. Friedrich Heiler, *Prayer: A Study in the History and Psychology of Religion,*
trans. and ed., Samuel McComb (Oxford: Oxford University Press, 1932), Ch. 6 ff.

VI. Religion and the Religious

Sigmund Freud

The Future of an Illusion

Sigmund Freud, M.D., is recognized as the founder of psychoanalysis. His books include: *Studies on Hysteria* (1895, with Josef Breuer); *The Interpretation of Dreams* (1900); *The Psychopathology of Everyday Life* (1904); *Three Essays on the Theory of Sexuality* (1905); *Jokes and Their Relation to the Unconscious* (1905); *The Origin and Development of Psychoanalysis* (1909); *Leonardo da Vinci and a Memory of His Childhood* (1910); *Totem and Taboo* (1912); *General Introduction to Psychoanalysis* (1920); *Beyond the Pleasure Principle* (1920); *The Ego and the Id* (1923); *Inhibitions, Symptoms and Anxiety* (1926); *The Future of an Illusion* (1927); and *Problems of Lay-analysis* (1927). Freud wrote a number of case histories and articles dealing with the subject of therapy.

1

In what does the peculiar value of religious ideas lie?

We have spoken of the hostility to civilization which is produced by the pressure that civilization exercises, the renunciations of instinct which it demands. If one imagines its prohibitions lifted—if, then, one may take any woman one pleases as a sexual object, if one may without hesitation kill one's rival for her love or anyone else who stands in one's way, if, too, one can carry off any of the other man's belongings without asking leave— how splendid, what a string of satisfactions one's life would be! True, one soon comes across the first difficulty: everyone else has exactly the same wishes as I have and will treat me with no more consideration than I treat him. And so in reality only one person could be made unrestrictedly happy by such a removal of the restrictions of civilization, and he would be a tyrant, a dictator, who had seized all the means to power. And even he would have every reason to wish that the others would observe at least one cultural commandment: "thou shalt not kill."

But how ungrateful, how short-sighted after all, to strive for the abolition of civilization! What would then remain would be a state of nature, and that would be far harder to bear. It is true that nature would not demand any restrictions of instinct from us, she would let us do as we liked; but she has her own particularly effective method of restricting us. She destroys us—coldly, cruelly, relentlessly, as it seems to us, and possibly through the very things that occasioned our satisfaction. It was precisely because of these dangers with which nature threatens us that we came together and created civilization, which is also, among other things, intended to make our communal life possible. For the principal task of civilization, its actual raison d'être, is to defend us against nature.

We all know that in many ways civilization does this fairly well already, and clearly as time goes on it will do it much better. But no one is under the illusion that nature has already been vanquished; and few dare hope that she will ever be entirely subjected to man. There are the ele-

Reprinted from The Future of an Illusion *by Sigmund Freud. Newly translated from the German and edited by James Strachey. Copyright © 1961 by James Strachey. W. W. Norton & Company, Inc., New York. Acknowledgment also made to Sigmund Freud Copyrights Ltd., The Institute of Psycho-Analysis, and The Hogarth Press Ltd. for permission to quote from "The Future of an Illusion" in volume 21 of* The Standard Edition of the Complete Psychological Works of Sigmund Freud, *revised and edited by James Strachey.*

ments, which seem to mock at all human control: the earth, which quakes and is torn apart and buries all human life and its works; water, which deluges and drowns everything in a turmoil; storms, which blow everything before them; there are diseases, which we have only recently recognized as attacks by other organisms; and finally there is the painful riddle of death, against which no medicine has yet been found, nor probably will be. With these forces nature rises up against us, majestic, cruel and inexorable; she brings to our mind once more our weakness and helplessness, which we thought to escape through the work of civilization. One of the few gratifying and exalting impressions which mankind can offer is when, in the face of an elemental catastrophe, it forgets the discordancies of its civilization and all its internal difficulties and animosities, and recalls the great common task of preserving itself against the superior power of nature.

For the individual, too, life is hard to bear, just as it is for mankind in general. The civilization in which he participates imposes some amount of privation on him, and other men bring him a measure of suffering, either in spite of the precepts of his civilization or because of its imperfections. To this are added the injuries which untamed nature—he calls it fate—inflicts on him. One might suppose that this condition of things would result in a permanent state of anxious expectation in him and a severe injury to his natural narcissism. We know already how the individual reacts to the injuries which civilization and other men inflict on him: he develops a corresponding degree of resistance to the regulations of civilization and of hostility to it. But how does he defend himself against the superior powers of nature, of fate, which threaten him as they threaten all the rest?

Civilization relieves him of this task; it performs it in the same way for all alike; and it is noteworthy that in this almost all civilizations act alike. Civilization does not call a halt in the task of defending man against nature, it merely pursues it by other means. The task is a manifold one. Man's self-regard, seriously menaced, calls for consolation; life and the universe must be robbed of their terrors; moreover his curiosity, moved, it is true, by the strongest practical interest, demands an answer.

A great deal is already gained with the first step: the humanization of nature. Impersonal forces and destinies cannot be approached; they remain eternally remote. But if the elements have passions that rage as they do in our own souls, if death itself is not something spontaneous but the violent act of an evil will, if everywhere in nature there are beings around us of a kind that we know in our own society, then we can breathe freely, can feel at home in the uncanny and can deal by psychical means with our senseless anxiety. We are still defenseless, perhaps, but we are no longer helplessly paralyzed; we can at least react. Perhaps, indeed, we are not even defenseless. We can apply the same methods against these violent supermen outside that we employ in our own society; we can try to adjure them, to appease them, to bribe them, and, by so influencing them, we may rob them of a part of their power. A replacement like this of natural science by psychology not only provides immediate relief, but also points the way to a further mastering of the situation.

For this situation is nothing new. It has an infantile prototype, of which it is in fact only the continuation. For once before, one has found oneself in a similar state of helplessness: as a small child, in relation to one's parents. One had reason to fear them, and especially one's father; and yet one was sure of his protection against the dangers one knew. Thus it was natural to assimilate the two situations. Here, too, wishing played its part, as it does in dream life. The sleeper may be seized with a presentiment of death, which threatens to place him in the grave. But the dreamwork knows how to select a condition that will turn even that dreaded event into a wish-fulfillment: the dreamer sees himself in an ancient Etruscan grave which he has climbed down into, happy to find his archaeological interests satisfied.[1] In the same way, a man makes the forces of nature not simply into persons with whom he can associate as he would with his equals—that would not do justice to the overpowering impression which those forces make on him—but he gives them the character of a father. He turns them into gods, following in this, as I have tried to show,[2] not only an infantile prototype but a phylogenetic one.

In the course of time the first observations were made of regularity and conformity to law in natural phenomena, and with this the forces of nature lost their human traits. But man's helplessness remains and along with it his longing for his father, and the gods. The gods retain their threefold task: they must exorcize the terrors of nature, they must reconcile men to the cruelty of fate, particularly as it is shown in death, and they must compensate them for the sufferings and privations which a civilized life in common has imposed on them.

But within these functions there is a gradual displacement of accent. It was observed that the phenomena of nature developed automatically according to internal necessities. Without doubt the gods were the lords of nature; they had arranged it to be as it was and now they could leave it to itself. Only occasionally, in what are known as miracles, did they intervene in its course, as though to make it plain that they had relinquished nothing of their original sphere of power. As regards the apportioning of destinies, an unpleasant suspicion persisted that the perplexity and helplessness of the human race could not be remedied. It was here that the gods were most apt to fail. If they themselves created fate, then their counsels must be deemed inscrutable. The notion dawned on the most gifted people of antiquity that Moira [Fate] stood above the gods and that the gods themselves had their own destinies. And the more autonomous nature became and the more the gods withdrew from it, the more earnestly were all expectations directed to the third function of the gods—the more did morality become their true domain. It now became the task of the gods to even out the defects and evils of civilization, to attend to the sufferings which men inflict on one another in their life together and to watch over the fulfillment of the precepts of civilization, which men obey so imperfectly. Those precepts themselves were credited with a divine origin; they were elevated beyond human society and were extended to nature and the universe.

And thus a store of ideas is created, born from man's need to make his helplessness tolerable and built up from the material of memories of the helplessness of his own childhood and the childhood of the human race. It can clearly be seen that the possession of these ideas protects him in two directions—against the dangers of nature and fate, and against the injuries that threaten him from human society itself. Here is the gist of the matter. Life in this world serves a higher purpose; no doubt it is not easy to guess what the purpose is, but it certainly signifies a perfecting of man's nature. It is probably the spiritual part of man, the soul, which in the course of time has so slowly and unwillingly detached itself from the body, that is the object of this elevation and exaltation. Everything that happens in this world is an expression of the intentions of an intelligence superior to us, which in the end, though its ways and byways are difficult to follow, orders everything for the best—that is, to make it enjoyable for us. Over each one of us there watches a benevolent Providence, which is only seemingly stern and which will not suffer us to become a plaything of the overmighty and pitiless forces of nature. Death itself is not extinction, is not a return to inorganic lifelessness, but the beginning of a new kind of existence which lies on the path of development to something higher. And, looking in the other direction, this view announces that the same moral laws which our civilizations have set up govern the whole universe as well, except that they are maintained by a supreme court of justice with incomparably more power and consistency. In the end all good is rewarded and all evil punished, if not actually in this form of life then in the later existences that begin after death. In this way all the terrors, the sufferings and the hardships of life are destined to be obliterated. Life after death, which continues life on earth, just as the invisible part of the spectrum joins onto the visible part, brings us all the perfection that we may perhaps have missed here. And the superior wisdom which directs this course of things, the infinite goodness that expresses itself in it, the justice that achieves its aim in it—these are the attributes of the divine beings who also created us and the world as a whole, or rather, of the one divine being into which, in our civilization, all the gods of antiquity have been condensed. The people which first succeeded in thus concentrating the divine attributes was not a little proud of the advance. It had laid open to view the father who had all along been hidden behind every divine figure as its nucleus. Fundamentally this was a return to the historical beginnings of the idea of God. Now that God was a single person, man's relations to him could recover the intimacy and intensity of the child's relation to his father. But if one had done so much for one's father, one wanted to have a reward, or at least to be his only beloved child, his Chosen People. Very much later, pious America laid claim to being "God's own Country"; and, as regards one of the shapes in which men worship the deity, the claim is undoubtedly valid.

The religious ideas that have been summarized above have of course passed through a long process of development and have been adhered to in various phases by various civilizations. I have singled out one such phase, which roughly corresponds to the final form taken by our present-day, white, Christian civilization. It is easy to see that not all the parts of this picture tally equally well with one another, that not all the questions that press for an answer receive one, and that it is difficult to dismiss the contradiction of daily experience. Nevertheless, such as they are, those ideas— ideas which are religious in the widest sense—are prized as the most precious possession of civilization, as the most precious thing it has to offer its participants. It is far more highly prized than all the devices for winning treasures from the earth or providing men with sustenance or preventing their illnesses, and so forth. People feel that life would not be tolerable if they did not attach to these ideas the value that is claimed for them. And now the question arises: What are these ideas in the light of psychology? Whence do they derive the esteem in which they are held? And, to take a further timid step, what is their real worth?

2

Let us now take up the thread of our inquiry. What, then, is the psychological significance of religious ideas and under what heading are we to classify them? The question is not at all easy to answer immediately. After rejecting a number of formulations, we will take our stand on the following one. Religious ideas are teachings and assertions about facts and conditions of external (or internal) reality which tell one something one has not discovered for oneself and which lay claim to one's belief. Since they give us information about what is most important and interesting to us in life, they are particularly highly prized. Anyone who knows nothing of them is very ignorant; and anyone who has added them to his knowledge may consider himself much the richer.

There are, of course, many such teachings about the most various things in the world. Every school lesson is full of them. Let us take geography. We are told that the town of Constance lies on the Bodensee.[3] A student song adds: "If you don't believe it, go and see." I happen to have been there and can confirm the fact that that lovely town lies on the shore of a wide stretch of water which all those who live round it call the Bodensee; and I am now completely convinced of the correctness of this geographical assertion. In this connection I am reminded of another, very remarkable, experience. I was already a man of mature years when I stood for the first time on the hill of the Acropolis in Athens, between the temple ruins, looking out over the blue sea. A feeling of astonishment mingled with my joy. It seemed to say: "So it really *is* true, just as we learnt at school!" How shallow and weak must have been the belief I then acquired in the real truth of what I heard, if I could be so astonished now! But I will not lay too much stress on the significance of this experience; for my astonishment could have had another explanation, which did not occur to me at the time and which is of a wholly subjective nature and has to do with the special character of the place.[4]

All teachings like these, then, demand belief in their contents, but not without producing grounds for their claim. They are put forward as the epitomized result of a longer process of thought based on observation and certainly also on inferences. If anyone wants to go through this process himself instead of accepting its result, they show him how to set about it. Moreover, we are always in addition given the source of the knowledge conveyed by them, where that source is not self-evident, as it is in the case of geographical assertions. For instance, the earth is shaped like a sphere; the proofs adduced for this are Foucault's pendulum experiment,[5] the behavior of the horizon and the possibility of circumnavigating the earth. Since it is impracticable, as everyone concerned realizes, to send every schoolchild on a voyage round the world, we are satisfied with letting what is taught at school be taken on trust; but we know that the path to acquiring a personal conviction remains open.

Let us try to apply the same test to the teachings of religion. When we ask on what their claim to be believed is founded, we are met with three answers, which harmonize remarkably badly with one another. Firstly, these teachings deserve to be believed because they were already believed by our primal ancestors; secondly, we possess proofs which have been handed down to us from those same primaeval times; and thirdly, it is forbidden to raise the question of their authentication at all. In former days anything so presumptuous was visited with the severest penalties, and even today society looks askance at any attempt to raise the question again.

This third point is bound to rouse our strongest suspicions. After all, a prohibition like this can only be for one reason—that society is very well aware of the insecurity of the claim it makes on behalf of its religious doctrines. Otherwise it would certainly be very ready to put the necessary data at the disposal of anyone who wanted to arrive at a conviction. This being so, it is with a feeling of mistrust which is hard to allay that we pass on to an examination of the other two grounds of proof. We ought to believe because our forefathers believed. But these ancestors of ours were far more ignorant than we are. They believed in things we could not possibly accept today; and the possibility occurs to us that the doctrines of religion may belong to that class too. The proofs they have left us are set down in writings which themselves bear every mark of untrustworthiness. They are full of contradictions, revisions and falsifications, and where they speak of factual confirmations they are themselves unconfirmed. It does not help much to have it asserted that their wording, or even their content only, originates from divine revelation; for this assertion is itself one of the doctrines whose authenticity is under examination, and no proposition can be a proof of itself.

Thus we arrive at the singular conclusion that of all the information provided by our cultural assets it is precisely the elements which might be of the greatest importance to us and which have the task of solving the riddles of the universe and of reconciling us to the sufferings of life—it is precisely those elements that are the least well authenticated of any. We should not be able to bring ourselves to accept anything of so little concern to us as the fact that whales bear young instead of laying eggs, if it were not capable of better proof than this.

This state of affairs is in itself a very remarkable psychological problem. And let no one suppose that what I have said about the impossibility of proving the truth of religious doctrines contains anything new. It has been felt at all times—undoubtedly, too, by the ancestors who bequeathed us this legacy. Many of them probably nourished the same doubts as ours, but the pressure imposed on them was too strong for them to have dared to utter them. And since then, countless people have been tormented by similar doubts, and have striven to suppress them, because they thought it was their duty to believe; many brilliant intellects have broken down over this conflict, and many characters have been impaired by the compromises with which they have tried to find a way out of it.

If all the evidence put forward for the authenticity of religious teachings originates in the past, it is natural to look round and see whether the present, about which it is easier to form judgments, may not also be able to furnish evidence of the sort. If by this means we could succeed in clearing even a single portion of the religious system from doubt, the whole of it would gain enormously in credibility. The proceedings of the spiritualists meet us at this point; they are convinced of the survival of the individual soul, and they seek to demonstrate to us, beyond doubt, the truth of this one religious doctrine. Unfortunately they cannot succeed in refuting the fact that the appearance and utterances of their spirits are merely the products of their own mental activity. They have called up the spirits of the greatest men and of the most eminent thinkers, but all the pronouncements and information which they have received from them have been so foolish and so wretchedly meaningless that one can find nothing credible in them but the capacity of the spirits to adapt themselves to the circle of people who have conjured them up.

I must now mention two attempts that have been made—both of which convey the impression of being desperate efforts—to evade the problem. One, of a violent nature, is ancient; the other is subtle and modern. The first is the "Credo quia absurdum" of an early Father of the Church.[6] It maintains that religious doctrines are outside the jurisdiction of reason—are above reason. Their truth must be felt inwardly, and they need not be comprehended. But this Credo is only of interest as a self-confession. As an authoritative statement it has no binding force. Am I to be obliged to believe *every* absurdity? And if not, why this one in particular? There is no appeal to a court above that of reason. If the truth of religious doctrines is dependent on an inner experience which bears witness to that truth, what is one to do about the many people who do not have this rare experience? One may require every man to use the gift of reason which he possesses, but one cannot erect, on the basis of a motive that exists only for a very few, an obligation that shall apply to everyone. If one man has gained an unshakable conviction of the true reality of religious doctrines from a state of ecstasy which has deeply moved him, of what significance is that to others?

The second attempt is the one made by the philosophy of "As if." This asserts that our thought-activity includes a great number of hypotheses whose groundlessness and even absurdity we fully realize. They are called "fictions," but for a variety of practical reasons we have to behave "as if" we believed in these fictions. This is the case with religious doctrines because of their incomparable importance for the maintenance of human society.[7] This line of argument is not far removed from the "Credo quia absurdum." But I think the demand made by the "As if" argument is one that only a philosopher could put forward. A man whose thinking is not influenced by the artifices of philosophy will never be able to accept it; in such a man's view, the admission that something is absurd or contrary to reason leaves no more to be said. It cannot be expected of him that precisely in treating his most important interests he shall forgo the guarantees he requires for all his ordinary activities. I am reminded of one of my children who was distinguished at an early age by a peculiarly marked matter-of-factness. When the children were being told a fairy story and were listening to it with rapt attention, he would come up and ask: "Is that a true story?" When he was told it was not, he would turn away with a look of disdain. We may expect that people will soon behave in the same way towards the fairy tales of religion, in spite of the advocacy of "As if."

But at present they still behave quite differently; and in past times religious ideas, in spite of their incontrovertible lack of authentication, have exercised the strongest possible influence on mankind. This is a fresh psychological problem. We must ask where the inner force of those doctrines lies and to what it is that they owe their efficacy, independent as it is of recognition by reason.

NOTES

1. This was an actual dream of Freud's, reported in Chapter VI (G) of *The Interpretation of Dreams* (1900a), *Standard Ed.*, 5, 454-5.

2. See Section 6 of the fourth essay in *Totem and Taboo* (1912-13), *Standard Ed.*, 13, 146 ff.

3. The German name for what we call the Lake of Constance.

4. This had happened in 1904, when Freud was almost fifty. He wrote a full account of the episode in an open letter to Romain Rolland some ten years after the present essay.

5. J. B. L. Foucault (1819-68) demonstrated the diurnal motion of the earth by means of a pendulum in 1851.

6. "I believe because it is absurd." This is attributed to Tertullian.

7. I hope I am not doing him an injustice if I take the philosopher of "As if" as the representative of a view which is not foreign to other thinkers: "We include as fictions not merely indifferent theoretical operations but ideational constructs emanating from the noblest minds, to which the noblest part of mankind cling and of which they will not allow themselves to be deprived. Nor is it our object so to deprive them—for as *practical fictions* we leave them all intact; they perish only as *theoretical truths*" (Hans Vaihinger, 1922. 68 [C. K. Ogden's translation, 1924, pp. 48-9]).

Erich Fromm

An Analysis of Some Types of Religious Experience

Erich Fromm, psychoanalyst, psychologist and social philosopher, received his doctorate from Heidelberg. He has taught and lectured at many universities throughout the world. He holds professorships at New York University and at the National University of Mexico. His books include: *Escape from Freedom* (1941); *Man for Himself: An Inquiry into the Psychology of Ethics* (1947); *Psychoanalysis and Religion* (1950); *The Forgotten Language: An Introduction to the Understanding of Dreams, Fairy Tales, and Myths* (1951); *The Sane Society* (1955); *The Art of Loving* (1956); *Sigmund Freud's Mission: An Analysis of His Personality and Influence* (1959); *Zen Buddhism and Psychoanalysis* (1960); *May Man Prevail? An Inquiry into the Facts and Fictions of Foreign Policy* (1961); *Marx's Concept of Man* (1961); *Beyond the Claims of Illusion: My Encounter With Marx and Freud* (1962); *The Dogma of Christ and Other Essays on Religion, Psychology, and Culture* (1963); *The Heart of Man: Its Genius for Good and Evil* (1964); and *You Shall Be as Gods: A Radical Interpretation of the Old Testament and Its Tradition* (1966). Fromm edited the volume *Socialist Humanism: An International Symposium* (1965).

Any discussion of religion is handicapped by a serious terminological difficulty. While we know that there were and are many religions outside of monotheism, we nevertheless associate the concept religion with a system centered around God and supernatural forces; we tend to consider monotheistic religion as a frame of reference for the understanding and evaluation of all other religions. It thus becomes doubtful whether religions without God like Buddhism, Taoism, or Confucianism can be properly called religions. Such secular systems as contemporary authoritarianism are not called religions at all, although psychologically speaking they deserve this name. We simply have no word to denote religion as a general human phenomenon in such a way that some association with a specific type of religion does not creep in and color the concept. For lack of such a word I shall use the term *religion* in these chapters, but I want to make it clear at the outset that I understand by "religion" *any system of thought and action shared by a group which gives the individual a frame of orientation and an object of devotion.*

There is indeed no culture of the past, and it seems there can be no culture in the future, which does not have religion in this broad sense of our definition. We need not, however, stop at this merely descriptive statement. The study of man permits us to recognize that the need for a common system of orientation and for an object of devotion is deeply rooted in the conditions of human existence. I have attempted in *Man for Himself* to analyze the nature of this need, and I quote from that book:

"Self-awareness, reason, and imagination have disrupted the 'harmony' which characterizes animal existence. Their emergence has made man into an anomaly, into the freak of the universe. He is part of nature, subject to her physical laws and unable to change them, yet he transcends the rest of nature. He is set apart while being a part; he is homeless, yet chained to the home he shares with all creatures. Cast into this world at an accidental place and time, he is forced out of it, again accidentally. Being aware of himself, he realizes his powerlessness and the limitations of his existence. He visualizes his own end: death. Never is he free from the dichotomy of his existence: he cannot rid himself of his mind, even if he should want to; he cannot rid himself of his body as long as he is alive—and his body makes him want to be alive.

From Erich Fromm, Psychoanalysis and Religion *(New Haven, Conn.: Yale University Press, 1950), pp. 21-64. Copyright 1950 by Erich Fromm. Reprinted by permission of the author and Yale University Press, New Haven, Connecticut.*

"Reason, man's blessing, is also his curse; it forces him to cope everlastingly with the task of solving an insoluble dichotomy. Human existence is different in this respect from that of all other organisms; it is in a state of constant and unavoidable disequilibrium. Man's life cannot 'be lived' by repeating the pattern of his species; *he* must live. Man is the only animal that can be *bored,* that can be *discontented,* that can feel evicted from paradise. Man is the only animal for whom his own existence is a problem which he has to solve and from which he cannot escape. He cannot go back to the prehuman state of harmony with nature; he must proceed to develop his reason until he becomes the master of nature, and of himself.

"The emergence of reason has created a dichotomy within man which forces him to strive everlastingly for new solutions. The dynamism of his history is intrinsic to the existence of reason which causes him to develop and, through it, to create a world of his own in which he can feel at home with himself and his fellow men. Every stage he reaches leaves him discontented and perplexed, and this very perplexity urges him to move toward new solutions. There is no innate 'drive for progress' in man; it is the contradiction in his existence that makes him proceed on the way he set out. Having lost paradise, the unity with nature, he has become the eternal wanderer (Odysseus, Oedipus, Abraham, Faust); he is impelled to go forward and with everlasting effort to make the unknown known by filling in with answers the blank spaces of his knowledge. He must give account to himself of himself, and of the meaning of his existence. He is driven to overcome this inner split, tormented by a craving for 'absoluteness,' for another kind of harmony which can lift the curse by which he was separated from nature, from his fellow men, and from himself."

. . . . .

"The disharmony of man's existence generates needs which far transcend those of his animal origin. These needs result in an imperative drive to restore a unity and equilibrium between himself and the rest of nature. He makes the attempt to restore this unity and equilibrium in the first place in thought by constructing an all-inclusive mental picture of the world which serves as a frame of reference from which he can derive an answer to the question of where he stands and what he ought to do. But such thought-systems are not sufficient. If man were only a disembodied intellect his aim would be achieved by a comprehensive thought-system.

But since he is an entity endowed with a body as well as a mind he has to react to the dichotomy of his existence not only in thinking but also in the process of living, in his feelings and actions. He has to strive for the experience of unity and oneness in all spheres of his being in order to find a new equilibrium. Hence any satisfying system of orientation implies not only intellectual elements but elements of feeling and sense to be realized in action in all fields of human endeavor. Devotion to an aim, or an idea, or a power transcending man such as God, is an expression of this need for completeness in the process of living."

. . . . .

"Because the need for a system of orientation and devotion is an intrinsic part of human existence we can understand the intensity of this need. Indeed, there is no other more powerful source of energy in man. Man is not free to choose between having or not having 'ideals,' but he is free to choose between different kinds of ideals, between being devoted to the worship of power and destruction and being devoted to reason and love. All men are 'idealists' and are striving for something beyond the attainment of physical satisfaction. They differ in the kinds of ideals they believe in. The very best but also the most satanic manifestations of man's mind are expressions not of his flesh but of his 'idealism,' of his spirit. Therefore a relativistic view which claims that to have some ideal or some religious feeling is valuable in itself is dangerous and erroneous. We must understand every ideal including those which appear in secular ideologies as expressions of the same human need and we must judge them with respect to their truth, to the extent to which they are conducive to the unfolding of man's powers and to the degree to which they are a real answer to man's need for equilibrium and harmony in his world." [1]

What I have said about man's idealism holds true equally for his religious need. There is no one without a religious need, a need to have a frame of orientation and an object of devotion; but this statement does not tell us anything about a specific context in which this religious need is manifest. Man may worship animals, trees, idols of gold or stone, an invisible god, a saintly man or diabolic leaders; he may worship his ancestors, his nation, his class or party, money or success; his religion may be conducive to the development of destructiveness or of love, of domination or of brotherliness; it may further his power of reason or paralyze it; he may be aware of his system as being a religious one, different from those of the secular realm, or he may think that he has no religion and interpret his devotion to certain allegedly secular aims like power, money or success as nothing but his concern for the practical and expedient. The question is not *religion or not* but *which kind of religion*, whether it is one furthering man's development, the unfolding of his specifically human powers, or one paralyzing them.

Curiously enough the interests of the devoted religionist and of the psychologist are the same in this respect. The theologian is keenly interested in the specific tenets of a religion, his own and others, because what matters to him is the truth of his belief against the others. Equally, the psychologist must be keenly interested in the specific contents of religion, for what matters to him is what human attitude a religion expresses and what kind of effect it has on man, whether it is good or bad for the development of man's powers. He is interested not only in an analysis of the *psychological roots* of various religions but also in their *value*.

The thesis that the need for a frame of orientation and an object of devotion is rooted in the conditions of man's existence seems to be amply verified by the fact of the universal occurrence of religion in history. This point has been made and elaborated by theologians, psychologists, and anthropologists, and there is no need for me to discuss it any further. I only want to stress that in making this point the adherents of traditional religion have often indulged in a fallacious bit of reasoning. Starting out with so broad a definition of religion as to include every possible religious phenomenon, their concept has remained associated with monotheistic religion, and thus they proceed to look upon all nonmonotheistic forms as precursors of or deviations from the "true" religion, and they end demonstrating that the belief in God in the sense of the Western religious tradition is inherent in man's equipment.

The psychoanalyst whose "laboratory" is the patient and who is a participant observer to another person's thoughts and feelings is able to add another proof to the fact that the need for some frame of orientation and object of devotion is inherent in man. In studying neuroses he discovers that he is studying religion. It was Freud who saw the connection between neurosis and religion; but while he interpreted religion as a collective childhood neurosis of mankind, the statement can also be reversed. We can interpret neurosis *as a private form of religion,* more specifically, as a regression to primitive forms of religion conflicting with officially recognized patterns of religious thought.

One can look at a neurosis from two aspects. One can focus on the neurotic phenomena themselves, the symptoms and other specific difficulties in living which the neurosis produces. The other aspect is not concerned with the positive as it were, with the neurosis, but with the negative, the failure of the neurotic individual to accomplish the fundamental aims of human existence, independence and the ability to be productive, to love, to think. Anyone who has failed to achieve maturity and integration develops a neurosis of one kind or another. He does not "just live," unbothered by this failure, satisfied to eat and drink, sleep and have sexual satisfaction and do his work; if this were the case then indeed we would have the proof that the religious attitude, while perhaps desirable, is not an intrinsic part of human nature. But the study of man shows that this is not so. If a person has not succeeded in integrating his energies in the direction of his higher self, he canalizes them in the direction of lower goals; if he has no picture of the world and his position in it which approximates the truth, he will create a picture which is illusory and cling to it with the same tenacity with which the religionist believes in his dogmas. Indeed, "man does not live by bread alone." He has only the choice of better or worse, higher or lower, satisfactory or destructive forms of religions and philosophies.

What is the religious situation in contemporary Western society? It resembles in curious fashion the picture which the anthropologist gets in studying the religion of the North American Indians. They have been converted to the Christian religion but their old pre-Christian religions have by no means been uprooted. Christianity is a veneer laid over this old religion and blended with it in many ways. In our own culture monotheistic religion and also atheistic and agnostic philosophies are a thin veneer built upon religions which are in many ways far more "primitive" than the Indian religions and, being sheer idolatry, are also more incompatible with the essential teachings of monotheism. As a collective and potent form of modern idolatry we find the worship of power, of success and of the authority of the market; but aside from these collective forms we find something else. If we scratch the surface of modern man we discover any number of individualized primitive forms of religion. Many of these are called neuroses, but one might just as well call them by their respective religious names: ancestor worship, totemism, fetishism, ritualism, the cult of cleanliness, and so on.

Do we actually find ancestor worship? Indeed, ancestor worship is one of the most widespread primitive cults in our society, and it does not alter its picture if we call it, as the psychiatrist does, neurotic fixation to father or mother. Let us consider such a case of ancestor worship. A beautiful, highly talented woman, a painter, was attached to her father in such a way that she would refuse to have any close contact with men; she spent all her free time with her father, a pleasant but rather dull gentleman who had been widowed early. Aside from her painting, nothing but her father was of any interest to her. The picture she gave of him to others was grotesquely different from reality. After he died she committed suicide and left a will stipulating only that she was to be buried by his side.

Another person, a very intelligent and gifted man, highly respected by everyone, led a secret life completely devoted to the worship of his father who, viewed most charitably, could be described as a shrewd go-getter, interested solely in acquiring money and social prestige. The son's picture of the father was, however, that of the wisest, most loving, and devoted parent, ordained by God to show him the right way to live; the son's every action and thought was considered from the standpoint of whether his father would approve or not, and since in real life his father had usually disapproved, the patient felt "out of grace" most of the time and frantically attempted to regain his father's approval even many years after his father had died.

The psychoanalyst tries to discover the causes of such pathological attachments and hopes to help the patient to free himself from such crippling father worship. But we are not interested here in the causes or in the problem of cure but in the phenomenology. We find a dependency on a father enduring with undiminished intensity many years after the parent's death, which cripples the patient's judgment, renders him unable to love, makes him feel like a child, constantly insecure and frightened. This centering one's life around an ancestor, spending most of one's energy in his worship, is not different from a religious ancestor cult. It gives a frame of reference and a unifying principle of devotion. Here too is the reason the patient cannot be cured by simply pointing out the irrationality of his behavior and the damage he does to himself. He often knows this intellectually in one compartment of himself, as it were, but emotionally he is completely devoted to his cult. Only if a profound change in his total personality occurs, if he becomes free *to* think, *to* love, *to* attain a new focus of orientation and devotion, can he be free *from* the slavish devotion to his parent; only if he is capable of adopting a higher form of religion can he free himself from his lower form.

Compulsive neurotic patients exhibit numerous forms of private ritual. The person whose life is centered around the feeling of guilt and the need for atonement may choose a washing compulsion as the dominant ritual of his life; another whose compulsion is exhibited in thinking rather than actions will have a ritual which forces him to think or say certain formulas which are supposed to avert disaster and others which are supposed to guarantee success. Whether we call these neurotic symptoms or ritual depends on our point of view; in substance these symptoms *are* rituals of a private religion.

Do we have totemism in our culture? We have a great deal—although the people suffering from it usually do not consider themselves in need of psychiatric help. A person whose exclusive devotion is to the state or his political party, whose only criterion of value and truth is the interest of state or party, for whom the flag as a symbol of his group is a holy object, has a religion of clan and totem worship, even though in his own eyes it is a perfectly rational system (which, of course, all devotees to any kind of primitive religion believe). If we want to understand how systems like fascism or Stalinism can possess millions of people, ready to sacrifice their integrity and reason to the principle, "my country, right or wrong," we are forced to consider the totemistic, the religious quality of their orientation.

Another form of private religion, very widespread although not dominant in our culture, is the religion of cleanliness. The adherents of this religion have one major standard of value according to which they judge people—cleanliness and orderliness. The phenomenon was strikingly apparent in the reaction of many American soldiers during the last war. Often at odds with their political convictions, they judged allies and enemies from the standpoint of this religion. The English and the Germans ranked high, the French and Italians low in this scale of values. This religion of cleanliness and orderliness is, in substance, not too different from certain highly ritualistic religious systems which are centered around the attempt to get rid of evil by cleansing rituals and to find security in the strict performance of ritualistic orderliness.

There is one important difference between a religious cult and neurosis, which makes the cult vastly superior to the neurosis as far as the satisfaction gained is concerned. If we imagine that the patient with his neurotic fixation to his father lived in a culture where ancestor worship is generally practiced as a cult, he could share his feelings with his fellow men rather than feel himself isolated. And it is the feeling of isolation, of being shut out, which is the painful sting of every neurosis. Even the most irrational orientation, if it is shared by a considerable body of men, gives the individual the feeling of oneness with others, a certain amount of security and stability which the neurotic person lacks. There is nothing inhuman, evil, or irrational which does not give some comfort, provided it is shared by a group. The most convincing proof for this statement can be found in those incidents of mass madness to which we have been and still are witnesses. Once a doctrine, however irrational, has gained power in a society, millions of people will believe in it rather than feel ostracized and isolated.

These ideas lead to an important consideration concerning the function of religion. If man regresses so easily into a more primitive form of religion, have not the monotheistic religions today the function of saving man from such regression? Is not the belief in God a safeguard against falling back into ancestor, totem, or golden-calf worship? Indeed, this would be so if religion had succeeded in molding man's character according to its stated ideals. But historical religion has capitulated before and compromised with secular power again and again. It has been concerned far more with certain dogmas rather than with the practice of love and humility in everyday life. It has failed to challenge secular power relentlessly and unceasingly where such power has violated the spirit of the religious ideal; on the contrary, it has shared again and again in such violations. If the churches were the representatives not only of the words but of the spirit of the Ten Commandments or the Golden Rule, they could be potent forces blocking the regression to idol worship. But since this is an exception rather than the rule, the question must be asked, not from an antireligious point of view but out of concern for man's soul: Can we trust religion to be the representative of religious needs or must we not separate these needs from organized, traditional religion in order to prevent the collapse of our moral structure?

In considering an answer to this question we must remember that no intelligent discussion of the problem is possible as long as we deal with religion in general instead of differentiating between various types of religion and religious experience. It would far transcend the scope of this ... [essay] to attempt a review of all types of religion. Even to discuss only those types which are relevant from the psychological standpoint cannot be undertaken here. I shall therefore deal with only one distinction, but one which in my opinion is the most important, and which cuts across nontheistic and theistic religions: that between *authoritarian* and *humanistic* religions.

What is the principle of authoritarian religion? The definition of religion given in the *Oxford Dictionary*, while attempting to define religion as such, is a rather accurate definition of authoritarian religion. It reads: "[Religion is] recognition on the part of man of some higher unseen power as having control of his destiny, and as being entitled to obedience, reverence, and worship."

Here the emphasis is on the recognition that man is controlled by a higher power outside of himself. But this alone does not constitute authoritarian religion. What makes it so is the idea that this power, because of the control it exercises, is *entitled* to "obedience, reverence and worship." I italicize the word "entitled" because it shows that the reason for worship, obedience, and reverence lies not in the moral qualities of the deity, not in love or justice, but in the fact that it has control, that is, has power over man. Furthermore it shows that the higher power has a right to force man to worship him and that lack of reverence and obedience constitutes sin.

The essential element in authoritarian religion and in the authoritarian religious experience is the surrender to a power transcending man. The main virtue of this type of religion is obedience, its cardinal sin is disobedience. Just as the deity is conceived as omnipotent or omniscient, man is conceived as being powerless and insignificant. Only as he can gain grace or help from the deity by complete surrender can he feel strength. Submission to a powerful authority is one of the avenues by which man escapes from his feeling of aloneness and limitation. In the act of surrender he loses his independence and integrity as an individual but he gains the feeling of being protected by an awe-inspiring power of which, as it were, he becomes a part.

In Calvin's theology we find a vivid picture of authoritarian, theistic thinking. "For I do not call it humility," says Calvin, "if you suppose that we have anything left. . . . We cannot think of ourselves as we ought to think without utterly despising everything that may be supposed an excellence in us. This humility is unfeigned submission of a mind overwhelmed with a weighty sense of its own misery and poverty; for such is the uniform description of it in the word of God."[2]

The experience which Calvin describes here, that of despising everything in oneself, of the submission of the mind overwhelmed by its own poverty, is the very essence of all authoritarian religions, whether they are couched in secular or in theological language.[3] In authoritarian religion God is a symbol of power and force, He is supreme because He has supreme power, and man in juxtaposition is utterly powerless.

Authoritarian secular religion follows the same principle. Here the

Führer or the beloved "Father of His People" or the State or the Race or the Socialist Fatherland becomes the object of worship; the life of the individual becomes insignificant and man's worth consists in the very denial of his worth and strength. Frequently authoritarian religion postulates an ideal which is so abstract and so distant that it has hardly any connection with the real life of real people. To such ideals as "life after death" or "the future of mankind" the life and happiness of persons living here and now may be sacrificed; the alleged ends justify every means and become symbols in the names of which religious or secular "elites" control the lives of their fellow men.

Humanistic religion, on the contrary, is centered around man and his strength. Man must develop his power of reason in order to understand himself, his relationship to his fellow men and his position in the universe. He must recognize the truth, both with regard to his limitations and his potentialities. He must develop his powers of love for others as well as for himself and experience the solidarity of all living beings. He must have principles and norms to guide him in this aim. Religious experience in this kind of religion is the experience of oneness with the All, based on one's relatedness to the world as it is grasped with thought and with love. Man's aim in humanistic religion is to achieve the greatest strength, not the greatest powerlessness; virtue is self-realization, not obedience. Faith is certainty of conviction based on one's experience of thought and feeling, not assent to propositions on credit of the proposer. The prevailing mood is that of joy, while the prevailing mood in authoritarian religion is that of sorrow and of guilt.

Inasmuch as humanistic religions are theistic, God is a symbol of *man's own powers* which he tries to realize in his life, and is not a symbol of force and domination, having *power over man*.

Illustrations of humanistic religions are early Buddhism, Taoism, the teachings of Isaiah, Jesus, Socrates, Spinoza, certain trends in the Jewish and Christian religions (particularly mysticism), the religion of Reason of the French Revolution. It is evident from these that the distinction between authoritarian and humanistic religion cuts across the distinction between theistic and nontheistic, and between religions in the narrow sense of the word and philosophical systems of religious character. What matters in all such systems is not the thought system as such but the human attitude underlying their doctrines.

One of the best examples of humanistic religions is early Buddhism. The Buddha is a great teacher, he is the "awakened one" who recognizes the truth about human existence. He does not speak in the name of a supernatural power but in the name of reason. He calls upon every man to make use of his own reason and to see the truth which he was only the first to find. Once man takes the first step in seeing the truth, he must apply his efforts to live in such a way that he develops his powers of reason and of love for all human creatures. Only to the degree to which he succeeds in this can he free himself from the bondage of irrational passions. While man must recognize his limitations according to Buddhistic teaching, he must also become aware of the powers in himself. The concept of Nirvana as the state of mind the fully awakened one can achieve is not one of man's helplessness and submission but on the contrary one of the development of the highest powers man possesses.

The following story of Buddha is very characteristic.

Once a hare sat under a mango tree and slept. Suddenly he heard a loud noise. He thought the world was coming to an end and started to run. When the other hares saw him running they asked, "Why do you run so fast?" He replied, "The world is coming to an end." Upon hearing this they all joined him in his flight. When the deer saw the hares running they asked them, "Why do you run so fast?" and the hares answered, "We run because the world is coming to an end." Upon which the deer joined them in their flight. Thus one species after another joined the animals already running until the whole animal kingdom was in a panicky flight which would have ended in its destruction. When Buddha, who at that time was living as a wise man, one of his many forms of existence, saw all the animals running in their panic, he asked the last group that had joined the flight why they were running. "Because the world is coming to an end," they answered. "This cannot be true," Buddha said. "The world is not coming to an end. Let us find out why they think so." He then inquired of one species after another, tracing the rumor back to the deer and then at last to the hares. When the hares told him that they were running because the world was coming to an end, he asked which particular hare had told them so. They pointed to the one who had started the report, and Buddha turned to him and asked, "Where were you and what did you do when you thought the world was coming to an end?" The hare answered, "I was sitting under a mango tree and was asleep." "You probably heard a mango fruit fall," Buddha told him. "The noise awakened you, you got frightened and thought the world was coming to an end. Let us go back to the tree where you sat and find out whether this was so." They both went to the tree. They found that indeed a mango had fallen where the hare had sat. Thus Buddha saved the animal kingdom from destruction.

I quote this story not primarily because it is one of the earliest examples of analytic inquiry into the origins of fright and rumors but because it is so expressive of the Buddhistic spirit. It shows loving concern for the creatures of the animal world and at the same time penetrating, rational understanding and confidence in man's powers.

Zen Buddhism, a later sect within Buddhism, is expressive of an even more radical anti-authoritarian attitude. Zen proposes that no knowledge is of any value unless it grows out of ourselves; no authority, no teacher can really teach us anything except to arouse doubts in us; words and thought systems are dangerous because they easily turn into authorities whom we worship. Life itself must be grasped and experienced as it flows, and in this lies virtue. Characteristic of this unauthoritarian attitude toward supreme beings is the following story:

"When Tanka of the T'ang dynasty stopped at Yerinji in the Capitol, it was severely cold; so taking down one of the Buddha images enshrined there, he made a fire of it and warmed himself. The keeper of the shrine, seeing this, was greatly incensed, and exclaimed: 'How dare you burn my wooden image of the Buddha?'

"Tanka began to search in the ashes as if he were looking for something, and said: 'I am gathering the holy sariras [a kind of mineral deposit found in the human body after cremation and believed to correspond to the saintliness of life] from the burnt ashes.'

"'How,' said the keeper, 'can you get sariras from a wooden Buddha?'

"Tanka retorted, 'If there are no sariras to be found in it, may I have the remaining two Buddhas for my fire?'

"The shrine-keeper later lost both his eyebrows for remonstrating against this apparent impiety of Tanka, while the Buddha's wrath never fell on the latter."[4]

Another illustration of a humanistic religious system is to be found in Spinoza's religious thinking. While his language is that of medieval theology, his concept of God has no trace of authoritarianism. God could not have created the world different from what it is. He cannot change anything; in fact, God is identical with the totality of the universe. Man must see his own limitations and recognize that he is dependent on the totality of forces outside himself over which he has no control. Yet his are the powers of love and of reason. He can develop them and attain an optimum of freedom and of inner strength.

The distinction between authoritarian and humanistic religion not only cuts across various religions, it can exist within the same religion. Our own religious tradition is one of the best illustrations of this point. Since it is of fundamental importance to understand fully the distinction between authoritarian and humanistic religion, I shall illustrate it further from a source with which every reader is more or less familiar, the Old Testament.

The beginning of the Old Testament[5] is written in the spirit of authoritarian religion. The picture of God is that of the absolute ruler of a patriarchal clan, who has created man at his pleasure and can destroy him at will. He has forbidden him to eat from the tree of knowledge of good and evil and has threatened him with death if he transgresses this order. But the serpent, "more clever than any animal," tells Eve, "Ye shall not surely die: For God doth know that in the day ye eat thereof, then your eyes shall be opened, and ye shall be as gods, knowing good and evil."[6] God proves the serpent to be right. When Adam and Eve have transgressed he punishes them by proclaiming enmity between man and nature, between man and the soil and animals, and between men and women. But man is not to die. However, "the man has become as one of us, to know good and evil: and now, lest he put forth his hand, and take also of the tree of life, and eat, and live for ever,"[7] God expells Adam and Eve from the garden of Eden and puts an angel with a flaming sword at the east "to keep the way of the tree of life."

The text makes very clear what man's sin is: it is rebellion against God's command; it is disobedience and not any inherent sinfulness in the act of eating from the tree of knowledge. On the contrary, further religious development has made the knowledge of good and evil the cardinal virtue to which man may aspire. The text also makes it plain what God's motive is: it is concern with his own superior role, the jealous fear of man's claim to become his equal.

A decisive turning point in the relationship between God and man is to be seen in the story of the Flood. When God saw "that the wickedness of man was great on the earth . . . it repented the Lord that he had made man and the earth, and it grieved him at his heart. And the Lord said, I will destroy man whom I have created from the face of the earth; both man, and beast, and the creeping thing, and the fowls of the air; for it repenteth me that I have made them."[8]

There is no question here but that God has the right to destroy his own creatures; he has created them and they are his property. The text defines their wickedness as "violence," but the decision to destroy not only man but animals and plants as well shows that we are not dealing here with a sentence commensurate with some specific crime but with God's angry regret over his own action which did not turn out well. "But Noah found grace in the eyes of the Lord," and he, together with his family and a representative of each animal species, is saved from the Flood. Thus far the destruction of man and the salvation of Noah are arbitrary acts of God. He could do as he pleased, as can any powerful tribal chief. But after the Flood the relationship between God and man changes fundamentally. A covenant is concluded between God and man in which God promises that "neither shall all flesh be cut off any more by the waters of a flood; neither shall there any more be a flood to destroy the earth." [9] God obligates himself never to destroy all life on earth, and man is bound to the first and most fundamental command of the Bible, not to kill: "At the hand of every man's brother will I require the life of man." [10] From this point on the relationship between God and man undergoes a profound change. God is no longer an absolute ruler who can act at his pleasure but is bound by a constitution to which both he and man must adhere; he is bound by a principle which he cannot violate, the principle of respect for life. God can punish man if he violates this principle, but man can also challenge God if he is guilty of its violation.

The new relationship between God and man appears clearly in Abraham's plea for Sodom and Gomorrah. When God considers destroying the cities because of their wickedness, Abraham criticizes God for violating his own principles. "That be far from thee to do after this manner, to slay the righteous with the wicked: and that the righteous should be as the wicked, that be far from thee. Shall not the Judge of all the earth do right?" [11]

The difference between the story of the Fall and this argument is great indeed. There man is forbidden to know good and evil and his position toward God is that of submission—or sinful disobedience. Here man uses his knowledge of good and evil, criticizes God in the name of justice, and God has to yield.

Even this brief analysis of the authoritarian elements in the biblical story shows that at the root of the Judaeo-Christian religion both principles, the authoritarian and the humanistic, are present. In the development of Judaism as well as of Christianity both principles have been preserved and their respective preponderance marks different trends in the two religions.

The following story from the Talmud expresses the unauthoritarian, humanistic side of Judaism as we find it in the first centuries of the Christian era.

A number of other famous rabbinical scholars disagreed with Rabbi Eliezar's views in regard to a point of ritual law. "Rabbi Eliezar said to them: 'If the law is as I think it is then this tree shall let us know.' Whereupon the tree jumped from its place a hundred yards (others say four hundred yards). His colleagues said to him, 'One does not prove anything from a tree.' He said, 'If I am right then this brook shall let us know.' Whereupon the brook ran upstream. His colleagues said to him, 'One does not prove anything from a brook.' He continued and said, 'If the law is as I think then the walls of this house will tell.' Whereupon the walls began to fall. But Rabbi Joshua shouted at the walls and said, 'If scholars argue a point of law, what business have you to fall?' So the walls fell no further out of respect for Rabbi Joshua but out of respect for Rabbi Eliezar did not straighten up. And that is the way they still are. Rabbi Eliezar took up the argument again and said, 'If the law is as I think, they shall tell us from heaven.' Whereupon a voice from heaven said, 'What have you against Rabbi Eliezar, because the law is as he says.' Whereupon Rabbi Joshua got up and said, 'It is written in the Bible: The law is not in heaven. What does this mean? According to Rabbi Jirmijahu it means since the Torah has been given on Mount Sinai we no longer pay attention to voices from heaven because it is written: You make your decision according to the majority opinion.' It then happened that Rabbi Nathan [one of the participants in the discussion] met the Prophet Elijah [who had taken a stroll on earth] and he asked the Prophet, 'What did God himself say when we had this discussion?' The Prophet answered, 'God smiled and said, My children have won, my children have won.'" [12]

This story is hardly in need of comment. It emphasizes the autonomy of man's reason with which even the supernatural voices from heaven cannot interfere. God smiles, man has done what God wanted him to do, he has become his own master, capable and resolved to make his decisions by himself according to rational, democratic methods.

The same humanistic spirit can be found in many stories from the Chassidic folklore of more than a thousand years later. The Chassidic movement was a rebellion of the poor against those who had the monopoly of learning or of money. Their motto was the verse of the Psalms: "Serve God in joy." They emphasized feeling rather than intellectual accomplishment, joy rather than contrition; to them (as to Spinoza) joy was the equivalent of virtue and sadness the equivalent of sin. The following story is characteristic of the humanistic and anti-authoritarian spirit of this religious sect:

A poor tailor came to a Chassidic rabbi the day after the Day of Atonement and said to him, "Yesterday I had an argument with God. I told him, 'Oh God, you have committed sins and I have committed sins. But you have committed grave sins and I have committed sins of no great importance. What have you done? You have separated mothers from their children and permitted people to starve. What have I done? I have sometimes failed to return a piece of cloth to a customer or have not been strict in the observance of the law. But I will tell you, God. I will forgive you your sins and you forgive me mine. Thus we are even.'" Whereupon the Rabbi answered, "You fool! Why did you let him get away that easily? Yesterday you could have forced him to send the Messiah."

This story demonstrates even more drastically than that of Abraham's argument with God the idea that God must live up to his promises just as man must live up to his. If God fails to put an end to the suffering of man as he has promised, man has the right to challenge him, in fact to force him to fulfill his promise. While the two stories quoted here are within the frame of reference of monotheistic religion, the human attitude behind them is profoundly different from that behind Abraham's readiness to sacrifice Isaac or Calvin's glorification of God's dictatorial powers.

That early Christianity is humanistic and not authoritarian is evident from the spirit and text of all Jesus' teachings. Jesus' precept that "the kingdom of God is within you" is the simple and clear expression of non-authoritarian thinking. But only a few hundred years later, after Christianity had ceased to be the religion of the poor and humble peasants, artisans, and slaves (the *Am haarez*) and had become the religion of those ruling the Roman Empire, the authoritarian trend in Christianity became dominant. Even so, the conflict between the authoritarian and humanistic principles in Christianity never ceased. It was the conflict between Augustine and Pelagius, between the Catholic Church and the many "heretic" groups and between various sects within Protestantism. The humanistic, democratic element was never subdued in Christian or in Jewish history, and this element found one of its most potent expressions in the mystic thinking within both religions. The mystics have been deeply imbued with the experience of man's strength, his likeness to God, and with the idea that God needs man as much as man needs God; they have understood the sentence that man is created in the image of God to mean the fundamental identity of God and man. Not fear and submission but love and the assertion of one's own powers are the basis of mystical experience. *God is not a symbol of power over man but of man's own powers.*

Thus far we have dealt with the distinctive features of authoritarian and humanistic religions mainly in descriptive terms. But the psychoanalyst must proceed from the description of attitudes to the analysis of their dynamics, and it is here that he can contribute to our discussion from an area not accessible to other fields of inquiry. The full understanding of an attitude requires an appreciation of those conscious and, in particular, unconscious processes occurring in the individual which provide the necessity for and the conditions of its development.

While in humanistic religion God is the image of man's higher self, a symbol of what man potentially is or ought to become, in authoritarian religion God becomes the sole possessor of what was originally man's: of his reason and his love. The more perfect God becomes, the more imperfect becomes man. He *projects* the best he has onto God and thus impoverishes himself. Now God has all love, all wisdom, all justice—and man is deprived of these qualities, he is empty and poor. He had begun with the feeling of smallness, but he now has become completely powerless and without strength; all his powers have been projected onto God. This mechanism of projection is the very same which can be observed in interpersonal relationships of a masochistic, submissive character, where one person is awed by another and attributes his own powers and aspirations to the other person. It is the same mechanism that makes people endow the leaders of even the most inhuman systems with qualities of superwisdom and kindness.[13]

When man has thus projected his own most valuable powers onto God, what of his relationship to his own powers? They have become separated from him and in the process he has become *alienated* from himself. Everything he has is now God's and nothing is left in him. *His only access to himself is through God.* In worshipping God he tries to get in touch with that part of himself which he has lost through projection. After having given God all he has, he begs God to return to him some of what originally was his own. But having lost his own he is completely at God's mercy. He necessarily feels like a "sinner" since he has deprived himself of everything that is good, and it is only through God's mercy or grace that he can regain that which alone makes him human. And in order to persuade God to give him some of his love, he must prove to him how utterly deprived he is of love; in order to persuade God to guide him by his superior wisdom he must prove to him how deprived he is of wisdom when he is left to himself.

But this alienation from his own powers not only makes man feel slavishly dependent on God, it makes him bad too. He becomes a man without faith in his fellow men or in himself, without the experience of his own love, of his own power of reason. As a result the separation between the "holy" and the "secular" occurs. In his worldly activities man acts without love, in that sector of his life which is reserved to religion he feels himself to be a sinner (which he actually is, since to live without love is to live in sin) and tries to recover some of his lost humanity by being in touch with God. Simultaneously, he tries to win forgiveness by emphasizing his own helplessness and worthlessness. Thus the attempt to obtain forgiveness results in the activation of the very attitude from which his sins stem. He is caught in a painful dilemma. The more he praises God, the emptier he becomes. The emptier he becomes, the more sinful he feels. The more sinful he feels, the more he praises his God—and the less able is he to regain himself.

Analysis of religion must not stop at uncovering those psychological processes within man which underly his religious experience; it must proceed to discover the conditions which make for the development of authoritarian and humanistic character structures, respectively, from which different kinds of religious experience stem. Such a sociopsychological analysis goes far beyond the context of . . . [this essay]. However, the principle point can be made briefly. What people think and feel is rooted in their character, and their character is molded by the total configuration of their practice of life—more precisely, by the socioeconomic and political structure of their society. In societies ruled by a powerful minority which holds the masses in subjection, the individual will be so imbued with fear, so incapable of feeling strong or independent, that his religious experience will be authoritarian. Whether he worships a punishing, awesome God or a similarly conceived leader makes little difference. On the other hand, where the individual feels free and responsible for his own fate, or among minorities striving for freedom and independence, humanistic religious experience develops. The history of religion gives ample evidence of this correlation between social structure and kinds of religious experience. Early Christianity was a religion of the poor and downtrodden; the history of religious sects fighting against authoritarian political pressure shows the same principle again and again. Judaism, in which a strong anti-authoritarian tradition could grow up because secular authority never had

much of a chance to govern and to build up a legend of its wisdom, therefore developed the humanistic aspect of religion to a remarkable degree.
Whenever, on the other hand, religion allied itself with secular power, the
religion had by necessity to become authoritarian. The real fall of man is
his alienation from himself, his submission to power, his turning against
himself even though under the guise of his worship of God.

From the spirit of authoritarian religion stem two fallacies of reasoning which have been used again and again as arguments for theistic
religion. One argument runs as follows: How can you criticize the emphasis on dependence on a power transcending man; is not man dependent on
forces outside himself which he cannot understand, much less control?

Indeed, man is dependent; he remains subject to death, age, illness,
and even if he were to control nature and to make it wholly serviceable to
him, he and his earth remain tiny specks in the universe. But it is one thing
to recognize one's dependence and limitations, and it is something entirely
different to indulge in this dependence, to worship the forces on which one
depends. To understand realistically and soberly how limited our power is
is an essential part of wisdom and of maturity; to worship it is masochistic
and self-destructive. The one is humility, the other self-humiliation.

We can study the difference between the realistic recognition of our
limitations and the indulgence in the experience of submission and powerlessness in the clinical examination of masochistic character traits. We
find people who have a tendency to incur sickness, accidents, humiliating
situations, who belittle and weaken themselves. They believe that they get
into such situations against their will and intention, but a study of their
unconscious motives shows that actually they are driven by one of the most
irrational tendencies to be found in man, namely, by an unconscious
desire to be weak and powerless; they tend to shift the center of their life to
powers over which they feel no control, thus escaping from freedom and
from personal responsibility. We find furthermore that this masochistic
tendency is usually accompanied by its very opposite, the tendency to rule
and to dominate others, and that the masochistic and the dominating
tendencies form the two sides of the authoritarian character structure.[14]
Such masochistic tendencies are not always unconscious. We find them
overtly in the sexual masochistic perversion, where the fulfillment of the
wish to be hurt or humiliated is the condition for sexual excitement and
satisfaction. We find it also in the relationship to the leader and the state
in all authoritarian secular religions. Here the explicit aim is to give up
one's own will and to experience submission under the leader or the state

as profoundly rewarding.

Another fallacy of theological thinking is closely related to the one concerning dependence. I mean here the argument that there must be a power or being outside of man because we find that man has an ineradicable longing to relate himself to something beyond himself. Indeed, any sane human being has a need to relate himself to others; a person who has lost that capacity completely is insane. No wonder that man has created figures outside of himself to which he relates himself, which he loves and cherishes because they are not subject to the vacillations and inconsistencies of human objects. That God is a symbol of man's need to love is simple enough to understand. But does it follow from the existence and intensity of this human need that there exists an outer being who corresponds to this need? Obviously that follows as little as our strongest desire to love someone proves that there is a person with whom we are in love. All it proves is our need and perhaps our capacity.

In this . . . [essay] I have attempted to psychoanalyze various aspects of religion. I might have started it with the discussion of a more general problem, the psychoanalytic approach to thought systems, religious, philosophical, and political. But I believe that it is more helpful to the reader to consider this general problem now after the discussion of the specific issues has permitted a more concrete approach.

Among the most important findings of psychoanalysis are those concerning the validity of thoughts and ideas. Traditional theories took as their basic data in the study of man's mind his own ideas about himself. Men were supposed to start wars motivated by their concern for honor, patriotism, freedom—because they thought they did. Parents were supposed to punish children out of their sense of duty and concern for their children—because they thought they did. People were supposed to kill unbelievers prompted by the wish to please God—because they thought they did. A new attitude toward man's thought slowly made its appearance, of which the first utterance is Spinoza's statement: "What Paul says about Peter tells us more about Paul than about Peter." With this attitude, our interest in Paul's statement is not in what *he* thinks it should be, namely, in Peter; we take it as a statement about Paul. We say that we know Paul better than he knows himself; we can decipher his thoughts because we are not taken in by the fact that he intends to communicate only a statement about Peter; we listen, as Theodor Reik phrased it, with "a third ear." Spinoza's statement contains an essential point of Freud's theory of man: that a great deal of what matters goes on behind one's hack, and that people's conscious ideas are only *one* datum, which has no greater relevancy than any other behavior datum; in fact often less.

Does this dynamic theory of man mean that reason, thought, and consciousness are of no importance and ought to be disregarded? In an understandable reaction to the traditional overestimation of conscious thought some psychoanalysts have tended to be skeptical toward any kind of thought system, interpreting it as being nothing but the rationalization of impulses and desires rather than considering it in terms of its own logical frame of reference. They have been particularly skeptical of all kinds of religious or philosophical statements and have been prone to view them as obsessional thinking which in itself must not be taken seriously. We must call this attitude an error not only from a philosophical standpoint but from the standpoint of psychoanalysis itself; because psychoanalysis, while debunking rationalizations, has made reason the tool with which we achieve such critical analyses of rationalization.

Psychoanalysis has demonstrated the ambiguous nature of our thinking processes. Indeed, the power of rationalization, this counterfeit of reason, is one of the most puzzling human phenomena. If we were not so accustomed to it, man's rationalizing effort would clearly appear to us as similar to a paranoid system. The paranoid person can be very intelligent, make excellent use of his reason in all areas of life except in that isolated part where his paranoid system is involved. The rationalizing person does exactly the same. We talk to an intelligent Stalinist who exhibits a great capacity to make use of his reason in many areas of thought. When we come to discuss Stalinism with him, however, we are suddenly confronted with a closed system of thought, the only function of which is to prove that his allegiance to Stalinism is in line with and not contradictory to reason. He will deny certain obvious facts, distort others, or, inasmuch as he agrees to certain facts and statements, he will explain his attitude as logical and consistent. He will at the same time declare that the fascist cult of the leader is one of the most obnoxious features of authoritarianism and claim that the Stalinist cult of the leader is something entirely different, that it is the genuine expression of the people's love for Stalin. When you tell him that is what the Nazis claimed too, he will smile tolerantly about your want of perception or accuse you of being the lackey of capitalism. He will find a thousand and one reasons why Russian nationalism is not nationalism, why authoritarianism is democracy, why slave labor is designed to educate and improve antisocial elements. The arguments which are used to defend or explain the deeds of the Inquisition or those used to explain racial or sex prejudices are illustrations of the same rationalizing capacity.

The degree to which man uses his thinking to rationalize irrational passions and to justify the actions of his group shows how great the distance is which man has still to travel in order to become Homo sapiens. But we must go beyond such an awareness. We must try to understand the reasons for this phenomenon lest we fall into the error of believing that man's readiness for rationalization is a part of "human nature," which nothing can change.

Man by origin is a herd animal. His actions are determined by an instinctive impulse to follow the leader and to have close contact with the other animals around him. Inasmuch as we are sheep, there is no greater threat to our existence than to lose this contact with the herd and to be isolated. Right and wrong, true and false are determined by the herd. But we are not only sheep. We are also human; we are endowed with awareness of ourselves, endowed with reason which by its very nature is independent of the herd. Our actions can be determined by the results of our thinking regardless of whether or not the truth is shared by others.

The split between our sheep nature and our human nature is the basis for two kinds of orientations: *the orientation by proximity to the herd and the orientation by reason.* Rationalization is a compromise between our sheep nature and our human capacity to think. The latter forces us to make believe that everything we do can stand the test of reason, and that is why we tend to make it appear that our irrational opinions and decisions are reasonable. But inasmuch as we are sheep, reason is not our real guide; we are guided by an entirely different principle, that of herd allegiance.

The ambiguity of thinking, the dichotomy between reason and a rationalizing intellect, is the expression of a basic dichotomy in man, the coextensive need for bondage and freedom. The unfolding and full emergence of reason is dependent on the attainment of full freedom and independence. Until this is accomplished man will tend to accept for truth that which the majority of his group wants to be true; his judgment is determined by the need for contact with the herd and by fear of being isolated from it. A few individuals can stand this isolation and say the truth in spite of the danger of losing touch. They are the true heroes of the human race, but for whom we should still be living in caves. Yet for the vast majority of men who are not heroes the development of reason depends on the emergence of a social order in which each individual is fully respected and not made a tool by the state or by any other group, a social order in which he need not be afraid to criticize and in which the pursuit of truth does not isolate man from his brothers but makes him feel one with them. It follows that man will attain the full capacity for objectivity and reason only when a society of man is established above all particular divisions of the human race, when loyalty to the human race and to its ideals is considered the prime loyalty that exists.

The minute study of the process of rationalization is perhaps the most significant contribution of psychoanalysis to human progress. It has opened up a new dimension of the truth, it has shown that the fact that someone sincerely believes in a statement is not enough to determine his sincerity, that only by understanding the unconscious processes going on in him can we know whether he rationalizes or whether he speaks the truth.[15]

Psychoanalysis of thought processes is not only concerned with those rationalizing thoughts which tend to distort or hide the true motivation but also with such thoughts which are untrue in another sense, that of not having the weight and significance which is attributed to them by those who profess them. A thought may be an empty shell, nothing but an opinion held because it is the thought pattern of the culture which one adopts easily and could shed easily, provided public opinion changes. A thought, on the other hand, may be the expression of the person's feelings and genuine convictions. In the latter case it is rooted in his total personality and has an *emotional matrix*. Only those thoughts which are thus rooted determine effectively the person's action.

A recent survey[16] offers a good illustration. Two questions were asked of whites in the North and South of the United States: (1) Are all men created equal? (2) Are the Negroes equal to the whites? Even in the South 61 per cent answered the first question in the affirmative but only 4 per cent answered the second question in the affirmative. (For the North the figures were 79 per cent and 21 per cent, respectively.) The person who assented only to the first question undoubtedly remembered it as a thought learned in classes and retained because it is still part of a generally recognized, respectable ideology, but it has no relation to what the person really feels; it is, as it were, in his head, without any connection with his heart and hence without any power to influence his action. The same holds true for any number of respectable ideas. A survey today in the United States would show almost complete unanimity that democracy is the best form of government. But this result does not prove that all those who expressed an opinion in favor of democracy would fight for it if it were threatened; even most of those who in their hearts are authoritarian personalities would express democratic opinions as long as the majority does so.

Any idea is strong only if it is grounded in a person's character structure. No idea is more potent than its emotional matrix. The psychoanalytic approach to religion then aims at the *understanding of human reality behind thought systems*. It inquires whether a thought system is expressive of the feeling which it portrays or whether it is a rationalization hiding opposite attitudes. Furthermore it asks whether the thought system grows from a strong emotional matrix or whether it is an empty opinion.

While it is relatively easy to describe the principle of this approach, the analysis of any thought system is exceedingly difficult. The analyst, in trying to determine the human reality behind a thought system, must in the first place consider the system as a whole. The meaning of any single part of a philosophical or religious system can be determined only within the whole context of that system. Should a part become isolated from its context the door is open to any kind of arbitrary misinterpretation. In the process of scrutinizing a system as a whole it is particularly important to watch any inconsistencies or contradictions within the system; these usually will point to discrepancies between consciously held opinion and underlying feeling. Calvin's views on predestination, for instance, which claim that the decision whether a man is to be saved or sentenced to eternal damnation is made before he is born and without his possessing the ability to change his own fate are in blatant contradiction to the idea of God's love. The psychoanalyst must study the personality and character structure of those who profess certain thought systems, both as individuals and as groups. He will inquire into the consistencies of character structure with professed opinion and will interpret the thought system in terms of the unconscious forces which can be inferred from minute details of manifest behavior. He finds, for instance, that the way a man looks at his neighbor or talks to a child, the way he eats, walks, or shakes hands, or the way in which a group behaves toward minorities is more expressive of faith and love than any stated belief. From the study of thought systems in connection with the character structure he will attempt to find an answer to the question whether and to what extent the thought system is a rationalization and how great the weight of the thought system is.

If the psychoanalyst is primarily interested in the human reality behind religious doctrines, he will find the same reality underlying different religions and opposite human attitudes underlying the same religion. The human reality, for instance, underlying the teachings of Buddha, Isaiah, Christ, Socrates, or Spinoza is essentially the same. It is determined by the striving for love, truth, and justice. The human reality behind Calvin's theological system and that of authoritarian political systems is also very similar. Their spirit is one of submission to power and lack of love and of respect for the individual.

Just as a parent's consciously felt or expressed concern for a child can be an expression of love or can express a wish for control and domination, a religious statement can be expressive of opposite human attitudes. We do not discard that statement but look at it in perspective, the human reality behind it providing the third dimension. Particularly concerning the sincerity of the postulate of love the words hold true: "By their fruits shall ye know them." If religious teachings contribute to the growth, strength, freedom, and happiness of their believers, we see the fruits of love. If they contribute to the constriction of human potentialities, to unhappiness and lack of productivity, they cannot be born of love, regardless of what the dogma intends to convey.

NOTES

1. *Man for Himself,* pp. 40-41, 46-47, 49-50.
2. Johannes Calvin, *Institutes of the Christian Religion* (Presbyterian Board of Christian Education, 1928), p. 681.
3. See Erich Fromm, *Escape from Freedom* (Farrar & Rinehart, 1941), pp. 141 ff. This attitude toward authority is described there in detail.
4. D. T. Suzuki, *An Introduction to Zen Buddhism* (Rider and Company, 1948), p. 124. Cf. also Professor Suzuki's other works on Zen, and Christmas Humphreys, *Zen Buddhism* (W. Heinemann, Ltd., 1949). An anthology of religious documents expressive of humanistic religion, drawn from all the great sources of the East and West, edited by Victor Gollancz, will be published this year. Here the reader will find a wealth of documentation on humanistic religious thinking.
5. The historical fact that the beginning of the Bible may not be its oldest part does not need to be considered here since we use the text as an illustration of two principles and not to establish a historical sequence.
6. Genesis 3:4-5.
7. *Ibid.* 3:22.
8. *Ibid.* 6:5 ff.
9. *Ibid.* 9:11.
10. *Ibid.* 9:5.
11. *Ibid.* 18:25.

12. Talmud, Baba Meziah, 59, b. (My translation.)

13. Cf. the discussion about symbiotic relationship in *Escape from Freedom*, pp. 158 ff.

14. See *Escape from Freedom*, pp. 141 ff.

15. One misunderstanding which easily arises at this point must be dispelled. The truth in the sense in which we speak of it here refers to the question of whether a motive given by a person as reason for his action is the true motivation as far as he is concerned. It does not refer to the truth of the rationalizing statement as such. To give a simple example: if someone who is afraid of meeting a certain person gives as the reason why he does not want to see him that it is raining heavily, he is rationalizing. The true reason is his fear and not the rain. The rationalizing statement, namely, that it is raining, may in itself be a true statement.

16. *Negro Digest,* 1945.

John Dewey

L Religion Versus the Religious

John Dewey was professor of philosophy at Columbia University from 1904 until his retirement in 1930. His first degree was
from the University of Vermont and his doctorate was from
Johns Hopkins University. He held a number of university
teaching positions prior to becoming a professor at Columbia,
such as at Michigan and Minnesota and at the University of
Chicago, where he organized an experimental elementary
school. He was a prolific writer, having written thirty-six books
and over eight hundred articles. Among his books are: *Psychology* (1887); *School and Society* (1899); *Studies in Logical
Theory* (1903); *How We Think* (1910); *The Influence of Darwin
on Philosophy and Other Essays in Contemporary Thought*
(1910); *Democracy and Education* (1916); *Creative Intelligence*
(1917); *Reconstruction in Philosophy* (1920); *Human Nature
and Conduct* (1922); *Experience and Nature* (1925); *The Quest
for Certainty: A Study of the Relation of Knowledge and Action*
(1929); *Philosophy and Civilization* (1931); *A Common Faith*
(1934); *Art as Experience* (1934); *Liberalism and Social Action*
(1935); *Logic: The Theory of Inquiry* (1938); *Experience and
Education* (1938); *Freedom and Culture* (1939); *Education
Today* (1940); *Problems of Men* (1946); and *Knowing and the
Known* (1949).

Never before in history has mankind been so much of two minds, so divided into two camps, as it is today. Religions have traditionally been allied with ideas of the supernatural, and often have been based upon explicit beliefs about it. Today there are many who hold that nothing worthy of being called religious is possible apart from the supernatural. Those who hold this belief differ in many respects. They range from those who accept the dogmas and sacraments of the Greek and Roman Catholic church as the only sure means of access to the supernatural to the theist or mild deist. Between them are the many Protestant denominations who think the Scriptures, aided by a pure conscience, are adequate avenues to supernatural truth and power. But they agree in one point: the necessity for a Supernatural Being and for an immortality that is beyond the power of nature.

The opposed group consists of those who think the advance of culture and science has completely discredited the supernatural and with it all religions that were allied with belief in it. But they go beyond this point. The extremists in this group believe that with elimination of the supernatural not only must historic religions be dismissed but with them everything of a religious nature. When historical knowledge has discredited the claims made for the supernatural character of the persons said to have founded historic religions; when the supernatural inspiration attributed to literatures held sacred has been riddled, and when anthropological and psychological knowledge has disclosed the all-too-human source from which religious beliefs and practices have sprung, everything religious must, they say, also go.

There is one idea held in common by these two opposite groups: identification of the religious with the supernatural. The question I shall raise in ... [this essay] concerns the ground for and the consequences of this identification: its reasons and its value. In the discussion I shall develop another conception of the nature of the religious phase of experience, one that separates it from the supernatural and the things that have grown up about it. I shall try to show that these derivations are encumbrances and that what is genuinely religious will undergo an emancipation when it is relieved from them; that then, for the first time, the religious aspect of experience will be free to develop freely on its own account.

This view is exposed to attack from both the other camps. It goes contrary to traditional religions, including those that have the greatest hold upon the religiously minded today. The view announced will seem to them to cut the vital nerve of the religious element itself in taking away the basis upon which traditional religions and institutions have been founded. From the other side, the position I am taking seems like a timid halfway position, a concession and compromise unworthy of thought that is thoroughgoing. It is regarded as a view entertained from mere tendermindedness, as an emotional hangover from childhood indoctrination, or even as a manifestation of a desire to avoid disapproval and curry favor.

The heart of my point, as far as I shall develop it in this first section, is that there is a difference between religion, *a* religion, and the religious; between anything that may be denoted by a noun substantive and the quality of experience that is designated by an adjective. It is not easy to find a definition of religion in the substantive sense that wins general acceptance. However, in the *Oxford Dictionary* I find the following: "Recognition on the part of man of some unseen higher power as having control of his destiny and as being entitled to obedience, reverence and worship."

This particular definition is less explicit in assertion of the supernatural character of the higher unseen power than are others that might be cited. It is, however, surcharged with implications having their source in ideas connected with the belief in the supernatural characteristic of historic religions. Let us suppose that one familiar with the history of religions, including those called primitive, compares the definition with the variety of known facts and by means of the comparison sets out to determine just what the definition means. I think he will be struck by three facts that reduce the terms of the definition to such a low common denominator that little meaning is left.

He will note that the "unseen powers" referred to have been conceived in a multitude of incompatible ways. Eliminating the differences, nothing is left beyond the bare reference to something unseen and powerful. This has been conceived as the vague and undefined Mana of the Melanesians; the Kami of primitive Shintoism; the fetish of the Africans; spirits, having some human properties, that pervade natural places and animate natural forces; the ultimate and impersonal principle of Buddhism; the unmoved mover of Greek thought; the gods and semidivine heroes of the Greek and Roman Pantheons; the personal and loving Providence of Christianity, omnipotent, and limited by a corresponding evil power; the arbitrary Will of Moslemism; the supreme legislator and judge of deism. And these are but a few of the outstanding varieties of ways in which the invisible power has been conceived.

There is no greater similarity in the ways in which obedience and reverence have been expressed. There has been worship of animals, of ghosts, of ancestors, phallic worship, as well as of a Being of dread power and of love and wisdom. Reverence has been expressed in the human sacrifices of the Peruvians and Aztecs; the sexual orgies of some Oriental religions; exorcisms and ablutions; the offering of the humble and contrite mind of the Hebrew prophet, the elaborate rituals of the Greek and Roman churches. Not even sacrifice has been uniform; it is highly sublimated in Protestant denominations and in Moslemism. Where it has existed it has taken all kinds of forms and been directed to a great variety of powers and spirits. It has been used for expiation, for propitiation and for buying special favors. There is no conceivable purpose for which rites have not been employed.

Finally, there is no discernible unity in the moral motivations appealed to and utilized. They have been as far apart as fear of lasting torture, hope of enduring bliss in which sexual enjoyment has sometimes been a conspicuous element; mortification of the flesh and extreme asceticism; prostitution and chastity; wars to extirpate the unbeliever; persecution to convert or punish the unbeliever, and philanthropic zeal; servile acceptance of imposed dogma, along with brotherly love and aspirations for a reign of justice among men.

I have, of course, mentioned only a sparse number of the facts which fill volumes in any well-stocked library. It may be asked by those who do not like to look upon the darker side of the history of religions why the darker facts should be brought up. We all know that civilized man has a background of bestiality and superstition and that these elements are still with us. Indeed, have not some religions, including the most influential forms of Christianity, taught that the heart of man is totally corrupt? How could the course of religion in its entire sweep not be marked by practices that are shameful in their cruelty and lustfulness, and by beliefs that are degraded and intellectually incredible? What else than what we find could be expected, in the case of people having little knowledge and no secure method of knowing; with primitive institutions, and with so little control of natural forces that they lived in a constant state of fear?

I gladly admit that historic religions have been relative to the conditions of social culture in which peoples lived. Indeed, what I am concerned with is to press home the logic of this method of disposal of outgrown traits of past religions. Beliefs and practices in a religion that now prevails are by this logic relative to the present state of culture. If so much flexibility has obtained in the past regarding an unseen power, the way it affects human destiny, and the attitudes we are to take toward it, why should it be assumed that change in conception and action has now come to an end? The logic involved in getting rid of inconvenient aspects of past religions compels us to inquire how much in religions now accepted are survivals from outgrown cultures. It compels us to ask what conception of unseen powers and our relations to them would be consonant with the best achievements and aspirations of the present. It demands that in imagination we wipe the slate clean and start afresh by asking what would be the idea of the unseen, of the manner of its control over us and the ways in which reverence and obedience would be manifested, if whatever is basically religious in experience had the opportunity to express itself, free from all historic encumbrances.

So we return to the elements of the definition that has been given. What boots it to accept, in defense of the universality of religion, a definition that applies equally to the most savage and degraded beliefs and practices that have related to unseen powers and to noble ideals of a religion having the greatest share of moral content? There are two points involved. One of them is that there is nothing left worth preserving in the notions of unseen powers, controlling human destiny to which obedience, reverence and worship are due, if we glide silently over the nature that has been attributed to the powers, the radically diverse ways in which they have been supposed to control human destiny, and in which submission and awe have been manifested. The other point is that when we begin to select, to choose, and say that some present ways of thinking about the unseen powers are better than others; that the reverence shown by a free and self-respecting human being is better than the servile obedience rendered to an arbitrary power by frightened men; that we should believe that control of human destiny is exercised by a wise and loving spirit rather than by madcap ghosts or sheer force—when I say, we begin to choose, we have entered upon a road that has not yet come to an end. We have reached a point that invites us to proceed farther.

For we are forced to acknowledge that concretely there is no such thing as religion in the singular. There is only a multitude of religions. "Religion" is a strictly collective term and the collection it stands for is not even of the kind illustrated in textbooks of logic. It has not the unity of a regiment or assembly but that of any miscellaneous aggregate. Attempts to prove the universality prove too much or too little. It is probable that religions have been universal in the sense that all the peoples we know anything about have had *a* religion. But the differences among them are so great and so shocking that any common element that can be extracted is meaningless. The idea that religion is universal proves too little in that the older apologists for Christianity seem to have been better advised than some modern ones in condemning every religion but one as an impostor, as at bottom some kind of demon worship or at any rate a superstitious figment. Choice among religions is imperative, and the necessity for choice leaves nothing of any force in the argument from universality. Moreover, when once we enter upon the road of choice, there is at once presented a possibility not yet generally realized.

For the historic increase of the ethical and ideal content of religions suggests that the process of purification may be carried further. It indicates that further choice is imminent, in which certain values and functions in experience may be selected. This possibility is what I had in mind in speaking of the difference between the religious and a religion. I am not proposing a religion, but rather the emancipation of elements and outlooks that may be called religious. For the moment we have a religion, whether that of the Sioux Indian or of Judaism or of Christianity, that moment the ideal factors in experience that may be called religious take on a load that is not inherent in them, a load of current beliefs and of institutional practices that are irrelevant to them.

I can illustrate what I mean by a common phenomenon in contemporary life. It is widely supposed that a person who does not accept any religion is thereby shown to be a non-religious person. Yet it is conceivable that the present depression in religion is closely connected with the fact that religions now prevent, because of their weight of historic encumbrances, the religious quality of experience from coming to consciousness and finding the expression that is appropriate to present conditions, intellectual and moral. I believe that such is the case. I believe that many persons are so repelled from what exists as a religion by its intellectual and moral implications, that they are not even aware of attitudes in themselves that if they came to fruition would be genuinely religious. I hope that this remark may help make clear what I mean by the distinction between "religion" as a noun substantive and "religious" as adjectival.

To be somewhat more explicit, a religion (and as I have just said there is no such thing as religion in general) always signifies a special body of beliefs and practices having some kind of institutional organization, loose or tight. In contrast, the adjective "religious" denotes nothing in the way of a specifiable entity, either institutional or as a system of beliefs. It does not denote anything to which one can specifically point as one can point to this and that historic religion or existing church. For it does not denote anything that can exist by itself or that can be organized into a particular and distinctive form of existence. It denotes attitudes that may be taken toward every object and every proposed end or ideal.

Before, however, I develop my suggestion that realization of the distinction just made would operate to emancipate the religious quality from encumbrances that now smother or limit it, I must refer to a position I have taken, but that in fact is a whole world removed from it. I have several times used the phrase "religious elements of experience." Now at present there is much talk, especially in liberal circles, of religious experience as vouching for the authenticity of certain beliefs and the desirability of certain practices, such as particular forms of prayer and worship. It is even asserted that religious experience is the ultimate basis of religion itself. The gulf between this position and that which I have taken is what I am now concerned to point out.

Those who hold to the notion that there is a definite kind of experience which is itself religious, by that very fact make out of it something specific, as a kind of experience that is marked off from experience as aesthetic, scientific, moral, political; from experience as companionship and friendship. But "religious" as a quality of experience signifies something that may belong to all these experiences. It is the polar opposite of some type of experience that can exist by itself. The distinction comes out clearly when it is noted that the concept of this distinct kind of experience is used to validate a belief in some special kind of object and also to justify some special kind of practice.

For there are many religionists who are now dissatisfied with the older "proofs" of the existence of God, those that go by the name of ontological, cosmological and teleological. The cause of the dissatisfaction is perhaps not so much the arguments that Kant used to show the insufficiency of these alleged proofs, as it is the growing feeling that they are too formal to offer any support to religion in action. Anyway, the dissatisfaction exists. Moreover, these religionists are moved by the rise of the experimental method in other fields. What is more natural and proper, accordingly, than that they should affirm they are just as good empiricists as anybody else—indeed, as good as the scientists themselves? As the latter rely upon certain kinds of experience to prove the existence of certain kinds of objects, so the religionists rely upon a certain kind of experience to prove the existence of the object of religion, especially the supreme object, God.

The discussion may be made more definite by introducing, at this point, a particular illustration of this type of reasoning. A writer says: "I broke down from overwork and soon came to the verge of nervous prostration. One morning after a long and sleepless night . . . I resolved to stop drawing upon myself so continuously and begin drawing upon God. I determined to set apart a quiet time every day in which I could relate my life to its ultimate source, regain the consciousness that in God I live, move and have my being. That was thirty years ago. Since then I have had literally not one hour of darkness or despair."

This is an impressive record. I do not doubt its authenticity nor that of the experience related. It illustrates a religious aspect of experience. But it illustrates also the use of that quality to carry a superimposed load of a particular religion. For having been brought up in the Christian religion, its subject interprets it in the terms of the personal God characteristic of that religion. Taoists, Buddhists, Moslems, persons of no religion, including those who reject all supernatural influence and power, have had experiences similar in their effect. Yet another author commenting upon the passage says: "The religious expert can be more sure that this God exists than he can of either the cosmological God of speculative surmise or the Christlike God involved in the validity of moral optimism," and goes on to add that such experiences "mean that God the savior, the power that gives victory over sin on certain conditions that man can fulfill, is an existent, accessible and scientifically knowable reality." It should be clear that this inference is sound only if the conditions, of whatever sort, that produce the effect are called "God." But most readers will take the inference to mean that the existence of a particular Being, of the type called "God" in the Christian religion, is proved by a method akin to that of experimental science.

In reality, the only thing that can be said to be "proved" is the existence of some complex of conditions that have operated to effect an adjustment in life, an orientation, that brings with it a sense of security and peace. The particular interpretation given to this complex of conditions is not inherent in the experience itself. It is derived from the culture with which a particular person has been imbued. A fatalist will give one name to it; a Christian Scientist another, and the one who rejects all supernatural being still another. The determining factor in the interpretation of the experience is the particular doctrinal apparatus into which a person has been inducted. The emotional deposit connected with prior teaching floods the whole situation. It may readily confer upon the experience such a peculiarly sacred preciousness that all inquiry into its causation is barred. The stable outcome is so invaluable that the cause to which it is referred is usually nothing but a reduplication of the thing that has occurred, plus some name that has acquired a deeply emotional quality.

The intent of this discussion is not to deny the genuineness of the result nor its importance in life. It is not, save incidentally, to point out the possibility of a purely naturalistic explanation of the event. My purpose is to indicate what happens when religious experience is already set aside as something *sui generis*. The actual religious quality in the experience described is the *effect* produced, the better adjustment in life and its conditions, not the manner and cause of its production. The way in which the experience operated, its function, determines its religious value. If the reorientation actually occurs, it, and the sense of security and stability accompanying it, are forces on their own account. It takes place in different persons in a multitude of ways. It is sometimes brought about by devotion to a cause; sometimes by a passage of poetry that opens a new perspective; sometimes as was the case with Spinoza—deemed an atheist in his day—through philosophical reflection.

The difference between an experience having a religious force because of what it does in and to the processes of living and religious experience as a separate kind of thing gives me occasion to refer to a previous remark. If this function were rescued through emancipation from dependence upon specific types of beliefs and practices, from those elements that constitute a religion, many individuals would find that experiences having the force of bringing about a better, deeper and enduring adjustment in life are not so rare and infrequent as they are commonly supposed to be. They occur frequently in connection with many significant moments of living. The idea of invisible powers would take on the meaning of all the conditions of nature and human association that support and deepen the sense of values which carry one through periods of darkness and despair to such an extent that they lose their usual depressive character.

I do not suppose for many minds the dislocation of the religious from a religion is easy to effect. Tradition and custom, especially when emotionally charged, are a part of the habits that have become one with our very being. But the possibility of the transfer is demonstrated by its actuality. Let us then for the moment drop the term "religious," and ask what are the attitudes that lend deep and enduring support to the processes of living. I have, for example, used the words "adjustment" and "orientation." What do they signify?

While the words "accommodation," "adaptation," and "adjustment" are frequently employed as synonyms, attitudes exist that are so different that for the sake of clear thought they should be discriminated. There are conditions we meet that cannot be changed. If they are particular and limited, we modify our own particular attitudes in accordance with them. Thus we accommodate ourselves to changes in weather, to alterations in income when we have no other recourse. When the external conditions are lasting we become inured, habituated, or, as the process is now often called, conditioned. The two main traits of this attitude, which I should like to call accommodation, are that it affects *particular* modes of conduct, not the entire self, and that the process is mainly *passive*. It may, however, become general and then it becomes fatalistic resignation or submission. There are other attitudes toward the environment that are also particular but that are more active. We react against conditions and endeavor to change them to meet our wants and demands. Plays in a foreign language are "adapted" to meet the needs of an American audience. A house is rebuilt to suit changed conditions of the household; the telephone is invented to serve the demand for speedy communication at a distance; dry soils are irrigated so that they may bear abundant crops. Instead of accommodating ourselves to conditions, we modify conditions so that they will be accommodated to our wants and purposes. This process may be called adaptation.

Now both of these processes are often called by the more general name of adjustment. But there are also changes in ourselves in relation to the world in which we live that are much more inclusive and deep-seated. They relate not to this and that want in relation to this and that condition of our surroundings, but pertain to our being in its entirety. Because of their scope, this modification of ourselves is enduring. It lasts through any amount of vicissitude of circumstances, internal and external. There is a composing and harmonizing of the various elements of our being such that, in spite of changes in the special conditions that surround us, these conditions are also arranged, settled, in relation to us. This attitude includes a note of submission. But it is voluntary, not externally imposed; and as voluntary it is something more than a mere stoical resolution to endure unperturbed throughout the buffetings of fortune. It is more outgoing, more ready and glad, than the latter attitude, and it is more active than the former. And in calling it voluntary, it is not meant that it depends upon a particular resolve or volition. It is a change *of* will conceived as the organic plenitude of our being, rather than any special change *in* will.

It is the claim of religions that they effect this generic and enduring change in attitude. I should like to turn the statement around and say that whenever this change takes place there is a definitely religious attitude. It is not *a* religion that brings it about, but when it occurs, from whatever cause and by whatever means, there is a religious outlook and function. As I have said before, the doctrinal or intellectual apparatus and the institutional accretions that grow up are, in a strict sense, adventitious to the intrinsic quality of such experiences. For they are affairs of the traditions of the culture with which individuals are inoculated. Mr. Santayana has connected the religious quality of experience with the imaginative, as that is expressed in poetry. "Religion and poetry," he says, "are identical in essence, and differ merely in the way in which they are attached to practical affairs. Poetry is called religion when it intervenes in life, and religion, when it merely supervenes upon life, is seen to be nothing but poetry." The difference between intervening *in* and supervening *upon* is as important as is the identity set forth. Imagination may play upon life or it may enter profoundly into it. As Mr. Santayana puts it, "poetry has a universal and a moral function," for "its highest power lies in its relevance to the ideals and purposes of life." Except as it intervenes, "all observation is observation of brute fact, all discipline is mere repression, until these facts digested and this discipline embodied in humane impulses become the starting point for a creative movement of the imagination, the firm basis for ideal constructions in society, religion, and art."

If I may make a comment upon this penetrating insight of Mr. Santayana, I would say that the difference between imagination that only supervenes and imagination that intervenes is the difference between one that completely interpenetrates all the elements of our being and one that is interwoven with only special and partial factors. There actually occurs extremely little observation of brute facts merely for the sake of the facts, just as there is little discipline that is repression and nothing but repression. Facts are usually observed with reference to some practical end and purpose, and that end is presented only imaginatively. The most repressive discipline has some end in view to which there is at least imputed an ideal quality; otherwise it is purely sadistic. But in such cases of observation and discipline imagination is limited and partial. It does not extend far; it does not permeate deeply and widely.

The connection between imagination and the harmonizing of the self is closer than is usually thought. The idea of a whole, whether of the whole personal being or of the world, is an imaginative, not a literal, idea. The limited world of our observation and reflection becomes the Universe only through imaginative extension. It cannot be apprehended in knowledge nor realized in reflection. Neither observation, thought, nor practical activity can attain that complete unification of the self which is called a whole. The *whole* self is an ideal, an imaginative projection. Hence the idea of a thoroughgoing and deep-seated harmonizing of the self with the Universe (as a name for the totality of conditions with which the self is connected) operates only through imagination—which is one reason why this composing of the self is not voluntary in the sense of an act of special volition or resolution. An "adjustment" possesses the will rather than is its express product. Religionists have been right in thinking of it as an influx from sources beyond conscious deliberation and purpose—a fact that helps explain, psychologically, why it has so generally been attributed to a supernatural source and that, perhaps, throws some light upon the reference of it by William James to unconscious factors. And it is pertinent to note that the unification of the self throughout the ceaseless flux of what it does, suffers, and achieves, cannot be attained in terms of itself. The self is always directed toward something beyond itself and so its own unification depends upon the idea of the integration of the shifting scenes of the world into that imaginative totality we call the Universe.

The intimate connection of imagination with ideal elements in experience is generally recognized. Such is not the case with respect to its connection with faith. The latter has been regarded as a substitute for knowledge, for insight. It is defined, in the Christian religion, as *evidence* of things not seen. The implication is that faith is a kind of anticipatory vision of things that are now invisible because of the limitations of our finite and erring nature. Because it is a substitute for knowledge, its material and object are intellectual in quality. As John Locke summed up the matter, faith is "assent to a proposition . . . on the credit of its proposer." Religious faith is then given to a body of propositions as true on the credit of their supernatural author, reason coming in to demonstrate the reasonableness of giving such credit. Of necessity there results the development of theologies, or bodies of systematic propositions, to make explicit in organized form the content of the propositions to which belief is attached and assent given. Given the point of view, those who hold that religion necessarily implies a theology are correct.

But belief or faith has also a moral and practical import. Even devils, according to the older theologians, believe—and tremble. A distinction was made, therefore, between "speculative" or intellectual belief and an act called "justifying" faith. Apart from any theological context, there is a difference between belief that is a conviction that some end should be supreme over conduct, and belief that some object or being exists as a truth for the intellect. Conviction in the moral sense signifies being conquered, vanquished, in our active nature by an ideal end; it signifies acknowledgment of its rightful claim over our desires and purposes. Such acknowledgement is practical, not primarily intellectual. It goes beyond evidence that can be presented to *any* possible observer. Reflection, often long and arduous, may be involved in arriving at the conviction, but the import of thought is not exhausted in discovery of evidence that can justify intellectual assent. The authority of an ideal over choice and conduct is the authority of an ideal, not of a fact, of a truth guaranteed to intellect, not of the status of the one who propounds the truth.

Such moral faith is not easy. It was questioned of old whether the Son of Man should find faith on the earth in his coming. Moral faith has been bolstered by all sorts of arguments intended to prove that its object is not ideal and that its claim upon us is not primarily moral or practical, since the ideal in question is already embedded in the existent frame of things. It is argued that the ideal is already the final reality at the heart of things that exist, and that only our senses or the corruption of our natures prevent us from apprehending its prior existential being. Starting, say, from such an idea as that justice is more than a moral ideal because it is embedded in the very make-up of the actually existent world, men have gone on to build up vast intellectual schemes, philosophies, and theologies, to prove that ideals are real not as ideals but as antecedently existing actualities. They have failed to see that in converting moral realities into matters of intellectual assent they have evinced lack of *moral* faith. Faith that something should be in existence as far as lies in our power is changed into the intellectual belief that it is already in existence. When physical existence does not bear out the assertion, the physical is subtly changed into the metaphysical. In this way, moral faith has been inextricably tied up with intellectual beliefs about the supernatural.

The tendency to convert ends of moral faith and action into articles of an intellectual creed has been furthered by a tendency of which psychologists are well aware. What we ardently desire to have thus and so, we tend to believe is already so. Desire has a powerful influence upon intellectual beliefs. Moreover, when conditions are adverse to realization of the objects of our desire—and in the case of significant ideals they are extremely adverse—it is an easy way out to assume that after all they are already embodied in the ultimate structure of what is, and that appearances to the contrary are *merely* appearances. Imagination then merely supervenes and is freed from the responsibility for intervening. Weak natures take to reverie as a refuge as strong ones do to fanaticism. Those who dissent are mourned over by the first class and converted through the use of force by the second.

What has been said does not imply that all moral faith in ideal ends is by virtue of that fact religious in quality. The religious is "morality touched by emotion" only when the ends of moral conviction arouse emotions that are not only intense but are actuated and supported by ends so inclusive that they unify the self. The inclusiveness of the end in relation to both self and the "universe" to which an inclusive self is related is indispensable. According to the best authorities, *religion* comes from a root that means being bound by vows to a particular way of life—as *les religieux* were monks and nuns who had assumed certain vows. The religious attitude signifies something that is bound through imagination to a *general* attitude. This comprehensive attitude, moreover, is much broader than anything indicated by "moral" in its usual sense. The quality of attitude is displayed in art, science and good citizenship.

If we apply the conception set forth to the terms of the definition earlier quoted, these terms take on a new significance. An unseen power controlling our destiny becomes the power of an ideal. All possibilities, as possibilities, are ideal in character. The artist, scientist, citizen, parent, as far as they are actuated by the spirit of their callings, are controlled by the unseen. For all endeavor for the better is moved by faith in what is possible, not by adherence to the actual. Nor does this faith depend for its moving power upon intellectual assurance or belief that the things worked for must surely prevail and come into embodied existence. For the authority of the object to determine our attitude and conduct, the right that is given it to claim our allegiance and devotion is based on the intrinsic nature of the ideal. The outcome, given our best endeavor, is not with us. The inherent vice of all intellectual schemes of idealism is that they convert the idealism of action into a system of beliefs about antecedent reality. The character assigned this reality is so different from that which observation and reflection lead to and support that these schemes inevitably glide into alliance with the supernatural.

All religions, marked by elevated ideal quality, have dwelt upon the power of religion to introduce perspective into the piecemeal and shifting episodes of existence. Here too we need to reverse the ordinary statement and say that whatever introduces genuine perspective is religious, not that religion is something that introduces it. There can be no doubt (referring to the second element of the definition) of our dependence upon forces beyond our control. Primitive man was so impotent in the face of these forces that, especially in an unfavorable natural environment, fear became a dominant attitude, and, as the old saying goes, fear created the gods.

With increase of mechanisms of control, the element of fear has, relatively speaking, subsided. Some optimistic souls have even concluded that the forces about us are on the whole essentially benign. But every crisis, whether of the individual or of the community, reminds man of the precarious and partial nature of the control he exercises. When man, individually and collectively, has done his uttermost, conditions that at different times and places have given rise to the ideas of Fate and Fortune, of Chance and Providence, remain. It is the part of manliness to insist upon the capacity of mankind to strive to direct natural and social forces to humane ends. But unqualified absolutistic statements about the omnipotence of such endeavors reflect egoism rather than intelligent courage.

The fact that human destiny is so interwoven with forces beyond human control renders it unnecessary to suppose that dependence and the humility that accompanies it have to find the particular channel that is prescribed by traditional doctrines. What is especially significant is rather the form which the sense of dependence takes. Fear never gave stable perspective in the life of anyone. It is dispersive and withdrawing. Most religions have in fact added rites of communion to those of expiation and propitiation. For our dependence is manifested in those relations to the environment that support our undertakings and aspirations as much as it is in the defeats inflicted upon us. The essentially unreligious attitude is that which attributes human achievement and purpose to man in isolation from the world of physical nature and his fellows. Our successes are dependent upon the cooperation of nature. The sense of the dignity of human nature is as religious as is the sense of awe and reverence when it rests upon a sense of human nature as a cooperating part of a larger whole. Natural piety is not of necessity either a fatalistic acquiescence in natural happenings or a romantic idealization of the world. It may rest upon a just sense of nature as the whole of which we are parts, while it also recognizes that we are parts that are marked by intelligence and purpose, having the capacity to strive by their aid to bring conditions into greater consonance with what is humanly desirable. Such piety is an inherent constituent of a just perspective in life.

Understanding and knowledge also enter into a perspective that is religious in quality. Faith in the continued disclosing of truth through directed cooperative human endeavor is more religious in quality than is any faith in a completed revelation. It is of course now usual to hold that revelation is not completed in the sense of being ended. But religions hold that the essential framework is settled in its significant moral features at least, and that new elements that are offered must be judged by conformity to this framework. Some fixed doctrinal apparatus is necessary for *a* religion. But faith in the possibilities of continued and rigorous inquiry does not limit access to truth to any channel or scheme of things. It does not first say that truth is universal and then add there is but one road to it. It does not depend for assurance upon subjection to any dogma or item of doctrine. It trusts that the natural interactions between man and his environment will breed more intelligence and generate more knowledge, provided the scientific methods that define intelligence in operation are pushed further into the mysteries of the world, being themselves promoted and improved in the operation. There is such a thing as faith in intelligence becoming religious in quality—a fact that perhaps explains the efforts of some religionists to disparage the possibilities of intelligence as a force. They properly feel such faith to be a dangerous rival.

Lives that are consciously inspired by loyalty to such ideals as have been mentioned are still comparatively infrequent to the extent of that comprehensiveness and intensity which arouse an ardor religious in function. But before we infer the incompetency of such ideals and of the actions they inspire, we should at least ask ourselves how much of the existing situation is due to the fact that the religious factors of experience have been drafted into supernatural channels and thereby loaded with irrelevant encumbrances. A body of beliefs and practices that are apart from the common and natural relations of mankind must, in the degree in which it is influential, weaken and sap the force of the possibilities inherent in such relations. Here lies one aspect of the emancipation of the religious from religion.

Any activity pursued in behalf of an ideal end against obstacles and in spite of threats of personal loss because of conviction of its general and enduring value is religious in quality. Many a person, inquirer, artist, philanthropist citizen—men and women in the humblest walks of life, have achieved, without presumption and without display, such unification of themselves and of their relations to the conditions of existence. It remains to extend their spirit and inspiration to ever wider numbers. If I have said anything about religions and religion that seems harsh, I have said those things because of a firm belief that the claim on the part of religions to possess a monopoly of ideals and of the supernatural means by which alone, it is alleged, they can be furthered, stands in the way of the realization of distinctively religious values inherent in natural experience. For that reason, if for no other, I should be sorry if any were misled by the frequency with which I have employed the adjective "religious" to conceive of what I have said as a disguised apology for what have passed as religions. The opposition between religious values as I conceive them and religions is not to be bridged. Just because the release of these values is so important, their identification with the creeds and cults of religions must be dissolved.

VII. God and the Existence of Evil

H. J. McCloskey

God and Evil

Henry J. McCloskey, professor of philosophy at La Trobe University, Victoria, Australia, received his education at the University of Melbourne. His books include: *Meta-Ethics and Normative Ethics* (1969); *John Stuart Mill: A Critical Study* (1971); and *God and Evil* (1974). Two interesting articles he has written in journals are "On Being an Atheist," *Question 1* (February 1968) and "The Problem of Evil," *The Journal of Bible and Religion* 30, no. 3 (July 1962).

THE PROBLEM STATED

Evil is a problem for the theist in that a contradiction is involved in the fact of evil on the one hand, and the belief in the omnipotence and perfection of God on the other. God cannot be both all-powerful and perfectly good if evil is real. This contradiction is well set out in its detail by Mackie

From The Philosophical Quarterly *10, no. 39 (April 1960) pp. 97-114. Reprinted by permission of the author and editor.*

in his discussion of the problem.[1] In his discussion Mackie seeks to show that this contradiction cannot be resolved in terms of man's free will. In arguing in this way Mackie neglects a large number of important points, and concedes far too much to the theist. He implicitly allows that whilst physical evil creates a problem, this problem is reducible to the problem of moral evil and that therefore the satisfactoriness of solutions of the problem of evil turns on the compatibility of free will and absolute goodness. In fact physical evils create a number of distinct problems which are not reducible to the problem of moral evil. Further, the proposed solution of the problem of moral evil in terms of free will renders the attempt to account for physical evil in terms of moral good, and the attempt thereby to reduce the problem of evil to the problem of moral evil, completely untenable. Moreover, the account of moral evil in terms of free will breaks down on more obvious and less disputable grounds than those indicated by Mackie. Moral evil can be shown to remain a problem whether or not free will is compatible with absolute goodness. I therefore propose in this paper to reopen the discussion of "the problem of evil," by approaching it from a more general standpoint, examining a wider variety of solutions than those considered by Mackie and his critics.

The fact of evil creates a problem for the theist; but there are a number of simple solutions available to a theist who is content seriously to modify his theism. He can either admit a limit to God's power, or he can deny God's moral perfection. He can assert either (1) that God is not powerful enough to make a world that does not contain evil, or (2) that God created only the good in the universe and that some other power created the evil, or (3) that God is all-powerful but morally imperfect, and chose to create an imperfect universe. Few Christians accept these solutions, and this is no doubt partly because such "solutions" ignore the real inspiration of religious beliefs, and partly because they introduce embarrassing complications for the theist in his attempts to deal with other serious problems. However, if any one of these solutions is accepted, then the problem of evil is avoided, and a weakened version of theism is made secure from attacks based upon the fact of the occurrence of evil.

For more orthodox theism, according to which God is both omnipotent and perfectly good, evil creates a real problem; and this problem is well-stated by the Jesuit, Father G. H. Joyce. Joyce writes:

> The existence of evil in the world must at all times be the greatest of all problems which the mind encounters when it reflects on God and His relation to the world. If He is, indeed, all-good and all-powerful, how has evil

any place in the world which He has made? Whence came it? Why is it here? If He is all-good why did He allow it to arise? If all-powerful why does He not deliver us from the burden? Alike in the physical and moral order creation seems so grievously marred that we find it hard to understand how it can derive in its entirety from God.[2]

The facts which give rise to the problem are of two general kinds, and give rise to two distinct types of problem. These two general kinds of evil are usually referred to as physical and as moral evil. These terms are by no means apt—suffering for instance is not strictly physical evil—and they conceal significant differences. However, this terminology is too widely accepted, and too convenient to be dispensed with here, the more especially as the various kinds of evil, whilst important as distinct kinds, need not for our purposes be designated by separate names.

Physical evil and moral evil then are the two general forms of evil which independently and jointly constitute conclusive grounds for denying the existence of God in the sense defined, namely as an all-powerful, perfect Being. The acuteness of these two general problems is evident when we consider the nature and extent of the evils of which account must be given. To take physical evils, looking first at the less important of these.

Physical evils. Physical evils are involved in the very constitution of the earth and animal kingdom. There are deserts and icebound areas; there are dangerous animals of prey, as well as creatures such as scorpions and snakes. There are also pests such as flies and fleas and the hosts of other insect pests, as well as the multitude of lower parasites such as tapeworms, hookworms and the like. Secondly, there are the various natural calamities and the immense human suffering that follows in their wake— fires, floods, tempests, tidal waves, volcanoes, earthquakes, droughts and famines. Thirdly, there are the vast numbers of diseases that torment and ravage man. Diseases such as leprosy, cancer, poliomyelitis appear prima facie not to be creations which are to be expected of a benevolent Creator. Fourthly, there are the evils with which so many are born—the various physical deformities and defects such as misshapen limbs, blindness, deafness, dumbness, mental deficiency and insanity. Most of these evils contribute towards increasing human pain and suffering; but not all physical evils are reducible simply to pain. Many of these evils are evils whether or not they result in pain. This is important, for it means that, unless there is one solution to such diverse evils, it is both inaccurate and positively misleading to speak of *the* problem of physical evil. Shortly I shall be arguing that no one solution covers all these evils, so we shall have to conclude that physical evils create not one problem but a number of distinct problems for the theist.

The nature of the various difficulties referred to by the theist as the problem of physical evil is indicated by Joyce in a way not untypical among the more honest, philosophical theists, as follows:

> The actual amount of suffering which the human race endures is immense. Disease has store and to spare of torments for the body: and disease and death are the lot to which we must all look forward. At all times, too, great numbers of the race are pinched by want. Nor is the world ever free for very long from the terrible sufferings which follow in the track of war. If we concentrate our attention on human woes, to the exclusion of the joys of life, we gain an appalling picture of the ills to which the flesh is heir. So too if we fasten our attention on the sterner side of nature, on the pains which men endure from natural forces—on the storms which wreck their ships, the cold which freezes them to death, the fire which consumes them—if we contemplate this aspect of nature alone we may be led to wonder how God came to deal so harshly with His Creatures as to provide them with such a home.[3]

Many such statements of the problem proceed by suggesting, if not by stating, that the problem arises at least in part by concentrating one's attention too exclusively on one aspect of the world. This is quite contrary to the facts. The problem is not one that results from looking at only one aspect of the universe. It may be the case that overall pleasure predominates over pain, and that physical goods in general predominate over physical evils, but the opposite may equally well be the case. It is both practically impossible and logically impossible for this question to be resolved. However, it is not an unreasonable presumption, with the large bulk of mankind inadequately fed and housed and without adequate medical and health services, to suppose that physical evils at present predominate over physical goods. In the light of the facts at our disposal, this would seem to be a much more reasonable conclusion than the conclusion hinted at by Joyce and openly advanced by less cautious theists, namely, that physical goods in fact outweigh physical evils in the world.

However, the question is not, Which predominates, physical good or physical evil? The problem of physical evil remains a problem whether the balance in the universe is on the side of physical good or not, because the problem is that of accounting for the fact that physical evil occurs at all.

Moral evil. Physical evils create one of the groups of problems referred to by the theist as "the problem of evil." Moral evil creates quite a distinct problem. Moral evil is simply immorality—evils such as selfishness, envy, greed, deceit, cruelty, callousness, cowardice and the larger scale evils such as wars and the atrocities they involve.

Moral evil is commonly regarded as constituting an even more serious problem than physical evil. Joyce so regards it, observing: "The man who sins thereby offends God. . . . We are called on to explain how God came to create an order of things in which rebellion and even final rejection have such a place. Since a choice from among an infinite number of possible worlds lay open to God, how came He to choose one in which these occur? Is not such a choice in flagrant opposition to the Divine Goodness?"[4]

Some theists seek a solution by denying the reality of evil or by describing it as a "privation" or absence of good. They hope thereby to explain it away as not needing a solution. This, in the case of most of the evils which require explanation, seems to amount to little more than an attempt to sidestep the problem simply by changing the name of that which has to be explained. It can be exposed for what it is simply by describing some of the evils which have to be explained. That is why a survey of the data to be accounted for is a most important part of the discussion of the problem of evil.

In *The Brothers Karamazov,* Dostoyevsky introduces a discussion of the problem of evil by reference to some then recently committed atrocities. Ivan states the problem:

> "By the way, a Bulgarian I met lately in Moscow," Ivan went on . . . "told me about the crimes committed by Turks in all parts of Bulgaria through fear of a general rising of the Slavs. They burn villages, murder, outrage women and children, and nail their prisoners by the ears to the fences, leave them till morning, and in the morning hang them—all sorts of things you can't imagine. People talk sometimes of bestial cruelty, but that's a great injustice and insult to the beasts; a beast can never be so cruel as a man, so artistically cruel. The tiger only tears and gnaws and that's all he can do. He would never think of nailing people by the ears, even if he were able to do it. These Turks took a pleasure in torturing children too; cutting the unborn child from the mother's womb, and tossing babies up in the air and catching them on the points of their bayonets before their mothers' eyes. Doing it before the mother's eyes was what gave zest to the amusement. Here is another scene that I thought very interesing. Imagine a trembling mother with her baby in her arms, a circle of invading Turks around her. They've planned a diversion: they pet the baby to make it laugh. They succeed; the baby laughs. At that moment, a Turk points a pistol four inches from the baby's face. They baby laughs with glee, holds out its little hands to the pistol, and he pulls the trigger in the baby's face and blows out its brains. Artistic, wasn't it?"[5]

Ivan's statement of the problem was based on historical events. Such happenings did not cease in the nineteenth century. *The Scourge of the Swastika* by Lord Russell of Liverpool contains little else than descriptions of such atrocities; and it is simply one of a host of writings giving documented lists of instances of evils, both physical and moral.

Thus the problem of evil is both real and acute. There is a clear *prima facie* case that evil and God are incompatible—both cannot exist. Most theists admit this, and that the onus is on them to show that the conflict is not fatal to theism; but a consequence is that a host of proposed solutions are advanced.

The mere fact of such a multiplicity of proposed solutions, and the widespread repudiation of each other's solutions by theists, in itself suggests that the fact of evil is an insuperable obstacle to theism as defined here. It also makes it impossible to treat of all proposed solutions, and all that can be attempted here is an examination of those proposed solutions which are most commonly invoked and most generally thought to be important by theists.

Some theists admit the reality of the problem of evil, and then seek to sidestep it, declaring it to be a great mystery which we poor humans cannot hope to comprehend. Other theists adopt a rational approach and advance rational arguments to show that evil, properly understood, is compatible with and even a consequence of God's goodness. The arguments to be advanced in this paper are directed against the arguments of the latter theists; but insofar as these arguments are successful against the rational theists, to that extent they are also effective in showing that the nonrational approach in terms of great mysteries is positively irrational.

PROPOSED SOLUTIONS TO THE PROBLEM OF PHYSICAL EVIL

Of the large variety of arguments advanced by theists as solutions to the problem of physical evil, five popularly used and philosophically significant solutions will be examined. They are, in brief: (1) physical good (pleasure) requires physical evil (pain) to exist at all; (2) physical evil is God's punishment of sinners; (3) physical evil is God's warning and reminder to man; (4) physical evil is the result of the natural laws, the operations of which are on the whole good; (5) physical evil increases the total

Physical good is impossible without physical evil. Pleasure is possible only by way of contrast with pain. Here the analogy of color is used. If everything were blue we should, it is argued, understand neither what color is nor what blue is. So with pleasure and pain.

The most obvious defect of such an argument is that it does not cover all physical goods and evils. It is an argument commonly invoked by those who think of physical evil as creating only one problem, namely the problem of human pain. However, the problems of physical evils are not reducible to the one problem, the problem of pain; hence the argument is simply irrelevant to much physical evil. Disease and insanity are evils, but health and sanity are possible in the total absence of disease and insanity. Further, if the argument were in any way valid even in respect of pain, it would imply the existence of only a speck of pain, and not the immense amount of pain in the universe. A speck of yellow is all that is needed for an appreciation of blueness and of color generally. The argument is therefore seen to be seriously defective on two counts even if its underlying principle is left unquestioned. If its underlying principle is questioned, the argument is seen to be essentially invalid. Can it seriously be maintained that if an individual were born crippled and deformed and never in his life experienced pleasure, that he could not experience pain, not even if he were severely injured? It is clear that pain is possible in the absence of pleasure. It is true that it might not be distinguished by a special name and called "pain," but the state we now describe as a painful state would nonetheless be possible in the total absence of pleasure. So too the converse would seem to apply. Plato brings this out very clearly in Book 9 of the *Republic* in respect to the pleasures of taste and smell. These pleasures seem not to depend for their existence on any prior experience of pain. Thus the argument is unsound in respect of its main contention; and in being unsound in this respect, it is at the same time ascribing a serious limitation of God's power. It maintains that God cannot create pleasure without creating pain, although as we have seen, pleasure and pain are not correlatives.

Physical evil is God's punishment for sin. This kind of explanation was advanced to explain the terrible Lisbon earthquake in the eighteenth century, in which 40,000 people were killed. There are many replies to this argument, for instance Voltaire's. Voltaire asked: "Did God in this earthquake select the 40,000 least virtuous of the Portuguese citizens?" The distribution of disease and pain is in no obvious way related to the virtue of the persons afflicted, and popular saying has it that the distribution is slanted in the opposite direction. The only way of meeting the fact that evils are not distributed proportionately to the evil of the sufferer is by suggesting that all human beings, including children, are such miserable sinners, that our offences are of such enormity, that God would be justified in punishing all of us as severely as it is possible for humans to be punished; but even then, God's apparent caprice in the selection of His victims requires explanation. In any case it is by no means clear that young children who very often suffer severely are guilty of sin of such an enormity as would be necessary to justify their sufferings as punishment.

Further, many physical evils are simultaneous with birth—insanity, mental defectiveness, blindness, deformities, as well as much disease. No crime of sin of *the child* can explain and justify these physical evils as punishment; and, for a parent's sin to be punished in the child is injustice or evil of another kind.

Similarly, the sufferings of animals cannot be accounted for as punishment. For these various reasons, therefore, this argument must be rejected. In fact it has dropped out of favor in philosophical and theological circles, but it continues to be invoked at the popular level.

Physical evil is God's warning to men. It is argued, for instance of physical calamities, that "they serve a moral end which compensates the physical evil which they cause. The awful nature of these phenomena, the overwhelming power of the forces at work, and man's utter helplessness before them, rouse him from the religious indifference to which he is so prone. They inspire a reverential awe of the Creator who made them, and controls them, and a salutary fear of violating the laws which He has imposed."[6] This is where immortality is often alluded to as justifying evil.

This argument proceeds from a proposition that is plainly false; and that the proposition from which it proceeds is false is conceded implicitly by most theologians. Natural calamities do not necessarily turn people to God, but rather present the problem of evil in an acute form; and the problem of evil is said to account for more defections from religion than any other cause. Thus if God's object in bringing about natural calamities is to inspire reverence and awe, He is a bungler. There are many more reliable methods of achieving this end. Equally important, the use of physical evil to achieve this object is hardly the course one would expect a benevolent God to adopt when other, more effective, less evil methods are available to Him, for example, miracles, special relevation, etc.

Evils are the results of the operation of laws of nature. This fourth argument relates to most physical evil, but it is more usually used to account for animal suffering and physical calamities. These evils are said to result from the operation of the natural laws which govern these objects, the relevant natural laws being the various causal laws, the law of pleasure-pain as a law governing sentient beings, etc. The theist argues that the non-occurrence of these evils would involve either the constant intervention by God in a miraculous way, and contrary to his own natural laws, or else the construction of a universe with different components subject to different laws of nature; for God, in creating a certain kind of being, must create it subject to its appropriate law; He cannot create it and subject it to any law of His own choosing. Hence He creates a world which has components and laws good in their total effect, although calamitous in some particular effects.

Against this argument three objections are to be urged. First, it does not cover all physical evil. Clearly not all disease can be accounted for along these lines. Secondly, it is not to give a reason against God's miraculous intervention simply to assert that it would be unreasonable for Him constantly to intervene in the operation of His own laws. Yet this is the only reason that theists seem to offer here. If, by intervening in respect to the operation of His laws, God could thereby eliminate an evil, it would seem to be unreasonable and evil of Him not to do so. Some theists seek a way out of this difficulty by denying that God has the power miraculously to intervene; but this is to ascribe a severe limitation to His power. It amounts to asserting that when His Creation has been effected, God can do nothing else except contemplate it. The third objection is related to this, and is to the effect that it is already to ascribe a serious limitation to God's omnipotence to suggest that He could not make sentient beings which did not experience pain, nor sentient beings without deformities and deficiencies, nor natural phenomena with different laws of nature governing them. There is no reason why better laws of nature governing the existing objects are not possible on the divine hypothesis. Surely, if God is all-powerful, He could have made a better universe in the first place, or one with better laws of nature governing it, so that the operation of its laws did not produce calamities and pain. To maintain this is not to suggest that an omnipotent God should be capable of achieving what is logically impossible. All that has been indicated here is logically possible, and therefore not beyond the powers of a being Who is really omnipotent.

This fourth argument seeks to exonerate God by explaining that He created a universe sound on the whole, but such that He had no direct control over the laws governing His creations, and had control only in His selection of His creations. The previous two arguments attribute the detailed results of the operations of these laws directly to God's will. Theists commonly use all three arguments. It is not without significance that they betray such uncertainty as to whether God is to be *commended* or *exonerated.*

The universe is better with evil in it. This is the important argument. One version of it runs: "Just as the human artist has in view the beauty of his composition as a whole, not making it his aim to give to each several part the highest degree of brilliancy, but that measure of adornment which most contributes to the combined effect, so it is with God."[7]

Another version of this general type of argument explains evil not so much as *a component* of a good whole, seen out of its context as a mere component, but rather as a *means* to a greater good. Different as these versions are, they may be treated here as one general type of argument, for the same criticisms are fatal to both versions.

This kind of argument, if valid, simply shows that some evil may enrich the universe; it tells us nothing about *how much* evil will enrich this particular universe, and how much will be too much. So, even if valid in principle—and shortly I shall argue that it is not valid—such an argument does not in itself provide a justification for the evil in the universe. It shows simply that the evil which occurs might have a justification. In view of the immense amount of evil the probabilities are against it.

This is the main point made by Wisdom in his discussion of this argument. Wisdom sums up his criticism as follows: "It remains to add that, unless there are independent arguments in favour of this world's being the best logically possible world, it is probable that some of the evils in it are not logically necessary to a compensating good; it is probable because there are so many evils."[8]

Wisdom's reply brings out that the person who relies upon this argument as a conclusive and complete argument is seriously mistaken. The argument, if valid, justifies only some evil. A belief that it justifies all the evil that occurs in the world is mistaken, for a second argument, by way of a supplement to it, is needed. This supplementary argument would take the form of a proof that all the evil that occurs is *in fact* valuable and necessary as a means to greater good. Such a supplementary proof is in principle impossible; so, at best, this fifth argument can be taken to show only that some evil *may be* necessary for the production of good, and that the evil in the world may perhaps have a justification on this account. This is not to justify a physical evil, but simply to suggest that physical evil might nonetheless have a justification, although we may never come to know this justification.

Thus the argument, even if it is valid as a general form of reasoning, is unsatisfactory because inconclusive. It is, however, also unsatisfactory in that it follows on the principle of the argument that, just as it is possible that evil in the total context contributes to increasing the total ultimate good, so equally, it will hold that good in the total context may increase the ultimate evil. Thus if the principle of the argument were sound, we could never know whether evil is really evil, or good really good. (Aesthetic analogies may be used to illustrate this point.) By implication it follows that it would be dangerous to eliminate evil because we may thereby introduce a discordant element into the divine symphony of the universe; and, conversely, it may be wrong to condemn the elimination of what is good, because the latter may result in the production of more, higher goods.

So it follows that, even if the general principle of the argument is not questioned, it is still seen to be a defective argument. On the one hand, it proves too little—it justifies only some evil and not necessarily all the evil in the universe; on the other hand it proves too much because it creates doubts about the goodness of apparent goods. These criticisms in themselves are fatal to the argument as a solution to the problem of physical evil. However, because this is one of the most popular and plausible accounts of physical evil, it is worthwhile considering whether it can properly be claimed to establish even the very weak conclusion indicated above.

Why, and in what way, is it supposed that physical evils, such as pain and misery, disease and deformity, will heighten the total effect and add to the value of the moral whole? The answer given is that physical evil enriches the whole by giving rise to moral goodness. Disease, insanity, physical suffering and the like are said to bring into being the noble moral virtues—courage, endurance, benevolence, sympathy and the like. This is what the talk about the enriched whole comes to. W. D. Niven makes this explicit in his version of the argument: "Physical evil has been the goad which has impelled men to most of those achievements which made the history of man so wonderful. Hardship is a stern but fecund parent of invention. Where life is easy because physical ills are at a minimum we find man degenerating in body, mind, and character." And Niven concludes by asking: "Which is preferable—a grim fight with the possibility of splendid triumph; or no battle at all?" [9]

The argument is: Physical evil brings moral good into being, and in fact is an essential precondition for the existence of some moral goods. Further, it is sometimes argued in this context that those moral goods which are possible in the total absence of physical evils are more valuable in themselves if they are achieved as a result of a struggle. Hence physical evil is said to be justified on the grounds that moral good plus physical evil is better than the absence of physical evil.

A common reply, and an obvious one, is that urged by Mackie.[10] Mackie argues that while it is true that moral good plus physical evil together are better than physical good alone, the issue is not as simple as that, for physical evil also gives rise to and makes possible many moral evils that would not or could not occur in the absence of physical evil. It is then urged that it is not clear that physical evils (for example, disease and pain) plus some moral goods (for example courage) plus some moral evil (for example, brutality) are better than physical good and those moral goods which are possible and which would occur in the absence of physical evil.

This sort of reply, however, is not completely satisfactory. The objection it raises is a sound one, but it proceeds by conceding too much to the theist, and by overlooking two more basic defects of the argument. It allows implicitly that the problem of physical evil may be reduced to the problem of moral evil; and it neglects the two objections which show that the problem of physical evil cannot be so reduced.

The theist therefore happily accepts this kind of reply, and argues that, if he can give a satisfactory account of moral evil he will then have accounted for both physical and moral evil. He then goes on to account for moral evil in terms of the value of free will and/or its goods. This general argument is deceptively plausible. It breaks down for the two reasons indicated here, but it breaks down at another point as well. If free will alone is used to justify moral evil, then even if no moral good occurred, moral evil would still be said to be justified; but physical evil would have no justification. Physical evil is not essential to free will; it is only justified if moral good actually occurs, and if the moral good which results from physical evils outweighs the moral evils. This means that the argument from free will cannot alone justify physical evil along these lines; and it means that the argument from free will and its goods does not justify physical evil, because such an argument is incomplete, and necessarily incomplete. It needs to be supplemented by factual evidence that is logically and practically impossible to obtain.

The correct reply, therefore, is first that the argument is irrelevant to many instances of physical evil, and secondly that it is not true that physical evil plus the moral good it produces is better than physical good and its moral goods. Much pain and suffering, in fact much physical evil generally, for example in children who die in infancy, animals and the insane passes unnoticed; it therefore has no morally uplifting effects upon others, and cannot by virtue of the examples chosen have such effects on the sufferers. Further, there are physical evils such as insanity and much disease to which the argument is inapplicable. So there is a large group of significant cases not covered by the argument. And where the argument is relevant, its premise is plainly false. It can be shown to be false by exposing its implications in the following way.

We either have obligations to lessen physical evil or we have not. If we have obligations to lessen physical evil then we are thereby reducing the total good in the universe. If, on the other hand, our obligation is to increase the total good in the universe it is our duty to prevent the reduction of physical evil and possibly even to increase the total amount of physical evil. Theists usually hold that we are obliged to reduce the physical evil in the universe; but in maintaining this, the theist is, in terms of this account of physical evil, maintaining that it is his duty to reduce the total amount of real good in the universe, and thereby to make the universe worse. Conversely, if by eliminating the physical evil he is not making the universe worse, then that amount of evil which he eliminates was unnecessary and in need of justification. It is relevant to notice here that evil is not always eliminated for morally praiseworthy reasons. Some discoveries have been due to positively unworthy motives, and many other discoveries which have resulted in a lessening of the sufferings of mankind have been due to no higher a motive than a scientist's desire to earn a reasonable living wage.

This reply to the theist's argument brings out its untenability. The theist's argument is seen to imply that war plus courage plus the many other moral virtues war brings into play are better than peace and its virtues; that famine and its moral virtues are better than plenty; that disease and its moral virtues are better than health. Some Christians in the past, in consistency with this mode of reasoning, opposed the use of anaesthetics to leave scope for the virtues of endurance and courage, and they opposed state aid to the sick and needy to leave scope for the virtues of charity and sympathy. Some have even contended that war is a good in disguise, again in consistency with this argument. Similarly the theist should, in terms of this fifth argument, in his heart if not aloud regret the discovery of the Salk polio vaccine because Dr. Salk has in one blow destroyed infinite possibilities of moral good.

There are three important points that need to be made concerning this kind of account of physical evil. (1) We are told, as by Niven, Joyce and others, that pain is a goad to action and that part of its justification lies in this fact. This claim is empirically false as a generalization about all people and all pain. Much pain frustrates action and wrecks people and personalities. On the other hand many men work and work well without being goaded by pain or discomfort. Further, to assert that men need goading is to ascribe another evil to God, for it is to claim that God made men naturally lazy. There is no reason why God should not have many men naturally industrious; the one is no more incompatible with free will than the other. Thus the argument from physical evil being a goad to man breaks down on three distinct counts. Pain often frustrates human endeavor, pain is not essential as a goad with many men, and where pain is a goad to higher endeavours, it is clear that less evil means to this same end are available to an omnipotent God. (2) The real fallacy in the argument is in the assumption that all or the highest moral excellence results from physical evil. As we have already seen, this assumption is completely false. Neither all moral goodness nor the highest moral goodness is triumph in the face of adversity or benevolence towards others in suffering. Christ Himself stressed this when He observed that the two great commandments were commandments to love. Love does not depend for its possibility on the existence and conquest of evil. (3) The "negative" moral virtues which are brought into play by the various evils—courage, endurance, charity, sympathy and the like—besides not representing the highest forms of moral virtue, are in fact commonly supposed by the theist and atheist alike not to have the value this fifth argument ascribes to them. We—theists and atheists alike—reveal our comparative valuations of these virtues and of physical evil when we insist on state aid for the needy; when we strive for peace, for plenty, and for harmony within the state.

In brief, the good man, the morally admirable man, is he who loves what is good knowing that it is good and preferring it because it is good. He does not need to be torn by suffering or by the spectacle of another's sufferings to be morally admirable. Fortitude in his own sufferings, and sympathetic kindness in others' may reveal to us his goodness; but his goodness is not necessarily increased by such things.

Five arguments concerning physical evil have now been examined. We have seen that the problem of physical evil is a problem in its own right, and one that cannot be reduced to the problem of moral evil; and further, we have seen that physical evil creates not one but a number of problems to which no one nor any combination of the arguments examined offers a solution.

PROPOSED SOLUTIONS TO THE PROBLEM OF MORAL EVIL

The problem of moral evil is commonly regarded as being the greater of the problems concerning evil. As we shall see, it does create what appears to be insuperable difficulties for the theist; but so too, apparently, do physical evils.

For the theist moral evil must be interpreted as a breach of God's law and as a rejection of God Himself. It may involve the eternal damnation of the sinner, and in many of its forms it involves the infliction of suffering on other persons. Thus it aggravates the problem of physical evil, but its own peculiar character consists in the fact of sin. How could a morally perfect, all-powerful God create a universe in which occur such moral evils as cruelty, cowardice and hatred, the more especially as these evils constitute a rejection of God Himself by His creations, and as such involve them in eternal damnation?

The two main solutions advanced relate to free will and to the fact that moral evil is a consequence of free will. There is a third kind of solution more often invoked implicitly than as an explicit and serious argument, which need not be examined here as its weaknesses are plainly evident. This third solution is to the effect that moral evils and even the most brutal atrocities have their justification in the moral goodness they make possible or bring into being.

Free will alone provides a justification for moral evil. This is perhaps the more popular of the serious attempts to explain moral evil. The argument in brief runs: men have free will; moral evil is a consequence of free will; a universe in which men exercise free will even with lapses into moral evil is better than a universe in which men become *automata* doing good always because predestined to do so. Thus on this argument it is the mere fact of the supreme value of free will itself that is taken to provide a justification for its corollary, moral evil.

The goods made possible by free will provide a basis for accounting for moral evil. According to this second argument, it is not the mere fact of free will that is claimed to be of such value as to provide a justification of moral evil, but the fact that free will makes certain goods possible. Some indicate the various moral virtues as the goods that free will makes possible, whilst others point to beatitude, and others again to beatitude achieved by man's own efforts or the virtues achieved as a result of one's own efforts. What all these have in common is the claim that the good consequences of free will provide a justification of the bad consequences of free will, namely moral evil.

Each of these two proposed solutions encounters two specific criticisms, which are fatal to their claims to be real solutions.

To consider first the difficulties to which the former proposed solution is exposed. A difficulty for the first argument—that it is free will alone that provides a justification for moral evil—lies in the fact that the theist who argues in this way has to allow that it is logically possible on the free will hypothesis that all men should always will what is evil, and that even so, a universe of completely evil men possessing free will is better than one in which men are predestined to virtuous living. It has to be contended that the value of free will itself is so immense that it more than outweighs the total moral evil, the eternal punishment of the wicked, and the sufferings inflicted on others by the sinners in their evilness. It is this paradox that leads to the formulation of the second argument; and it is to be noted that the explanation of moral evil switches to the second argument or to a combination of the first and second argument, immediately the theist refuses to face the logical possibility of complete wickedness, and insists instead that in fact men do not always choose what is evil.

The second difficulty encountered by the first argument relates to the possibility that free will is compatible with less evil, and even with no evil, that is, with absolute goodness. If it could be shown that free will is compatible with absolute goodness, or even with less moral evil than actually occurs, then all or at least some evil will be left unexplained by free will alone.

Mackie, in his recent paper, and Joyce, in his discussion of this argument, both contend that free will is compatible with absolute goodness. Mackie argues that if it is not possible for God to confer free will on men and at the same time ensure that no moral evil is committed, He cannot really be omnipotent. Joyce directs his argument rather to fellow-theists, and it is more of an *ad hominem* argument addressed to them. He writes:

> Free will need not (as is often assumed) involve the power to choose wrong. Our ability to misuse the gift is due to the conditions under which it is exercised here. In our present state we are able to reject what is truly good, and exercise our power of preference in favour of some baser attrac- 'ion. Yet it is not necessary that it should be so. And all who accept Christian revelation admit that those who attain their final beatitude exercise

freedom of will, and yet cannot choose aught but what is truly good. They possess the knowledge of Essential Goodness; and to it, not simply to good in general, they refer every choice. Moreover, even in our present condition it is open to omnipotence so to order our circumstances and to confer on the will such instinctive impulses that we should in every election adopt the right course and not the wrong one. [11]

To this objection, that free will is compatible with absolute goodness and that therefore a benevolent, omnipotent God would have given man free will and ensured his absolute virtue, it is replied that God is being required to perform what is logically impossible. It is logically impossible, so it is argued, for free will and absolute goodness to be combined, and hence, if God lacks omnipotence only in this respect, He cannot be claimed to lack omnipotence in any sense in which serious theists have ascribed it to Him.

Quite clearly, if free will and absolute goodness are logically incompatible, then God, in not being able to confer both on man, does not lack omnipotence in any important sense of the term. However, it is not clear that free will and absolute goodness are logically opposed; and Joyce does point to considerations which suggest that they are not logical incompatibles. For my own part I am uncertain on this point; but my uncertainty is not a factual one but one concerning a point of usage. It is clear that an omnipotent God could create rational agents predestined always to make virtuous "decisions"; what is not clear is whether we should describe such agents as having free will. The considerations to which Joyce points have something of the status of test cases, and they would suggest that we should describe such agents as having free will. However, no matter how we resolve the linguistic point, the question remains—Which is more desirable, free will and moral evil and the physical evil to which free will gives rise, or this special free will or pseudo-free-will which goes with absolute goodness? I suggest that the latter is clearly preferable. Later I shall endeavor to defend this conclusion; for the moment I am content to indicate the nature of the value judgment on which the question turns at this point.

The second objection to the proposed solution of the problem of moral evil in terms of free will alone is related to the contention that free will is compatible with less moral evil than occurs, and possibly with no moral evil. We have seen what is involved in the latter contention. We may now consider what is involved in the former. It may be argued that free will is compatible with less moral evil than in fact occurs, on various grounds.

(1) God, if He were all-powerful, could miraculously intervene to prevent some or perhaps all moral evil; and He is said to do so on occasions in answer to prayers (for example, to prevent wars) or of His own initiative (for instance, by producing calamities which serve as warnings, or by working miracles, and so forth). (2) God has made man with a certain nature. This nature is often interpreted by theologians as having a bias to evil. Clearly God could have created man with a strong bias to good, whilst still leaving scope for a decision to act evilly. Such a bias to good would be compatible with freedom of the will. (3) An omnipotent God could so have ordered the world that it was less conducive to the practice of evil.

These are all considerations advanced by Joyce, and separately and jointly, they establish that God could have conferred free will upon us, and at least very considerably *reduced* the amount of moral evil that would have resulted from the exercise of free will. This is sufficient to show that *not all* the moral evil that exists can be justified by reference to free will alone. This conclusion is fatal to the account of moral evil in terms of free will alone. The more extreme conclusion that Mackie seeks to establish—that absolute goodness is compatible with free will—is not essential as a basis for refuting the free will argument. The difficulty is as fatal to the claims of theism whether all moral evil or only some moral evil is unaccountable. However, whether Mackie's contentions are sound is still a matter of logical interest, although not of any real moment in the context of the case against theism, once the fact that less moral evil is compatible with free will has been established.

The second free will argument arises out of an attempt to circumvent these objections. It is not free will, but the value of the goods achieved through free will that is said to be so great as to provide a justification for moral evil.

This second argument meets a difficulty in that it is now necessary for it to be supplemented by a proof that the number of people who practice moral virtue or who attain beatitude or who attain beatitude and/or virtue after a struggle is sufficient to outweigh the evilness of moral evil, the evilness of their eternal damnation and the physical evil they cause to others. This is a serious defect in the argument, because it means that the argument can at best show that moral evil *may have* a justification, and not that it has a justification. It is both logically and practically impossible to supplement and complete the argument. It is necessarily incomplete and inconclusive, even if its general principle is sound.

This second argument is designed also to avoid the other difficulty of the first argument—that free will may be compatible with no evil and certainly with less evil. It is argued that even if free will is compatible with absolute goodness it is still better that virtue and beatitude be attained after a genuine personal struggle; and this, it is said, would not occur if God, in conferring free will, nonetheless prevented moral evil or reduced the risk of it. Joyce argues in this way: "To receive our final beatitude as the fruit of our labours, and as the recompense of a hard-won victory, is an incomparably higher destiny than to receive it without any effort on our part. And since God in His wisdom has seen fit to give us such a lot as this, it was inevitable that man should have the power to choose wrong. We could not be called to merit the reward due to victory without being exposed to the possibility of defeat." [12]

There are various objections which may be urged here. First, this argument implies that the more intense the struggle, the greater is the triumph and resultant good, and the better the world; hence we should apparently, on this argument, court temptation and moral struggles to attain greater virtue and to be more worthy of our reward. Secondly, it may be urged that God is being said to be demanding too high a price for the goods produced. He is omniscient. He knows that many will sin and not attain the goods or the Good free will is said to make possible. He creates men with free will, with the natures men have, in the world as it is constituted, knowing that in His doing so He is committing many to moral evil and eternal damnation. He could avoid all this evil by creating men with rational wills predestined to virtue, or He could eliminate much of it by making men's natures and the conditions in the world more conducive to the practice of virtue. He is said not to choose to do this. Instead, at the cost of the sacrifice of the many, He is said to have ordered things so as to allow fewer men to attain this higher virtue and higher beatitude that result from the more intense struggle.

In attributing such behavior to God, and in attempting to account for moral evil along these lines, theists are, I suggest, attributing to God immoral behaviour of a serious kind—of a kind we should all unhesitatingly condemn in a fellow human being.

We do not commend people for putting temptation in the way of others. On the contrary, anyone who today advocated, or even allowed where he could prevent it, the occurrence of evil and the sacrifice of the many—even as a result of their own freely chosen actions—for the sake of the higher virtue of the few, would be condemned as an immoralist. To put severe temptation in the way of the many, knowing that many and perhaps even most will succumb to the temptation, for the sake of the higher virtue of the few, would be blatant immorality; and it would be immoral whether or not those who yielded to the temptation possessed free will. This point can be brought out by considering how a conscientious moral agent would answer the question: Which should I choose for other people, a world in which there are intense moral struggles and the possibility of magnificent triumphs and the certainty of many defeats, or a world in which there are less intense struggles, less magnificent triumphs but more triumphs and fewer defeats, or a world in which there are no struggles, no triumphs and no defeats? We are constantly answering less easy questions than this in a way that conflicts with the theist's contentions. If by modifying our own behavior we can save someone else from an intense moral struggle and almost certain moral evil, for example if by refraining from gambling or excessive drinking ourselves we can help a weaker person not to become a confirmed gambler or an alcoholic, or if by locking our car and not leaving it unlocked and with the key in it we can prevent people yielding to the temptation to become car thieves, we feel obliged to act accordingly, even though the person concerned would freely choose the evil course of conduct. How much clearer is the decision with which God is said to be faced—the choice between the higher virtue of some and the evil of others, or the higher but less high virtue of many more, and the evil of many fewer. None of the alternatives denies free will to men.

These various difficulties dispose of each of the main arguments relating to moral evil. There are in addition to these difficulties two other objections that might be urged.

If it could be shown that man has not free will both arguments collapse; and even if it could be shown that God's omniscience is incompatible with free will they would still break down. The issues raised here are too great to be pursued in this paper; and they can simply be noted as possible additional grounds from which criticisms of the main proposed solutions of the problem of moral evil may be advanced.

The other general objection is by way of a follow-up to points made in the second objection to both arguments above. It concerns the relative value of free will and its goods and evils and the value of the best of the alternatives to free will and its goods. Are free will and its goods so much more valuable than the next best alternatives that their superior value can really justify the immense amount of evil that is introduced into the world by free will?

Theologians who discuss this issue ask, Which is better—men with free will striving to work out their destinies, or automata, machine-like creatures, who never make mistakes because they never make decisions? When put in this form we naturally doubt whether free will plus moral evil plus the possibility of the eternal damnation of the many and the physical evil of untold billions are quite so unjustified after all; but the fact of the matter is that the question has not been fairly put. The real alternative is, on the other hand, rational agents with free wills making many bad and some good decisions on rational and nonrational grounds, and "rational" agents predestined always "to choose" the right things for the right reasons—that is, if the language of automata must be used, rational automata. Predestination does not imply the absence of rationality in all senses of that term. God, were He omnipotent, could preordain the decisions and the reasons upon which they were based; and such a mode of existence would seem to be in itself a worthy mode of existence, and one preferable to an existence with free will, irrationality and evil.

CONCLUSION

In this paper it has been maintained that God, were He all-powerful and perfectly good, would have created a world in which there was no unnecessary evil. It has not been argued that God ought to have created a perfect world, nor that He should have made one that is in any way logically impossible. It has simply been argued that a benevolent God could, and would, have created a world devoid of superfluous evil. It has been contended that there is evil in this world—unnecessary evil—and that the more popular and philosophically more significant of the many attempts to explain this evil are completely unsatisfactory. Hence we must conclude from the existence of evil that there cannot be an omnipotent, benevolent God.

NOTES

1. Mackie, "Evil and Omnipotence," *Mind*, 1955.
2. Joyce, *Principles of Natural Theology*, chapter 17. All subsequent quotations from Joyce in this paper are from this chapter of this work.
3. Ibid.
4. Ibid.
5. P. 244, Garnett translation, Heinemann.
6. Joyce, chapter 17.

7. Ibid.

8. Wisdom, *Mind*, 1931.

9. W. D. Niven, *Encyclopedia of Religion and Ethics.* Joyce's corresponding argument runs:

"Pain is the great stimulant to action. Man no less than animals is impelled to work by the sense of hunger. Experience shows that, were it not for this motive the majority of men would be content to live in indolent ease. Man must earn his bread.

"One reason plainly why God permits suffering is that man may rise to a height of heroism which would otherwise have been beyond his scope. Nor are these the only benefits which it confers. That sympathy for others which is one of the most precious parts of our experience, and one of the most fruitful sources of well-doing, has its origin in the fellow-feeling engendered by endurance of similar trials. Furthermore, were it not for these trials, man would think little enough of a future existence, and of the need of striving after his last end. He would be perfectly content with his existence, and would reck little of any higher good. These considerations here briefly advanced suffice at least to show how important is the office filled by pain in human life, and with what little reason it is asserted that the existence of so much suffering is irreconcilable with the wisdom of the Creator."

And:

"It may be asked whether the Creator could not have brought man to perfection without the use of suffering. Most certainly He could have conferred upon him a similar degree of virtue without requiring any effort on his part. Yet it is easy to see that there is a special value attaching to a conquest of difficulties such as man's actual demands, and that in God's eyes this may well be an adequate reason for assigning this life to us in preference to another. . . . Pain has value in respect to the next life, but also in respect to this. The advance of scientific discovery, the gradual improvement of the organization of the community, the growth of material civilization are due in no small degree to the stimulus afforded by pain."

10. Mackie, "Evil and Omnipotence," *Mind*, 1955.

11. Joyce, chapter 17.

12. Ibid.

VIII. God and a Fated Universe

Antony Flew

Divine Omnipotence and Human Freedom

Antony Flew, professor of philosophy at the University of Reading, was educated at St. John's College, Oxford University. His books include: *A New Approach to Psychical Research* (1953); *Hume's Philosophy of Belief* (1961); *God and Philosophy* (1966); *Evolutionary Ethics* (1967); and *An Introduction to Western Philosophy* (1971). He has edited or co-edited such anthologies as: *Logic and Language*, volume I (1951), volume II (1953); *New Essays in Philosophical Theology* (1955, with A. C. MacIntyre); *Essays in Conceptual Analysis* (1956); *Hume on Human Nature and the Understanding* (1962); and *Body, Mind and Death* (1964). He has contributed articles to many professional journals and encyclopedias.

"Either God cannot abolish evil, or he will not; if he cannot, then he is not all-powerful; if he will not, then he is not all good." [1] Perhaps the most powerful of all skeptical arguments, this has appealed especially to the clearest and most direct minds, striking straight and decisively to the heart

From the Hibbert Journal *53 (January 1955): 135-44. Reprinted by permission of the author and the Hibbert Trust.*

of the matter. It was, for instance, central to J. S. Mill's rejection of Christianity. He returns to it repeatedly, and often angrily, throughout his *Three Essays on Religion*[2]. Consider, for instance, his reference to "the impossible problem of reconciling infinite benevolence and justice with infinite power in the Creator of such a world as this. The attempt to do so not only involves absolute contradiction in an intellectual point of view but exhibits to excess the revolting spectacle of a jesuitical defence of moral enormities."

(1) These are robust words, yet not quite final. Several determined efforts have been made to escape from the dilemma. One favorite—which might be dubbed the Freewill Defense—runs like this. The first move is to point out: "Nothing which implies contradiction falls under the omnipotence of God"[3]; that is, even God cannot do what is *logically* impossible; that is, if you make up a self-contradictory, a nonsense sentence it won't miraculously become sense just because you have put the word *God* as its subject. The third formulation is greatly superior to the other two, because it brings out the nature of *logical* impossibility. It should appeal to theologians, as being free of the unwanted and of course entirely incorrect suggestion that being unable to do the *logically* impossible is some sort of limitation on or weakness in Omnipotence; whereas, they should say, the only limitation or weakness lies in men who contradict themselves and talk nonsense about God.[4] The second move in this defense is to claim: "God gave men free will"; and that this necessarily implies the possibility of doing evil as well as good, that is to say that there would be a contradiction in speaking, it would be nonsense to speak, of creatures with freedom to choose good or evil but not able to choose evil. (Which, no blame to him, is what his creatures, men, have done.) This may be followed by a third rather less common move: to point out that certain good things, namely, certain virtues, logically presuppose not merely beings with freedom of choice (which alone are capable of either virtue or vice), and consequently the possibility of evil, but also the actual occurrence of certain evils. Thus what we might call the second-order goods of sympathetic feeling and action logically could not occur without (at least the appearance of) the first-order evils of suffering or misfortune. And the moral good of forgiveness presupposes the prior occurrence of (at least the appearance of) some lower-order moral evil to be forgiven. This may be already a second-order evil such as callousness, thus making the forgiveness a third-order good. Here one recalls: *O felix culpa quae tantum et talem meruit habere redemptorem.*[5]

The upshot is that there are certain goods, e.g. moral virtues, which logically presuppose the possibility of correlative evils, and others, e.g. the virtues of forgiveness and sympathetic action, which logically presuppose the actuality (of at least the appearance) of certain evils, in this case the doing of injuries and the suffering of misfortunes. Thus it would not make sense to suggest that God might have chosen to achieve these goods without the possibility in the one case, the actuality in the other, of the correlative and presupposed evils. Unfortunately men have chosen to misuse their freedom by choosing to exploit the possibility of wrongdoing necessarily involved in the possibility of rightdoing. But this is not God's fault: or at any rate it does not show that God *cannot* be both all powerful and all good.

(2) This is a powerful defense, which has satisfied many believers, and routed, or at least rattled, many skeptics. The usual counterattacks, which we have here no space to deploy, lack the simple, seemingly decisive force of the original dilemma. Although they still constitute a formidable challenge, they leave the believer with some freedom of maneuver.

(3) This account in terms of move and counter-move is only a crudely stylized cartoon, without the panoply of distinctions and refinements required to do justice to the full complexity of the logical situation. But its purpose is merely to set the stage for the launching of a further new, or at least unusual, skeptical counterattack. This is directed at the key position of the whole Freewill Defense: the idea that there is a contradiction involved in saying that God might have made people so that they always in fact *freely* chose the right. If there is no contradiction here then Omnipotence might have made a world inhabited by wholly virtuous people; the entire Freewill Defense collapses; and we are back again with the original intractable antinomy.

(a) The first phase consists in bringing out what is meant by "acting freely," "being free to choose" and so on: particularly that none of these concepts necessarily involve unpredictable or uncaused action. A paradigm case of acting freely, of being free to choose, would be the marriage of two normal young people, when there was no question of the parties "having to get married," and no social or parental pressure on either of them—a case which is scarcely rare. To say that Murdo was free to ask whichever eligible girl of his acquaintance he wanted, and that he chose to ask, was accepted by, and has now of his own free will married Mairi, is not to say: that his actions and choices were uncaused or in principle unpredictable; but precisely and only that, being of an age to know his own mind, he did what he did and rejected possible alternative courses of action without being under any pressure to act in this way. Indeed those who know Murdo and Mairi may have known what was going to happen long before the day of the wedding. And if it is the case that one day a team of psychologists and physiologists will be able to predict a person's behavior far more completely and successfully than even his best friends now can, even up to 100 percent completely and successfully, still this will not show that he never acts freely, can never choose between alternatives, deciding for himself on the one which most appeals to him (or on the one which is most uncongenial for that matter, if that is what he chooses to do). Unless they produce evidence that there was obstruction or pressure or an absence of alternatives, their discoveries will not even be relevant to questions about his freedom of choice, much less a decisive disproof of the manifest fact that sometimes he has complete, sometimes restricted, and sometimes no freedom.

Again: to say that a person could have helped doing something is not to say that what he did was in principle unpredictable nor that there were no causes anywhere which in some sense determined that he would as a matter of fact act in this way. It is to say that *if* he had chosen to do otherwise he would have been able to do so; that there were alternatives, within the capacities of one of his physical strength, of his IQ, with his knowledge, and open to a person in his situation. As before, the meaning of the key phrase "could have helped it" can be elucidated by looking at simple paradigm cases—such as those in which fastidious language-users employ it when the madness of metaphysics is not upon them; such as those by reference to which the expression is, and ultimately has always to be explained. If, as Damon Runyon might have put it, these are not cases of acting freely (etc.), still they will at least do till such cases come along.

Now if this sort of argument is sound, then there is no contradiction involved in saying that a particular action or choice was: *both* free, and could have been helped, and so on; *and* predictable, or even foreknown, and explicable in terms of caused causes. Of course it is not possible here to establish that it *is* sound, but it is to the point to mention that this is the line taken by Hobbes and Hume and—though the problem did not present itself to him in quite the same terms—even Aristotle among the classical philosophers; and which is now being confidently pursued with great subtlety through many ramifications by the majority of those contemporary English-speaking philosophers who have tackled any of the puzzles about free will.[6] Again, it is the doctrine of the Roman Church that God's foreknowledge is not incompatible with man's freedom. Again, if this sort of compatibilism is wrong then it will be possible to fit human freedom into the world only in the gaps of scientific ignorance. Finally, if it is wrong then it is hard to see what meaning these expressions have and how if at all they could ever be taught, understood, or correctly used.

(b) The second phase, once we are clear of misconceptions about the meaning of "acting freely" and so on, is to argue that: not only is there no necessary conflict between acting freely and behaving predictably and/or as a result of caused causes; but also Omnipotence might have, could without contradiction be said to have, created only people who would always as a matter of fact freely have chosen to do the right thing. Now we have already argued to the effect that there is no contradiction in saying both that Murdo chose to marry Mairi of his own free will; and that he would not have chosen to do this if his endocrine glands had not as a matter of fact been in such and such a state, that is, that his glandular condition was one of many causes of his choice. Whether or not it is the case that hypothetical propositions of this sort could be truly asserted of any and every piece of human behavior; whether or not, that is, every human action, decision and reaction actually has physiological causes: still to say that this is so and to say that people sometimes can help doing what they do, do act freely, and so on is not necessarily to contradict oneself.

It might be objected that if Murdo acted because his glands were in such and such a state then he cannot have chosen Mairi because he wanted to be married to her: that the one explanation excludes the other.[7] But this is not so. For the one assigns a physiological cause, gives a, but not presumably the only, such precondition, the absence of which would have been followed by the absence of Murdo's action; while the other indicates his motive, again perhaps not the only one. But to say that and in what way a piece of behavior was motivated is not to deny that it was caused. Compare the analogous mistake of thinking: that if I think as I do because of such and such physiological causes or because of such and such motives (i.e. if there are physiological conditions without which I should not think as I do, or if I want to think as I do); then it *cannot* also be the case that there are, and I have sufficient reasons, arguments, grounds for thinking as I do. The word *because* is multiply ambiguous: there are many different sorts of explanations, which do not necessarily exclude one another, as many sorts as there are sorts of questions.[8]

It might be objected—this is really the same objection differently wrapped—that in one situation described it is not really Murdo or Mairi but their glands which made the decision. But again we appeal to the Argument of the Paradigm Case.[9] If this is not a case of Murdo deciding, then what is? What then would be *meant* by "Murdo deciding"? Again, glands are not people. So it is only a misleading metaphor to speak of glands *deciding* anything. And someone's glands are not *other people* taking decisions out of his hands, railroading him into action against his will or fixing things irrevocably before he comes along. They are *parts* of him, without which he would not be what he is.[10]

Returning to the thesis from these objections: if it really is logically possible for an action to be both freely chosen and yet fully determined by caused causes, what has become of the keystone argument of the Freewill Defense, that there is a contradiction in speaking of God so arranging the laws of nature that all men always as a matter of fact freely choose to do the right? If this goes it looks as if the third move in that Defense can involve little more than a delaying action by the believer, a mopping-up operation for the triumphant skeptic.

The skeptic might try to say that only some of those higher-order goods which logically presuppose their appropriate lower-order evils necessarily require for their display the actual occurrence of the evils in question, and that not all the moral goods are second order. (However, they all without exception do presuppose freedom; see Kant and everybody else.) For someone could exercise forgiveness when he thought, but mistakenly, he had been injured; and virtues such as honesty and intellectual integrity are not in any way parasitical on antecedent evils, moral or non-moral. But this would leave the argument untouched insofar as it applied to virtues such as fortitude in bearing pain, which requires for its actual exercise actual pain; and someone could also reply, rather lamely, that even the appearance of injury, which is the minimum requirement for the exercise of forgiveness, must be counted as some sort of lower-order evil.

What the skeptic should say is that if there is no contradiction in suggesting that Omnipotence might so arrange his creation that all men always would freely choose the right, then there would be no need for any vale of soul-making. The end product, a person who, no matter what the temptations, always would choose the right, could have been produced without: *either* the evil involved in the creation of those who wickedly choose damnation and therefore have to pay the penalty; *or* the evil necessary for the actual exercise of those virtues which cannot be exercised without the actual occurrence of the evil logically required to make them possible. Omnipotence could have evolved creatures who he could have been sure *would* respond to the appropriate challenge by a willing exercise of fortitude, without these creatures having to acquire this character by any *actual* exercise of fortitude. What it would still make no sense to suggest would be that God could have had *actual* displays of, say, fortitude or could himself have *actually* forgiven anyone without there being the evil of pain to be endured or of sin to be forgiven.[11]

(4) We cannot hope here even to begin to meet objections to the theses of (3) based on the rejection of the idea that freedom and universal causal determinism are not necessarily incompatible. In any case the argument in this section is to take a turn which will put an entirely new complexion on everything said so far. But suppose now that someone who accepted this reconciling idea raised the objection that what has been shown is: *not* that there is no contradiction in speaking of God so arranging His creation that all men always would as a matter of fact freely choose the right; *but* that there is no contradiction in speaking of a world in which there are always antecedent conditions of all human action sufficient to ensure that agents always will as a matter of fact freely choose the right.

The nerve of this distinction lies in the personality of God, which makes a crucial difference. In the former case a quasi-personal being has fixed everything that everyone will do, and choose, and suffer. In the latter case it has not been fixed by some personal or quasi-personal agent, but it just happens to be the case that there always have been, are, and will be, antecedent conditions sufficient to ensure that human agents will act in the particular way they do act, and not in any other. This latter is the doctrine of determinism, carefully formulated to specify only conditions sufficient to ensure that that agent will in fact act in particular ways, not conditions which make such action in the most fundamental sense inevitable and unavoidable. (That second, carefully eschewed specification would be incoherent; since the very idea of action surely involves that in that same fundamental sense the agent always could do other than he does.)[12] The former doctrine is the doctrine of predestination: "God from all eternity did by the most wise and holy counsel of His own will, freely and unchangeably ordain whatsoever comes to pass."[13]

Now, the argument would run, whereas determinism is perhaps compatible with human freedom and the fair ascription of responsibility to human agents, predestination certainly is not. For consider the phenomenon of post-hypnotic suggestion: "A subject is hypnotized, and told that after a precise time interval ... he is to carry out some series of actions. . . . When he is awakened from the hypnotic trance he remembers nothing of these instructions. Nevertheless, when the prescribed time is up, he will carry out the program in every detail. If he is asked why he is behaving in this curious fashion, he will usually produce some highly ingenious rationalization. . . . "[14]

Predestination seems to make out that all of us, all the time, whether we know it or not, *both* when by ordinary standards we are acting freely and could help doing what we choose to do *and* when we are acting under compulsion or when we are not acting at all but are asleep or paralyzed— all of us are, really and ultimately, as it were, acting out the irresistible suggestions of the Great Hypnotist. This idea is incompatible with that of our being free agents, properly accountable for what we do. Hence there is, after all, "a contradiction in speaking of God so arranging the laws of nature that all men always as a matter of fact freely choose to do the right."

This is an apparently conclusive argument. Yet it is completely though subtly mistaken. Certainly if we were to discover that a particular person or a particular group of people, whom previously we had thought to be acting freely, and properly accountable for what they did, had in fact been acting out the post-hypnotic suggestions of some master hypnotist— then indeed we should need to reconsider all questions of their accountability in the light of this fresh information. It would not prove that they were not *in any degree* responsible, even if we knew that this hypnotist's suggestions were irresistible. For there would remain the question whether they willingly put themselves in his power knowing what this might involve. Here the analogy is with the man who knows that he is not responsible for what he does when he is drunk but who could have helped getting into that state.[15] What our information would be sufficient to prove is that there was someone else besides the apparent agent, namely the hypnotist, who is at least partly responsible, at least an accessory before the fact. Here the analogy is to the boss who sends one of his gang to do a job, or to the man who sets a booby-trap and leaves it where his victim will certainly spring it.

But the case of predestination, where the hypnotist would not be a human being but God, is essentially different. First, because here there is no question of any of us being in any way responsible for allowing ourselves to fall under the spell of this hypnotist. Second, because here it is not a matter of some being divinely hypnotized, and some not; or all being so for part of the time, and part not; but of absolutely everyone from the beginning to the end of time being hypnotized all the time. The first reaction to the idea of God, the Great Hypnotist, is that this would mean that no one ever was or had been or would be *really* responsible, that none of the people who we should otherwise have been certain could have helped doing things *really* could. And so on. But this is at least very misleading. Certainly it would be monstrous to suggest that anyone, however truly responsible to and in the eyes of men, could fairly be called to account and be punished by the God who had rigged his every move. All the bitter words which have ever been written against the wickedness of the God of predestinationism—especially when he is also thought of as filling Hell with all but the elect—are amply justified.[16] But this is not sufficient to show that every application of the phrases "acted freely," "had a choice," "made his own decisions" and so forth must have been wrong if predestination is true. Again remember the Argument of the Paradigm Case. The *meaning* of these phrases has been given in terms of certain familiar human situations. No new information, not even on a matter of theological fact, can conceivably show that such phrases cannot correctly be applied to such defining cases.[17]

The objection therefore cannot be sustained. The true position seems to be: that while there is no "contradiction in speaking of God as so arranging the laws of nature that all men always as a matter of fact freely choose to do the right"; still the idea of God arraigning and punishing anyone who freely chose the wrong, if he had so arranged the laws of nature that his victim would so act, "outrages . . . the most ordinary justice and humanity."[18] Thus while the Calvinist picture—the Great Hypnotist—is appropriate in its appreciation of the implications of Omnipotence, it is morally obnoxious insofar as it presents human creatures as *justly* accountable to that Omnipotence. The usual alternative—the Father sending his sons out into the world—is appropriate insofar as it recognizes the facts of human freedom and responsibility in a human context, but quite wrong in making out that Omnipotence could, like a human father, justly rebuke and even punish a prodigal for what in the human sense he freely did.

Either God cannot abolish evil or he will not: if he cannot then he is not all powerful; if he will not then he is not all good.

NOTES

1. In the first version of this article, published in the *Hibbert Journal* in 1955, and in the later and longer version published in A. Flew and A. C. MacIntyre (eds.) *New Essays in Philosophical Theology* (London and New York: SCM Press and Macmillan, 1955 and 1956), I mistakenly attributed this formulation to St. Augustine of Hippo. My error was pointed out to me by Dr. John Burnaby of St. John's College, Cambridge. I welcome this first opportunity both to thank him and to correct the mistake publicly.

2. London: Longmans, 1874: The passage about to be quoted is at pp. 186-87. This powerful and lucid book has been curiously neglected: even such a philosophical scholar as the late Professor A. N. Prior overlooked the essay on "Nature," which is centrally relevant to his *Logic and the Basis of Ethics* (Oxford: Clarendon, 1949). The essay "Theism" is chiefly remarkable for the fact that Mill, though rejecting the Christian revelation, and consequently not "incumbered with the necessity of admitting the omnipotence of the Creator" (p. 186), was still, in spite of Hume and Darwin, sufficiently impressed with the Argument to Design to explore at length the idea of a finite God, allowing "a large balance of probability in favour of creation by intelligence" (p. 174).

3. St. Thomas Aquinas, *Summa Theologica*, IA XXV, Art. 4.

4. Compare J. M. E. McTaggart, *Some Dogmas of Religion* (London: Arnold, 1906 and 1930), S 166; where the whole notion of Divine Omnipotence is attacked, and rejected, on these inept grounds.

5. "O happy fault, which deserved to have such and so great a Redeemer": the sentence is taken from the Roman Catholic *Missal*.

6. See, for instance, *Leviathan*, Ch. XXI and the pamphlet "Of Liberty and Necessity"; *An Enquiry Concerning Human Understanding*, S VII and *A Treatise of Human Nature*, II (iii) 1-3; and *Nicomachean Ethics*, III (i-v) and V (viii).

7. Compare *Phaedo* 98 B7ff.

8. See my "A Rational Animal" in J. R. Smythies (ed.) *Brain and Mind* (London: Routledge and Kegan Paul, 1965).

9. See J. O. Urmson's article under that title, in the *Revue Internationale de Philosophie* for 1963; and compare my "Again the Paradigm," in P. Feyerabend and G. Maxwell (eds.) *Mind, Matter and Method* (Minneapolis: University of Minnesota Press, 1966).

10. Hence the Alice in Wonderland quality of "I sat down to interview my brains"—John Dalmas in R. Chandler, *Trouble Is My Business* (Harmondsworth: Penguin, undated), p. 145.

11. Professor C. S. Lewis offered, in *The Problem of Pain* (London: Bles, 1940), pp. 89-90, an extraordinary argument to meet the objection "If God is omniscient He must have known what Abraham would do, without any experiment; why then this needless torture?" (of actually going through with it). "The reality of Abraham's obedience was the act itself; and what God knew in knowing that Abraham 'would obey' was Abraham's actual obedience on that mountain top at that moment. To say that God 'need not have tried the experiment' is to say that because God knows, the thing known by God need not exist." But this is not so at

all. Any plausibility Lewis's argument may have derives from an ambiguity in *would*. For the objector is saying that Omniscience must know how people *would* behave if they *were* to be tested, whereas Lewis is replying that He could not know that they *will* in future so behave unless they *are* in fact going so to behave. The reply is simply irrelevant.

12. I try in several later papers to explain what this most fundamental sense of "could have done otherwise" is, and how it is presupposed by but differs from the sense in which we might say that one of the victims of *The Godfather* received an offer which he could not refuse or that Luther at Worms could do no other than he did. See, for instance, "Is There a Problem of Freedom?" in E. Pivcevic (ed.), *Phenomenology and Philosophical Understanding* (Cambridge University Press, 1975) especially pp. 84-86; and "Hume and Historical Inevitability" in my *A Rational Animal* (London and New York: Oxford University Press, forthcoming).

13. The *Westminster Confession* of 1649.

14. R. and M. Knight, *A Modern Introduction to Psychology* (London: University Tutorial Press, 1948), p. 212.

15. Compare Aristotle, *Nicomachean Ethics*, III (v) 8: 1113 b 31ff.

16. "The recognition, for example, of the object of highest worship in a being who could make a Hell; and who could create countless generations of human beings with the certain foreknowledge that he was creating them for this fate. . . . Any other of the outrages to the most ordinary justice and humanity involved in the common Christian conception of the moral character of God sinks into insignificance beside this dreadful idealization of wickedness." (*Three Essays on Religion*, pp. 113-114). Compare the *Westminster Confession:* "By the decree of God, for the manifestation of His glory, some men and angels are predestined unto everlasting life, and others foreordained to everlasting death."

17. Thus the Calvinists and other clearheaded predestinarian theologians were quite right to insist that "God from all eternity did . . . freely and unchangeably ordain whatsoever comes to pass. Yet . . . thereby" is no "violence offered to the will of the creatures." What was wrong was to suggest that in such a case "neither is God the author of sin" and that *God* could fairly hold men accountable. (All the quotations in this note come from the *Westminster Confession*.)

18. Thus Calvin said that the damned are damned "by a just and irreprehensible, but incomprehensible judgment." Luther agrees: "The highest degree of faith is to believe He is just, though of His own will He makes us . . . proper subjects for damnation. . . . If I could by any means understand how this same God . . . can yet be merciful and just, there would be no need for faith" (*The Bondage of the Will*, tr. J. I. Packer and O. R. Johnson [London: J. Clarke, 1957], II 7).

IX. Ethics Without God

Kai Nielsen

⌐ Morality and the Will of God

Kai Nielsen, professor of philosophy at the University of Calgary, was educated at Duke University and has taught at New York University, Amherst College, University of Ottawa and Brooklyn College, and has lectured in Europe and Africa. He is an editor of the *Canadian Journal of Philosophy*. His books include: *Reason and Practice* (1971); *Contemporary Critiques of Religion* (1971); *Scepticism* (1973); and *Ethics Without God* (1973), from which this selection is taken. He has written extensively on a variety of subjects in professional journals and encyclopedias.

1

It is the claim of many influential Jewish and Christian theologians (Brunner, Buber, Barth, Niebuhr and Bultmann—to take outstanding examples) that the only genuine basis for morality is in religion. And any old religion is not good enough. The only truly adequate foundation for moral belief is a religion that acknowledges that absolute sovereignty of

This article first appeared in the book Ethics Without God, *by Kai Nielsen, published by Prometheus Books, Buffalo, N.Y., and is reprinted by permission.*

the Lord, found in the prophetic religions.

These theologians will readily grant what is plainly true, namely, that as a matter of fact many nonreligious people behave morally, but they contend that without a belief in God and his law there is no ground or reason for being moral. The sense of moral relativism, skepticism and nihilism rampant in our age is due in large measure to the general weakening of religious belief in an age of science. Without God there can be no objective foundation for our moral beliefs. As Brunner puts it,[1] "The believer alone clearly perceives that the Good, as it is recognized in faith, is the sole Good, and all that is otherwise called good cannot lay claim to this title, at least in the ultimate sense of the word . . . The Good consists in always doing what God wills at any particular moment." Moreover, this moral Good can only be attained by our "unconditional obedience" to God, the ground of our being. Without God life would have no point and morality would have no basis. Without religious belief, without the Living God, there could be no adequate answer to the persistently gnawing questions: What ought we to do? How ought I to live?

Is this frequently repeated claim justified? Are our moral beliefs and conceptions based on or grounded in a belief in the God of Judaism, Christianity and Islam? In trying to come to grips with this question, we need to ask ourselves three fundamental questions.

(1) Is being willed by God the, or even a, *fundamental* criterion for that which is so willed being morally good or for its being something that ought to be done?

(2) Is being willed by God the *only* criterion for that which is so willed being morally good or for its being something that ought to be done?

(3) Is being willed by God the only *adequate* criterion for that which is so willed being morally good or being something that ought to be done?

I shall argue that the fact that God wills something—if indeed that is a fact—cannot be a fundamental criterion for its being morally good or obligatory and thus it cannot be the only criterion or the only adequate criterion for moral goodness or obligation.

By way of preliminaries we should first get clear what is meant by a fundamental criterion. When we speak of the criterion for the goodness of an action or attitude, we speak of some measure or test by virtue of which we may decide which actions or attitudes are good or desirable, or, at least, are the least undesirable of the alternate actions or attitudes open to us. A moral criterion is the measure we use for determining the value or worth of an action, principle, rule or attitude. We have such a measure or test when we have some generally relevant considerations by which we may decide whether something is whatever it is said to be. A fundamental moral criterion is (1) a test or measure used to judge the legitimacy of moral rules and/or acts or attitudes, and (2) a measure that one would give up last if one were reasoning morally. (In reality, there probably is no single fundamental criterion, although there are fundamental criteria.)

There is a further preliminary matter we need to consider. In asking about the basis or authority for our moral beliefs we are not asking about how we came to have them. If you ask someone where he got his moral beliefs, he, to be realistic, should answer that he got them from his parents, parent surrogates, teachers.[2] They are beliefs which he has been conditioned to accept. But the validity or soundness of a belief is independent of its origin. When one person naïvely asks another where he got his moral beliefs, most likely he is not asking how he came by them, but rather (1) on what authority he holds these beliefs, or (2) what good reasons or justification he has for these moral beliefs. He should answer that he does not and cannot hold these beliefs on any authority. It is indeed true that many of us turn to people for moral advice and guidance in moral matters, but if we do what we do simply because it has been authorized, we cannot be reasoning and acting as moral agents; for to respond as a moral agent, one's moral principle must be something which is subscribed to by one's own deliberate commitment, and it must be something for which one is prepared to give reasons.

Keeping these preliminary clarifications in mind, we can return to my claim that the fact (if indeed it is a fact) that God has commanded, willed or ordained something cannot, in the very nature of the case, be a fundamental criterion for claiming that whatever is commanded, willed or ordained *ought* to be done.

2

Some perceptive remarks made by A. C. Ewing will carry us part of the way.[3] Theologians like Barth and Brunner claim that ethical principles gain their justification because they are God's decrees. But as Ewing points out, if "being obligatory" means just "willed by God," it becomes unintelligible to ask why God wills one thing rather than another. In fact, there can be no reason for his willing one thing rather than another, for his willing it *eo ipso* makes whatever it is he wills good, right or obligatory. "God wills it because it ought·to be done" becomes "God wills it because

God wills it"; but the first sentence, even as used by the most ardent believer, is not a tautology. "If it were said in reply that God's commands determine what we ought to do but that these commands were only issued
because it was good that they should be or because obedience to them did
good, this would still make judgments about the good, at least, independent of the will of God, and we should not have given a definition of all
fundamental ethical concepts in terms of God or made ethics dependent
on God."[4] Furthermore, it becomes senseless to say what the believer very
much wants to say, namely, "I ought always to do what God wills" if
"what I ought to do" and "what God wills" have the same meaning. And
to say I ought to do what God wills because I love God makes the independent assumption that I ought to love God and that I ought to do what God
wills if I love him.

Suppose we say instead that we ought to do what God wills because
God will punish us if we do not obey him. This may indeed be a cogent,
self-interested or prudential reason for doing what God commands, but it
is hardly a morally good reason for doing what he commands since such
considerations of self-interest cannot be an adequate basis for morality. A
powerful being—an omnipotent and omniscient being—speaking out of
the whirlwind cannot by his mere commands create an obligation. Ewing
goes on to assert: "Without a prior conception of God as good or his
commands as right, God would have no more claim on our obedience than
Hitler or Stalin except that he would have more power than even they had
to make things uncomfortable for those who disobey him."[5] Unless we assume that God is morally perfect, unless we assume the perfect goodness
of God, there can be no necessary "relation between being commanded or
willed by God and being obligatory or good."[6]

To this it is perfectly correct to reply that as believers we must believe
that God is wholly and completely good, the most perfect of all conceivable
beings.[7] It is not open for a Jew or a Christian to question the goodness of
God. He must start with that assumption. Any man who seriously questions God's goodness or asks why he should obey God's commands shows
by this very response that he is not a Jew or a Christian. Believers must
claim that God is wholly and utterly good and that what he wills or commands is of necessity good, though this does not entail that the believer is
claiming that the necessity here is a logical necessity. For a believer, God is
all good; he is the perfect good. This being so, it would seem that the believer is justified in saying that he and we—if his claim concerning God is
correct—ought to do what God wills and that our morality is after all

grounded in a belief in God. But this claim of his is clearly dependent on his assumption that God is good. Yet I shall argue that even if God is good, indeed, even if God is the perfect good, it does not follow that morality can be based on religion and that we can know what we ought to do simply by knowing what God wishes us to do.

3

To come to understand the grounds for this last, rather elliptical claim, we must consider the logical status of "God is good." Is it a nonanalytic and in some way substantive claim, or is it analytic? (Can we say that it is neither?) No matter what we say, we get into difficulties.

Let us try to claim that it is nonanalytic, that it is in some way a substantive statement. So understood, God cannot then be by definition good. If the statement is synthetic and substantive, its denial cannot be self-contradictory; that is, it cannot be self-contradictory to assert that X is God but X is not good. It would always in fact be wrong to assert this, for God is the perfect good, but the denial of this claim is not self-contradictory, it is just false or in some way mistaken. The *is* in "God is the perfect good" is not the *is* of identity; perfect goodness is being predicated of God in some logically contingent way. It is the religious experience of the believer and the events recorded in the Bible that lead the believer to the steadfast conviction that God has a purpose or vocation for him which he can fulfill only by completely submitting to God's will. God shall lead him and guide him in every thought, word and deed. Otherwise he will be like a man shipwrecked, lost in a vast and indifferent universe. Through careful attention to the Bible, he comes to understand that God is a wholly good being who has dealt faithfully with his chosen people. God is not by definition perfectly good or even good, but in reality, though not of logical necessity, he never falls short of perfection.

Assuming that "God is good" is not a truth of language, how, then, do we know that God is good? Do we know or have good grounds for believing that the remarks made at the end of the above paragraph are so? The believer can indeed make such a claim, but how do we or how does he know that this is so? What grounds have we for believing that God is good? Naïve people, recalling how God spoke to Job out of the whirlwind may say that God is good because he is omnipotent and omniscient. But this clearly will not do, for, as Hepburn points out, there is nothing logically improper about saying "X is omnipotent and omniscient and morally wicked."[8] Surely in the world as we know it there is no logical connection between being powerful and knowledgeable and being good. As far as I can see, all that God proved to Job when he spoke to him out of the whirl-wind was that God was an immeasurably powerful being; but he did not prove his moral superiority to Job and he did nothing at all even to exhibit his moral goodness. (One might even argue that he exhibited moral wick-edness.) We need not assume that omnipotence and omniscience bring with them goodness or even wisdom.

What other reason could we have for claiming that God is good? We might say that he is good because he tells us to do good in thought, word and deed and to love one another. In short, in his life and in his precepts God exhibits for us his goodness and love. Now one might argue that chil-dren's hospitals and concentration camps clearly show that such a claim is false. But let us assume that in some way God does exhibit his goodness to man. Let us assume that if we examine God's works we cannot but affirm that God is good.[9] We come to understand that he is not cruel, callous or indifferent. But in order to make such judgments or to gain such an understanding, we must use our own logically independent moral criteria. In taking God's goodness as not being true by definition or as being some kind of conceptual truth, we have, in asserting "God is good," of necessity made a moral judgment, a moral appraisal, using a criterion that cannot be based on a knowledge that God exists or that he issues commands. We call God good because we have experienced the goodness of his acts, but in order to do this, in order to know that he is good or to have any grounds for believing that he is good, we must have an independent moral criterion which we use in making this predication of God. So if "God is good" is taken to be synthetic and substantive, then morality cannot simply be based on a belief in God. We must of logical necessity have some criterion of goodness that is not derived from any statement asserting that there is a deity.

4

Let us alternatively, and more plausibly, take "God is good" to be a truth of language. Now some truths of language (some analytic statements) are statements of identity, such as "puppies are young dogs" or "a father is a male parent." Such statements are definitions and the *is* indicates identity. But "God is good" is clearly not such a statement of identity, for [the fact] that *God* does not have the same meaning as *good* can easily be seen from the following case: Jane says to Betsy, after Betsy helps on old lady across the street, "That was good of you." "That was good of you" most certainly does not mean "that was God of you." And when we say "conscientiousness is good" we do not mean to say "conscientiousness is God." To say, as a believer does, that God is good is not to say that God is God. This clearly indicates that the word *God* does not have the same meaning as the word *good*. When we are talking about God we are not talking simply about morality.

"God is the perfect good" is somewhat closer to "a father is a male parent," but even here *God* and *the perfect good* are not identical in meaning. "God is the perfect good" in some important respects is like "a triangle is a trilateral." Though something is a triangle if and only if it is a trilateral, it does not follow that *triangle* and *trilateral* have the same meaning. Similarly, something is God if and only if that something is the perfect good, but it does not follow that *God* and *the perfect good* have the same meaning. When we speak of God we wish to say other things about him as well, though indeed what is true of God will also be true of the perfect good. Yet what is true of the evening star will also be true of the morning star, since they both refer to the same object, namely Venus, but, as Frege has shown, it does not follow that the two terms have the same meaning if they have the same referent.

Even if it could be made out that "God is the perfect good" is in some way a statement of identity, (1) it would not make "God is good" a statement of identity. and (2) we could know that X is the perfect good only if we already knew how to decide that X is good.[10] So even on the assumption that "God is the perfect good" is a statement of identity, we need an independent way of deciding whether something is good; we must have an independent criterion for goodness.

Surely the alternative presently under consideration is more plausible than the alternative considered in section 3. "God is good" most certainly appears to be analytic in the way "puppies are young," "a bachelor is unmarried" or "unjustified killing is wrong" are analytic. These statements are not statements of identity; they are not definitions, though they all follow from definitions and to deny any of them is self-contradictory.

In short, it seems to me correct to maintain that "God is good," "puppies are young" and "triangles are three-sided" are all truths of language; the predicates partially define their subjects. That is to say—to adopt for a moment, a Platonic-sounding idiom—goodness is partially definitive of Godhood, as youngness is partially definitive of puppyhood and as three-sidedness is partially definitive of triangularity.

To accept this is not at all to claim that we can have no understanding of good without an understanding of God; and the truth of the above claim that God is good will not show that God is the, or even a, fundamental criterion for goodness. Let us establish first that and then how the fact of such truths of language does not show that we could have no understanding of good without having an understanding of God. We could not understand the full religious sense of what is meant by God without knowing that whatever is denoted by this term is said to be good; but, as *young* or *three-sided* are understood without reference to puppies or triangles, though the converse cannot be the case, so *good* is also understood quite independently of any reference to God. We can intelligibly say, "I have a three-sided figure here that is most certainly not a triangle" and "colts are young but they are not puppies." Similarly, we can well say "conscientiousness, under most circumstances at least, is good even in a world without God." Such an utterance is clearly intelligible, to believer and nonbeliever alike. It is a well-formed English sentence with a use in the language. Here we can use the word *good* without either asserting or assuming the reality of God. Such linguistic evidence clearly shows that good is a concept which can be understood quite independently of any reference to the deity, that morality without religion, without theism is quite possible. In fact, just the reverse is the case. Christianity, Judaism and theistic religions of that sort could not exist if people did not have a moral understanding that was, logically speaking, quite independent of such religions. We could have no understanding of the truth of "God is good" or of the concept God unless we had an independent understanding of goodness.

That this is so can be seen from the following considerations. If we had no understanding of the word *young*, and if we did not know the criteria for deciding whether a dog was young, we could not know how correctly to apply the word *puppy*. Without such a prior understanding of what it is to be young, we could not understand the sentence "puppies are young." Similarly, if we had no understanding of the use of the word *good*, and if we did not know the criteria for deciding whether a being (or if you will, a power or a force) was good, we could not know how correctly to apply the word *God*. Without such a prior understanding of goodness, we could not understand the sentence "God is good." This clearly shows that our understanding of morality and knowledge of goodness are independent of any knowledge that we may or may not have of the divine. Indeed, without a prior and logically independent understanding of good and without some nonreligious criterion for judging something to be good, the religious person could have no knowledge of God, for he could not know whether that powerful being who spoke out of the whirlwind and laid the foundations of the earth was in fact worthy of worship and perfectly good.

From my argument we should conclude that we cannot decide whether something is good or whether it ought to be done simply from finding out (assuming that we can find out) that God commanded it, willed it, enjoined it. Furthermore, whether "God is good" is synthetic (substantive) or analytic (a truth of language), the concept of good must be understood as something distinct from the concept of God; that is to say, a man could know how to use *good* properly and still not know how to use *God*. Conversely, a man could not know how to use *God* correctly unless he already understood how to use *good*. An understanding of goodness is logically prior to, and is independent of, any understanding or acknowledgment of God.

5

In attempting to counter my argument for the necessary independence of morality—including a central facet of religious morality—from any beliefs about the existence or powers of the deity, the religious moralist might begin by conceding that (1) there are secular moralities that are logically independent of religion, and (2) that we must understand the meanings of moral terms independently of understanding what it means to speak of God. He might even go so far as to grant that only a man who understood what good and bad were could come to believe in God. *Good,* he might grant, does not mean "willed by God" or anything like that; and "there is no God, but human happiness is nonetheless good" is indeed perfectly intelligible as a moral utterance. But granting that, it is still the case that Jew and Christian do and must—on pain of ceasing to be Jew or Christian—take God's will as their final court of appeal in the making of moral appraisals or judgments. Any rule, act or attitude that conflicts with what the believer sincerely believes to be the will of God must be rejected by him. It is indeed true that in making moral judgments the Jew or Christian does not always use God's will as a criterion for what is good or what ought to be done. When he says "fluoridation is a good thing" or "the resumption of nuclear testing is a crime," he need not be using God's will as a criterion for his moral judgment. But where any moral judgment or any other moral criterion conflicts with God's ordinances, or with what the person making the judgment honestly takes to be God's ordinances, he must accept those ordinances, or he is no longer a Jew or a Christian. This acceptance is a crucial test of his faith. In this way, God's will is his fundamental moral criterion.

That the orthodox Jew or Christian would reason in this way is perfectly true, but though he says that God's will is his fundamental criterion, it is still plain that he has a yet more fundamental criterion which he must use in order to employ God's will as a moral criterion. Such a religious moralist must believe and thus be prepared to make the moral claim that there exists a being whom he deems to be perfectly good or worthy of worship and whose will should always be obeyed. But to do this he must have a moral criterion (a standard for what is morally good) that is independent of God's will or what people believe to be God's will. In fact, the believer's moral criterion—"because it is willed by God"—is in logical dependence on some distinct criterion in virtue of which the believer judges that something is perfectly good, is worthy of worship. And in making this very crucial judgment he cannot appeal to God's will as a criterion, for, that there is a being worthy of the appellation *God*, depends in part on the above prior moral claim. Only if it is correct, can we justifiably say that there is a God.

It is crucial to keep in mind that "a wholly good being exists who is worthy of worship" is not analytic, is not a truth of language, though "God is wholly good" is. The former is rather a substantive moral statement (expressing a moral judgment) and a very fundamental one indeed, for the believer's whole faith rests on it. Drop this and everything goes.

It is tempting to reply to my above argument in this vein: "But it is blasphemy to judge God; no account of the logical structure of the believer's argument can be correct if it says that the believer must judge that God is good." Here we must beware of verbal magic and attend very carefully to precisely what it is we are saying. I did not—and could not on pain of contradiction—say that God must be judged worthy of worship, perfectly good; for God by definition is worthy of worship, perfectly good. I said something quite different, namely that the believer and nonbeliever alike must decide whether there exists or could conceivably exist a force, a being ("ground of being") that is worthy of worship or perfectly good; and I further said that in deciding this, one makes a moral judgment that can in no way be logically dependent on God's will. Rather, the moral standard, "because it is willed by God," is dependent for its validity on the acceptance of the claim that there is a being worthy of worship. And as our little word *worthy* indicates, this is unequivocally a moral judgment for believer and nonbeliever alike.

There is a rather more baroque objection[11] to my argument that (1) nothing could count as the Judaeo-Christian God unless that reality is worthy of worship, and (2) it is our own moral insight that must tell us if anything at all is or ever possibly could be worthy of worship or whether there is a being who possesses perfect goodness. My conclusion from (1) and (2) was that rather than morality being based on religion, it can be seen that religion in a very fundamental sense must be based on morality. The counterargument claims that such a conclusion is premature because the judgment that something is worthy of worship is not a moral judgment; it is an evaluative judgment, a religious evaluation, but not a moral judgment. The grounds for this counterclaim are that if the judgment is a moral judgment, as I assumed, then demonolatry—the worship of evil spirits—would be self-contradictory. But although demonolatry is morally and religiously perverse, it is not self-contradictory. Hence my argument must be mistaken.

However, if we say "Z is worthy of worship" or that, given Judaeo-Christian attitudes, "if Z is what ought to be worshipped then Z must be good," it does not follow that demonolatry is self-contradictory or incoherent. Not everyone uses language as Jews and Christians do and not everyone shares the conventions of those religious groups. To say that nothing can be God, the Judaeo-Christian God, unless it is worthy of worship, and to affirm that the judgment of something as worthy of worship is a moral judgment, is not to deny that some people on some grounds could judge that what they believe to be evil spirits are worthy of worship. By definition, they could not be Jews or Christians—they show by their linguistic behavior that they do not believe in the Judaeo-Christian God who, by definition, is perfectly good. Jews and Christians recognize that believers in demonolatry do not believe in God but in evil spirits whom such Joycean characters judge to be worthy of worship. The Christian and the demonolater make different moral judgments of a very fundamental sort reflecting different views of the world.

6

The dialectic of our general argument about morality and divine commands should not end here. There are some further considerations which need to be brought to the forefront. Consider the theological claim that there is an infinite self-existent being, upon whom all finite realities depend for their existence, but who in turn depends on nothing. Assuming the intelligibility of the key concepts in this claim and assuming also that we know this claim to be true, it still needs to be asked how we can know, except by the use of our own moral understanding, that this infinite, self-existent being is good or is a being whose commands we ought to obey. Since he—to talk about this being anthropomorphically by the use of personal pronouns—is powerful enough, we might decide that it would be "the better part of valour" to obey him, but this decision would not at all entail that we *ought* to obey him. How do we know that this being is good, except by our own moral discernment? We could not discover that this being is good or just by discovering that he "laid the foundation of the world" or "created man in his image and likeness." No information about the behavior patterns of this being would of itself tell us that he was good, righteous or just. We ourselves would have to decide that, or, to use the misleading idiom of the ethical intuitionist, we would have to intuit or somehow come to perceive or understand that the unique ethical properties of goodness, righteousness and justness apply to this strange being or "ground of all being" that we somehow discover to exist. Only if we independently knew what we would count as good, righteous, just, would we be in a position to know whether this being is good or whether his commands ought to be obeyed. That most Christians most of the time unquestionably assume that he is good only proves that this judgment is for them a fundamental moral judgment. But this should hardly be news.

At this point it is natural to reply: "Still, we would not even call this being God unless he was thought to be good. God, whatever else he may or may not be, in a fitting or proper object of worship." A person arguing thus might continue: "This is really a material mode statement about the use of the word *God*; that is to say, we would not call Z God unless that Z were a fitting or proper object of worship or a being that ought to be worshipped. And if we say 'Z is a fitting object of worship' or 'Z ought to be worshipped,' we must also be prepared to say 'Z is good.' Z could not be one without being the other; and if Z is a fitting object of worship, Z necessarily is a being we would call God. Thus, if Z is called God, then Z must also of necessity be called good since in Judaeo-Christian contexts what ought to be worshipped must also be good. (This is a logical remark about the use of the phrase 'ought to be worshipped' in Judaeo-Christian contexts.) God, by definition, is good. Though the word *God* is not equivalent to the word *good*, we would not call a being or power *God* unless that being was thought to be good."

The above point is well taken, but it still remains the case that the believer has not derived a moral claim from a nonmoral religious one. Rather, he has only indicated that the word *God*, like the words *Saint, Santa Claus, Honky, Nigger, Mick* or *Kike*, is not a purely descriptive term. *God*, like *Saint*, and so forth, has an evaluative force; it expresses a pro-attitude on the part of the believer and does not just designate or even describe a necessary being or transcendent power or immanent force. Such a believer—unlike Schopenhauer—means by *God* something toward which he has an appropriate pro-attitude; employing this word with its usual evaluative force, he could not say, "God commands it but it is really evil to do it." If, on the other hand, we simply think of what is purportedly designated or described by the word *God*—the descriptive force of the word—we can say, for example, without paradox, "an objective power commands it but it is evil to do it." By simply considering the reality allegedly denoted by the word *God*, we cannot discover whether this "reality" is good. If we simply let Z stand for this reality, we can always ask, "Is it good?" This is never a self-answering question in the way it is if we ask, "Is murder evil?" Take away the evaluative force of the word *God* and you have no ground for claiming that it must be the case that God is good; to make this claim, with our admittedly fallible moral understanding, we must decide if this Z is good.

"But"—it will be countered—"you have missed the significance of the very point you have just made. As you say yourself, *God* is not just a descriptive word and God-sentences are not by any means used with a purely descriptive aim. *God* normally has an evaluative use and God-sentences have a directive force. You cannot begin to understand them if you do not take this into consideration. You cannot just consider what Z designates or purports to designate."

My reply to this is that we can and must if we are going to attain clarity in these matters. Certain crucial and basic sentences like "God created the Heavens and earth" and "God is in Christ," are by no means just moral or practical utterances, and they would not have the evaluative force they do if it were not thought that in some strange way they described a mysterious objective power. The religious quest is a quest to find a Z such that Z is worthy of worship. This being the case, the evaluative force of the words and of the utterance is dependent on the descriptive force. How else but by our own moral judgment that Z is a being worthy to be worshipped are we enabled to call this Z "my Lord and my God"? Christians say there is a Z such that Z should be worshipped. Nonbelievers deny this or remain skeptical. Findlay,[12] for example, points out that this atheism is in part moral because he does not believe that there can possibly be a Z such that Z is a worthy object of worship. Father Copleston,[13] on the other hand, says there is a Z such that Z ought to be worshipped. This Z, Father Copleston claims, is a "necessary being" whose nonexistence is in some important sense inconceivable. But both Findlay and Copleston are using their own moral understanding in making their respective moral judgments. Neither is deriving or deducing his moral judgment from the statement "there is a Z" or from noticing or adverting to the fact—if it is a fact—that Z is "being-itself," "a reality whose nonexistence is unthinkable," "the ground of being" or the like.

Morality cannot be based on religion. If anything, the opposite is partly true, for nothing can be God unless he or it is an object worthy of worship, and it is our own moral insight that must tell us if anything at all could possibly be worthy of worship.

It is true that if some Z is God, then, by definition, Z is an object worthy of worship. But this does not entail there is such a Z; that there is such a Z would depend both on what is the case and on what we, as individuals, judge to be worthy of worship. "God is worthy of worship" is—for most uses of *God*—analytic. To understand this sentence requires no insight at all but only a knowledge of English; but that there is or can be a Z such that Z is worthy of worship depends, in part at least, on the moral insight—or lack thereof—of that fallible creature that begins and ends in dust.

In her puzzling article, "Modern Moral Philosophy,"[14] Miss Anscombe has made a different sort of objection to the type of approach taken here. Moral uses of obligation statements, she argues, have no reasonable sense outside a divine-law conception of ethics. Without God, such conceptions are without sense. There was once a context, a religious way of life, in which these conceptions had a genuine application. *Ought* was once equated, in the relevant context, with *being obliged, bound* or *required*. This came about because of the influence of the Torah. Because of the "dominance of Christianity for many centuries the concepts of being bound, permitted or excused became deeply embedded in our language and thought."[15] But since this is no longer so unequivocally the case these conceptions have become rootless. Shorn of this theistic Divine Law, shorn of the Hebrew-Christian tradition, these conceptions can only retain a "mere mesmeric force" and cannot be "inferred from anything whatever."[16] I think Miss Anscombe would say that I have shown nothing more than this in my above arguments. What I have said about the independence of morality from religion is quite correct for this "corrupt" age, where the basic principles of a divine-law conception of ethics appear merely as practical major premises on a par with the principle of utility and the like. In such contexts a moral *ought* can only have a psychological force. Without God, it can have no "discernible content," for the conception of moral obligation "only operates in the context of law."[17] By such moves as I have made above, I have, in effect, indicated how moral obligation *now* has only a delusive appearance of content. And in claiming that without God these still can be genuine moral obligations, I have manifested "a detestable desire to retain the atmosphere of the term "morally obligatory" where the term itself no longer has a genuine use."[18] "Only if we believe in God as a law-giver can we come to believe that there is anything a man is categorically bound to do on pain of being a bad man."[19] The concept of obligation has, without God, become a Holmesless Watson. In our present context, Miss Anscombe argues, we should, if "psychologically possible," jettison the concepts of moral obligation, moral duty and the like and approach ethics only after we have developed a philosophical psychology which will enable us to clarify what pleasure is, what a human action is and what constitutes human virtue and a distinctively "human flourishing."[20]

I shall not be concerned here with the larger issues raised by Miss Anscombe's paradoxical, excessively obscure, yet strangely challenging remarks. I agree, of course, that philosophical psychology is important, but I am not convinced that we have not "done" ethics and cannot profitably "do" ethics without such a philosophical psychology. I shall, however, be concerned here only to point out that Miss Anscombe has not shown us that the notion of moral obligation is unintelligible or vacuous without God and his laws.

We have already seen that if so-and-so is called a divine command or an ordinance of God, then it is obviously something that the person who behave like this it is not because you base morals on religion or on a law ought to obey, for he would not call anything a *divine* command or an ordinance of *God* unless he thought he ought to obey it. But we ourselves, by our own moral insight, must judge that such commands or promulgations are worthy of such an appellation. Yet no moral conceptions follow from a command or law as such. And this would be true at any time whatsoever. It is a logical and not a historical consideration.

Now it is true that if you believe in God in such a way as to accept God as your Lord and Master, and if you believe that something is an ordinance of God, then you ought to try to follow this ordinance. But if you believe like this it is not because you base morals on religion or on a law concept of morality, but because he who can bring himself to say "my God" uses *God* and cognate words evaluatively. To use such an expression is already to make a moral evaluation; the man expresses a decision, that he is morally bound to do whatever God commands. "I ought to do whatever this Z commands" is an expression of moral obligation. To believe in God, as we have already seen, involves the making of a certain value judgment; that is to say, the believer believes that there is a Z such that Z is worthy of worship. But his value judgment cannot be derived from just examining Z, or from hearing Z's commands or laws. Without a pro-attitude on the part of the believer toward Z, without a decision by the individual concerned that Z is worthy of worship, nothing of moral kind follows. But no decision of this sort is entailed by discoveries about Z or by finding out what Z commands or wishes. It is finally up to the individual to decide that this Z is worthy of worship, that this Z ought to be worshipped, that this Z ought to be called his Lord and Master. We have here a moral use of *ought* that is logically prior to any law conception of ethics. The command gains obligatory force because it is judged worthy of obedience. If someone says, "I do not pretend to appraise God's laws, I just simply accept them because God tells me to," similar considerations obtain. This person judges that there is a Z that is a proper object of obedience. This expresses his own moral judgment, his own sense of what he is obliged to do.

A religious belief depends for its viability on our sense of good and bad—our own sense of worth—and not vice versa. It is crucial to an understanding of morality that this truth about the uses of our language be understood. Morality cannot be based on religion, and I (like Findlay) would even go so far as to deny in the name of morality that any Z whatsoever could be an object or being worthy of worship. But whether or not I am correct in this last judgment, it remains the case that each person with his own finite and fallible moral awareness must make decisions of this sort for himself. This would be so whether he was in a Hebrew-Christian tradition or in a "corrupt" and "shallow" consequentialist tradition or in any tradition whatsoever. A moral understanding must be logically prior to any religious assent.

NOTES

1. Brunner, Emil (1947), *The Divine Imperative,* translated by Olive Wyon, London: Lutterworth Press, chapter IX.

2. Nowell-Smith, P. H. (1966), "Morality: Religious and Secular" in Ramsey, Ian (ed.), *Christian Ethics and Contemporary Philosophy*, London: SCM Press.

3. Ewing, A. C. (1961), "The Autonomy of Ethics" in Ramsey, Ian (ed.), *Prospect for Metaphysics,* London: Allen and Unwin.

4. *Ibid.,* p. 39.

5. *Ibid.,* p. 40.

6. *Ibid.,* p. 41.

7. See Rees, D. A. (1961), "Metaphysical Schemes and Moral Principles" in *Prospect for Metaphysics*, op. cit. p. 23.

8. Hepburn, Ronald (1958), *Christianity and Paradox,* London: C. A. Watts, p. 132.

9. This is surely to assume a lot.

10. Finally we must be quite clear that X's being good is but a necessary condition for X's being the perfect good. But what would be a sufficient condition? Do we really know? I think we do not. We do not know how to identify the referent of "the Perfect Good." Thus in one clear sense we do not understand what such a phrase means.

11. This objection has been made in an unpublished paper by Professor T. P. Brown.

12. Findlay, J. N. (1955), "Can God's Existence be Disproved?" in Antony Flew and Alasdair MacIntyre (eds.), *New Essays in Philosophical Theology,* New York: Macmillan Company, pp. 47-56.

13. Russell, Bertrand and Copleston, F. C. (1957), "The Existence of God: A Debate" in Bertrand Russell, *Why I Am Not a Christian,* London: Allen and Unwin, pp. 145-47.

14. Anscombe, Elizabeth (January 1958), "Modern Moral Philosophy" in *Philosophy*, vol. 33, no. 8.

15. *Ibid.,* p. 5.

16. *Ibid.,* p. 8.

17. *Ibid.,* p. 18.

18. *Ibid.,* p. 18.

19. *Ibid.,* p. 6.

20. *Ibid.,* pp. 1, 15, 18.

X. God and Survival of the Personality After Death

Corliss Lamont

L___The Illusion of Immortality

Corliss Lamont received his bachelor's degree from Harvard University and his doctorate from Columbia University. He has taught at Columbia University, the New School for Social Research, Cornell University, and the Harvard Graduate School of Education. Among his writings are *The Illusion of Immortality* (1935); *The Philosophy of Humanism* (1965); *Freedom of Choice Affirmed* (1967); and *Voice in the Wilderness: Collected Essays of Fifty Years* (1975). He has edited *A Humanist Wedding Service* (1952); *Man Answers Death: An Anthology of Poetry* (1952); and *A Humanist Funeral Service* (1962).

THE "DESIRE" FOR IMMORTALITY

That in practically all cultures, at least until recently, there is to be found belief in some sort of after-existence is not be questioned. But to infer from this that there is an inherent and universal *desire* for a life beyond is a highly illegitimate procedure. As we have seen, many primitive peoples, including the Old Testament Hebrews and the Homeric Greeks, believed

Reprinted from Corliss Lamont, The Illusion of Immortality *(New York: Frederick Ungar, 1965), pp. 198-235. Reprinted by permission of Corliss Lamont.*

that there existed beyond the grave an unhappy and gloomy underworld where the feeble shades of the departed wandered about in unmitigated melancholy. Naturally enough, peoples with such a conception of the afterlife had no burning enthusiasm to go to the abode of the dead. They viewed it as a far from attractive inevitability, frequently took an interest in it mainly for the sake of warding off the harm that the ghosts of the deceased might do the living, and sometimes simply regarded it with a bored indifference. It is quite possible, too, that at certain periods and among certain peoples the emergence of human individuality as such was not sufficiently pronounced to make a splendid immortality seem warranted for the average man.

As to the after-existence beliefs of Buddhism and Hinduism, there is considerable disagreement among scholars and even among the adherents of these religions themselves. One group claims that the ultimate goal of Nirvana means complete extinction or absorption of the individual personality; another that it is a state of conscious bliss comparable to the Christian's beatific vision of God. Whatever the correct interpretation, there can be no doubt that millions of Buddhists and Hindus look forward to their successive reincarnations after death with dread and despair, hoping for nothing so much as the total annihilation of their selves. And the beliefs and feelings of these Easterners should alone be sufficient to demonstrate that there is no innate and universal desire for immortality. For proof of this, however, we need not go outside of the Christian West. Even in the Middle Ages, the great centuries of faith, thoughts of the life beyond were likely to throw the majority of men into paroxysms of fear rather than ecstasies of joy; to arouse an attitude of melancholy resignation in face of the inevitable rather than one of overflowing gladness in anticipation of the glorious.

The supposed age-long, worldwide urge for immortality is a fine-sounding fiction that carries considerable plausibility because it does make some approach to the actual truth. For we do seem to find a universal law to the effect that every normal man, *if* the idea enters firmly enough into his consciousness and the counteracting forces of education and reason are not too potent, can be stimulated to desire a *worthwhile* immortality. And this means that the longing for an after-existence is a longing only *potentially* present in every human heart, since it does not become an actuality until the right kind of survival is offered in the right kind of way.

This constitutes no mystery, however, since as every modern advertiser knows, the same principle holds in regard to the exciting of desire for any object, real or imaginary. But because of various psychological and affectional factors that I shall take up later in detail, it is particularly easy to arouse the appetite for life everlasting; and when once set astir, this yearning can be developed through the appropriate techniques into such a powerful and seemingly permanent emotional pattern that it is readily mistaken for a human instinct. Presumably even in regions where the Hindu and Buddhist priesthoods hold out extinction as the final goal, the inhabitants, if exposed to the proper influences, could be taught deeply to desire immortality.

The early Greeks and the early Hebrews did not crave immortality, mainly for the simple reason that they could not conceive of a desirable one, being unable to imagine a man as enjoying a decent existence when deprived of this earthly body. The religious revolution based on the life, passion and rising of Jesus Christ from the tomb supplied the necessary foundation for a satisfactory future life by promising the resurrection of the body. For a time there was a glad and glorious sense of complete victory over death; a psychological release of mind and soul perhaps unknown before that day. These feelings were buttressed by the belief that the world would shortly come to an end and that therefore the victory would soon become apparent and unmistakable to all. But the world stubbornly refused to enact this grand finale.

The Church Fathers proceeded to do their duty and to remind the faithful of original sin and the torments of hell. Their inventive minds, worried by what the soul should do between death and resurrection, seized upon the concept of purgatory and gave it a conspicuous place in the complex Christian theology. The holy Catholic Church then created the system of indulgences, providing for the remission of human souls' punishment in purgatory; and, incidentally, made the granting of these indulgences so much a matter of cash contributions to ecclesiastical coffers that the scandal of it occasioned Martin Luther's revolt that became the Reformation.

Hell and purgatory came to be so emphasized in Catholic doctrine and practice that the masses of men could hardly be expected to look forward to immortality with a consuming eagerness. Apparently every effort was made to impress constantly on the minds of the people the dire penalties of retribution awaiting them as soon as they passed away. To aid in this, through the processes of association, death itself was represented in the most frightful manner possible. Revolting emblems of it everywhere met the eye; in the churches and the cloisters, on bridges and highways, in the carvings of tables and chairs, in the hangings of apartments, in rings and breviaries. Artists turned out series upon series of the gruesome "Dance of Death," depicting death as a ghastly skeleton leading his victims to an untimely end. He plays the fiddle at weddings; beats the drum in battle; shadows the scholar, the sculptor, the painter; stands leering beside the newborn baby in its cradle. The result was, as W. E. H. Lecky says, to make "the terrors of death for centuries the nightmare of the imagination."[1] St. Francis of Assisi was clearly out of step with the times when he referred mystically to "Brother Death."

Even Dante in his magnificent *Divine Comedy* devoted most of his space and his genius to the varied and exciting aspects of the next world's lower regions. But the more successful his vivid portrayals of hell and purgatory as art, the more effective they were in filling the minds of his readers with grim forebodings of the life beyond. Dante's heaven was far less convincing than his other conceptions and constituted a distinct anti-climax. The saintly Thomas Aquinas would not permit hell to be forgotten even in paradise, declaring that "in order that nothing may be wanting to the happiness of the blessed in Heaven, a perfect view is granted them of the tortures of the damned."[2] This statement was based on the general principle that an awareness of the opposite misery always increases the relish of any pleasure.

The priests and high priests of the Church no doubt sincerely believed for the most part that their terrifying doctrines were morally necessary and entirely true, but it was altogether natural for the plain man to recoil in dismay from their dread prophecies. With what cruel and awful literalness these doctrines could be taken is well shown by the remark of "Bloody Mary," Catholic queen of England in the sixteenth century, to the effect that: "As the souls of heretics are hereafter to be eternally burning in hell, there can be nothing more proper than for me to imitate the Divine vengeance by burning them on earth."[3]

The leaders of the new Protestant Church, while they eliminated purgatory, did not make the future state look any more attractive on the whole. Calvin, with his ruthless insistence on the very small number of God's predestined elect, frightened the multitude into piety. Fire and brimstone sermons became the order of the day. In England the great preacher, Jeremy Taylor, predicted: "Husbands shall see their wives, parents shall see their children tormented before their eyes. The bodies of the damned shall be crowded together in hell like grapes in a wine press, which shall press one another till they burst."[4] In America the stern voice of Jonathan Edwards, the noted Puritan theologian, rang out in warning to sinners: "The God that holds you over the pit of hell, much as one holds a spider, or some loathsome insect, over the fire, abhors you, and is dreadfully provoked: his wrath towards you burns like fire. . . . You are ten thousand times more abominable in his eyes than the most hateful venomous serpent is in ours. . . . It would be dreadful to suffer this fierceness and wrath of Almighty God one moment; but you must suffer it to all eternity. There will be no end to this exquisite horrible misery."[5]

The heads of the wicked, Edwards prophesies, "their eyes, their tongues, their hands, their feet, their loins, and their vitals shall forever be full of glowing, melting fire, fierce enough to melt the very rocks and elements; and, also, they shall eternally be full of the most quick and lively sense to feel the torment . . . not for one minute, nor for one day, nor for one year, nor for one age, nor for two ages, nor for an hundred ages, nor for ten thousand or million ages, one after another, but forever and ever, without any end at all, and never, never be delivered!"[6] These are but brief samples of the vast quantity of the dire exhortations that came forth from Protestant pulpits century after century. The average believer, feeling that there was more than an even chance that he and his would meet a most unwelcome fate, was inclined to shudder when he thought of the world to come. No assurance that his enemies and other malefactors would boil in hell could free him from the apprehension that he, too, might share the same destiny. No talk about the pearly gates and golden streets of heaven could counteract the creeping fear within his heart.

There were, of course, important exceptions to this state of mind, particularly among the cultured minority and the professional philosophers. Like their prototypes in all ages, they tended to rise above the more vulgar religious superstitions. It is true that the philosophers, ever intellectual imperialists *par excellence*, were always looking for another world to conquer and reared great systems demonstrating that mere death could never stop the invincible spirit of man. But on the whole they were lacking that queer quirk of the imagination which envisages hellfires and other devilish torments for the vast majority of mankind as a victory over the tomb. Some went so far as to deny altogether personal survival after death, the greatest of these being Benedict Spinoza in the seventeenth century.

At about the time that the advanced ideas of the French Enlightenment were spreading farthest throughout Europe, an important change regarding the nature of immortality began to become manifest in the

Church itself. Certain Protestant preachers, tired and disgusted with the doctrine of eternal punishment, reintroduced the old heresy of universalism and taught that all human souls would eventually be saved. For various reasons this theory of universalism grew stronger and stronger during the nineteenth century. A distinct trend set in towards slackening and indeed extinguishing, the everlasting flames of divine retribution. Today hell, even among religious groups which still formally include it in their theology, is decidedly out of fashion. At the same time there has developed among Christians, and among non-Christians, too, more and more of an active, positive desire for immortality. This modern longing for a future life is directly connected with the modern tendency to make that realm beyond the grave seem more worthwhile and less forbidding. And there are undoubtedly other influential factors behind this phenomenon, such as the added emphasis on the individual ego, which accompanied the rise of capitalism in the modern world.

On the terms now so frequently offered, with hell abolished and happiness guaranteed, few normal persons would choose to turn down the gift of immortality. For surely well-nigh all men would be glad to continue living in another world which promises to prolong an enjoyment already present or to bring an enjoyment so far absent; to have a chance to do and experience all those things for which there was not time or opportunity in this life; to go to a place where Ponce de Leon's romantic quest for the elixir of youth has been answered once and for all by the assurance that everyone shall possess eternally the health and vigor of the prime of life. It is begging the question to say, "An eternity of life, of happiness, of this same old self? How monotonous, how boring it would be!" For if there really is unceasing joy and bliss awaiting us on the other side of death, then boredom, monotony and other ills are excluded by definition.

Those comparatively few Westerners who insist that they want oblivion are motivated, I think, by several considerations. In the first place, they may be recoiling in horror and disgust from the orthodox and traditional Christian view of immortality that puts so much emphasis on eternal punishment. In the second place, they may be afflicted with the idea of endlessness. "Is it never to end?" protests one individual. "The thought appalls. I, little I, to live a million years—and another million—and another! My tiny light to burn forever!"[7] Another writes: "I feel time lasting indefinitely, space lengthening without end, something like a never stopping crescendo. It seems to me that my being gradually swells, substitutes itself to everything, grows by absorbing worlds and centuries, then bursts, and everything ceases, and I am left with an atrocious pain in the head and in the stomach. It is eternity which is frightful."[8]

Declares a third: "It is the aimlessness of the process which afflicts the mind; for it is a progress which leads nowhere, which has no goal, seeing that, after ages of forward movement, you are precisely as distant from the imagined end as when you started."[9] Comparatively few believers in the Christian West have thought through the full meaning of durational eternity, have ever asked themselves the simple question: Do I, who know so well the length of one earthly life, really believe that this conscious self of mine is to go on existing for 500 million years and then 500 hundred million more and so on *ad infinitum?* If persons who have faith in immortality asked themselves this question, they would perhaps pass into a temporary state of intellectual vertigo.

In the third place, the wooers of extinction may be genuinely tired of or dissatisfied with life on earth and be simply unable to imagine that the completely happy after-existence promised by the modern immortalists can possibly come true. And in this judgment they are certainly displaying considerable common sense. But the fact remains that, granting the reality of the paradise which the more optimistic immortalists portray, the average citizen would hardly decline the opportunity of going there. Sophisticated unbelievers will claim that interest in immortality is vulgar and that only Philistines could want a life beyond the grave; but their protestations smack of the grapes that have soured. It is only honest for those who do not feel able to take stock in a worthwhile immortality to admit that such a continuation of existence has often been at least a pleasant dream.

Professor James H. Leuba finds that a considerable number of those who do not believe would take great satisfaction in the assurance of a future life.[10] Analyzing the other unbelievers, he goes on to say: "With the normally constituted individual, the realization of the absence of ground for a belief usually abates and even removes the desire for it. . . . The reasonable man tries to suppress desire for the unattainable and sometimes succeeds."[11] The unbeliever may therefore be sincere in asserting that he does not desire immortality, but he is liable to forget that he might like to have it very much if he thought it within the bounds of possibility.

SPECIFIC MOTIVATIONS

I have stated that there are various psychological and affectional factors in human nature which make the desire for immortality easy to arouse. These same factors, of course, make the belief in immortality easy to inculcate. We shall now consider them. And we can begin no more appropriately than by examining that inborn tendency, already mentioned, of human beings to preserve and protect their lives amid the vicissitudes of fortune. This tendency includes an indefinite number of specific reactions to specific and often unique situations. Only in a very vague and summary way is the tendency classifiable as an instinct. It is by no means all-powerful, since human reason and emotions bent on other objectives can overrule it.

Men commit suicide by premeditation and knowingly risk their lives in all kinds of adventurous exploits below, upon and above the earth. Divers and submarine crews disappear beneath the waters never to be seen again; explorers go forth defiantly to die along the frozen wastes of the poles, and mountain climbers upon the icy precipices of unscaled peaks. Aviators daily live dangerously. Throughout history men have sacrificed themselves for the ideals they found compelling, as they did by the millions in the Second World War. Yet during all these most hazardous forms of activity men cling to life to the very last. Indeed, if the tendency towards self-preservation did not on the whole prevail, neither the human individual nor the human species would long endure. And if this tendency had not been a predominating force throughout the long course of evolution, there would have been no intense and competitive struggle for existence, no survival of the fittest, and therefore no man to meditate on the meaning of such things.

Such observations in the end amount to little more than the truism that life is life and will continue to be a forward-pushing and active enterprise as long as it is life at all. This is true of all forms of life, from the humblest to the highest; the lowliest plant will do battle for its place in the sun. The vital urge in any species or any individual is prior to the dawn of mind. It is not something rational or based on experience; it is innate and spontaneous. Newborn babes, hovering uncomprehending between life and death, will fight desperately for their niche in the world; octogenarians, fatally ill and lapsed into total unconsciousness, will struggle to the end to maintain the faintest foothold on existence.

But when mortality and its meaning once become clear, the native tendency towards self-preservation takes on the additional form of *conscious* fear of death and love of life. These two states of minds are different expressions of the same fundamental behavior pattern, and they alternate in human beings according to circumstance. It is readily seen how natural it is for men to interpret this fear of death and love of life as a positive wish for a hereafter; how natural it is for them to ease the fear and indulge the love by persuading themselves that there actually is a transcendental existence beyond the grave. Thus they express their simple desire for the continuation of present life in this world as a profound desire for a future life in another world.

The wholly natural desire of living forms to keep on living does not, in the main, noticeably abate among the aged of the human species. In fact, many old people cling to existence more determinedly than at any other time in their lives. At the age of eighty-eight, a few days before his death, Charles Renouvier stated: "When a man is old, very old, and accustomed to life, it is very difficult to die. I think that young men accept the idea of dying more easily, perhaps more willingly than old men. When one is more than eighty years old, one is cowardly and shrinks from death. And when one knows and can no longer doubt that death is coming near, deep bitterness falls on the soul."[12] This last thought of Renouvier is especially important. Though today the greater proportion of mankind still die in youth and middle age, almost all individuals in these age periods expect to go on living for a considerable time to come. But the elderly know for certain that death is waiting for them just around the corner and that before long they must meet the fate of all mortals. They may begin to feel something like the condemned prisoner awaiting execution on a set day. And they are bound to lose the relative unconcern of younger people for whom death is a matter of the vague and far-off future.

Another point worth noting is that those who have survived middle age can with some accuracy take the measure of their lives, judge just how far their achievements have fallen short of their aims, and see, also, that now it is too late to retrieve their weaknesses, their mistakes and their plain bad luck. In youth, no matter what missteps we make, there is always the prospect of a long future in which to correct or counteract them. So long as we are not beyond our fifties, it is never too late to mend; but in the sixties, the seventies and the eighties this proverb is far less applicable. Men in these latter stages of maturity are inclined to dream more insistently of a second life where they will have a second chance, where circumstances will be more propitious and where they will really be able to do justice to themselves. Rare indeed is the man who towards the close of life does not feel that he has been, in one respect or another, something of a failure and who does not wish that he might have an opportunity to remold his career.

Ilya Metchnikoff, the celebrated Russian biologist, found that "the desire to live, instead of diminishing tends, on the contrary, to increase with age."[13] This opinion is the more convincing because Metchnikoff himself was an ardent advocate of developing what he called the "instinct for death," that is, a positive desire to die on the part of old persons comparable to the wish to sleep when tired. He believed that almost all human deaths are premature and caused by some kind of simple violence or by that more complete form of violence known as disease, and that therefore this potential instinct has been prevented from expressing itself. His ideal was "orthobiosis," which is "the development of human life so that it passes through a long period of old age in active and vigorous health leading to the final period in which there shall be present a sense of satiety of life and a wish for death."[14]

Walter Savage Landor, on his seventy-fourth birthday, wrote four lines which give consummate expression to what Metchnikoff had in mind:

> *I strove with none, for none was worth my strife.*
> *Nature I loved and, next to Nature, Art:*
> *I warmed both hands before the fire of life;*
> *It sinks, and I am ready to depart.*[15]

In all his widespread and careful researches on the subject Metchnikoff discovered only two cases of old people in whom the instinct for death was sufficiently well advanced to accord with his theory. And it is doubtful whether his ideal of a universal instinct for death among human beings will ever be fulfilled. For besides meaning universal old age it would entail a perfect timing for the arrival of death that could be rarely expected. So long as there is a physiological energy in the body that serves to keep life going, there will usually be as its counterpart a psychological desire to keep life going. If death came only when the physical strength of the body was entirely exhausted, then we might well accept it with the same readiness as sleep. The trouble is that most people die when the physiological vitality of many parts of the organism is still strong and when, therefore, the psychological urge for life is also strong. For death is ordinarily due to a breakdown in one section of the organism which has fatal results for the body as a whole.

All this is not to overlook the fact that a number of the aged who are miserable, weak and losing the use of their faculties one by one, may devoutly wish for a speedy and painless end. But this is a wish likely to arise in intelligent people of any age who are afflicted with incurable illness and suffering. And in some cases the conscious will to have life terminate may overcome, through an act of suicide, all the factors, subconscious as well as conscious, that make for the continuance of life, no matter how distasteful it may be. Yet in practically all cases of suicide or would-be suicide it is to be remembered that the person desires to die because this life no longer seems *worthwhile* and not because he craves nonexistence. However unbearable his condition, he would normally accept with alacrity the offer of a rejuvenated life beyond the tomb where he would enjoy everlasting health and happiness. Thus, the positive desire or definite decision to depart this world by no means implies a predilection for oblivion.

The idea of extinction is so repulsive, according to Plutarch, that we may "almost say that all men and women would readily submit themselves to the teeth of Cerberus, and to the punishment of carrying water in a sieve, if only they might remain in existence and escape the doom of annihilation."[16] The poet Heine cries out: "How our soul struggles against the thought of the cessation of our personality, of eternal annihilation! The *horror vacui* which we ascribe to nature is really inborn in the human heart."[17] Unamuno takes the position of being a defiant conscientious objector against personal extinction: "If it is nothingness that awaits us, let us make an injustice of it; let us fight against destiny, even though without hope of victory; let us fight against it quixotically."[18] Dylan Thomas protests:

> *Do not go gentle into that good night.*
> *Rage, rage against the dying of the light.*[19]

Even Thomas Huxley, a very tough-minded scientist who had no faith in immortality and who died in 1895, wrote near the close of his life: "It is a curious thing that I find my dislike to the thought of extinction increasing as I get older and nearer the goal. It flashes across me at all sorts of times and with a sort of horror that in 1900 I shall probably know no more of what is going on than I did in 1800. I had sooner be in hell a good deal—at any rate in one of the upper circles where the climate and company are not too trying."[20]

In a questionnaire conducted by Professor F. C. S. Schiller 22 percent of those who answered asserted that they preferred any sort of a future life to annihilation.[21] Thus it is apparent that for some men the prospect of the most gloomy and hateful variety of after-existence can serve as a kind of psychological buffer against the stern and stark idea of annihilation. And this is understandable. For to try to realize that when once we close our eyes in death, we shall never, never open them again on any happy or absorbing scene, that this pleasant earth will roll on and on for ages with ourselves no more sensible of what transpires than a dull clod, that this brief and flickering and bittersweet life is our only glimpse, our only taste, of existence throughout the billion infinities of unending time—to try to realize this, even to phrase such thoughts, can occasion a black, sinking spell along the pathways of sensation.

To the profound aversion towards non-existence we can to a large degree attribute, among those unable to believe in personal survival, an interest in various substitute or vicarious types of immortality. . . . The most important of these are ideal immortality, the attainment of a certain high and noble quality in life and intellect; biological immortality in the ongoing generations of one's children and descendants; and social immortality through the continuing impact of one's personality, work, fame or even impersonal achievements on successive societies of the future. The strength of the bent towards fame is seen in the characteristic efforts to preserve one's name and memory among the living by means of countless different devices. And it is evidenced in the general preference among males for sons, who will carry on the family name.

In Plato's *Symposium*, Diotima says to Socrates: "Think only of the ambition of men, and you will wonder at the senselessness of their ways, unless you consider how they are stirred by the love of an immortality of fame. They are ready to run all risks greater by far than they would have run for their children, and to spend money and undergo any sort of toil, and even to die, for the sake of leaving behind them a name which shall be eternal."[22] The economic and social effects of this sentiment, operating through the distribution and expenditure of wealth, have been and are immense and incalulable. But even for the greatest men we can think of today, what will the immortality of fame amount to, one wonders, a million years from now?

The universal shrinking from death is often augmented by the fear of dying, that is, fear of the process, gradual or sudden, that brings to a final conclusion our stay upon this earth. This process, particularly if in the form of long-drawn-out illness may indeed entail much physical pain and mental anguish. Even when it is short it may involve terrible suffering, as when people meet death in some frightful automobile or airplane accident. Yet only a comparatively few men perish in this manner; and there can be no doubt that on the whole the terrors of dying have been greatly exaggerated. There is much good evidence to the effect that the last moments of life are for the vast majority far from an ordeal.

The eminent English physician, Sir Arbuthnot Lane, tells us:

> In the course of my life I must have seen scores of people die. Some of them were people who in life had been horribly afraid of death. Yet I don't think I can remember a single instance where, when their time came, this did not leave them, to be replaced by a wonderful state of peace and calm. I have never known anybody really to resent death when their last moment has come. They have clung desperately to life so long as they could; and may have regretted bitterly the parting with their friends and all that they held dear, but not one who was conscious to the end ever seemed to regard death as a horrible climax to life. In all such cases it came as a perfectly natural and undisturbed happening.[23]

Sir William Osler, the noted surgeon, gives testimony of the same nature. "I have careful records," he writes, "of about five hundred deathbeds, studied particularly with reference to the modes of death and the sensations of the dying. . . . Ninety suffered bodily pain or distress of one sort or another, eleven showed mental apprehension, two positive terror, one expressed spiritual exaltation, one bitter remorse. The great majority gave no sign one way or the other; like their birth, their death was a sleep and a forgetting."[24] Whatever the facts, however, men have long been accustomed to attach to death the blame for all the afflictions, actual and reputed, of the process of dying. Thus, they have placed on innocent death a guilt which properly belongs to life itself; and this miscarriage of justice has been of considerable influence on the philosophical and religious attitudes of mankind.

Much of the dismal and oppressive atmosphere that usually surrounds the disposal of the dead is also transferred, through the processes of association, to death. No matter how skillful the embalmer's art, no matter how calm and reposed the appearance of the body, no mattter how beautiful the floral decorations, it is at best not a pleasant thing to view the cold and unresponsive corpse of a beloved intimate, so appallingly like yet unlike the living person. That last intense look at the dead body lying in the coffin may haunt for years the inner recesses of the mind. Funeral services, however short and simple, however unaccompanied by crepe and tears, do not result in happy memories. And the final procession to the cemetery, behind a sable hearse, and the final lowering of the coffined body into the grave are experiences that leave grim and indelible traces on the souls of the living.

The fact that we have been accustomed to associate the personality of the departed with his body may lead us to half-imagine that the man himself is in the coffin and in the ground, as common idioms, such as "he would turn in his grave," well illustrate. So we may conceive of the deceased as perhaps overwhelmed by the absolute solitude, stillness and darkness. Thought of the inevitable decay and dissolution of his body may also come to plague us; and we may meditate, Hamlet-like, concerning the unflattering destiny that overtakes what was once a man. These painful reflections we may even carry forward to that day when our own familiar body may be interred. These are indeed morbid thoughts, but they are thoughts that not infrequently arise in conjunction with ordinary burial customs and the well-known fate of corpses.

Closely connected with the natural interest in immortality that results from the general tendency to seek life and avoid death is the fact that the very structure and functioning of the human personality encourage confidence in continued existence. "I not only postulate a morrow when I prepare for it, but ingenuously and heartily believe that the morrow will come. . . . Every moment of life accordingly trusts that life will continue; and this prophetic interpretation of action, so long as action lasts, amounts to continual faith in futurity."[25] By far the greater part of rational deliberation directly or indirectly concerns our future and confidently assumes that the future will occur.

William Hazlitt has a marvelous passage on the initial incredibility of extinction:

> To see the golden sun and the azure sky, the outstretched ocean, to walk upon the green earth, and to be lord of a thousand creatures, to look down the giddy precipices or over the distant flowery vales, to see the world spread out under one's finger in a map, to bring the stars near, to view the smallest insects in a microscope, to read history, and witness the revolutions of empire and the succession of generations, to hear of the glory of Sidon and Tyre, of Babylon and Susa, as of a faded pageant, and to say all these were, and are now nothing, to think that we exist in such a point of time, and in such a corner of space, to be at once spectators and a part of the moving scene, to watch the return of the seasons of spring and autumn, to hear
>
> *The stockdove plain amid the forest deep,*
> *That drowsy rustles to the sighing gale*

—to traverse wilderness, to listen to the midnight choir, to visit lighted halls, or plunge into the dungeon's gloom, or sit in crowded theatres and see life itself mocked, to feel heat and cold, pleasure and pain, right and wrong, truth and falsehood, to study the works of art and refine the sense of beauty to agony, to worship fame and to dream of immortality, to have read Shakespeare and belong to the same species as Sir Isaac Newton; to be and do all this, and then in a moment to be nothing, to have it all snatched from one like a juggler's ball or a phantasmagoria; there is something revolting and incredible to sense in the transition, and no wonder, that, aided by youth and warm blood and the flush of enthusiasm, the mind contrives for a long time to reject it with disdain and loathing as a monstrous and improbable fiction.[26]

But we must supplement Hazlitt to remark how very difficult, if not impossible, it is concretely to envision ourselves as non-existent. We may see with the mind's eye our own deathbed, view upon it our own rigid and lifeless corpse, witness our own funeral service, but we ourselves are always there as living observers. Whether we shift our imagination two thousand years back to the assassination of Julius Caesar or indefinitely forward to the first air flight for man's colonization of Mars—indeed no matter how many thousands of years our minds pry into the future or into the past or however far afield into space—*we* are at the scene of action busily playing the reporter's role. And in this sense we are truly egocentric.

Freud characteristically comments upon the matter:

> Our own death is indeed unimaginable, and whenever we make the attempt to imagine it we can perceive that we really survive as spectators. Hence the psychoanalytic school could venture on the assertion that at bottom no one believes in his own death; or to put the same thing in another way, in the unconscious every one of us is convinced of his own immortality. . . . What we call our "unconscious" (the deepest strata of our minds, made up of instinctual impulses) knows nothing whatever of negatives or denials—contradictions coincide in it—and so it knows nothing whatever of our own death, for to that we can give only a negative purport.[27]

Thus, as Edward Young writes in his famous poem, *Night Thoughts,* "All men think all men mortal but themselves."

Yet, while the *limitations* of the imagination help in some ways to make acceptable the belief in immortality, at the same time its very power and scope can have a like effect. One does not have to belong to any religious cult to have the experience of remembering a dead person so vividly on occasion that it seems as if he himself must still exist. We are habitually and normally able to recall images of departed personalities that have far more reality-tone than memories of places which we know for certain to be objectively existent. When someone close to us dies, especially if suddenly, the sheer momentum of our mental habits often makes us feel, "Why this is impossible. He *can't* be gone." It takes time for us to overcome a curious feeling of unreality and to readjust our minds to the new situation. Such mental states lead easily to the claim that one has a sure and dependable sense of the objective though invisible presence of the dead. In dreams we may see, talk with and even touch the dead. And in view of these well-known facts it does not seem surprising that the living should report in good faith that even during waking hours they carry on social intercourse with the souls of the deceased. Men will probably keep on "seeing" various species of ghosts and apparitions to the end of time. For those who will not let reason discipline their imaginations, such visions will always seem a reliable indication that there is another life.

A kindred motivation behind belief in immortality is the commonplace distinction . . . between body and personality, or soul. Among many peoples the phenomena of dreams, trances and the ordinary human shadow have encouraged credence in the soul as an entity able to exist separately and independently of the body. A more inclusive and modern position is that of Dr. Holmes: "I believe," he avers, "in immortality because not otherwise can we explain the discrepancy between soul and body. Early in life these two begin to pull apart—the body to fail and the soul to grow stronger and ever stronger. Physically we begin to die when spiritually we are most ready to live."[28] Dr. Harry Emerson Fosdick expresses much the same thought when he says that "the assertion of our immortality involves the faith that we are invisible, spiritual personalities."[29]

These and many other similar statements by immortalists seem to be in essence far more proclamations of the soul-body distinction and of the value of the soul than convincing arguments for immortality; they indicate that the immortalists think the very existence of the soul or personality to be in jeopardy unless it is eternal. The discerning Professor Woodbridge aptly phrases our point when he writes that proofs of immortality illustrate the radical difference between body and soul and turn the illustrations into evidence."[30] A comparable situation arises when men, utilizing familiar religious terminology, fight for the more individualistic values under the banner of the immortality of the soul.[31]

The strongest single motivation, however, supporting belief in a future life is in my opinion the effect on the living of the death of friends, relatives and even entire strangers. Unutterable grief over the loss of a beloved child or parent and intense desire to be with him again are natural and universal human feelings. And they lead, as there is abundant evidence to show, quite directly to hope or conviction of a hereafter. . . . The great biologist, Henri Pasteur, writes: "My philosophy is of the heart and not of the mind, and I give myself up, for instance, to those feelings about eternity which come naturally at the bedside of a cherished child drawing its last breath."[32] A young man of thirty-one says: "My belief in a future life and in recognition after death have been strengthened by the death of my little boy." Another confides: "The death of a near friend a year ago has profoundly affected my life; it seems as if a part of myself is being parted from the beloved dead. Paralleling these profound reactions again."[33]

Friedrich Schleiermacher leaves us a letter from a close friend who has just lost her husband: "Schleier, by all that is dear to God and sacred, give me, if you can, the certain assurance of finding and knowing him again. Tell me your inmost faith on this, dear Schleier; Oh! if it fails, I am undone. It is for this that I live, for this that I submissively and quietly endure: this is the only outlook that sheds a light on my dark life,—to find him again, to live for him again. O God! he cannot be destroyed!"[34] There are numerous cases on record of people killing themselves to preclude being parted from the beloved dead. Paralleling these profound reactions on the part of the bereaved are the strong hopes of those who are dying or whose time is short to meet again the loved ones they are leaving behind, or at least to watch their development. It is not difficult to understand why people should have such intense feelings in the face of death or why they should interpret these feelings as valid reasons for belief in a future life. Probably the greater proportion of believers in the world today would agree with William James that "the surest warrant for immortality is the yearning of our bowels for our dear ones."[35] There can be no doubt that the idea of immortality will continue to exercise an appeal "as long as love kisses the lips of death,"[36] in the words of Robert Ingersoll.

But it is not only *love* for the departed that leads to hope for their immortality. The attachment to them may be negative and in the form of secret dislike or hatred. In most families there exists a certain amount of antagonism among the different members; and in some, bitter quarrels are the rule rather than the exception. When one member of a family passes on, the others, no matter how innocent of being remiss, are likely to reproach themselves for neglect and harsh words. They may have a distinct sense of guilt and be anxious for an opportunity to show more affectionate feelings toward the relative who has died.[37] By their devotion to his memory and their hymns of praise to his good qualities they will try to prove to him that, after all, they loved him deeply. But unless he still exists somewhere as a conscious person, their efforts are in vain. Hence they cherish the thought that at least temporarily he has survived death and is able to appreciate their attitude.

Attesting to the far-reaching effects of the loss of dear ones is the fresh and absorbing interest which the matter of immortality often takes on for the sorrowing survivors. A widow or a grieving parent will order a whole shelf of books on the future life, will suddenly become devoutly religious or will go in for Spiritualism with a vengeance. Then as time passes and the hurt grows less, as the bereaved gradually becomes more and more adjusted to the new situation, his preoccupation with the hereafter diminishes. Thus Dr. Lawton finds that the normal Spiritualist attends services for only a relatively short period, usually not more than one or two years.[38] A merely temporary credence in survival, then, may function as a psychological shock-absorber, or therapeutic. And in general what many people really want is *belief* in immortality rather than immortality itself.

It should be noted here that the orthodox Spiritualist, Catholic and other religious practices in relation to the dead by no means always have a curative effect. By encouraging the bereaved to keep on constantly and indefinitely thinking about the departed, saying masses for his soul, or trying to converse with him through mediums, these practices sometimes keep open and raw the painful wound of death. They may prompt the mourners to withdraw from the world and its fruitful activities and to center their thoughts upon the memory of the beloved dead. Especially is this a danger in Spiritualism, with its continual and morbid emphasis on actual discourse with the personalities of the departed, its ghoulish spirit photographs and its experiments, following out the tradition of the Witch of Endor and other historical celebrities, in raising phantoms from the depths of nowhere. Nor is it exactly healthy to have constantly that eerie feeling that the dead are always present and perhaps watching your every move. Thus the natural concern with the theory of survival that results from the death of the near and dear may be abnormally stimulated.

When some great and well-loved public figure dies, members of the community may be moved to reflect upon a hereafter whether or not they knew the man personally. The passing of a president, a king, a leading statesman or, in some countries, a motion-picture star, will cause millions to speculate on the meaning of death. A similar result may follow the large-scale loss of human life in some terrible catastrophe, such as a mine disaster, the sinking of a ship at sea, a calamitous flood, fire or earthquake. During the First World War, when millions and millions of men were dying on the battlefields of Europe, concern over a life beyond registered a noticeable increase. "Not for a century," claims an observer, "has interest in the great themes of death, immortality and the life everlasting been so widespread and so profound. The war has made a new heaven; let us trust that it may aid in making a new earth."[39] One writer, Winifred Kirkland, impressed with how the war filled whole populations with the spirit of what she calls "the New Death," makes the astonishing statement: "If even for a few generations we act on our conjecture of immortality, the larger vision, the profounder basis of purpose, will so advance human existence *as to make this war worth its price.*"[40] [Italics mine— C.L.] And many a Christian clergyman rejoiced over the effect of the First World War in bringing a revival, through suffering, of belief in immortality and other religious doctrines.[41]

While reactions to the death of others differ considerably according to the individual temperament, it is not to be doubted that frequently the most bitter heartache occurs when persons are cut off prematurely or when their demise is sudden and totally unexpected. Often these two conditions of dying suddenly and long before one's time coincide. When we read in our morning newspaper of nine young and healthy college students being abruptly snuffed out by carbon monoxide gas as they lay sleeping during the night,[42] we are deeply shocked both at the swift horror of the accident and at the measureless unfulfilled potentialities that came to an end with the death of these youths. We sense, too, the unspeakable anguish of the families concerned, proud of these fine sons and brothers, devoted to them over long years, and bringing them up with loving and sacrificial care only to have them snatched away as they were about to step out into the world and show their mettle. Added to all this is the frustrated feeling of these families at having no chance to say good-bye, no opportunity to speak a last affectionate word or to make some gesture of endearment. On the other hand, to take a very different sort of case, when an old man full of years and honor passes peacefully away during the natural decline of senescence, we are not likely to feel that death is a cruel and awful thing. In fact, we may feel that it has carried out a function both proper and beneficial.

Hence we must classify the widespread reaction to *premature* death as one of the major motivations toward belief in immortality. It is appalling to realize that the First World War claimed some ten million lives, combatants and noncombatants. The comparable figure for the Second World War totaled fifty million. A majority of the victims of course were in their youth or middle age. In the United States accidents alone account for more than a hundred thousand deaths a year, while more than twenty thousand commit suicide. Each year more than twenty thousand children perish before reaching fifteen. No less than half of all deaths in America occur during youth or middle age, that is, before the age of sixty-five.

Now since the U.S. record as regards the deathrate and longevity is one of the best in the world, the situation in most other countries is measurably worse. In India, for example, the average expectation of life is approximately thirty-two years, according to latest estimates of the United Nations. These various figures show clearly why there is a common feeling that death cheats our friends, our families and all mankind out of a large portion of experience that is rightfully theirs. If every human being, both in the United States and elsewhere, lived to be seventy or eighty years old, one of the most potent factors leading to credence in immortality would disappear.

Mortals seek many different kinds of compensations in immortality besides those already mentioned. One man may primarily want another existence because he was unsuccessful in love, another because he never received proper recognition from the socially elite, another because his yearning for knowledge remains unsatisfied. This last motivation has often been strong among persons of high intelligence and scientific ability; it was, for instance, undoubtedly an important factor in Plato's interest in immortality. Among religious people the desire to attain a clearer vision of God and to be with Christ has of course been a sincere and powerful element in the hope for life eternal. Sometimes the thirst for knowledge after death takes the form of sheer curiosity as to what is going to happen on earth; and many an immortalist has had the quaint notion that from the other world, as from a ringside seat, he will look down upon this globe and behold the varying progress of men and nations, of friends and favorite causes.

There are additional motivations that might in general be called philosophical. Thus the English Hegelian, Bernard Bosanquet, is of the opinion that "the longing for continuance is at bottom the longing for the satisfactory whole. . . . What we really care about is not simple prolongation of our "personal" existence, but, whether accompanying prolongation or in the direct form of liberation, some affirmation of our main interests, or some refuge from the perpetual failure of satisfaction."[43] Closely akin to this is the notion that only if there is immortality does life have "meaning." This is merely another way of saying that without immortality life is futile or irrational. . . . Very far-reaching metaphysical and ethical assumptions are involved in such statements. They clearly depend on a whole philosophy of value which is of dubious validity, and which is little more than a rationalization of the all-too-human tendency to insist on a cosmic standing for human desires and ideals.

To borrow the phraseology of John Dewey, the immortalists have a craving for the sure, the fixed, the stable, as against the uncertain, the changing, the precarious.[44] Or, in Dr. Horace Kallen's language, they want perfect freedom, that is, "the smooth and uninterrupted flow of behavior; the flow of desire into fulfillment, of thought into deed, of act into fact" in a realm where "danger, evil and frustration are nonexistent."[45] So it becomes apparent that, in general, frustration of any human impulse, ambition or ideal may be influential in leading to belief in a beyond. Especially is this true of the more egoistic and self-assertive activities, though concern with a hereafter does not necessarily imply selfishness.

Just as bad health is one of the chief props of the modern religion known as Christian Science, so it can become one of the prime incentives towards belief in immortality. In heaven the sick, the halt and the blind will have glorious and perfect bodies no longer subject to the shortcomings of earthly development and the strains of medical experimentation. The chronic invalid will rise every morning with the vigor of a young athlete about to run a race; the nervous wreck will feel and exude nothing but strength, self-confidence and calm; the bent, ill old man, slow in mind and dull in sense, will step forth as in the prime of life, erect, handsome and alert. Such is the promise of paradise. And it extends not only to those who are definitely ill, but to all who were born with or acquired any sort of deformity. There will be no hunchbacks in the great beyond; and if a man loses a leg here, he can be sure that God will give him back a much better one in heaven. Even those who are rather plain of countenance can expect some improvement in the realm of immortality.

Most of the motivations behind belief in a future existence which I have been citing might become compelling for any human being regardless of his station in life or his share of this world's goods. But it is of the very highest importance to remember that the great masses of men since the beginning of history have been moved, in addition, to hope for a hereafter because of the sheer economic and social misery in which they have for the most part lived. Poverty-stricken, lacking the very necessities of life, crushed by grinding toil, they have had ample reason to flee for refuge and recompense to visions of a world beyond. Shut out from the rich empires of art and culture, denied access to education and opportunity, ever the most numerous victims of the bloody wars that have perpetually plagued mankind, these masses have easily and naturally fallen prey to hallucinations of a blessed hereafter where everything will be set aright. And they have listened with eager ears to the teachings of kings, priests and other henchmen of the status quo to the effect that if they remain resigned and humble on this earth, they will have a marvelous reward in heaven. Karl Marx makes a trenchant comment: "The mortgage held by the peasants on the heavenly estates guarantees the mortgage held by the bourgeoise on the peasant estates."[46]

While no doubt a number of upper-class religious propagandists have had their tongues in their cheeks, especially in modern times, there is no reason to think that most of them have not been devoutly sincere. Indeed, their very sincerity has enabled them to take with good conscience the position that since the well-deserving among the oppressed and suffering masses will in any case receive their proper recompense in paradise, it is not worthwhile to try to do much about their condition here. An ingenious variation of this attitude is the theory that since character-building is the purpose of existence, the trying and unhappy experiences of this life are simply God's inimitable way of developing and strengthening the soul.

Along with everything else, the common people have swallowed religion's bogeyman story about the terrible punishments in the afterlife for those who do not conform to established standards of conduct and who are too presumptuous in challenging the settled habits of exploitation. Fear of retribution after death, however, does not imply a weakening of the belief in immortality; and, on the contrary, by deeply involving the emotions, may serve to strengthen it. As I have already pointed out, for long periods of history the prevailing sentiment towards a future life was one of fear rather than of hope and joy. Since the precepts of the Church have always constituted for a large proportion of the workers and peasants their chief education, they have accepted whatever emphasis—whether on heaven or hell—that the Church has chosen to make. In general, the brute weight of authority and tradition has been one of the prime causes of belief in immortality.

A drastic change in the economic and social system, making the world a safer and saner place to live in, would have far-reaching effects on the extent and strength of belief in a hereafter. A more rational social order would, in my judgment, quickly result in a sweeping decline in the influence of immortality ideas. And we have here an excellent supporting illustration for the economic interpretation of history in which economic forces and relationships have a decisive influence on such important elements of the cultural superstructure as religion. This is not to say that in some species of economic Utopia the wish to believe and the belief in such a significant religious idea as that of immortality would automatically and completely disappear. There still would exist those motivations towards belief inherent in the biological and psychological structure of human beings. There still would exist personal frustration, due to such causes as unsatisfied ambition and unrequited love. There still would be premature death from accidents and disease.

But the frustrations would take place on a level unconnected with the maladjustments that come from strain and worry over the basic necessities of a decent existence. Mental and emotional security would increase with economic security, while devotion to the great objectives of the new society would drive personal troubles and Freudian complexes into the background. There can be no doubt that the emphasis in contemporary civilization on individualism and the expansion of the ego has tended to encourage psychological traits that foster the urge for self-perpetuation. The tendency, however, in a more cooperative commonwealth stressing collective effort would be to develop the altruistic rather than the egoistic impulses of men. Everyone would be taught the ideal of fulfilling himself in socially useful activities rather than in those with merely personal significance. In this much improved society of the future the increased freedom from disease, war and violence in general would bring about a corresponding decrease in premature death. All in all, in such a social order many of the most potent factors of the past and present that have led men to seek supernatural consolation in an afterlife would be reduced to a minimum.

The remaining factors, such as the drive towards self-preservation and the difficulty of imagining oneself nonexistent, would be relatively unaffected by the new social and economic conditions and would have to be specifically dealt with by education and science. Some people desire immortality, moreover, not because they are downtrodden and miserable on this earth, but because they are having such a fine time here that they want to go on with it in another life. In this connection Professor Taylor testifies that in his experience it is just "when we feel most alive and vigorous in soul and body"[47] that we are surest and most desirous of a life beyond. And it is possible that in a cooperative and peaceful world society, where a greater proportion of the people than ever before would presumably be enjoying full and happy lives, some might cast eyes of longing in the direction of an after-existence because of their very feeling of vitality. In such cases the idea of immortality would be compensatory in the sense of counteracting the sense of unhappiness that results from the reflection that a present happiness must end.

The converse of the proposition that a higher and happier form of society will weaken the belief in immortality is that a prior weakening in this belief will help to bring about a better society. If they fully realized that this life is all, men would be less prone to accept without the stiffest sort of resistance the rank injustices and irrationalities of present existence. Those who seem condemned by circumstance to poverty and misery would put up a much stronger fight to better their lot. It would not be so simple to persuade millions of men to sacrifice their lives in frightful wars if they recognized that death was the absolute end. Increasing lack of faith in a hereafter would also react against the general conservative influence of supernatural religion. The very fact that disbelief in immortality can be an important factor in stirring the masses of the people to militant action makes many sophisticated members of the upper classes reluctant to have the truth about death too widely broadcast.

It is, of course, grossly inaccurate to say, as some careless critics do, that all immortality ideas are merely compensatory or wish-fulfilling. This neglects the fact that among primitive tribes these ideas have been pseudo-scientific principles of explanation designed to make intelligible such phenomena as dreams, trances and apparitions in which the dead appear to play a part. More important still, it overlooks the dread with which large numbers of mankind have regarded existence beyond the grave. Where fear of an afterlife is the prevailing sentiment and desire for it weak or nonexistent, it is difficult to understand how the idea of immortality can be classed as a wish-fulfillment. This does not mean, however, that the inclusion of hell in the hereafter in itself deprives the future life of its quite common character of wish-fulfillment. It all depends on the emphasis given to hell and the extent to which men feel that they are likely to go there rather than to heaven.

The simple idea of hell has often functioned as a necessary complement of heaven in an all-embracing moral or hedonistic wish-fulfilment.

Men may devoutly desire hell—for other people. And the assumption that the powers-that-be in the universe, in the role of cosmic police officers, will deal severely with whatever man considers evil is no less a reading of wishes and ideals into existence than the assumption that they are supporting everything he deems good. In fact it is the same anthropomorphic assumption expressed differently. The concept of hell is compensatory in so far as it serves to provide a vicarious victory over the evils that so frequently win the day in this-earthly life. Like the idea of heaven it is only too likely to cut the nerve of effective action against the ills of this world. One of the most impassioned of the early church fathers, Tertullian, gives us a most instructive paean of transcendental triumph: "How shall I admire, how laugh, how exult when I behold so many proud monarchs groaning in the lower abyss of darkness, so many magistrates liquefying in fiercer flames than they ever kindled against the Christians; so many sage philosophers blushing in red-hot fires with their deluded pupils."[48]

Now if a Christian really believes, with Tertullian, not only that his virtuousness will bring him eternal reward in paradise, but also that the wickedness of his enemies and oppressors will be revenged and punished in hell, he can afford to take a very serene view of the woes of this life. If he himself happens to be a member of the ruling class instead of one of the underdogs, his pangs of conscience regarding some of the more brutal and nefarious practices of the governing authorities can easily be assuaged by his inner assurance that the guilty will receive their proper deserts in the next world. If God can be depended upon to wreak stern justice in the hereafter on the heads of tyrants and malefactors, then why should anyone bother too much about them in the here-now? And where hell is taken seriously, this logic applies just as much in the modern world as in the ancient and medieval.

Even ideas of hell can, then, to a certain extent be rightly designated as wish-fulfillments. When we turn to the idea of heaven, "the land of pure delight," we find that the wish-fulfillment interpretation is fully justified. Analyses of the motivations behind belief in a blessed immortality, of the arguments supporting it and of the descriptions that are part of it all point to this conclusion. . . . Ethical arguments stressed in modern times involve little more than turning human wishes into proofs. And if we call to mind any characteristic portrayals of paradise, we see at once that they conform to the familiar earthly life, needs and desires of the particular people concerned.

In the realm beyond, the Egyptians must have their River Nile, the

Mohammedans their alluring young females, the Scandinavians their warlike Valhalla, the American Indians their Happy Hunting Ground, the Christians their saints and angels. The Book of Revelation promises that the righteous in heaven "shall hunger no more, neither thirst any more; neither shall the sun light on them, nor any heat."[49] No vast penetration is required to realize that this passage was written by someone who thought that the climate in Palestine was more than a trifle too hot. On the other hand, when missionaries told the Eskimos about the excessive warmth of hell, these inhabitants of the frozen north, evidently rather tired of so much ice and snow, responded by asking eagerly the way to the infernal regions.[50]

Naturally enough, the ethical distinctions in heaven vary with the standards and ideals of this-worldly cultures. In one culture the brave will be awarded the choicest places in the next life, in another the humble; in one culture the strenuously active, in another the devoutly contemplative. In Christianity itself there have been shifts of emphasis according to time and place. In former ages, for example, paradise, reflecting common this-earthly attitudes, was conceived of as a state of inactive bliss, as an eternal rest home where the weary righteous could cease from their labors and bask forever in easeful ecstasy. Today, however, when joyous and rewarding work is comparatively more widespread and at least held out to everyone as an ideal, there is a tendency to picture heaven as a place where fruitful activity will continue and souls will press on to unending development and improvement.

A motivation akin to simple wish-fulfillment in leading support to dreams of immortality is the human predilection for the dramatic. An after-existence where you can be reunited with your friends and family is plainly a more exciting prospect than death as the absolute end. Then there are all the other imagined delights, beauties and adventures of the hereafter, including the chance to meet the many great and glamorous figures of the past. Add a purgatory and hell as colorfully described as in the *Divine Comedy*, and the panorama of immortality becomes an absorbing drama with enormous theatrical appeal, particularly for those whose lives are on the humdrum side.

That there should be such a large element of wish-fulfillment in immortality ideas does not in itself disestablish them. To desire a thing greatly no more *dis*proves than proves its existence. But if we deeply wish something to be true, we must be doubly on guard to prevent our emotions from influencing our judgment on the question. And in the case of immortality, with such a wide and powerful range of motivations encouraging belief in the idea, there is reason to regard an affirmative answer with considerable suspicion. Especially does this hold true today when there is so much emphasis on the pleasant aspects of the future life, and hell is considered so out-of-date. For these various reasons I believe that for the modern mind one of the most appropriate and penetrating comments that can be made on the points at issue is to be found in Rupert Brooke's satire entitled "Heaven."[51] I give this poem in full:

> *Fish (fly-replete in depth of June,*
> *Dawdling away their wat'ry noon)*
> *Ponder deep wisdom, dark or clear,*
> *Each secret fishy hope or fear.*
> *Fish say, they have their Stream and Pond;*
> *But is there anything Beyond?*
> *This life cannot be All, they swear,*
> *For how unpleasant, if it were!*
> *One may not doubt that somehow, Good*
> *Shall come of Water and of Mud;*
> *And, sure, the reverent eye must see*
> *A Purpose in Liquidity.*
> *We darkly know, by Faith we cry,*
> *The future is not Wholly Dry.*
> *Mud unto mud!—Death eddies near—*
> *Not here the appointed End, not here!*
> *But somewhere, beyond Space and Time*
> *Is wetter water, slimier slime!*
> *And there (they trust) there swimmeth One*
> *Who swam ere rivers were begun,*
> *Immense, of fishy form and mind,*
> *Squamous, omnipotent, and kind;*
> *And under that Almighty Fin,*
> *The littlest fish may enter in.*
> *Oh! never fly conceals a hook*
> *Fish say, in the Eternal Brook,*
> *But more than mundane weeds are there,*
> *And mud, celestially fair;*
> *Fat caterpillars drift around,*
> *And Paradisal grubs are found;*

Unfading moths, immortal flies,
And the worm that never dies.
And in that Heaven of all their wish
There shall be no more land, say fish!

NOTES

1. W. E. H. Lecky, *History of European Morals* (Appleton, 1927), Vol. I, p. 211.

2. Thomas Aquinas, *Summa Theologica,* Part III (Supplement), Q. 94, Art. 1.

3. Quoted in Alger, *A Critical History of the Doctrine of a Future Life* (W. J. Widdleton, 1871), p. 515.

4. Quoted in Chapman Cohen, *Essays in Free-thinking* (London: Pioneer Press, 1928), p. 26.

5. Jonathan Edwards, Sermon, "Sinners in the Hands of an Angry God," (Application).

6. President Edwards, *Works* (Worcester, Mass.: Isaiah Thomas, 1809), Vol. VIII, p. 167.

7. Quoted in Pringle-Pattison, *The Idea of Immortality* (Oxford University Press), p. 233.

8. Quoted in James H. Leuba, *The Belief in God and Immortality* (Open Court, 1921), p. 298.

9. Pringle-Pattison, *op. cit.*, p. 133.

10. Leuba, *op. cit.,* pp. 254 ff.

11. *Ibid.*, p. 256.

12. Quoted in Ilya Metchnikoff, *The Prolongation of Life* (Putnam, 1908), p. 127.

13. Quoted in G. Stanley Hall, *Senescence* (Appleton, 1923), p. 89.

14. *Ibid.,* p. 262.

15. Walter Savage Landor, "Dying Speech of an Old Philosopher."

16. Quoted in Pringle-Pattison, *op. cit.* p. 131.

17. *Ibid.,* p. 132.

18. Miguel de Unamuno, *The Tragic Sense of Life* (London: Macmillan, 1926), p. 268.

19. Dylan Thomas, "Do Not Go Gentle into That Good Night," *Collected Poems* (New Directions, 1946). (Copyright 1952, 1953 by Dylan Thomas. Reprinted by permission of New Directions.)

20. Leonard Huxley, *Life and Letters of Thomas Henry Huxley* (Appleton, 1900), Vol. II, p. 67.

21. Cited by Pratt, *The Religious Consciousness* (Macmillan, 1928), p. 235.

22. Plato, *Symposium*, 208.

23. Quoted in Chapman Cohen, *op. cit.,* p. 19.

24. William Osler, *Science and Immortality* (Houghton Mifflin, 1904), p. 19.

25. Santayana, *Reason in Religion* (Scribners', 1926), p. 235.

26. William Hazlitt, "On the Feeling of Immortality in Youth."

27. Sigmund Freud, "Thoughts on War and Death," Vol. IV, *Collected Papers* (International Psycho-Analytical Press, 1924), pp. 305-13. One of America's most acute philosophers, Professor F. J. E. Woodbridge of Columbia, thought that the impossibility of men's imagining themselves nonexistent was the most powerful motive of all towards belief in personal immortality.

28. *New York Times,* April 21, 1930.

29. Fosdick, *The Assurance of Immortality* (Association Press, 1926), p. 30.

30. F. J. E. Woodbridge, *The Son of Apollo* (Houghton Mifflin, 1929), p. 231.

31. See Cassirer, Kristeller, Randall (eds.) *The Renaissance Philosophy of Man* (University of Chicago Press, 1948), p. 11.

32. Quoted in Leuba, *op. cit.,* p. 317.

33. Quoted, *ibid.,* p. 316.

34. *Ibid.,* p. 315.

35. James, *The Principles of Psychology* (Holt, 1923), Vol. II, p. 308.

36. Robert G. Ingersoll, *Lectures and Essays,* First Series (London: Watts, 1926), p. 127.

37. See Lawton, *The Drama of Life After Death* (Holt, 1932), pp. 425-26.

38. *Ibid.,* p. 424.

39. Quoted in Winifred Kirkland, *The New Death* (Houghton Mifflin, 1918), p. 9.

40. *Ibid.,* pp. 163-64.

41. See Ray H. Abrams, "War Brings a Revival of Religion," Chap. XII in *Preachers Present Arms* (Round Table Press, 1933).

42. *New York Times,* Feb. 26, 1934.

43. Bernard Bosanquet, *The Value and Destiny of the Individual* (London: Macmillan, 1913), pp. 274-75.

44. John Dewey, *Experience and Nature* (Open Court, 1926), Ch. II.

45. Horace Kallen, in Dewey and others, *Creative Intelligence* (Holt, 1947), p. 434.

46. Karl Marx, *The Class Struggles in France* (New York: Labor News Company, 1924), p. 112.

47. Taylor, "The Belief in Immortality," in *The Faith and the War,* F. J. Fookes Jackson (ed.) (London: Macmillan, 1916), p. 139.

48. Quoted in Chapman Cohen, *op. cit.,* p. 25.

49. Revelation 7:16.

50. See Philip F. Waterman, *The Story of Superstition* (Knopf, 1929), p. 276.

51. Copyright, 1915, by Dodd, Mead & Co., Inc.

XI. Why Do Things Exist?

Kurt E. M. Baier

The Meaning of Life

Kurt Baier, professor of philosophy at the University of Pitts-
burgh, has degrees from the University of Vienna, the University of Melbourne and Oxford University. He has taught at
the University of Melbourne and at Canberra University College. He is the author of *The Moral Point of View* (1958), and
with Nicholas Rescher edited *Values and the Future.*

Tolstoy, in his autobiographical work, "A Confession," reports how, when
he was fifty and at the height of his literary success, he came to be obsessed
by the fear that life was meaningless.

"At first I experienced moments of perplexity and arrest of life, as
though I did not know what to do or how to live; and I felt lost and became
dejected. But this passed, and I went on living as before. Then these
moments of perplexity began to recur oftener and oftener, and always in
the same form. They were always expressed by the questions: What is it

From The Meaning of Life, *Inaugural Lecture delivered by K. E. M. Baier at the
Canberra University College, Canberra, Australia, on October 15, 1957, and reprinted with the permission of the author and the Australian National University.*

for? What does it lead to? At first it seemed to me that these were aimless and irrelevant questions. I thought that it was all well known, and that if I should ever wish to deal with the solution it would not cost me much effort; just at present I had no time for it, but when I wanted to, I should be able to find the answer. The questions however began to repeat themselves frequently, and to demand replies more and more insistently and like drops of ink always falling on one place they ran together into one black blot."[1]

A Christian living in the Middle Ages would not have felt any serious doubts about Tolstoy's questions. To him it would have seemed quite certain that life had a meaning and quite clear what it was. The medieval Christian world picture assigned to man a highly significant, indeed the central part in the grand scheme of things. The universe was made for the express purpose of providing a stage on which to enact a drama starring Man in the title role.

To be exact, the world was created by God in the year 4004 B.C. Man was the last and the crown of this creation, made in the likeness of God, placed in the Garden of Eden on earth, the fixed center of the universe, round which revolved the nine heavens of the sun, the moon, the planets and the fixed stars, producing as they revolved in their orbits the heavenly harmony of the spheres. And this gigantic universe was created for the enjoyment of man, who was originally put in control of it. Pain and death were unknown in paradise. But this state of bliss was not to last. Adam and Eve ate of the forbidden tree of knowledge, and life on this earth turned into a death-march through a vale of tears. Then, with the birth of Jesus, new hope came into the world. After He had died on the cross, it became at least possible to wash away with the purifying water of baptism some of the effects of Original Sin and to achieve salvation. That is to say, on condition of obedience to the law of God, man could now enter heaven and regain the state of everlasting, deathless bliss, from which he had been excluded because of the sin of Adam and Eve.

To the medieval Christian the meaning of human life was therefore perfectly clear. The stretch on earth is only a short interlude, a temporary incarceration of the soul in the prison of the body, a brief trial and test, fated to end in death, the release from pain and suffering. What really matters, is the life after the death of the body. One's existence acquires meaning not by gaining what this life can offer but by saving one's immortal soul from death and eternal torture, by gaining eternal life and everlasting bliss.

The scientific world picture which has found ever more general acceptance from the beginning of the modern era onwards is in profound conflict with all this. At first, the Christian conception of the world was discovered to be erroneous in various important details. The Copernican theory showed up the earth as merely one of several planets revolving round the sun, and the sun itself was later seen to be merely one of many fixed stars, each of which is itself the nucleus of a solar system similar to our own. Man, instead of occupying the center of creation, proved to be merely the inhabitant of a celestial body no different from millions of others. Furthermore, geological investigations revealed that the universe was not created a few thousand years ago, but was probably millions of years old.

Disagreements over details of the world picture, however, are only superficial aspects of a much deeper conflict. The appropriateness of the whole Christian outlook is at issue. For Christianity, the world must be regarded as the "creation" of a kind of Superman, a person possessing all the human excellences to an infinite degree and none of the human weaknesses, Who has made man in His image, a feeble, mortal, foolish copy of Himself. In creating the universe, God acts as a sort of playwright-cum-legislator-cum-judge-cum-executioner. In the capacity of playwright, He creates the historical world process, including man. He erects the stage and writes, in outline, the plot. He creates the *dramatis personae*, and watches over them with the eye partly of a father, partly of the law. While on stage, the actors are free to extemporise, but if they infringe the divine commandments, they are later dealt with by their creator in His capacity of judge and executioner.

Within such a framework, the Christian attitudes towards the world are natural and sound: it is natural and sound to think that all is arranged for the best even if appearances belie it; to resign oneself cheerfully to one's lot; to be filled with awe and veneration in regard to anything and everything that happens; to want to fall on one's knees and worship and praise the Lord. These are wholly fitting attitudes within the framework of the world view just outlined. And this world view must have seemed wholly sound and acceptable because it offered the best explanation which was then available of all the observed phenomena of nature.

As the natural sciences developed, however, more and more things in the universe came to be explained without the assumption of a supernatural creator. Science, moreover, could explain them better, that is, more accurately and more reliably. The Christian hypothesis of a supernatural maker, whatever other needs it was capable of satisfying, was at any rate no longer indispensable for the purpose of explaining the existence or occurrence of anything. In fact, scientific explanations do not seem to leave any room for this hypothesis. The scientific approach demands that we look for a natural explanation of anything and everything. The scientific way of looking at and explaining things has yielded an immensely greater measure of understanding of, and control over, the universe than any other way. And when one looks at the world in this scientific way, there seems to be no room for a personal relationship between human beings and a supernatural perfect being ruling and guiding men. Hence many scientists and educated men have come to feel that the Christian attitudes towards the world and human existence are inappropriate. They have become convinced that the universe and human existence in it are without a purpose and therefore devoid of meaning.[2]

THE EXPLANATION OF THE UNIVERSE

Such beliefs are disheartening and unplausible. It is natural to keep looking for the error that must have crept into our arguments. And if an error has crept in, then it is most likely to have crept in with science. For before the rise of science, people did not entertain such melancholy beliefs, while the scientific world picture seems literally to force them on us.

There is one argument which seems to offer the desired way out. It runs somewhat as follows. Science and religion are not really in conflict. They are, on the contrary, mutually complementary, each doing an entirely different job. Science gives provisional, if precise, explanations of small parts of the universe, religion gives final and overall, if comparatively vague, explanations of the universe as a whole. The objectionable conclusion, that human existence is devoid of meaning, follows only if we use scientific explanations where they do not apply, namely, where total explanations of the whole universe are concerned.[3]

After all, the argument continues, the scientific world picture is the inevitable outcome of rigid adherence to scientific method and explanation, but scientific, that is, causal explanations from their very nature are incapable of producing real illumination. They can at best tell us *how* things are or have come about, but never *why*. They are incapable of making the universe intelligible, comprehensible, meaningful to us. They represent the universe as meaningless, not because it *is* meaningless, but because scientific explanations are not designed to yield answers to investigations into the why and wherefore, into the meaning, purpose, or point of things. Scientific explanations (this argument continues) began, harmlessly enough, as partial and provisional explanations of the movement of material bodies, in particular the planets, within the general framework of the medieval world picture. Newton thought of the universe as a clock made, originally wound up, and occasionally set right by God. His laws of motion only revealed the ways in which the heavenly machinery worked. Explaining the movement of the planets by these laws was analogous to explaining the machinery of a watch. Such explanations showed *how* the thing worked, but not *what it was for* or *why* it existed. Just as the explanation of how a watch works can help our understanding of the watch only if, in addition, we assume that there is a watchmaker who has designed it for a purpose, made it, and wound it up, so the Newtonian explanation of the solar system helps our understanding of it only on the similar assumption that there is some divine artificer who has designed and made this heavenly clockwork for some purpose, has wound it up, and perhaps even occasionally sets it right, when it is out of order.

Socrates, in the *Phaedo*, complained that only explanations of a thing showing the good or purpose for which it existed could offer a *real* explanation of it. He rejected the kind of explanation we now call "causal" as no more than mentioning "that without which a cause could not be a cause," that is, as merely a necessary condition, but not the *real* cause, the real explanation.[4] In other words, Socrates held that *all* things can be explained in two different ways: either by mentioning merely a necessary condition, or by giving the *real* cause. The former is not an elucidation of the explicandum, not really a help in understanding it, in grasping its "why" and "wherefore."

This Socratic view, however, is wrong. It is not the case that there are two kinds of explanation for everything, one partial, preliminary, and not really clarifying, the other full, final, and illuminating. The truth is that these two kinds of explanation are equally explanatory, equally illuminating, and equally full and final, but that they are appropriate for different kinds of explicanda.

When in an uninhabited forest we find what looks like houses, paved streets, temples, cooking utensils, and the like, it is no great risk to say that these things are the ruins of a deserted city, that is to say, of something man-made. In such a case, the appropriate explanation is teleological, that is, in terms of the purposes of the builders of that city. On the other hand, when a comet approaches the earth, it is similarly a safe bet that, unlike the city in the forest, it was not manufactured by intelligent creatures and that, therefore, a teleological explanation would be out of place, whereas a causal one is suitable.

It is easy to see that in some cases causal, and in others teleological, explanations are appropriate. A small satellite circling the earth may or may not have been made by man. We may never know which is the true explanation, but either hypothesis is equally explanatory. It would be wrong to say that only a teleological explanation can *really* explain it. Either explanation would yield complete clarity although, of course, only one can be true. Teleological explanation is only one of several that are possible.

It may indeed be strictly correct to say that the question *"Why* is there a satellite circling the earth?" can only be answered by a teleological explanation. It may be true that "Why?" questions can really be used properly only in order to elicit *someone's reasons for* doing something. If this is so, it would explain our dissatisfaction with causal answers to "Why?" questions. But even if it is so, it does not show that "Why is the satellite there?" *must be answered by a teleological explanation.* It shows only that either it must be so answered or it must not be asked. The question "Why have you stopped beating your wife?" can be answered only by a teleological explanation, but if you have never beaten her, it is an improper question. Similarly, if the satellite is not man-made, "Why is there a satellite?" is improper since it implies an origin it did not have. Natural science can indeed only tell us *how* things in nature have come about and now *why,* but this is so not because something else can tell us the *why* and *wherefore,* but because there is none.

There is, however, another point which has not yet been answered. The objection just stated was that causal explanations did not even set out to answer the crucial question. We ask the question "Why?" but science returns an answer to the question "How?" It might now be conceded that this is no ground for a complaint, but perhaps it will instead be said that causal explanations do not give complete or full answers even to that latter question. In causal explanations, it will be objected, the existence of one thing is explained by reference to its cause, but this involves asking for the cause of that cause, and so on, ad infinitum. There is no resting place which is not as much in need of explanation as what has already been explained. Nothing at all is ever fully and completely explained by this sort of explanation.

Leibniz has made this point very persuasively. "Let us suppose a book of the elements of geometry to have been eternal, one copy always having been taken down from an earlier one; it is evident that, even though a reason can be given for the present book out of a past one, nevertheless out of any number of books, taken in order, going backwards, we shall never come upon a *full* reason; though we might well always wonder why there should have been such books from all time—why there were books at all, and why they were written in this manner. What is true of books is true also of the different states of the world; for what follows is in some way copied from what precedes . . . And so, however far you go back to earlier states, you will never find in those states a *full reason* why there should be any world rather than none, and why it should be such as it is."[5]

However, a moment's reflection will show that if any type of explanation is merely preliminary and provisional, it is teleological explanation, since it presupposes a background which itself stands in need of explanation. If I account for the existence of the man-made satellite by saying that it was made by some scientists for a certain purpose, then such an explanation can clarify the existence of the satellite only if I assume that there existed materials out of which the satellite was made, and scientists who made it for some purpose. It therefore does not matter what type of explanation we give, whether causal or teleological: either type, any type of explanation, will imply the existence of something by reference to which the explicandum can be explained. And this in turn must be accounted for in the same way, and so on forever.

But is not God a necessary being? Do we not escape the infinite regress as soon as we reach God? It is often maintained that, unlike ordinary intelligent beings, God is eternal and necessary; hence His existence, unlike theirs, is not in need of explanation. For what is it that creates the vicious regress just mentioned? It is that, if we accept the principle of sufficient reason (that there must be an explanation for the existence of anything and everything the existence of which is not logically necessary, but merely contingent[6]), the existence of all the things referred to in any explanation requires itself to be explained. If, however, God is a logically necessary being, then His existence requires no explanation. Hence the vicious regress comes to an end with God.

Now, it need not be denied that God is a necessary being in some sense of that expression. In one of these senses, I, for instance, am a necessary being: it is impossible that I should not exist, because it is self-refuting to say "I do not exist." The same is true of the English language and of the universe. It is self-refuting to say "There is no such thing as the English language" because this sentence is in the English language, or "There is no such thing as the universe" because whatever there is, *is* the universe. It is impossible that these things should not in fact exist since it is impossible that we should be mistaken in thinking that they exist. For what possible occurrence could even throw doubt on our being right on these matters, let alone show that we are wrong? I, the English language, and the universe are necessary beings, simply in the sense in which all is necessarily true which has been *proved* to be true. The occurrence of utterances such as "I exist," "the English language exists" and "the universe exists" is in itself sufficient proof of their truth. These remarks are therefore necessarily true, hence the things asserted to exist are necessary things.

But this sort of necessity will not satisfy the principle of sufficient reason, because it is only hypothetical or consequential necessity. *Given that* someone says "I exist," then it is logically impossible that he should not exist. Given the evidence we have, the English language and the universe most certainly do exist. But there is no necessity about the evidence. On the principle of sufficient reason, we must explain the existence of the evidence, for its existence is not logically necessary.[7]

In other words, the only sense of "necessary being" capable of terminating the vicious regress is "logically necessary being," but it is no longer seriously in dispute that the notion of a logically necessary being is self-contradictory.[8] Whatever can be conceived of as existing can equally be conceived of as not existing.

However, even if *per impossibile*, there were such a thing as a logically necessary being, we could still not make out a case for the superiority of teleological over causal explanation. The existence of the universe cannot be explained in accordance with the familiar model of manufacture by a craftsman. For that model presupposes the existence of materials out of which the product is fashioned. God, on the other hand, must create the materials as well. Moreover, although we have a simple model of "creation out of nothing," for composers create tunes out of nothing, yet there is a great difference between creating *something to be sung,* and making the sounds which are a singing of it, or producing the piano on which to play it. Let us, however, waive all these objections and admit, for argument's sake, that creation out of nothing is conceivable. Surely, even so, no one can claim that it is the kind of explanation which yields the clearest and fullest understanding. Surely, to round off scientific explanations of the origin of the universe with creation out of nothing does not add anything to our *understanding.* There may be merit of some sort in this way of speaking, but whatever it is, it is not greater clarity or explanatory power.[9]

What then, does all this amount to? Merely to the claim that scientific explanations are no worse than any other. All that has been shown is that all explanations suffer from the same defect: all involve a vicious infinite regress. In other words, no type of human explanation can help us to unravel the ultimate, unanswerable mystery. Christian ways of looking at things may not be able to render the world any more lucid than science can, but at least they do not pretend that there are no impenetrable mysteries. On the contrary, they point out untiringly that the claims of science to be able to elucidate everything are hollow. They remind us that science is not merely limited to the exploration of a tiny corner of the universe but that, however far our probing instruments may eventually reach, we can never even approach the answers to the last questions: "Why is there a world at all rather than nothing?" and "Why is the world such as it is and not different?" Here our finite human intellect bumps against its own boundary walls.

Is it true that scientific explanations involve an infinite vicious regress? Are scientific explanations really only provisional and incomplete? The crucial point will be this. Do *all* contingent truths call for explanation? Is the principle of sufficient reason sound? Can scientific explanations never come to a definite end? It will be seen that with a clear grasp of the nature and purpose of explanation we can answer these questions.[10]

Explaining something to someone is making him understand it. This involves bringing together in his mind two things, a model which is accepted as already simple and clear, and that which is to be explained, the explicandum, which is not so. Understanding the explicandum is seeing that it belongs to a range of things which could legitimately have been expected by anyone familiar with the model and with certain facts.

There are, however, two fundamentally different positions which a person may occupy relative to some explicandum. He may not be familiar with any model capable of leading him to expect the phenomenon to be explained. Most of us, for instance, are in that position in relation to the phenomena occurring in a good séance. With regard to other things people will differ. Someone who can play chess, already understands chess, already has a model. Someone who has never seen a game of chess has not. He sees the moves on the board, but he cannot understand, cannot follow, cannot make sense of what is happening. Explaining the game to him is giving him an explanation, is making him understand. He can understand or follow chess moves only if he can see them as conforming to a model of a chess game. In order to acquire such a model, he will, of course, need to know the constitutive rules of chess, that is, the permissible moves. But that is not all. He must know that a normal game of chess is a competition (not all games are) between two people, each trying to win, and he must know what it is to win at chess: to manoeuver the opponent's king into a position of checkmate. Finally, he must acquire some knowledge of what is and what is not conducive to winning: the tactical rules or canons of the game.

A person who has been given such an explanation and who has mastered it—which may take quite a long time—has now reached understanding, in the sense of the ability to follow each move. A person cannot in that sense understand merely one single move of chess and no other. If he does not understand any other moves, we must say that he has not yet mastered the explanation, that he does not really understand the single move either. If he has mastered the explanation, then he understands all those moves which he can see as being in accordance with the model of the game inculcated in him during the explanation.

However, even though a person who has mastered such an explanation will understand many, perhaps most, moves of any game of chess he cares to watch, he will not necessarily understand them all, as some moves of a player may not be in accordance with his model of the game. White, let us say, at his fifteenth move, exposes his queen to capture by Black's knight. Though in accordance with the constitutive rules of the game, this move is nevertheless perplexing and calls for explanation, because it is not conducive to the achievement by White of what must be assumed to be his aim: to win the game. The queen is a much more valuable piece than the knight against which he is offering to exchange.

An onlooker who has mastered chess may fail to understand this move, be perplexed by it, and wish for an explanation. Of course he may fail to be perplexed, for if he is a very inexperienced player he may not *see* the disadvantageousness of the move. But there is such a need whether anyone sees it or not. The move *calls for* explanation because to anyone who knows the game it must appear to be incompatible with the model which we have learnt during the explanation of the game, and by reference to which we all explain and understand normal games.

However, the required explanation of White's fifteenth move is of a very different kind. What is needed now is not the acquisition of an explanatory model, but the removal of the real or apparent incompatibility between the player's move and the model of explanation he has already acquired. In such a case the perplexity can be removed only on the assumption that the incompatibility between the model and the game is merely apparent. As our model includes a presumed aim of both players, there are the following three possibilities: (a) White has made a mistake: he has overlooked the threat to his queen. In that case, the explanation is that White thought his move conducive to his end, but it was not. (b) Black has made a mistake: White set a trap for him. In that case, the explanation is that Black thought White's move was not conducive to White's end, but it was. (c) White is not pursuing the end which any chess player may be presumed to pursue: he is not trying to win his game. In that case, the explanation is that White has made a move which he knows is not conducive to the end of winning his game because, let us say, he wishes to please Black, who is his boss.

Let us now set out the differences and similarities between the two types of understanding involved in these two kinds of explanation. I shall call the first kind "model"—understanding and explaining, respectively, because both involve the use of a model by reference to which understanding and explaining is effected. The second kind I shall call "unvexing," because the need for this type of explanation and understanding arises only when there is a perplexity arising out of the incompatibility of the model and the facts to be explained.

The first point is that unvexing presupposes model-understanding, but not vice versa. A person can neither have nor fail to have unvexing-understanding of White's fifteenth move at chess, if he does not already have model-understanding of chess. Obviously, if I don't know how to play chess, I shall fail to have model-understanding of White's fifteenth move. But I can neither fail to have nor, of course, can I have unvexing-understanding of it, for I cannot be perplexed by it. I merely fail to have model-understanding of this move as, indeed, of any other move of chess. On the other hand, I may well have model-understanding of chess without having unvexing-understanding of every move. That is to say, I may well know how to play chess without understanding White's fifteenth move. A person cannot fail to have unvexing-understanding of the move unless he is vexed or perplexed by it, hence he cannot even fail to have unvexing-understanding unless he already has model-understanding. It is not true that one either understands or fails to understand. On certain occasions, one neither understands nor fails to understand.

The second point is that there are certain things which cannot call for unvexing-explanations. No one can, for instance, call for an unvexing-explanation of White's first move, which is Pawn to King's Four. For no one can be perplexed or vexed by this move. Either a person knows how to play chess or he does not. If he does, then he must understand this move, for if he does not understand it, he has not yet mastered the game. And if he does not know how to play chess, then he cannot yet have, or fail to have, unvexing-understanding, he cannot therefore need an unvexing-explanation. Intellectual problems do not arise out of ignorance, but out of insufficient knowledge. An ignoramus is puzzled by very little. Once a student can see problems, he is already well into the subject.

The third point is that model-understanding implies being able, without further thought, to have model-understanding of a good many other things; unvexing-understanding does not. A person who knows chess, and therefore has model-understanding of it, must understand a good many chess moves, in fact all except those that call for unvexing-explanations. If he claims that he can understand White's first move, but no others, then he is either lying or deceiving himself or he really does not understand any move. On the other hand, a person who, after an unvexing-explanation, understands White's fifteenth move, need not be able, without further explanation, to understand Black's or any other further move which calls for unvexing-explanation.

What is true of explaining deliberate and highly stylized human behavior such as playing a game of chess is also true of explaining natural phenomena. For what is characteristic of natural phenomena—that they recur in essentially the same way, that they are, so to speak, repeatable—is also true of chess games, as it is not of games of tennis or cricket. There is only one important difference: man himself has invented and laid down the rules of chess, as he has not invented or laid down the "rules or laws governing the behavior of things." This difference between chess and phenomena is important, for it adds another way to the three already mentioned,[11] in which a perplexity can be removed by an unvexing-explanation, namely, by abandoning the original explanatory model. This is, of course, not possible in the case of games of chess, because the model for chess is not a "construction" on the basis of the already existing phenomena of chess, but an invention. The person who first thought up the model of chess could not have been mistaken. The person who first thought of a model explaining some phenomena could have been mistaken.

Consider an example. We may think that the following phenomena belong together: the horizon seems to recede however far we walk towards it; we seem to be able to see further the higher the mountain we climb; the sun and moon seem every day to fall into the sea on one side but to come back from behind the mountains on the other side without being any the worse for it. We may explain these phenomena by two alternative models: (a) that the earth is a large disk; (b) that it is a large sphere. However, to a believer in the first theory there arises the following perplexity: how is it that when we travel long enough towards the horizon in any one direction, we do eventually come back to our starting point without ever coming to the edge of the earth? We may at first attempt to "save" the model by saying that there is only an apparent contradiction. We may say either that the model does not require us to come to an edge, for it may be possible only to walk round and round on the flat surface. Or we may say that the person must have walked over the edge without noticing it, or perhaps that the travellers are all lying. Alternatively, the fact that our model is "constructed" and not invented or laid down enables us to say, what we could not do in the case of chess, that the model is inadequate or unsuitable. We can choose another model which fits all the facts, for instance, that the earth is round. Of course, then we have to give an unvexing-explanation for why it *looks* flat, but we are able to do that.

We can now return to our original question, "Are scientific explanations true and full explanations or do they involve an infinite regress, leaving them forever incomplete?"

Our distinction between model and unvexing-explanations will help here. It is obvious that only those things which are perplexing *call for* and *can be given* unvexing-explanations. We have already seen that in disposing of one perplexity, we do not necessarily raise another. On the contrary, unvexing-explanations truly and completely explain what they set out to explain, namely, how something is possible which, on our explanatory model, seemed to be impossible. There can therefore be no infinite regress here. Unvexing-explanations are real and complete explanations.

Can there be an infinite regress, then, in the case of model-explanations? Take the following example. European children are puzzled by the fact that their antipodean counterparts do not drop into empty space. This perplexity can be removed by substituting for their explanatory model another one. The European children imagine that throughout space there is an all-pervasive force operating in the same direction as the force that pulls them to the ground. We must, in our revised model, substitute for this force another acting anywhere in the direction of the center of the earth. Having thus removed their perplexity by giving them an adequate model, we can, however, go on to ask *why* there should be such a force as the force of gravity, why bodies should "naturally," in the absence of forces acting on them, behave in the way stated in Newton's laws. And we might be able to give such an explanation. We might for instance construct a model of space which would exhibit as derivable from it what in Newton's theory are "brute facts." Here we would have a case of the brute facts of one theory being explained within the framework of another, more general theory. And it is a sound methodological principle that we should continue to look for more and more general theories.

Note two points, however. The first is that we must distinguish, as we have seen, between *the possibility* and *the necessity* of giving an explanation. Particular occurrences can be explained by being exhibited as instances of regularities, and regularities can be explained by being exhibited as instances of more general regularities. Such explanations make things clearer. They organize the material before us. They introduce order where previously there was disorder. But absence of this sort of explanation (model-explanation) does not leave us with a puzzle or perplexity, an intellectual restlessness or cramp. The unexplained things are not unintelligible, incomprehensible, or irrational. Some things, on the other hand, call for, require, demand an explanation. As long as we are without such an explanation, we are perplexed, puzzled, intellectually perturbed. We need an unvexing-explanation.

Now, it must be admitted that we may be able to construct a more general theory, from which, let us say, Newton's theory can be derived. This would further clarify the phenomena of motion and would be intellectually satisfying. But failure to do so would not leave us with an intellectual cramp. The facts stated in Newton's theory do not require, or stand in need of, unvexing-explanations. They could do so only if we already had another theory or model with which Newton's theory was incompatible. They could not do so, by themselves, prior to the establishment of such another model.

The second point is that there is an objective limit to which such explanations tend, and beyond which they are pointless. There is a very good reason for wishing to explain a less general by a more general theory. Usually, such a unification goes hand in hand with greater precision in measuring the phenomena which both theories explain. Moreover, the more general theory, because of its greater generality, can explain a wider range of phenomena, including not only phenomena already explained by some other theories but also newly discovered phenomena, which the less general theory cannot explain. Now, the ideal limit to which such expansions of theories tend is an all-embracing theory which unifies all theories and explains all phenomena. Of course, such a limit can never be reached, since new phenomena are constantly discovered. Nevertheless, theories may be tending towards it. It will be remembered that the contention made against scientific theories was that there is no such limit because they involve an infinite regress. On that view, which I reject, there is no conceivable point at which scientific theories could be said to have explained the whole universe. On the view I am defending, there is such a limit, and it is the limit towards which scientific theories are actually tending. I claim that the nearer we come to this limit, the closer we are to a full and complete explanation of everything. For if we were to reach the limit, then though we could, of course, be left with a model which is itself unexplained and could be yet further explained by derivation from another model, there would be no need for, and no point in, such a further explanation. There would be no need for it, because any clearly defined model permitting us to expect the phenomena it is designed to explain offers full and complete explanations of these phenomena, however narrow the range. And while, at lower levels of generality, there is a good reason for providing more general models, since they further simplify, systematize, and organize the phenomena, this, which is the only reason for building more general theories, no longer applies once we reach the ideal limit of an all-embracing explanation.

It might be said that there is another reason for using different models: that they might enable us to discover new phenomena. Theories are not only instruments of explanation, but also of discovery. With this I agree. But it is irrelevant to my point: that *the needs of explanation* do not require us to go on forever deriving one explanatory model from another.

It must be admitted, then, that in the case of model-explanations there is a regress, but it is neither vicious nor infinite. It is not vicious because, in order to explain a group of explicanda, a model-explanation *need* not itself be derived from another more general one. It gives a perfectly full and consistent explanation by itself. And the regress is not infinite, for there is a natural limit, an all-embracing model, which can explain all phenomena, beyond which it would be pointless to derive model-explanations from yet others.

What about our most serious question, "Why is there anything at all?" Sometimes, when we think about how one thing has developed out of another and that one out of a third, and so on back throughout all time, we are driven to ask the same question about the universe as a whole. We want to add up all things and refer to them by the name, "the world," and we want to know why the world exists and why there is not nothing instead. In such moments, the world seems to us a kind of bubble floating on an ocean of nothingness. Why should such flotsam be adrift in empty space? Surely, its emergence from the hyaline billows of nothingness is more mysterious even than Aphrodite's emergence from the sea. Wittgenstein expressed in these words the mystification we all feel: "Not *how* the world is, is the mystical, but *that* it is. The contemplation of the world *sub specie aeterni* is the contemplation of it as a limited whole. The feeling of the world as a limited whole is the mystical feeling." [12]

Professor J. J. C. Smart expresses his own mystification in these moving words:

> That anything should exist at all does seem to me a matter for the deepest awe. But whether other people feel this sort of awe, and whether they or I ought to is another question. I think we ought to. If so, the question arises: if "Why should anything exist at all?" cannot be interpreted after the manner of the cosmological argument, that is, as an absurd request for the non-sensical postulation of a logically necessary being, what sort of question is it? What sort of question is this question "Why should anything exist at all?" All I can say is that I do not yet know. [13]

It is undeniable that the magnitude and perhaps the very existence of the universe is awe-inspiring. It is probably true that it gives many people "the mystical feeling." It is also undeniable that our awe, our mystical feeling, aroused by contemplating the vastness of the world, is justified, in the same sense in which our fear is justified when we realize we are in danger. There is no more appropriate object for our awe or for the mystical feeling than the magnitude and perhaps the existence of the universe, just as there is no more appropriate object for our fear than a situation of personal peril. However, it does not follow from this that it is a good thing to cultivate, or indulge in, awe or mystical feelings, any more than it is necessarily a good thing to cultivate, or indulge in, fear in the presence of danger.

In any case, whether or not we ought to have or are justified in having a mystical feeling or a feeling of awe when contemplating the universe, having such a feeling is not the same as asking a meaningful question, although having it may well *incline us* to utter certain forms of words. Our question "Why is there anything at all?" may be no more than the expression of our feeling of awe or mystification, and not a meaningful question at all. Just as the feeling of fear may naturally but illegitimately give rise to the question "What sin have I committed?" so the feeling of awe or mystification may naturally but illegitimately lead to the question "Why is there anything at all?" What we have to discover, then, is whether this question makes sense or is meaningless.

Yet, of course, it will be said, it makes perfectly good sense. There is an undeniable fact and it calls for explanation. The fact is that the universe exists. In the light of our experience, there can be no possible doubt that something or other exists, and the claim that the universe exists commits us to no more than that. And surely this calls for explanation, because the universe must have originated somehow. Everything has an origin and the universe is no exception. Since the universe is the totality of things, it must have originated out of nothing. If it had originated out of something, even something as small as one single hydrogen atom, what has so originated could not be the whole universe, but only the universe minus the atom. And then the atom itself would call for explanation, for it too must have had an origin, and it must be *an origin out of nothing*. And how can anything originate out of nothing? Surely that calls for some explanation.

However, let us be quite clear what is to be explained. There are two facts here, not one. The first is that the universe exists, which is undeniable. The second is that the universe must have originated out of nothing, and that is not undeniable. It is true that, *if it has originated at all,* then it must have originated out of nothing, or else it is not the universe that has originated. But need it have originated? Could it not have existed for ever?[14] It might be argued that nothing exists for ever, that everything has originated out of something else. That may well be true, but it is perfectly compatible with the fact that the universe is everlasting. We may well be able to trace the origin of any thing to the time when, by some transformation, it has developed out of some other thing, and yet it may be the case that no thing has its origin in nothing, and the universe has existed forever. For even if every *thing* has a beginning and an end, the total of mass and energy may well remain constant.

Moreover, the hypothesis that the universe originated out of nothing is, empirically speaking, completely empty. Suppose, for argument's sake, that the annihilation of an object without remainder is conceivable. It would still not be possible for any hypothetical observer to ascertain whether space was empty or not. Let us suppose that *within the range of observation of our observer* one object after another is annihilated without remainder and that only one is left. Our observer could not then tell whether in remote parts of the universe, beyond his range of observation, objects are coming into being or passing out of existence. What, moreover are we to say of the observer himself? Is he to count for nothing? Must we not postulate him away as well, if the universe is to have arisen out of nothing?

Let us, however, ignore all of these difficulties and assume that the universe really has originated out of nothing. Even that does not prove that the universe has not existed forever. If the universe can conceivably develop out of nothing, then it can conceivably vanish without remainder. And it can arise out of nothing again and subside into nothingness once more, and so on ad infinitum. Of course, *again* and *once more* are not quite the right words. The concept of time hardly applies to such universes. It does not make sense to ask whether one of them is earlier or later than, or perhaps simultaneous with, the other because we cannot ask whether they occupy the same or different spaces. Being separated from one another by "nothing," they are not separated from one another by "anything." We cannot therefore make any statements about their mutual spatio-temporal relations. It is impossible to distinguish between one long continuous universe and two universes separated by nothing. How, for instance, can we tell whether the universe including ourselves is not frequently annihilated and "again" reconstituted just as it was?

Let us now waive these difficulties as well. Let us suppose for a moment that we understand what is meant by saying that the universe originated out of nothing and that this has happened only once. Let us accept this as a fact. Does this fact call for explanation?

It does not call for an unvexing-explanation. That would be called for only if there were a perplexity due to the incompatibility of an accepted model with some fact. In our case, the fact to be explained is the origination of the universe out of nothing, hence there could not be such a perplexity, for we need not employ a model incompatible with this. If we had a model incompatible with our "fact," then that would be the wrong model and we would simply have to substitute another for it. The model we employ to explain the origin of the universe out of nothing could not be based on the similar origins of other things for, of course, there is nothing else with a similar origin.

All the same, it seems very surprising that something should have come out of nothing. It is contrary to the principle that everything has an origin, that is, has developed out of something else. It must be admitted that there is this incompatibility. However, it does not arise because a well-established model does not square with an undeniable fact; it arises because a well-established model does not square with *an assumption* of which it is hard even to make sense and for which there is no evidence whatsoever. In fact, the only reason we have for making this assumption is a simple logical howler: that because everything has an origin, the universe must have an origin, too, except, that, being the universe, it must have originated out of nothing. This is a howler, because it conceives of the universe as a big thing, whereas in fact it is the totality of things, that is, not *a* thing. That everything has an origin does not entail that the totality of things has an origin. On the contrary, it strongly suggests that it has not. For to say that everything has an origin implies that any given thing must have developed out of something else which in turn, being a thing, must have developed out of something else, and so forth. If we assume that everything has an origin, we need not, indeed it is hard to see how we can, assume that the totality of things has an origin as well. There is therefore no perplexity, because we need not and should not assume that the universe has originated out of nothing.

If, however, in spite of all that has been said just now, someone still wishes to assume, contrary to all reason, that the universe has originated out of nothing, there would still be no perplexity, for then he would simply have to give up the principle which is incompatible with this assumption, namely, that no thing can originate out of nothing. After all, this principle *could* allow for exceptions. We have no proof that it does not. Again, there is no perplexity, because no incompatibility between our assumption and an inescapable principle.

But, it might be asked, do we not need a model-explanation of our supposed fact? The answer is no. We do not need such an explanation, for there could not possibly be a model for this origin other than this origin itself. We cannot say that origination out of nothing is like birth, or emergence, or evolution, or anything else we know, for it is not like anything we know. In all these cases, there is *something* out of which the new thing has originated.

To sum up. The question, "Why is there anything at all?" looks like a perfectly sensible question modelled on "Why does *this* exist?" or "How has *this* originated?" It looks like a question about the origin of a thing. However, it is not such a question, for the universe is not a thing, but the totality of things. There is therefore no reason to assume that the universe has an origin. The very assumption that it has is fraught with contradictions and absurdities. If, nevertheless, it were true that the universe has originated out of nothing, then this would not call either for an unvexing- or a model-explanation. It would not call for the latter, because there could be no model of it taken from another part of our experience, since there is nothing analogous in our experience to origination out of nothing. It would not call for the former, because there can be no perplexity due to the incompatibility of a well-established model and an undeniable fact, since there is no undeniable fact and no well-established model. If, on the other hand, as is more probable, the universe has not originated at all, but is eternal, then the question why or how it has originated simply does not arise. There can then be no question about why anything at all exists, for it could not mean how or why the universe had originated, since *ex hypothesi* it has no origin. And what else could it mean?

Lastly, we must bear in mind that the hypothesis that the universe was made by God out of nothing only brings us back to the question of who made God or how God originated. And if we do not find it repugnant to say that God is eternal, we cannot find it repugnant to say that the universe is eternal. The only difference is that we know for certain that the universe exists, while we have the greatest difficulty in even making sense of the claim that God exists.

To sum up. According to the argument examined, we must reject the scientific world picture because it is the outcome of scientific types of explanation which do not really and fully explain the world around us, but only tell us *how* things have come about, not *why*, and can give no answer to the ultimate question, why there is anything at all rather than nothing. Against this, I have argued that scientific explanations are real and full, just like the explanations of everyday life and of the traditional religions. They differ from those latter only in that they are more precise and more easily disprovable by the observation of facts.

My main points dealt with the question of why scientific explanations were thought to be merely provisional and partial. The first main reason is the misunderstanding of the difference between teleological and causal explanations. It is first, and rightly, maintained that teleological explanations are answers to "Why?" questions, while causal explanations are answers to "How?" questions. It is further, and wrongly, maintained that, in order to obtain real and full explanations of anything, one must answer both "Why?" and "How?" questions. In other words, it is thought that all matters can and must be explained by both teleological and causal types of explanation. Causal explanations, it is believed, are merely provisional and partial, waiting to be completed by teleological explanations. Until a teleological explanation has been given, so the story goes, we have not *really* understood the explicandum. However, I have shown that both types are equally real and full explanations. The difference between them is merely that they are appropriate to different types of explicanda.

It should, moreover, be borne in mind that teleological explanations are not, in any sense, unscientific. They are rightly rejected in the natural sciences, not however because they are unscientific, but because no intelligences or purposes are found to be involved there. On the other hand, teleological explanations are very much in place in psychology, for we find intelligence and purpose involved in a good deal of human behavior. It is not only not unscientific to give teleological explanations of deliberate human behavior, but it would be quite unscientific to exclude them.

The second reason why scientific explanations are thought to be merely provisional and partial is that they are believed to involve a vicious infinite regress. Two misconceptions have led to this important error. The first is the general misunderstanding of the nature of explanation, and in particular the failure to distinguish between the two types which I have called model- and unvexing-explanations, respectively. If one does not draw this distinction, it is natural to conclude that scientific explanations lead to a vicious infinite regress. For while it is true of those perplexing matters which are elucidated by unvexing-explanations that they are incomprehensible and cry out for explanation, it is not true that after an unvexing-explanation has been given, this itself is again capable, let alone in need of, a yet further explanation of the same kind. Conversely, while it is true that model-explanations of regularities can themselves be further explained by more general model-explanations, it is not true that, in the absence of such more general explanations, the less general are incomplete, hang in the air, so to speak, leaving the explicandum incomprehensible and crying out for explanation. The distinction between the two types of explanation shows us that an explicandum is either perplexing and incomprehensible, in which case an explanation of it *is necessary* for clarification and, when given, *complete*, or it is a regularity capable of being subsumed under a model, in which case a further explanation *is possible* and often profitable, but *not necessary* for clarification.

The second misconception responsible for the belief in a vicious infinite regress is the misrepresentation of scientific explanation *as essentially causal*. It has generally been held that, in a scientific explanation, the explicandum is the effect of some event, the cause, temporally prior to the explicandum. Combined with the principle of sufficient reason (the principle that anything is in need of explanation which might conceivably have been different from what it is), this error generates the nightmare of determinism. Since any event might have been different from what it was, acceptance of this principle has the consequence that *every* event must have a reason or explanation. But if the reason is itself an event *prior in time*, then every reason must have a reason preceding it, and so the infinite regress of explanation is necessarily tied to the time scale stretching infinitely back into the endless past. It is, however, obvious from our account that science is not primarily concerned with the forging of such causal chains. The primary object of the natural sciences is not historical at all. Natural science claims to reveal, not the beginnings of things, but their underlying reality. It does not dig up the past, it digs down into the structure of things existing here and now. Some scientists do allow themselves to speculate, and rather precariously at that, about origins. But their hard work is done on the structure of what exists now. In particular, those explanations which are themselves further explained are not explanations linking event to event in a gapless chain reaching back to creation day, but generalizations of theories tending towards a unified theory.

THE PURPOSE OF MAN'S EXISTENCE

Our conclusion in the previous section has been that science is in principle able to give complete and real explanations of every occurrence and thing in the universe. This has two important corollaries: (1) Acceptance of the scientific world picture cannot be *one's reason for* the belief that the universe is unintelligible and therefore meaningless, though coming to accept it, after having been taught the Christian world picture, may well have been, in the case of many individuals, *the only or the main cause* of their belief that the universe and human existence are meaningless. (2) It is not in accordance with reason to reject this pessimistic belief on the grounds that scientific explanations are only provisional and incomplete and must be supplemented by religious ones.

In fact, it might be argued that the more clearly we understand the explanations given by science, the more we are driven to the conclusion that human life has no purpose and therefore no meaning. The science of astronomy teaches us that our earth was not specially created about 6,000 years ago, but evolved out of hot nebulae which previously had whirled aimlessly through space for countless ages. As they cooled, the sun and the planets formed. On one of these planets at a certain time the circumstances were propitious and life developed. But conditions will not remain favorable to life. When our solar system grows old, the sun will cool, our planet will be covered with ice, and all living creatures will eventually perish. Another theory has it that the sun will explode and that the heat generated will be so great that all organic life on earth will be destroyed. That is the comparatively short history and prospect of life on earth. Altogether it amounts to very little when compared with the endless history of the inanimate universe.

Biology teaches us that the species man was not specially created but is merely, in a long chain of evolutionary changes of forms of life, the last link, made in the likeness not of God but of nothing so much as an ape. The rest of the universe, whether animate or inanimate, instead of serving the ends of man, is at best indifferent, at worst savagely hostile. Evolution, to whose operation the emergence of man is due, is a ceaseless battle among members of different species, one species being gobbled up by another, only the fittest surviving. Far from being the gentlest and most highly moral, man is simply the creature best fitted to survive, the most efficient if not the most rapacious and insatiable killer. And in this unplanned, fortuitous, monstrous, savage world man is madly trying to snatch a few brief moments of joy, in the short intervals during which he is free from pain, sickness, persecution, war or famine until, finally, his life is snuffed out in death. Science has helped us to know and understand this world, but what purpose or meaning can it find in it?

Complaints such as these do not mean quite the same to everybody, but one thing, I think, they mean to most people: science shows life to be meaningless, because life is without purpose. The medieval world picture provided life with a purpose; hence medieval Christians could believe that life had a meaning. The scientific account of the world takes away life's purpose and with it its meaning.

There are, however, two quite different senses of "purpose." Which one is meant? Has science deprived human life of purpose in both senses? And if not, is it a harmless sense, in which human existence has been robbed of purpose? Could human existence still have meaning if it did not have a purpose in that sense?

What are the two senses? In the first and basic sense, purpose is normally attributed only to persons or their behavior as in "Did you have a purpose in leaving the ignition on?" In the second sense, purpose is normally attributed only to things, as in "What is the purpose of that gadget you installed in the workshop?" The two uses are intimately connected. We cannot attribute a purpose to a thing without implying that someone did something, in the doing of which he had some purpose, namely, to bring about the thing with the purpose. Of course, *his* purpose is not identical with *its* purpose. In hiring laborers and engineers and buying materials and a site for a factory and the like, the entrepreneur's purpose, let us say, is to manufacture cars, but the purpose of cars is to serve as a means of transportation.

There are many things that a man may do, such as buying and selling, hiring laborers, ploughing, felling trees, and the like, which it is foolish, pointless, silly, perhaps crazy, to do if one has no purpose in doing them. A man who does these things without a purpose is engaging in inane, futile pursuits. Lives crammed full with such activities devoid of purpose are pointless, futile, worthless. Such lives may indeed be dismissed as meaningless. But it should also be perfectly clear that acceptance of the scientific world picture does not force us to regard our lives as being without a purpose in this sense. Science has not only not robbed us of any purpose which we had before, but it has furnished us with enormously greater power to achieve these purposes. Instead of praying for rain or a good harvest or offspring, we now use ice pellets, artificial manure, or artificial insemination.

By contrast, having or not having a purpose, in the other sense, is value neutral. We do not think more or less highly of a thing for having or not having a purpose. "Having a purpose," in this sense, confers no kudos, "being purposeless" carries no stigma. A row of trees growing near a farm may or may not have a purpose: it may or may not be a windbreak, may or may not have been planted or deliberately left standing there in order to prevent the wind from sweeping across the fields. We do not in any way disparage the trees if we say they have no purpose but have just grown that way. They are as beautiful, made of as good wood, as valuable, as if they had a purpose. And, of course, they break the wind just as well. The same is true of living creatures. We do not disparage a dog when we say that it has no purpose, is not a sheep dog or a watchdog or a rabbit dog, but just a dog that hangs around the house and is fed by us.

Man is in a different category, however. To attribute to a human being a purpose in that sense is not neutral, let alone complimentary: it is offensive. It is degrading for a man to be regarded as merely serving a purpose. If, at a garden party, I ask a man in livery, "What is your purpose?" I am insulting him. I might as well have asked, "What are you *for*?" Such questions reduce him to the level of a gadget, a domestic animal, or perhaps a slave. I imply that *we* allot to *him* the tasks, the goals, the aims which he is to pursue; that *his* wishes and desires and aspirations and purposes are to count for little or nothing. We are treating him, in Kant's phrase, merely as a means to our ends, not as an end in himself.

The Christian and the scientific world pictures do indeed differ fundamentally on this point. The latter robs man of a purpose in this sense. It sees him as a being with no purpose allotted to him by anyone but himself. It robs him of any goal, purpose, or destiny appointed for him by any outside agency. The Christian world picture, on the other hand, sees man as a creature, a divine artifact, something halfway between a robot (manufactured) and an animal (alive), a homunculus, or perhaps Frankenstein, made in God's laboratory, with a purpose or task assigned him by his Maker.

However, lack of purpose in this sense does not in any way detract from the meaningfulness of life. I suspect that many who reject the scientific outlook because it involves the loss of purpose of life, and therefore meaning, are guilty of a confusion between the two senses of *purpose* just distinguished. They confusedly think that if the scientific world picture is true, then their lives must be futile because that picture implies that man has no purpose given him from without. But this is muddled thinking, for, as has already been shown, pointlessness is implied only by purposelessness in the other sense, which is not at all implied by the scientific picture of the world. These people mistakenly conclude that there can be no purpose *in* life because there is no purpose *of* life; that *men* cannot themselves adopt and achieve purposes because *man*, unlike a robot or a watchdog, is not a creature with a purpose.[15]

However, not all people taking this view are guilty of the above confusion. Some really hanker after a purpose of life in this sense. To some people the greatest attraction of the medieval world picture is the belief in an omnipotent, omniscient, and all-good Father, the view of themselves as His children who worship Him, of their proper attitude to what befalls them as submission, humility, resignation in His will, and what is often described as the "creaturely feeling."[16] All these are attitudes and feelings appropriate to a being that stands to another in the same sort of relation, though of course on a higher plane, in which a helpless child stands to his progenitor. Many regard the scientific picture of the world as cold, unsympathetic, unhomely, frightening, because it does not provide for any appropriate object of this creaturely attitude. There is nothing and no one in the world, as science depicts it, in which we can have faith or trust, on whose guidance we can rely, to whom we can turn for consolation, whom we can worship or submit to—except other human beings. This may be felt as a keen disappointment, because it shows that the meaning of life cannot lie in submission to His will, in acceptance of whatever may come, and in worship. But it does not imply that life can have *no* meaning. It merely implies that it must have a different meaning from that which it was thought to have. Just as it is a great shock for a child to find that he must stand on his own feet, that his father and mother no longer provide for him, so a person who has lost his faith in God must reconcile himself to the idea that he has to stand on his own feet, alone in the world except for whatever friends he may succeed in making.

But is not this to miss the point of the Christian teaching? Surely, Christianity can tell us the meaning of life because it tells us the grand and noble end for which God has created the universe and man. No human life, however pointless it may seem, is meaningless because in being part of God's plan, every life is assured of significance.

This point is well taken. It brings to light a distinction of some importance: we call a person's life meaningful not only if it is worthwhile, but also if he has helped in the realization of some plan or purpose transcending his own concerns. A person who knows he must soon die a painful death can give significance to the remainder of his doomed life by, say, allowing certain experiments to be performed on him which will be useful in the fight against cancer. In a similar way, only on a much more elevated plane, every man, however humble or plagued by suffering, is guaranteed significance by the knowledge that he is participating in God's purpose.

What, then, on the Christian view, is the grand and noble end for which God has created the world and man in it? We can immediately dismiss that still popular opinion that the smallness of our intellect prevents us from stating meaningfully God's design in all its imposing grandeur.[17] This view cannot possibly be a satisfactory answer to our question about the purpose of life. It is, rather, a confession of the impossibility of giving one. If anyone thinks that this "answer" can remove the sting from the impression of meaninglessness and insignificance in our lives, he cannot have been stung very hard.

If, then, we turn to those who are willing to state God's purpose in so many words, we encounter two insuperable difficulties. The first is to find a purpose grand and noble enough to explain and justify the great amount of undeserved suffering in this world. We are inevitably filled by a sense of bathos when we read statements such as this: " . . . history is the scene of a divine purpose, in which the whole of history is included, and Jesus of Nazareth is the centre of that purpose, both as revelation and as achievement, as the fulfillment of all that was past, and the promise of all that was to come. . . . If God is God, and if He made all these things, why did He do it? . . . God created a universe, bounded by the categories of time, space, matter, and causality, because He desired to enjoy for ever the society of a fellowship of finite and redeemed spirits which have made to His love the response of free and voluntary love and service."[18] Surely this cannot be right? Could a God be called omniscient, omnipotent, *and* all-good who, for the sake of satisfying his desire to be loved and served, imposes (or has to impose) on his creatures the amount of undeserved suffering we find in the world?

There is, however, a much more serious difficulty still: God's purpose in making the universe must be stated in terms of a dramatic story, many of whose key incidents symbolize religious conceptions and practices which we no longer find morally acceptable: the imposition of a taboo on the fruits of a certain tree, the sin and guilt incurred by Adam and Eve by violating the taboo, the wrath of God,[19] the curse of Adam and Eve and all their progeny, the expulsion from Paradise, the Atonement, by Christ's bloody sacrifice on the cross, which makes available by way of the sacraments God's Grace by which alone men can be saved (thereby, incidentally, establishing the valuable power of priests to forgive sins and thus alone make possible a man's entry to heaven[20]), Judgment Day on which the sheep are separated from the goats and the latter condemned to eternal torment in hell fire.

Obviously it is much more difficult to formulate a purpose for creating the universe and man that will justify the enormous amount of undeserved suffering which we find around us, if that story has to be fitted in as well. For now we have to explain not only why an omnipotent, omniscient, and all-good God should create such a universe and such a man, but also why, foreseeing every move of the feeble, weak-willed, ignorant, and covetous creature to be created, He should nevertheless have created him and, having done so, should be incensed and outraged by man's sin, and why He should deem it necessary to sacrifice His own son on the cross to atone for this sin which was, after all, only a disobedience of one of his commands, and why this atonement and consequent redemption could not have been followed by man's return to Paradise—particularly of those innocent children who had not yet sinned—and why, on Judgment Day, this merciful God should condemn some to eternal torment.[21] It is not surprising that in the face of these and other difficulties, we find, again and again, a return to the first view: that God's purpose cannot meaningfully be stated.

It will perhaps be objected that no Christian today believes in the dramatic history of the world as I have presented it. But this is not so. It is the official doctrine of the Roman Catholic, the Greek Orthodox, and a large section of the Anglican Church.[22] Nor does Protestantism substantially alter this picture. In fact, by insisting on "Justification by Faith Alone" and by rejecting the ritualistic, magical character of the medieval Catholic interpretation of certain elements in the Christian religion, such as indulgences, the sacraments, and prayer, while at the same time insisting on the necessity of grace, Protestantism undermined the moral element in medieval Christianity expressed in the Catholic's emphasis on personal merit.[23] Protestantism, by harking back to St. Augustine, who clearly realized the incompatibility of grace and personal merit,[24] opened the way for Calvin's doctrine of Predestination (the intellectual parent of that form of rigid determinism which is usually blamed on science) and Salvation or Condemnation for all eternity.[25] Since Roman Catholics, Lutherans, Calvinists, Presbyterians and Baptists officially subscribe to the views just outlined, one can justifiably claim that the overwhelming majority of professing Christians hold or ought to hold them.

It might still be objected that the best and most modern views are wholly different. I have not the necessary knowledge to pronounce on the accuracy of this claim. It may well be true that the best and most modern views are such as [those of] Professor Braithwaite, who maintains that Christianity is, roughly speaking, "morality plus stories," where the stories are intended merely to make the strict moral teaching both more easily understandable and more palatable.[26] Or it may be that one or the other of the modern views on the nature and importance of the dramatic story told in the sacred Scriptures is the best. My reply is that, even if it is true, it does not prove what I wish to disprove, that one can extract a sensible answer to our question "What is the meaning of life?" from the kind of story subscribed to by the overwhelming majority of Christians, who would, moreover, reject any such modernist interpretation at least as indignantly as the scientific account. Moreover, though such views can perhaps avoid some of the worst absurdities of the traditional story, they are hardly in a much better position to state the purpose for which God has created the universe and man in it, because they cannot overcome the difficulty of finding a purpose grand and noble enough to justify the enormous amount of undeserved suffering in the world.

Let us, however, for argument's sake, waive all these objections. There remains one fundamental hurdle which no form of Christianity can overcome: the fact that it demands of man a morally repugnant attitude towards the universe. It is now very widely held [27] that the basic element of the Christian religion is an attitude of worship towards a being supremely worthy of being worshipped and that it is religious feelings and experiences which apprise their owner of such a being and which inspire in him the knowledge or the feeling of complete dependence, awe, worship, mystery, and self-abasement. There is, in other words, a bi-polarity (the famous "I-Thou relationship") in which the object, "the wholly-other," is exalted whereas the subject is abased to the limit. Rudolf Otto has called this the "creature-feeling"[28] and he quotes as an expression of it, Abraham's words when venturing to plead for the men of Sodom: "Behold now, I have taken upon me to speak unto the Lord, which am but dust and ashes." (Genesis 18:27). Christianity thus demands of men an attitude inconsistent with one of the presuppositions of morality: that man is not wholly dependent on something else, that man has free will, that man is in principle capable of responsibility. We have seen that the concept of grace is the Christian attempt to reconcile the claim of total dependence and the claim of individual responsibility (partial independence), and it is obvious that such attempts must fail. We may dismiss certain doctrines, such as the doctrine of original sin or the doctrine of eternal hellfire or the doctrine that there can be no salvation outside the Church as extravagant and peripheral, but we cannot reject the doctrine of total dependence without rejecting the characteristically Christian attitude as such.

THE MEANING OF LIFE

Perhaps some of you will have felt that I have been shirking the real problem. To many people the crux of the matter seems as follows. How can there be any meaning in our life if it ends in death? What meaning can there be in it that our inevitable death does not destroy? How can our existence be meaningful if there is no afterlife in which perfect justice is meted out? How can life have any meaning if all it holds out to us are a few miserable earthly pleasures and even these to be enjoyed only rarely and for such a piteously short time?

I believe this is the point which exercises most people most deeply. Kirilov, in Dostoevsky's novel *The Possessed*, claims, just before commiting suicide, that as soon as we realize that there is no God, we cannot live any longer, we must put an end to our lives. One of the reasons which he gives is that when we discover that there is no paradise, we have nothing to live for:

> ... there was a day on earth, and in the middle of the earth were three crosses. One on the cross had such faith that He said to another, "Today thou shalt be with me in paradise." The day came to an end, both died, and they went, but they found neither paradise nor resurrection. The saying did not come true. Listen: that man was the highest of all on earth. . . . There has never been any one like Him before or since, and never will be. . . . And if that is so, if the laws of Nature did not spare even *Him*, and made even Him live in the midst of lies and die for a lie, then the whole planet is a lie and is based on a lie and a stupid mockery. So the very laws of the planet are a lie and a farce of the devil. What, then, is there to live for? [29]

And Tolstoy, too, was nearly driven to suicide when he came to doubt the existence of God and an afterlife.[30] And this is true of many.

What, then, is it that inclines us to think that if life is to have a meaning, there would be an afterlife? It is this. The Christian world view contains the following three propositions. The first is that since the Fall, God's curse on Adam and Eve, and the expulsion from Paradise, life on earth for mankind has not been worthwhile, but a vale of tears, one long chain of misery, suffering, unhappiness, and injustice. The second is that a perfect afterlife is awaiting us after the death of the body. The third is that we can enter this perfect life only on certain conditions, among which is also the condition of enduring our earthly existence to its bitter end. In this way, our earthly existence which, in itself, would not (at least for many people, if not all) be worth living, acquires meaning and significance; only if we endure it, can we gain admission to the realm of the blessed.

It might be doubted whether this view is still held today. However, there can be no doubt that even to-day we all imbibe a good deal of this view with our earlier education. In sermons, the contrast between the perfect life of the blessed and our life of sorrow and drudgery is frequently driven home and we hear it again and again that Christianity has a message of hope and consolation for all those "who are weary and heavy laden."[31]

It is not surprising, then, that when the implications of the scientific world picture begin to sink in, when we come to have doubts about the existence of God and another life, we are bitterly disappointed. For if there is no afterlife, then all we are left is our earthly life, which we have come to regard as a necessary evil, the painful fee of admission to the land of eternal bliss. But if there is no eternal bliss to come and if this hell on earth is all, why hang on till the horrible end?

Our disappointment therefore arises out of these two propositions, that the earthly life is not worth living, and that there is another perfect life of eternal happiness and joy which we may enter upon if we satisfy certain conditions. We can regard our lives as meaningful, if we believe both. We cannot regard them as meaningful if we believe merely the first and not the second. It seems to me inevitable that people who are taught something of the history of science, will have serious doubts about the second. If they cannot overcome these, as many will be unable to do, then they must either accept the sad view that their life is meaningless or they must abandon the first proposition: that this earthly life is not worth living. They must find the meaning of their life in this earthly existence. But is this possible?

A moment's examination will show us that the Christian evaluation of our earthly life as worthless, which we accept in our moments of pessimism and dissatisfaction, is not one that we normally accept. Consider only the question of murder and suicide. On the Christian view, other things being equal, the most kindly thing to do would be for every one of us to kill as many of our friends and dear ones as still have the misfortune to be alive, and then to commit suicide without delay, for every moment spent in this life is wasted. On the Christian view, God has not made it that easy for us. He has forbidden us to hasten others or ourselves into the next life. Our bodies are his private property and must be allowed to wear themselves out in the way decided by Him, however painful and horrible that may be. We are, as it were, driving a burning car. There is only one way out, to jump clear and let it hurtle to destruction. But the owner of the car has forbidden it on pain of eternal tortures worse than burning. And so we do better to burn to death inside.

On this view, murder is a less serious wrong than suicide. For murder can always be confessed and repented and therefore forgiven, suicide cannot—unless we allow the ingenious way out chosen by the heroine of Graham Greene's play, *The Living Room*, who swallows a slow but deadly poison and, while awaiting its taking effect, repents having taken it. Murder, on the other hand, is not so serious because, in the first place, it need not rob the victim of anything but the last lap of his march in the vale of tears, and, in the second place, it can always be forgiven. Hamlet, it will be remembered, refrains from killing his uncle during the latter's prayers because, as a true Christian, he believes that killing his uncle at that point, when the latter has purified his soul by repentance, would merely be doing him a good turn, for murder at such a time would simply despatch him to undeserved and everlasting happiness.

These views strike us as odd, to say the least. They are the logical consequence of the official medieval evaluation of this our earthly existence. If this life is not worth living, then taking it is not robbing the person concerned of much. The only thing wrong with it is the damage to God's property, which is the same, both in the case of murder and suicide. We do not take this view at all. Our view, on the contrary, is that murder is the most serious wrong because it consists in taking away from someone else against his will his most precious possession, his life. For this reason, when a person suffering from an incurable disease asks to be killed, the mercy killing of such a person is regarded as a much less serious crime than murder because, in such a case, the killer is not robbing the other of a good against his will. Suicide is not regarded as a real crime at all, for we take the view that a person can do with his own possessions what he likes.

However, from the fact that these are our normal opinions, we can infer nothing about their truth. After all, we could easily be mistaken. Whether life is or is not worthwhile, is a value judgment. Perhaps all this is merely a matter of opinion or taste. Perhaps no objective answer can be given. Fortunately, we need not enter deeply into these difficult and controversial questions. It is quite easy to show that the medieval evaluation of earthly life is based on a misguided procedure.

Let us remind ourselves briefly of how we arrive at our value judgments. When we determine the merits of students, meals, tennis players, bulls, or bathing belles, we do so on the basis of some criteria and some standard or norm. Criteria and standards notoriously vary from field to field and even from case to case. But that does not mean that we have *no* idea about what are the appropriate criteria or standards to use. It would not be fitting to apply the criteria for judging bulls to the judgment of students or bathing belles. They score on quite different points. And even where the same criteria are appropriate, as in the judgment of students enrolled in different schools and universities, the standards will vary from one institution to another. Pupils who would only just pass in one, would perhaps obtain honors in another. The higher the standard applied, the lower the marks, that is, the merit conceded to the candidate.

The same procedure is applicable also in the evaluation of a life. We examine it on the basis of certain criteria and standards. The medieval Christian view uses the criteria of the ordinary man: a life is judged by what the person concerned can get out of it: the balance of happiness over unhappiness, pleasure over pain, bliss over suffering. Our earthly life is judged not worthwhile because it contains much unhappiness, pain, and suffering, little happiness, pleasure, and bliss. The next life is judged worthwhile because it provides eternal bliss and no suffering.

Armed with these criteria, we can compare the life of this man and that, and judge which is more worthwhile, which has a greater balance of bliss over suffering. But criteria alone enable us merely to make compara-tive judgments of value, not absolute ones. We can say which is more and which is less worthwhile, but we cannot say which is worthwhile and which is not. In order to determine the latter, we must introduce a standard. But what standard ought we to choose?

Ordinarily, the standard we employ is the average of the kind. We call a man and a tree tall if they are well above the average of their kind. We do not say that Jones is a short man because he is shorter than a tree. We do not judge a boy a bad student because his answer to a question in the Leaving Examination is much worse than that given in reply to the same question by a young man sitting for his finals for the Bachelor's degree.

The same principles must apply to judging lives. When we ask whether a given life was or was not worthwhile, then we must take into consideration the range of worthwhileness which ordinary lives normally cover. Our end poles of the scale must be the best possible and the worst possible life that one finds. A good and worthwhile life is one that is well above average. A bad one is one well below.

The Christian evaluation of earthly lives is misguided because it adopts a quite unjustifiably high standard. Christianity singles out the major shortcomings of our earthly existence: there is not enough happi-ness; there is too much suffering; the good and bad points are quite un-equally and unfairly distributed; the underprivileged and underendowed do not get adequate compensation; it lasts only a short time. It then quite accurately depicts the perfect or ideal life as that which does not have any of these shortcomings. Its next step is to promise the believer that he will be able to enjoy this perfect life later on. And then it adopts as its stan-dard of judgment the perfect life, dismissing as inadequate anything that falls short of it. Having dismissed earthly life as miserable, it further damns it by characterizing most of the pleasures of which earthly existence allows as bestial, gross, vile, and sinful, or alternatively as not really pleasurable.

This procedure is as illegitimate as if I were to refuse to call anything tall unless it is infinitely tall, or anything beautiful unless it is perfectly flawless, or anyone strong unless he is omnipotent. Even if it were true that there is available to us an afterlife which is flawless and perfect, it would still not be legitimate to judge earthly lives by this standard. We do not fail every candidate who is not an Einstein. And if we do not believe in an afterlife, we must of course use ordinary earthly standards.

I have so far only spoken of the worthwhileness, only of what a person can get out of a life. There are other kinds of appraisal. Clearly, we evaluate people's lives not merely from the point of view of what they yield to the persons that lead them, but also from that of other men on whom these lives have impinged. We judge a life more significant if the person has contributed to the happiness of others, whether directly by what he did for others, or by the plans, discoveries, inventions, and work he performed. Many lives that hold little in the way of pleasure or happiness for their owners are highly significant and valuable, deserve admiration and respect on account of the contributions made.

It is now quite clear that death is simply irrelevant. If life can be worthwhile at all, then it can be so even though it be short. And if it is not worthwhile at all, then an eternity of it is simply a nightmare. It may be sad that we have to leave this beautiful world, but it is so only if and because it is beautiful. And it is no less beautiful for coming to an end. I rather suspect that an eternity of it might make us less appreciative, and in the end it would be tedious.

It will perhaps be objected now that I have not really demonstrated that life has a meaning, but merely that it can be worthwhile or have value. It must be admitted that there is a perfectly natural interpretation of the question, "What is the meaning of life?" on which my view actually proves that life has no meaning. I mean the interpretation discussed in [the] section ["The Purpose of Man's Existence"] of this lecture, where I attempted to show that, if we accept the explanations of natural science, we cannot believe that living organisms have appeared on earth in accordance with the deliberate plan of some intelligent being. Hence, on this view, life cannot be said to have a purpose, in the sense in which man-made things have a purpose. Hence it cannot be said to have a meaning or significance in that sense.

However, this conclusion is innocuous. People are disconcerted by the thought that *life as such* has no meaning in that sense only because they very naturally think it entails that no individual life can have meaning either. They naturally assume that *this* life or *that* can have meaning only if *life as such* has meaning. But it should by now be clear that your life and mine may or may not have meaning (in one sense) even if life as such has none (in the other). Of course, it follows from this that your life may have meaning while mine has not. The Christian view guarantees a meaning (in one sense) to every life, the scientific view does not (in any sense). By relating the question of the meaningfulness of life to the particular circumstances of an individual's existence, the scientific view leaves it an open question whether an individual's life has meaning or not. It is, however, clear that the latter is the important sense of "having a meaning." Christians, too, must feel that their life is wasted and meaningless if they have not achieved salvation. To know that even such lost lives have a meaning in another sense is no consolation to them. What matters is not that life should have a guaranteed meaning, whatever happens here or hereafter, but that, by luck (grace) or the right temperament and attitude (faith) or a judicious life (works) a person should make the most of his life.

"But here lies the rub," it will be said. "Surely, it makes all the difference whether there is an afterlife. This is where morality comes in." It would be a mistake to believe that. Morality is not the meting out of punishment and reward. To be moral is to refrain from doing to others what, if they followed reason, they would not do to themselves, and to do to others what, if they followed reason, they would want to have done. It is, roughly speaking, to recognize that others, too, have a right to a worthwhile life. Being moral does not make one's own life worthwhile; it helps others to make theirs so.

CONCLUSION

I have tried to establish three points: (1) that scientific explanations render their explicanda as intelligible as prescientific explanations: they differ from the latter only in that, having testable implications and being more precisely formulated, their truth or falsity can be determined with a high degree of probability; (2) that science does not rob human life of purpose, in the only sense that matters, but, on the contrary, renders many more of our purposes capable of realization; (3) that common sense, the Christian world view, and the scientific approach agree on the criteria but differ on the standard to be employed in the evaluation of human lives; judging human lives by the standards of perfection, as Christians do, is unjustified; if we abandon this excessively high standard and replace it by an everyday one, we have no longer any reason for dismissing earthly existence as not worthwhile.

On the basis of these three points I have attempted to explain why so many people come to the conclusion that human existence is meaningless and to show that this conclusion is false. In my opinion, this pessimism rests on a combination of two beliefs, both partly true and partly false: the belief that the meaningfulness of life depends on the satisfaction of at least three conditions, and the belief that this universe satisfies none of them. The conditions are, first, that the universe is intelligible, second, that life has a purpose, and third, that all men's hopes and desires can ultimately be satisfied. It seemed to medieval Christians and it seems to many Christians today that Christianity offers a picture of the world which can meet these conditions. To many Christians and non-Christians alike it seems that the scientific world picture is incompatible with that of Christianity, therefore with the view that these three conditions are met, therefore with the view that life has a meaning. Hence they feel that they are confronted by the dilemma of accepting either a world picture incompatible with the discoveries of science or the view that life is meaningless.

I have attempted to show that the dilemma is unreal because life can be meaningful even if not all of these conditions are met. My main conclusion, therefore, is that acceptance of the scientific world picture provides no reason for saying that life is meaningless, but on the contrary every reason for saying that there are many lives which are meaningful and significant. My subsidiary conclusion is that one of the reasons frequently offered for retaining the Christian world picture, namely, that its acceptance gives us a guarantee of a meaning for human existence, is unsound. We can see that our lives can have a meaning even if we abandon it and adopt the scientific world picture instead. I have, moreover, mentioned several reasons for rejecting the Christian world picture: (1) the biblical explanations of the details of our universe are often simply false; (2) the so-called explanations of the whole universe are incomprehensible or absurd; (3) Christianity's low evaluation of earthly existence (which is the main cause of the belief in the meaninglessness of life) rests on the use of an unjustifiably high standard of judgment.

NOTES

1. Count Leo Tolstoy, "A Confession," reprinted in *A Confession, The Gospel in Brief, and What I Believe*, No. 229, The World's Classics (London: Geoffrey Cumberlege, 1940).

2. See, e.g., Edwyn Bevan, *Christianity*, pp. 211-227. See also H. J. Paton, *The Modern Predicament* (London: George Allen and Unwin Ltd., 1955), pp. 103-116, 374.

3. See, for instance, L. E. Elliott-Binns, *The Development of English Theology in the Later Nineteenth Century* (London: Longmans, Green & Co., 1952), pp. 30-33.

4. See "Phaedo" (*Five Dialogues* by Plato, Everyman's Library No. 456), para. 99, p. 189.

5. "On the Ultimate Origination of Things" (*The Philosophical Writings of Leibniz*, Everyman's Library, No. 905), p. 32.

6. See "Monadology" (*The Philosophical Writings of Leibniz*, Everyman's Library, No. 905), para. 32-38, pp. 8-10.

7. To borrow the useful term coined by Professor D. A. T. Gasking of Melbourne University.

8. See, e.g., J. J. C. Smart, "The Existence of God," reprinted in *New Essays in Philosophical Theology*, ed. by A. Flew and A. MacIntyre (London: S.C.M. Press, 1957), pp. 35-39.

9. That creation out of nothing is not a clarificatory notion becomes obvious when we learn that "in the philosophical sense" it does not imply creation at a particular time. The universe could be regarded as a creation out of nothing even if it had no beginning. See e.g. E. Gilson, *The Christian Philosophy of St. Thomas Aquinas* (London: Victor Gollancz Ltd. 1957), pp. 147-155, and E. L. Mascall, *Via Media* (London: Longmans, Green & Co., 1956), pp. 28 ff.

10. In what follows I have drawn heavily on the work of Ryle and Toulmin. See for instance G. Ryle, *The Concept of Mind* (London: Hutchinson's University Library, 1949), pp. 56-60 and his article, "If, So, and Because," in *Philosophical Analysis* by Max Black, and S. E. Toulmin, *Introduction to the Philosophy of Science* (London: Hutchinson's University Library, 1953).

11. See p. 303, points (a)—(c).

12. L. Wittgenstein, *Tractatus Logico-Philosophicus* (London: Routledge & Kegan Paul Ltd., 1922), Sect. 6.44-6.45.

13. J. J. C. Smart, "The Existence of God," p. 46. See also Rudolf Otto, *The Idea of the Holy* (London: Geoffrey Cumberlege, 1952), esp. pp. 9-29.

14. Contemporary theologians would admit that it cannot be proved that the universe must have had a beginning. They would admit that we know it only through revelation. (See footnote 9.) I take it more or less for granted that Kant's attempted proof of the Thesis in his First Antinomy of Reason (Immanuel Kant's *Critique of Pure Reason*, trans. by Norman Kemp Smith [London: Macmillan and Co. Ltd., 1950], pp. 396-402) is invalid. It rests on a premise which is false: that the completion of the infinite series of succession of states, which must have preceded the present state if the world has had no beginning, is logically im-

possible. We can persuade ourselves to think that this infinite series is logically impossible if we insist that it is a series which must, literally, be *completed*. For the verb *to complete*, as normally used, implies an activity which, in turn, implies an agent who must have *begun* the activity at some time. If an infinite series is a whole that must be *completed* then, indeed, the world must have had a beginning. But that is precisely the question at issue. If we say, as Kant does at first, "that an eternity has elapsed," we do not feel the same impossibility. It is only when we take seriously the words *synthesis* and *completion*—both of which suggest or imply work or activity and therefore *beginning*—that it seems necessary that an infinity of successive states cannot have elapsed. (See also R. Crawshay-Williams, *Methods and Criteria of Reasoning* [London: Routledge & Kegan Paul, 1957], App. iv.)

15. See, e.g., "Is Life Worth Living?" B. B. C. Talk by the Rev. John Sutherland Bonnell in *Asking Them Questions,* Third Series, ed. by R. S. Wright (London: Geoffrey Cumberlege, 1950).

16. See, e.g., Rudolf Otto, *The Idea of the Holy,* pp. 9-11. See also C. A. Campbell, *On Selfhood and Godhood* (London: George Allen & Unwin Ltd., 1957), p. 246, and H. J. Paton, *The Modern Predicament,* pp. 69-71.

17. For a discussion of this issue, see the eighteenth-century controversy between deists and theists, for instance, in Sir Leslie Stephen's *History of English Thought in the Eighteenth Century* (London: Smith, Elder & Co., 1902), pp. 112-19 and pp. 134-63. See also the attacks by Toland and Tindal on "the mysterious" in *Christianity Not Mysterious* and *Christianity as Old as the Creation, or The Gospel a Republication of the Religion of Nature,* respectively, parts of which are reprinted in Henry Bettenson's *Doctrines of the Christian Church,* pp. 426-31. For modern views maintaining that mysteriousness is an essential element in religion, see Rudolf Otto, *The Idea of the Holy,* esp. pp. 25-40, and most recently M. B. Foster, *Mystery and Philosophy* (London: S. C. M. Press, 1957), esp. chapters 4 and 6. For the view that statements about God must be nonsensical or absurd, see e.g. H. J. Paton, *op. cit.,* pp. 119-20, 367-69. See also "Theology and Falsification" in *New Essays in Philosophical Theology,* ed. by A. Flew and A. MacIntyre (London: S. C. M. Press, 1955), pp. 96-131; also N. McPherson, "Religion as the Inexpressible," *ibid.,* esp. pp. 137-43.

18. Stephen Neill, *Christian Faith To-day* (London: Penguin Books, 1955), pp. 240-41.

19. It is difficult to feel the magnitude of this first sin unless one takes seriously the words "Behold, the man has eaten of the fruit of the tree of knowledge of good and evil, and is become as one of us; and now, may he not put forth his hand, and take also of the tree of life, and eat, and live for ever?" Genesis 3:22.

20. See in this connection the pastoral letter of 2nd February, 1905, by Johannes Katschtaler, Prince Bishop of Salzburg, on the honor due to priests, contained in *Quellen zur Geschichte des Papsttums,* by Mirbt, pp. 487-99, translated and reprinted in *The Protestant Tradition,* by J. S. Whale (Cambridge: University Press, 1955), pp. 259-62.

21. How impossible it is to make sense of this story has been demonstrated beyond any doubt by Tolstoy in his famous "Conclusion of a Criticism of Dogmatic

Theology," reprinted in *A Confession, The Gospel in Brief, and What I Believe.*

22. See "The Nicene Creed," "The Tridentine Profession of Faith," "The Syllabus of Errors," reprinted in *Documents of the Christian Church,* pp. 34, 373 and 380 respectively.

23. See, e.g., J. S. Whale, *The Protestant Tradition,* Ch. IV., esp. pp. 48-56.

24. See *ibid.,* pp. 61 ff.

25. See "The Confession of Augsburg," esp. Articles II, IV, XVIII, XIX, XX; "Christianae Religionis Institutio," "The Westminster Confession of Faith," esp. Articles III, VI, IX, X, XI, XVI, XVII; "The Baptist Confession of Faith," esp. Articles III, XXI, XXIII, reprinted in *Documents of the Christian Church,* pp. 294 ff., 298 ff., 344 ff., 349 ff.

26. See, e.g., Braithwaite's *An Empiricist's View of the Nature of Religious Belief* (Eddington Memorial Lecture).

27. See, e.g., the two series of Gifford Lectures most recently published: *The Modern Predicament* by H. J. Paton, pp. 69 ff., and *On Selfhood and Godhood* by C. A. Campbell, pp. 231-50.

28. Rudolf Otto, *The Idea of the Holy,* p. 9.

29. Fyodor Dostoyevsky, *The Devils* (London: The Penguin Classics, 1953) pp. 613-614.

30. Leo Tolstoy, *A Confession, The Gospel in Brief, and What I Believe,* p. 24.

31. See, for instance, J. S. Whale, *Christian Doctrine,* pp. 171, 176-78; see also Stephen Neill, *Christian Faith To-day,* p. 241.

XII. Science and the Religious Impulse

Bertrand Russell

Cosmic Purpose

Bertrand Russell, mathematician, philosopher, educator and author, was awarded the 1950 Nobel Prize for literature "in recognition of his many-sided and significant authorship, in which he has constantly figured as a defender of humanity and freedom of thought." He studied at Trinity College, Cambridge University. Russell lectured and taught at such universities as Harvard, University of California at Berkeley and at Los Angeles, Columbia, Chicago, Peking and Trinity College (where he accepted a fellowship in 1944). He wrote more than forty books and many articles on subjects ranging through such topics as mathematics, science, philosophy, psychology, morals, history, politics, economics and education. His *Principles of Mathematics* (1903) and the three-volume *Principia Mathematica* (1910-13, in collaboration with A. N. Whitehead) changed the philosophical foundations of logic and mathematics. Among Russell's important works are *Problems of Philosophy* (1912); *Our Knowledge of the External World as a Field for Scientific Method in Philosophy* (1914); *Political Ideals* (1917); *Roads to Freedom* (1918); *Mysticism and Logic*

(1918); *Introduction to Mathematical Philosophy* (1919); *The Analysis of Mind* (1921); *The Problems of China* (1922); *The ABC of Atoms* (1923); *The ABC of Relativity* (1925); *On Education* (1926); *The Analysis of Matter* (1927); *An Outline of Philosophy* (1927); *Sceptical Essays* (1929); *Marriage and Morals* (1929); *The Conquest of Happiness* (1930); *The Scientific Outlook* (1931); *Education and the Social Order* (1932); *Religion and Science* (1935); *Power: A New Social Analysis* (1938); *Inquiry into Meaning and Truth* (1940); *A History of Western Philosophy* (1945); *Human Knowledge: Its Scope and Limits* (1948); *In Praise of Idleness* (1948); *Authority and the Individual* (1949); *Unpopular Essays* (1950); *New Hopes for a Changing World* (1951); *The Impact of Science on Society* (1952); *Human Society in Ethics and Politics* (1954); *Logic and Knowledge* (1956); and *The Autobiography of Bertrand Russell* (1969).

Modern men of science, if they are not hostile or indifferent to religion, cling to one belief which, they think, can survive amid the wreck of former dogmas—the belief, namely, in cosmic purpose. Liberal theologians, equally, make this the central article of their creed. The doctrine has several forms, but all have in common the conception of evolution as having a direction towards something ethically valuable, which, in some sense, gives the reason for the whole long process. Sir J. Arthur Thomson, as we saw, maintained that science is incomplete because it cannot answer the question *why?* Religion, he thought, can answer it. Why were stars formed? Why did the sun give birth to planets? Why did the earth cool, and at last give rise to life? Because, in the end, something admirable was going to result—I am not quite sure what, but I believe it was scientific theologians and religiously-minded scientists.

The doctrine has three forms—theistic, pantheistic, and what may be called "emergent." The first which is the simplest and most orthodox, holds that God created the world and decreed the laws of nature because He foresaw that in time some good would be evolved. In this view the purpose exists consciously in the mind of the Creator, who remains external to His creation.

From Bertrand Russell, Religion and Science (*London: Oxford University Press, 1935*), pp. 190-222. Reprinted by permission of the Oxford University Press.

In the pantheistic form, God is not external to the universe, but is merely the universe considered as a whole. There cannot therefore be an act of creation, but there is a kind of creative force *in* the universe, which causes it to develop according to a plan which this creative force may be said to have had in mind throughout the process.

In the "emergent" form, the purpose is more blind. At an earlier stage, nothing in the universe foresees a later stage, but a kind of blind impulsion leads to those changes which bring more developed forms into existence, so that, in some rather obscure sense, the end is implicit in the beginning.

All these three forms are represented in ... [a group of] B.B.C. talks. . . . The Bishop of Birmingham advocated the theistic form, Professor J. S. Haldane the pantheistic form, and Professor Alexander the "emergent" form—though Bergson and Professor Lloyd Morgan are perhaps more typical representatives of this last. The doctrines will perhaps become clearer by being stated in the words of those who hold them.

The Bishop of Birmingham maintains that "there is a rationality in the universe akin to the rational mind of man," and that "this makes us doubt whether the cosmic process is not directed by a mind." The doubt does not last long. We learn immediately that "there has obviously, in this vast panorama, been a progress which has culminated in the creation of civilized man. Is that progress the outcome of blind forces? It seems to me fantastic to say 'yes' in answer to this question. . . . In fact, the natural conclusion to draw from the modern knowledge won by scientific method is that the Universe is subject to the sway of thought—of thought directed by will towards definite ends. Man's creation was thus not a quite incomprehensible and wholly improbable consequence of the properties of electrons and protons, or, if you prefer so to say, of discontinuities in space-time: it was the result of some Cosmic Purpose. And the ends towards which that Purpose acted must be found in man's distinctive qualities and powers. In fact, man's moral and spiritual capacities, at their highest, show the nature of the Cosmic Purpose which is the source of his being."

The Bishop rejects pantheism, as we saw, because, if the world is God, the evil in the world is in God; and also because "we must hold that God is *not,* like his Universe, in the making." He candidly admits the evil in the world, adding: "We are puzzled that there should be so much evil, and this bewilderment is the chief argument against Christian theism." With admirable honesty, he makes no attempt to show that our bewilderment is irrational.

Dr. Barnes's exposition raises problems of two kinds—those concerned with cosmic purpose in general, and those specially concerned with its theistic form. The former I will leave to a later stage, but on the latter a few words must be said now.

The conception of purpose is a natural one to apply to a human artificer. A man who desires a house cannot, except in the Arabian Nights, have it rise before him as a result of his mere wish; time and labor must be expended before his wish can be gratified. But Omnipotence is subject to no such limitations. If God really thinks well of the human race—an unplausible hypothesis, as it seems to me—why not proceed, as in Genesis, to create man at once? What was the point of the ichthyosaurs, dinosaurs, diplodochi, mastodons, and so on? Dr. Barnes himself confesses, somewhere, that the purpose of the tapeworm is a mystery. What useful purpose is served by rabies and hydrophobia? It is no answer to say that the laws of nature inevitably produce evil as well as good, for God decreed the laws of nature. The evil which is due to sin may be explained as the result of our free will, but the problem of evil in the prehuman world remains. I hardly think Dr. Barnes will accept the solution offered by William Gillespie, that the bodies of beasts of prey were inhabited by devils, whose first sins antedated the brute creation; yet it is difficult to see what other logically satisfying answer can be suggested. The difficulty is old, but nonetheless real. An omnipotent Being who created a world containing evil not due to sin must Himself be at least partially evil.[1]

To this objection the pantheistic and emergent forms of the doctrine of cosmic purpose are less exposed.

Pantheistic evolution has varieties according to the particular brand of pantheism involved; that of Professor J. S. Haldane, which we are now to consider, is connected with Hegel, and, like everything Hegelian, is not very easy to understand. But the point of view is one which has had considerable influence throughout the past hundred years and more, so that it is necessary to examine it. Moreover, Professor Haldane is distinguished for his work in various special fields, and he has exemplified his general philosophy by detailed investigations, particularly in physiology, which appeared to him to demonstrate that the science of living bodies has need of other laws besides those of chemistry and physics. This fact adds weight to his general outlook.

According to this philosophy, there is not, strictly speaking, any such thing as "dead" matter, nor is there any living matter without something of the nature of consciousness; and, to go one step further, there is no consciousness which is not in some degree divine. The distinction between appearance and reality is involved in Professor Haldane's views, although he does not mention it; but now, as with Hegel, it has become a distinction of degree rather than of kind. Dead matter is least real, living matter a little more so, human consciousness still more, but the only complete reality is God, i.e., the universe conceived as divine. Hegel professes to give logical proofs of these propositions, but we will pass these by, as they would require a volume. We will, however, illustrate Professor Haldane's views by some quotations from his B.B.C. talk.

"If we attempt," he says, "to make mechanistic interpretation the sole basis of our philosophy of life, we must abandon completely our traditional religious beliefs and many other ordinary beliefs." Fortunately, however, he thinks, there is no need to explain everything mechanistically, i.e. in terms of chemistry and physics, nor, indeed, is this possible, since biology needs the conception of *organism*. "From the physical standpoint life is nothing less than a standing miracle." "Hereditary transmission . . . itself implies the distinguishing feature of life as co-ordinated unity always tending to maintain and reproduce itself." "If we assume that life is not inherent in Nature, and that there must have been a time before life existed, this is an unwarranted assumption which would make the appearance of life totally unintelligible." "The fact that biology bars decisively the door against a final mechanistic or mathematical interpretation of our experience is at least very significant in connection with our ideas as to religion." "The relations of conscious behavior to life are analogous to those of life to mechanism." "For psychological interpretation the present is no mere fleeting moment: it holds within it both the past and the future." As biology needs the concept of *organism*, so (he maintains) psychology needs that of *personality*; it is a mistake to think of a person as made up of a soul *plus* a body, or to suppose that we know only sensations, not the external world, for in truth the environment is not *outside* us. "Space and time do not isolate personality; they express an order within it, so that the immensities of space and time are within it, as Kant saw." "Personalities do not exclude one another. It is simply a fundamental fact in our experience that an active ideal of truth, justice, charity and beauty is always present to us, and is our interest, but not our mere individual interest. The ideal is, moreover, one ideal, though it has different aspects."

From this point, we are ready to take the next step, from single personalities to God. "Personality is not merely individual. It is in this fact that we recognize the presence of God—God present not merely as a being outside us, but within and around us as Personality of personalities." "It is only within ourselves, in our active ideals of truth, right, charity and beauty, and consequent fellowship with others, that we find the revelation of God." Freedom and immortality, we are told, belong to God, not to human individuals, who, in any case, are not quite "real." "Were the whole human race to be blotted out, God would still, as from all eternity, be the only reality, and in His existence what is real in us would continue to live."

One lasting consoling reflection: from the sole reality of God, it follows that the poor ought not to mind being poor. It is foolish to grasp at "unreal shadows of the passing moment, such as useless luxury. . . . The real standard of the poor may be far more satisfying than that of the rich." For those who are starving, one gathers, it will be a comfort to remember that "the only ultimate reality is the spiritual or personal reality which we denote by the existence of God."

Many questions are raised by this theory. Let us begin with the most definite: in what sense, if any, is biology not reducible to physics and chemistry, or psychology to biology?

As regards the relation of biology to chemistry and physics, Professor Haldane's view is not that now held by most specialists. An admirable, though not recent, statement of the opposite point of view will be found in *The Mechanistic Conception of Life* by Jacques Loeb (published in 1912), some of the most interesting chapters of which give the results of experiments on reproduction, which is regarded by Professor Haldane as obviously inexplicable on mechanical principles. The mechanistic point of view is sufficiently accepted to be that set forth in the last edition of the *Encyclopaedia Britannica,* where Mr. E. S. Goodrich, under the heading "Evolution," says: "A living organism, then, from the point of view of the scientific observer, is a self-regulating, self-repairing, physico-chemical complex mechanism. What, from this point of view, we call 'life' is the sum of its physico-chemical processes, forming a continuous interdependent series without break, and without the interference of any mysterious extraneous force."

You will look in vain through this article for any hint that in living matter there are processes not reducible to physics and chemistry. The author points out that there is no sharp line between living and dead matter: "No hard-and-fast line can be drawn between the living and the non-living. There is no special living chemical substance, no special vital element differing from dead matter, and no special vital force can be found at work. Every step in the process is determined by that which pre-ceded it and determines that which follows." As to the origin of life, "it must be supposed that long ago, when conditions became favorable, relatively high compounds of various kinds were formed. Many of these would be quite unstable, breaking down almost as soon as formed; others might be stable and merely persist. But still others might tend to reform, to assimilate, as fast as they broke down. Once started on this track such a growing compound or mixture would inevitably tend to perpetuate itself, and might combine with or feed on others less complex than itself." This point of view, rather than that of Professor Haldane, may be taken as that which is prevalent among biologists at the present day. They agree that there is no sharp line between living and dead matter, but while Professor Haldane thinks that what we call dead matter is really living, the majority of biologists think that living matter is really a physico-chemical mechanism.

The question of the relation between physiology and psychology is more difficult. There are two distinct questions: Can our bodily behavior be supposed due to physiological causes alone? and, What is the relation of mental phenomena to concurrent actions of the body? It is only bodily behavior that is open to public observation; our thoughts may be *inferred* by others, but can only be *perceived* by ourselves. This, at least, is what common sense would say. In theoretical strictness, we cannot observe the actions of bodies, but only certain effects which they have on us; what others observe at the same time may be similar, but will always differ, in a greater or less degree, from what we observe. For this and other reasons, the gap between physics and psychology is not so wide as was formerly thought. Physics may be regarded as predicting what we shall see in certain circumstances, and in this sense it is a branch of psychology, since our seeing is a "mental" event. This point of view has come to the fore in modern physics through the desire to make only assertions that are empir-ically verifiable, combined with the fact that a verification is always an observation by some human being, and therefore an occurrence such as psychology considers. But all this belongs to the philosophy of the two sciences rather than to their practice; their technique remains distinct in spite of the *rapprochement* between their subject matters.

To return to the two questions at the beginning of the preceding paragraph: if our bodily actions all have physiological causes, our minds become causally unimportant. It is only by bodily acts that we can com-municate with others, or have any effect upon the outer world; what we think only matters if it can affect what our bodies do. Since, however, the distinction betwen what is mental and what is physical is only one of convenience, our bodily acts may have causes lying wholly within physics, and yet mental events may be among their causes. The practical issue is not to be stated in terms of mind and body. It may, perhaps, be stated as follows: Are our bodily acts determined by physico-chemical laws? And, if they are, is there nevertheless an independent science of psychology, in which we study mental events directly, without the intervention of the artifically constructed concept of matter?

Neither of these questions can be answered with any confidence, though there is some evidence in favor of an affirmative answer to the first of them. The evidence is not direct; we cannot calculate a man's movements as we can those of the planet Jupiter. But no sharp line can be drawn between human bodies and the lowest forms of life; there is nowhere such a gap as would tempt us to say: here physics and chemistry cease to be adequate. And as we have seen, there is also no sharp line between living and dead matter. It seems probable, therefore, that physics and chemistry are supreme throughout.

With regard to the possibility of an independent science of psychology, even less can be said at present. To some extent, psychoanalysis has attempted to create such a science, but the success of this attempt, in so far as it avoids physiological causation, may still be questioned. I incline—though with hesitation—to the view that there will ultimately be a science embracing both physics and psychology, though distinct from either as at present developed. The technique of physics was developed under the influence of a belief in the metaphysical reality of "matter," which now no longer exists, and the new quantum mechanics has a different technique which dispenses with false metaphysics. The technique of psychology, to some extent, was developed under a belief in the metaphysical reality of the "mind." It seems possible that, when physics and psychology have both been completely freed from these lingering errors, they will both develop into one science dealing neither with mind nor with matter, but with events, which will not be labelled either "physical" or "mental." In the meantime, the question of the scientific status of psychology must remain open.

Professor Haldane's views on psychology raise, however, a narrower issue, as to which much more definite things can be said. He maintains that the distinctive concept of psychology is "personality." He does not define the term, but we may take it as meaning some unifying principle which binds together the constituents of one mind, causing them all to modify each other. The idea is vague; it stands for the "soul," in so far as this is still thought to be defensible. It differs from the soul in not being a bare entity, but a kind of quality of wholeness. It is thought, by those who believe in it, that everything in the mind of John Smith has a John-Smithy quality which makes it impossible for anything quite similar to be in anyone else's mind. If you are trying to give a scientific account of John Smith's mind, you must not be content with general rules, such as can be given for all pieces of matter indiscriminately; you must remember that the events concerned are happening to that particular man, and are what they are because of his whole history and character.

There is something attractive about this view, but I see no reason to regard it as true. It is, of course, obvious that two men in the same situation may react differently because of differences in their past histories, but the same is true of two bits of iron, of which one has been magnetized and the other not. Memories, one supposes, are engraved on the brain, and affect behavior through a difference of physical structure. Similar considerations apply to character. If one man is choleric and another phlegmatic, the difference is usually traceable to the glands, and could, in most cases, be obliterated by the use of suitable drugs. The belief that personality is mysterious and irreducible has no scientific warrant, and is accepted chiefly because it is flattering to our human self-esteem.

Take again the two statements: "For psychological interpretation the present is no mere fleeting moment: it holds within it both the past and the future"; and "space and time do not isolate personality: they express an order within it." As regards past and future, I think Professor Haldane has in mind such matters as our condition when we have just seen a flash of lightning, and are expecting the thunder. It may be said that the lightning, which is past, and the thunder, which is future, both enter into our present mental state. But this is to be misled by metaphor. The recollection of lightning is not lightning, and the expectation of thunder is not thunder. I am not thinking merely that recollection and expectation do not have physical effects; I am thinking of the actual quality of the subjective experience: seeing is one thing, recollecting is another; hearing is one thing, expecting is another. The relations of the present to the past and the future, in psychology as elsewhere, are causal relations, not relations of interpenetration. (I do not mean, of course, that my expectation causes the thunder, but that past experiences of lightning followed by thunder, together with present lightning, cause expectation of thunder.) Memory does not prolong the existence of the past; it is merely one way in which the past has effects.

With regard to space, the matter is similar but more complicated. There are two kinds of space, that in which one person's private experiences are situated, and that of physics, which contains other people's bodies, chairs and tables, the sun, moon and stars, not merely as reflected in our private sensations, but as we suppose them to be in themselves. This second sort is hypothetical, and can, with perfect logic, be denied by any man who is willing to suppose that the world contains nothing but his own experiences. Professor Haldane is not willing to say this, and must therefore admit the space which contains things other than his own experiences. As for the subjective kind of space, there is the visual space containing all my visual experiences; there is the space of touch; there is, as William James pointed out, the voluminousness of a stomach ache; and so on. When I am considered as one thing among a world of things, every form of subjective space is inside me. The starry heavens that I see are not the remote starry heavens of astronomy, but an effect of the stars on me; what I see is in me, not outside of me. The stars of astronomy are in physical space, which is outside of me, but which I only arrive at by inference, not through analysis of my own experience. Professor Haldane's statement that space expresses an order within personality is true of my private space, not of physical space; his accompanying statement that space does not isolate personality would only be correct if physical space also were inside me. As soon as this confusion is cleared up, his position ceases to be plausible.

Professor Haldane, like all who follow Hegel, is anxious to show that nothing is really separate from anything else. He has now shown—if one could accept his arguments—that each man's past and future co-exist with his present, and that the space in which we all live is also inside each of us. But he has a further step to take in the proof that "personalities do not exclude one another." It appears that a man's personality is constituted by his ideals, and that our ideals are all much the same. I will quote his words once more: "an active ideal of truth, justice, charity and beauty is always present to us. . . . The ideal is, moreover, one ideal, though it has different aspects. It is these common ideals, and the fellowship they create, from which comes the revelation of God."

Statements of this kind, I must confess, leave me gasping, and I hardly know where to begin. I do not doubt Professor Haldane's word when he says that "an active ideal of truth, justice, charity, and beauty" is *always* present to *him*; I am sure it must be so, since he asserts it. But when it comes to attributing this extraordinary degree of virtue to mankind in general, I feel that I have as good a right to my opinion as he has to his. I find, for my part, untruth, injustice, uncharitableness and ugliness pursued, not only in fact, but as ideals. Does he really think that Hitler and Einstein have "one ideal, though it has different aspects"? It seems to me that each might bring a libel action for such a statement. Of course it may be said that one of them is a villain, and is not really pursuing the ideals in which, at heart, he believes. But this seems to me too facile a solution. Hitler's ideals come mainly from Nietzsche, in whom there is every evidence of complete sincerity. Until the issue has been fought out— by other methods than those of the Hegelian dialectic—I do not see how we are to know whether the God in whom *the* ideal is incarnate is Jehovah or Wotan.

As for the view that God's eternal blessedness should be a comfort to the poor, it has always been held by the rich, but the poor are beginning to grow weary of it. Perhaps, at this date, it is scarcely prudent to seem to associate the idea of God with the defence of economic injustice.

The pantheistic doctrine of cosmic purpose, like the theistic doctrine, suffers, though in a somewhat different way, from the difficulty of explaining the necessity of a temporal evolution. If time is not ultimately real—as practically all pantheists believe—why should the best things in the history of the world come late rather than early? Would not the reverse order have done just as well? If the idea that events have dates is an illusion, from which God is free, why should He choose to put the pleasant events at the end and the unpleasant ones at the beginning? I agree with Dean Inge in thinking this question unanswerable.

The "emergent" doctrine, which we have next to consider, avoids this difficulty, and emphatically upholds the reality of time. But we shall find that it incurs other difficulties at least as great.

The only representative of the "emergent" view, in the volume of B.B.C. talks from which I have been quoting, is Professor Alexander. He begins by saying that dead matter, living matter, and mind, have appeared successively, and continues: "Now this growth is one of what, since Mr. Lloyd Morgan introduced or reintroduced the idea and the term, is called emergence. Life emerges from matter and mind from life. A living being is also a material being, but one so fashioned as to exhibit a new quality which is life. . . . And the same thing may be said of the transition from life to mind. A 'minded' being is also a living being, but one of such complexity of development, so finely organized in certain of its parts, and particularly in its nervous system, as to carry mind—or, if you please to use the word, consciousness."

He goes on to say that there is no reason why this process should cease with mind. On the contrary, it "suggests a further quality of existence beyond mind, which is related to mind as mind to life or life to matter. That quality I call deity, and the being which possesses it is God. It seems to me, therefore, that all things point to the emergence of this quality, and that is why I said that science itself, when it takes the wider view, requires deity." The world, he says, is "striving or tending to deity," but "deity has not in its distinctive nature as yet emerged at this stage of the world's existence." He adds that, for him, God "is not a creator as in historical religions, but created."

There is a close affinity between Professor Alexander's views and those of Bergson's "creative evolution." Bergson holds that determinism is mistaken because, in the course of evolution, genuine novelties emerge, which could not have been predicted in advance, or even imagined. There is a mysterious force which urges everything to evolve. For example, an animal which cannot see has some mystic foreboding of sight, and proceeds to act in a way that leads to the development of eyes. At each moment something new emerges, but the past never dies, being preserved in memory—for forgetting is only apparent. Thus the world is continually growing richer in content, and will in time become quite a nice sort of place. The one essential is to avoid the intellect, which looks backward and is static; what we must use is intuition, which contains within itself the urge to creative novelty.

It must not be supposed that reasons are given for believing all this, beyond occasional bits of bad biology, reminiscent of Lamarck. Bergson is to be regarded as a poet, and on his own principles avoids everything that might appeal to the mere intellect.

I do not suggest that Professor Alexander accepts Bergson's philosophy in its entirety, but there is a similarity in their views, though they have developed them independently. In any case, their theories agree in emphasizing time, and in the belief that, in the course of evolution, unpredictable novelties emerge.

Various difficulties make the philosophy of emergent evolution unsatisfactory. Perhaps the chief of these is that, in order to escape from determinism, prediction is made impossible, and yet the adherents of this theory predict the future existence of God. They are exactly in the position of Bergson's shellfish, which wants to see although it does not know what seeing is. Professor Alexander maintains that we have a vague awareness of "deity" in some experiences, which he descibes as "numinous." The feeling which characterizes such experiences is, he says, "the sense of mystery, of something which may terrify us or may support us in our helplessness, but at any rate which is other than anything we know by our senses or our reflection." He gives no reason for attaching importance to this feeling, or for supposing that, as his theory demands, mental development makes it become a larger element in life. From anthropologists one would infer the exact opposite. The sense of mystery, of a friendly or hostile nonhuman force, plays a far greater part in the life of savages than in that of civilized men. Indeed, if religion is to be identified with this feeling, every step in known human development has involved a diminution of religion. This hardly fits in with the supposed evolutionary argument for an emergent Deity.

The argument, in any case, is extraordinarily thin. There have been, it is urged, three stages in evolution: matter, life, and mind. We have no reason to suppose that the world has finished evolving, and there is therefore likely, at some later date, to be a fourth phase—and a fifth and a sixth and so on, one would have supposed. But no, with the fourth phase evolution is to be complete. Now matter could not have foreseen life, and life could not have foreseen mind, but mind can, dimly, foresee the next stage, particularly if it is the mind of a Papuan or a Bushman. It is obvious that all this is the merest guesswork. It may happen to be true, but there is no rational ground for supposing so. The philosophy of emergence is quite right in saying that the future is unpredictable, but, having said this, it at once proceeds to predict the future. People are more unwilling to give up the word *God* than to give up the idea for which the word has hitherto stood. Emergent evolutionists, having become persuaded that God did not create the world, are content to say that the world is creating God. But beyond the name, such a God has almost nothing in common with the object of traditional worship.

With regard to cosmic purpose in general, in whichever of its forms, there are two criticisms to be made. In the first place, those who believe in cosmic purpose always think that the world will go on evolving in the same direction as hitherto; in the second place, they hold that what has already happened is evidence of the good intentions of the universe. Both these propositions are open to question.

As to the direction of evolution, the argument is mainly derived from

what has happened on this earth since life began. Now this earth is a very
small corner of the universe, and there are reasons for supposing it by no
means typical of the rest. Sir James Jeans considers it very doubtful
whether, at the present time, there is life anywhere else. Before the Copernican revolution, it was natural to suppose that God's purposes were
specially concerned with the earth, but now this has become an unplausible hypothesis. If it is the purpose of the cosmos to evolve mind, we must
regard it as rather incompetent in having produced so little in such a long
time. It is, of course, *possible* that there will be more mind later on somewhere else, but of this we have no jot of scientific evidence. It may seem
odd that life should occur by accident, but in such a large universe accidents will happen.

And even if we accept the rather curious view that the cosmic purpose is specially concerned with our little planet, we still find that there is
reason to doubt whether it intends quite what the theologians say it does.
The earth (unless we use enough poison gas to destroy all life) is likely to
remain habitable for some considerable time, but not forever. Perhaps
our atmosphere will gradually fly off into space; perhaps the tides will
cause the earth to turn always the same face to the sun, so that one hemi-
sphere will be too hot and the other too cold; perhaps (as in a moral tale by
J. B. S. Haldane) the moon will tumble into the earth. If none of these
things happen first, we shall in any case be all destroyed when the sun
explodes and becomes a cold white dwarf, which, we are told by Jeans, is to
happen in about a million million years, though the exact date is still
somewhat uncertain.

A million million years gives us some time to prepare for the end, and
we may hope that in the meantime both astronomy and gunnery will have
made considerable progress. The astronomers may have discovered another
star with inhabitable planets, and the gunners may be able to fire us off to
it with a speed approaching that of light, in which case, if the passengers
were all young to begin with, some might arrive before dying of old age. It
is perhaps a slender hope, but let us make the best of it.

Cruising round the universe, however, even if it is done with the most
perfect scientific skill, cannot prolong life forever. The second law of thermodynamics tells us that, on the whole, energy is always passing from
more concentrated to less concentrated forms, and that, in the end, it will
have all passed into a form in which further change is impossible. When
that has happened, if not before, life must cease. To quote Jeans once
more, "with universes as with mortals, the only possible life is progress to

the grave." This leads him to certain reflections which are very relevant to our theme:

> The three centuries which have elapsed since Giordano Bruno suffered martyrdom for believing in the plurality of worlds have changed our conception of the universe almost beyond description, but they have not brought us appreciably nearer to understanding the relation of life to the universe. We can still only guess as to the meaning of this life, which, to appearances, is so rare. Is it the final climax towards which the whole creation moves, for which the millions of millions of years of transformation of matter in uninhabited stars and nebulae, and of the waste of radiation in desert space, have been only an incredibly extravagant preparation? Or is it a mere accidental and possibly quite unimportant by-product of natural processes, which have some other and more stupendous end in view? Or, to glance at a still more modest line of thought, must we regard it as something of the nature of a disease, which affects matter in its old age when it has lost the high temperature and the capacity for generating high-frequency radiation with which younger and more vigorous matter would at once destroy life? Or, throwing humility aside, shall we venture to imagine that it is the only reality, which creates, instead of being created by, the colossal masses of the stars and nebulae and the almost inconceivably long vistas of astronomical time?

This, I think, states the alternatives, as presented by science, fairly and without bias. The last possibility, that mind is the only reality, and that the spaces and times of astronomy are created by it, is one for which, logically, there is much to be said. But those who adopt it, in the hope of escaping from depressing conclusions, do not quite realize what it entails. Everything that I know directly is part of my "mind," and the inferences by which I arrive at the existence of other things are by no means conclusive. It may be, therefore, that nothing exists except my mind. In that case, when I die the universe will go out. But if I am going to admit minds other than my own, I must admit the whole astronomical universe, since the evidence is exactly equally strong in both cases. Jeans's last alternative, therefore, is not the comfortable theory that other people's minds exist, though not their bodies; it is the theory that I am alone in an empty universe, inventing the human race, the geological ages of the earth, the sun and stars and nebulae, out of my own fertile imagination. Against this theory there is, so far as I know, no valid logical argument; but against any other form of the doctrine that mind is the only reality there is the fact that our evidence for other people's minds is derived by inference from our evidence for their bodies. Other people, therefore, if they have minds, have bodies; oneself alone may possibly be a disembodied mind, but only if oneself alone exists.

I come now to the last question in our discussion of cosmic purpose, namely: is what has happened hitherto evidence of the good intentions of the universe? The alleged ground for believing this, as we have seen, is that the universe has produced US. I cannot deny it. But are we really so splendid as to justify such a long prologue? The philosophers lay stress on values: they say that we think certain things good, and that since these things are good, we must be very good to think them so. But this is a circular argument. A being with other values might think ours so atrocious as to be proof that we were inspired by Satan. Is there not something a trifle absurd in the spectacle of human beings holding a mirror before themselves, and thinking what they behold so excellent as to prove that a cosmic purpose must have been aiming at it all along? Why, in any case, this glorification of man? How about lions and tigers? They destroy fewer animal or human lives than we do, and they are much more beautiful than we are. How about ants? They manage the corporate state much better than any Fascist. Would not a world of nightingales and larks and deer do better than our human world of cruelty and injustice and war? The believers in cosmic purpose make much of our supposed intelligence, but their writings make one doubt it. If I were granted omnipotence, and millions of years to experiment in, I should not think man much to boast of as the final result of all my efforts.

Man, as a curious accident in a backwater, is intelligible: his mixture of virtues and vices is such as might be expected to result from a fortuitous origin. But only abysmal self-complacency can see in man a reason which Omniscience could consider adequate as a motive for the Creator. The Copernican revolution will not have done its work until it has taught men more modesty than is to be found among those who think man sufficient evidence of cosmic purpose.

NOTES

1. As Dean Inge puts it: "We magnify the problem of evil by our narrow moralism, which we habitually impose upon the Creator. There is no evidence for the theory of God is a merely moral Being, and what we observe of His laws and operations here indicates strongly that He is not." *Outspoken Essays*, Vol. II, p. 24.

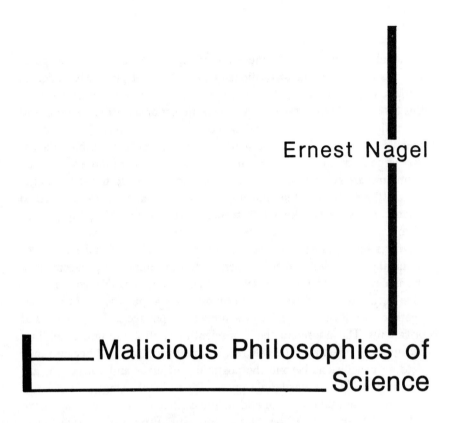

Ernest Nagel

Malicious Philosophies of Science

There is no substantial evidence for the widely held view that changes in the content and standards of theoretical inquiry are uniquely determined by changes in the economic and political structure of society. To be sure, scientific inquiries are often initiated and subsidized by those concerned with problems of commerce and technology, and the manner in which scientific discoveries are assimilated by a society depends on its economic and political organization. But once a department of inquiry establishes its traditions and workmanship, so the history of science seems to indicate, the course of subsequent developments in it is determined by the materials explored, by the talents and skills available, and by the logic of theoretical investigation.

In almost every age, however, the attitudes which men assume toward personal and social issues have often been justified by them in terms of their understanding of the methods and latest findings of science. Pro-

Reprinted with permission of Macmillan Publishing Company, Inc., from Sovereign Reason *by Ernest Nagel. Copyright 1954 by The Free Press.*

fessional scientists have frequently used their specialized knowledge to buttress or criticize the institutions of their day; but publicists, religious leaders, and philosophers have usually played a more prominent role in this task of evaluating the general social import of scientific methods and scientific theories. Such evaluations do not, in most cases, flow from the specific character of scientific methods or their technical achievements; they issue from the social and religious commitments of those who make them, and are symptomatic of the stresses and strains in the social scene.

In the midst of actual and impending disaster, men are inclined to listen to any voice speaking with sufficient authority; and during periods of social crisis, when rational methods of inquiry supply no immediate solutions for pressing problems, spokesmen for institutional and philosophic theologies find a ready audience for a systematic disparagement of the achievements of empirical science. Ideas which the advance of knowledge had partially driven underground during periods of fair social weather are then insolently proclaimed as panaceas for public and private ills. The assured methods of scientific control and understanding, because they effect no wholesale resolution of problems and because they yield no conclusions beyond the possibility of error and correction, are then declared to be unsuitable guides for rational living.

The mounting economic and political tensions of our own age have not failed to produce a literature of this type. From various quarters— from men of science, historians of ideas, as well as outspoken representatives of theological systems—there has come a flood of criticism of modern science and of the secular naturalism which has accompanied its growth. The criticism has been neither uniform nor consistent. But the common objective of much of it has been the limitation of the authority of science, and the institution of methods other than those of controlled experimentation for discovering the natures and values of things. Many recent evaluations of science have thus had an obviously malicious intent; and the present essay will seek to determine briefly to what extent, in the case of several influential types of philosophies of science, good sense has been sacrificed to such malice.

1

Undoubtedly the most solidly entrenched intellectual basis for the current disparagement of science is a well-known but nonetheless questionable theory of knowledge upon which experimental method is made to rest. This type of critique starts with the familiar fact that in many theories of the natural sciences, especially physics, the various sensory qualities (such as colors and sounds) receive no *explicit* mention, and that it is only the quantifiable traits of things (such as mass and length) which are noticed. The immediate conclusion which is then drawn is that sensory qualities are not properties of objects in their own right, but are dependent on the activity of an *immaterial mind*. The remainder of the argument may then proceed along either of two lines of interpretation. According to one of them, more common in earlier centuries than in our own, the traits studied by the natural sciences are the only genuinely real things, while the directly experienced qualities are only a passing appearance. The sights and sounds and smells of the human scene are thus taken to have only a "subjective" existence and to be the otiose by-products of the true executive order of nature. According to the second interpretation, currently highly fashionable, the qualities apprehended in daily experience are the concrete and exclusive reality. It is these qualities which are held to constitute the intrinsic natures of things; and since these qualities are allegedly psychic products, it is they which are regarded as the intelligible substance of the world. In putting to one side the qualitative character of existence the natural sciences are consequently preoccupied with shadowy abstractions, which have at best only a mean practical value; and the laws which are the outcome of scientific inquiry, far from expressing the true nature of things, fail to grasp and convey the dynamic reality of existence.

On either interpretation, therefore, the world is split into two discontinuous realms. One of them, the proper domain of natural science, is a "mysterious universe" forever foreign and essentially unintelligible to the common experience of mankind; the other, the locus of enjoyments and values, is the theater of the mind's activities and creations, and is the only reality in which mind can feel confidently at home. On either alternative, the human scene is endowed with character so distinctive that the procedures of the empirical sciences can provide no guide to it. For the controlled methods of experimentation are held to be relevant only to the realm of abstract quantity, so that the entire field of valuation, of deliberation and moral choice, is exempted from the norms of experimental inquiry. Qualitative reality, which by hypothesis has an inherent connection with mind and consciousness, must therefore be explored by techniques different from those employed in the positive sciences; and in this realm, claims to truth must be subjected to canons of a radically different kind. Imagination, intuition, introspection, and modes of emotional experience are some of the ways which have been recommended for grasping genuine reality and for understanding human affairs.[1]

Nevertheless, the actual character of scientific method offers warrant neither for such attempts to limit its authority, nor for the radical dualism of the qualitative and the quantitative, the mental and the physical, upon which those attempts thrive. A brief mention of some obvious features of experimental procedure will be sufficient to show how inadequate are the analyses on whose basis the authority of scientific method is impugned.

In the first place, however "abstract" scientific theories may be, those theories can be neither understood nor used except in contexts of familiar qualitative discriminations. These contexts are tacitly taken for granted in the explicit formulation of theories, and are neither ignored nor contemned by the practicing scientists. Consider, for example, some of the operations involved in even so elementary a process as the measurement of spatial magnitude: standards of magnitude must be constructed, requiring the use of familiar bodies of daily experience; the relative constancy of the standards must be established, thus necessitating the noting of qualitative changes such as temperature; and the mutual relations of bodies must be discriminated, thus involving the identification and distinction of bodies on the basis of such qualities as color and the texture of surfaces. In general, no metaphysical opposition between the qualitative and the quantitative is forced upon us in this process, since the institution of quantitative standards is simply the ordering and the discrimination of qualitative continua. The view that the subject-matter and the data of the physicist are opaque pointer-readings is clearly a falsification of the scientist's procedure—a falsification which becomes more evident the more thorough is our examination of the full spectrum of scientific operations.

In the second place, there can be no doubt that the colors, sounds, and other characteristics we perceive in our everyday affairs owe their existence not only to the objects they are commonly believed to qualify, but also to complicated mechanisms (including physiological ones) of which common sense is frequently unaware. But it does not follow that these qualities are therefore constituted out of some "mental stuff," or that a "mind" (in the sense of a disembodied, experimentally unidentifiable agent) is required for bringing them into existence. Whatever the conditions may be for the occurrence of colors, for example, experience shows extended *surfaces* to be colored; and if it is held that colors are "mental," traits (such as that of being extended) must be attributed to the mind which are the presumptive distinguishing marks of physical objects. In that case, however, what becomes of the notion of mind as a disembodied entity? But dialectic aside, there is no shred of evidence that in addition to complicated physico-organic processes any other "agents" are required to produce the qualitative manifolds of experience. The postulation of an additional agent (held to be something distinctively "mental") is on a par with the caprice of endowing the planets with souls in order to account for their motions. The actual procedures of the natural sciences thus offer no ground for the alleged dualism between the mental and the physical; and accordingly, even the semblance of a reason for limiting the scope of experimental techniques disappears.

And in the third place, the "abstractness" with which natural science is charged as a fatal weakness is in fact a trait of all cognition. All cognition involves the making of distinctions and the recognition of some things as relevant and others as not; in this sense, therefore, all cognition abstracts from its subject-matter and prescinds those features from it which bear on the problems at issue. To *know* the course of the planets is not to engage in periodic journeys around the sun; to *know* the factors and conditions of a human transaction is not the same as to participate in its joys and sorrows. More generally, it is not the function of knowledge to reproduce its own subject-matter; and to refuse to make abstractions of any sort is to abandon knowledge in favor of uninformed feeling and blind experience. Accordingly, just what is the quarrel of those critics who find fault with the abstractness of science? Do they seriously claim that the theories of science are not relevant to their subject-matters? Do they maintain that there are ways essentially different from and superior to those employed in the natural sciences for ascertaining the conditions for the occurrence of things and events? Or do they disdain science simply because it does not supply what no knowledge worthy of the name can offer—an unanalyzed reduplication of its own subject-matter? In either event, their discontent flows from a willful romanticism and a disregard of the historical achievements of the natural sciences; it provides no valid ground for excluding the operations of experimental inquiry from the domain of human affairs.

2

A second widespread critique of scientific methods is at bottom a variant of the one already considered. It does not *explicitly* disown the authority of science in human affairs; but it does recommend the adoption of such vague and irresponsible canons of experimental control that it in effect argues for the exclusion of the logical methods employed in the positive sciences from the study of social problems. This view rests its case on two major claims; that in the past the natural sciences have mistakenly tried to "reduce" all features of the world to "mechanical" or "materialistic" properties; and that recent advances in our knowledge have demonstrated the breakdown of the "mechanical" categories of classical science. The present view, like the previous one, maintains that the human scene is so discontinuous with the "lower levels" of nature that a common logic of inquiry cannot be adequate to all of them; it therefore concludes that problems affecting human destiny must be investigated on the basis of canons of validity and intelligibility which differ radically from those used in the natural sciences.

Let us examine these contentions. And first, what are we to understand by the terms "mechanical" and "materialistic"? When practicing physicists characterize an explanation as "mechanical," they mean a theory which, like the one developed by Galileo and Newton, explains a class of changes *entirely* on the basis of the masses and the spatial and temporal relations of bodies. In this quite precise sense of the word, Maxwell's electromagnetic theory is not a mechanical theory, and with its advent in the nineteenth century the earlier hope that the science of mechanics would become the universal science of nature was gradually abandoned. But those who accuse classical science of being "mechanical" are anything but so definite as to the real point of their charge. For according to them the Darwinian theory of organic evolution as well as Maxwell's theory of electromagnetism are mechanical, although neither of these theories satisfies the physicist's definition of "mechanical." The only clear meaning which can be given to the accusation is that classical science is *deterministic*—in the sense that it attempts to discover the precise conditions for the occurrence of phenomena, without benefit of final causes and without invoking experimentally unidentifiable causal agents.

But if this is the meaning of the charge, the claim that modern science no longer operates with mechanical categories is singularly ill-founded. As already noted, even classical physics recognized that mechanical theories (in the technical sense of the word) are not universally adequate; and recent researches into atomic phenomena have only fortified this conclusion. There is, however, nothing in modern research which requires the abandonment of the *generic* ideal of classical science: to find the determining conditions for the occurrence of phenomena, expressible in terms capable of overt empirical control. Thus, even modern quantum-theory—although it employs technical modes of specifying the character of physical systems which are different from those used in classical mechanics—is deterministic or mechanical (in the loose sense) in so far as it rigorously specifies the unique physical conditions under which certain types of changes will occur. Similarly, modern genetics is no less deterministic than the Darwinian theory, since the former, even more completely than the latter, has succeeded in disclosing the mechanisms or structures involved in the transmission of characteristics from one generation to another. It is therefore simply not true that recent advances in knowledge have demonstrated the untenability of the logical canons of classical science.

The claim that the world picture according to natural science "reduces" everything to blind, undifferentiated collocations of material particles, and thus fails to do justice to the distinctive traits of human behavior, likewise rests on a misconception as to what the sciences in fact accomplish. Consider, for example, the following comments of the late Lord Balfour:

> What are we to say about a universe reduced without remainder to collections of electric charges radiating throughout a hypothetical ether? . . . We can certainly act on our environment, and as certainly our actions can never be adequately explained in terms of entities which neither think, nor feel, nor purpose, nor know. It constitutes a spiritual invasion of the physical world:—it is a miracle. . . . We are spiritual beings, and must take account of spiritual values. The story of a man is something more than a mere continuation of the story of matter. It is different in kind.[2]

That this represents a caricature of what the achievements of physics imply will be evident if we recall that the sciences seek to determine the precise *conditions* under which events come into being and continue to exist. For in ascertaining those conditions the sciences do not *thereby deny* the existence of any traits found in nature, whether in the human scene or elsewhere. In particular, physics has assumed the task of finding the most general and pervasive constituents and circumstances of existing things; it does not legislate away as unreal or nonexistent—and could not do so without contradiction—the things and events into whose conditions of existence it inquires. The explanations which physics offers for the traits and changes it studies, consist of careful specifications of the conditions under which those traits and changes occur; and no other sense of "explanation" is relevant in discussing its findings. Whether these explanations can be stated entirely in terms of a special class of entities and their relations (for example, in terms of the distribution of electrically charged particles) is a specific empirical issue which can be resolved only by detailed empirical inquiry; it cannot be settled by dialectic, or by an a priori fiat such as that the living cannot be explained in terms of the non-living.

Criticisms of natural science such as the following are therefore altogether pointless, since they operate with mythological conceptions as to the character of its explanations: "With the faintest and simplest element of consciousness, natural science meets something for which it has no pigeon-hole anywhere in its system. . . . Mind at its best is autonomous. Granting that it is connected mysteriously and intimately with physical processes that natural science claims as its own, it cannot be reduced to those processes, nor can it be explained by the laws of those processes."[3]

Explanations of "mind" in terms of physical processes do not wipe out the distinction between the behavior of inorganic masses and the distinctive activities of men; nor do they pretend to deduce somehow the direction of those activities from physical laws containing no mention of purposive behavior. Such explanations simply state the generalized conditions for the occurrence of "mind." Accordingly, the only form of "reduction" with which the natural sciences may rightly be charged is the form which consists in ascertaining the structures under which specific traits are manifested; and it is clear that if those sciences failed in effecting such a reduction, they would fail in achieving the objective of knowledge. The conclusion seems unavoidable that those who would exclude the logical methods of the natural sciences from fields of social inquiry, on the score that these methods commit their users to the "reductive fallacy," are in effect recommending the abandonment of the quest for the causal determinants of human affairs.

One final claim, associated with the charge that the logic of natural science is "reductive," remains to be considered—the claim that human traits are "emergent properties" on a "higher level" of existence than are those with which physics and chemistry are concerned, so that the methods employed by these disciplines cannot be adequate to the study of the higher emergent qualities. Some examples will make clear the chief features of the theory of emergence. However much we may know about the interaction of hydrogen and oxygen with *other* elements, so it is said, it is impossible to infer from such knowledge the fact that they combine to form water; and in particular, the qualities which emerge when water is formed could never be predicted from those data. Similarly, no amount of knowledge concerning the physics and physiology of the human body makes it possible to deduce the "spiritual" characteristics of the organism as a thinking, purposive creature. Nature is thus conceived as a system of levels of emergence, each level requiring a peculiar mode of study; and a fortiori, the distinctive qualities of human beings can be satisfactorily explored and understood only when inquiry into them is conducted on the basis of a logic specific to "spiritual" subject matter.

But the following brief remarks will be sufficient to blunt whatever force the argument from the alleged facts of emergence may be supposed to have. It is indeed not possible to *deduce* the properties of water (for example, its transparency or its ability to quench thirst) from those of hydrogen and oxygen, *if* the former properties do not enter into the premises from which the deduction is attempted. For in general, no statement containing a given term P can be deduced from a class of statements unless the latter also contain that term. In one sense, therefore, the main contention of emergent evolution is simply a logical truism. In the second place, although the occurrence of certain traits may be left unexplained by one theory, a different theory (perhaps a revised form of the first one) may supply a satisfactory explanation. For example, the theories of physics which were accepted in the early nineteenth century were unable to account for any chemical facts, although present-day physics is in the position to explain the occurrence of many chemical reactions. Accordingly, whether a quality is to be regarded as an "emergent" or not is relative to a specific theory, and is not an *inherent* fact about that quality. It also follows that since no theory of science can be regarded as necessarily final, traits which at one time are taken to fall into the province of one specialized discipline, may at some later date be explained on the basis of theories developed in a different branch of science. This has certainly been the history of such sciences as chemistry, biology, and even psychology, in their relation to physics. And finally, if the doctrine of emergence is seen in this light, no clear reasons remain why the logic of experimental inquiry—as conducted in the natural sciences—has no authority over investigations into human affairs. Indeed, as the natural sciences have become more comprehensive they have provided an enriched understanding of human traits. No theoretical limits can be set to such a progressively widening scope of the sciences of nature. And what is no less to the point, these fresh achievements have involved no surrender, on the part of the natural sciences, of the procedural principles under whose guidance they obtained their historical successes.

3

The views which have been noticed thus far attempt to limit the scope of scientific methods on the basis of considerations that are at least nominally scientific in character. The criticisms of science to which attention must next be directed do not even pretend to adduce scientific grounds for their claims, and are frankly based upon explicit theological and metaphysical commitments for which no experimental evidence is invoked. The chief burden of their complaints is that science offers no "ultimate explanation" for the facts of existence; and their chief recommendation is the cultivation of "ontological wisdom" as the sole method for making "ultimately intelligible" both the order of the cosmos and the nature of the good life.

Some citations from recent writers will exhibit more clearly than would a paraphrase the unique mixture of pontifical dogmatism, oracular wisdom, and condescending obscurantism which seems to be the indispensable intellectual apparatus of this school of criticism. Professor Gilson characterizes the plight of science as follows:

> This world of ours is a world of change; physics, chemistry, biology can teach us the laws according to which change actually happens to it; what these sciences cannot teach us is why this world, taken together with its laws, its order, and its intelligibility is, or exists. . . . Scientists never ask themselves *why* things happen, but *how* they happen. Now as soon as you substitute the positivist's notion of relation for the metaphysical notion of cause, you at once lose all right to wonder *why* things are, and why they are what they are. . . . Why anything at all is, or exists, science knows not, precisely because it cannot even ask the question. To this supreme question the only answer is that each and every particular existential energy, and each and every particular existing thing depends for its existence upon a pure Act of existence. In order to be the ultimate answer to all existential problems, this supreme cause has to be absolute existence. Being absolute, such a cause is self-sufficient; if it creates, its creative act must be free. Since it creates not only being but order, it must be something which at least eminently contains the only principle of order known to us in experience, namely, thought.[4]

And Professor Maritain, building on the alleged subordination of science to metaphysics, indicates some of the immediate consequences of this hierarchial arrangement:

> Science . . . is distinguished from wisdom in this, that science aims at the detail of some special field of knowing and deals with the secondary,

proximate or apparent causes, while wisdom aims at some universal knowing and deals with prime and deepest causes, with the highest sources of being. . . . Wisdom is not only distinct from but also superior to science, in the sense that its object is more universal and more deeply immersed in the mystery of things, and in the sense that the function of defending the first principles of knowledge and of discovering the fundamental structure and organization thereof belongs to wisdom, not to science. . . . Science puts means in man's hands, and teaches men how to apply these means for the happiest outcome, not for him who acts, but for the work to be done. Wisdom deals with ends in man's heart, and teaches man how to use means and apply science for the real goodness and happiness of him who acts, of the person himself. . . . Science is like art in this, that though both are good in themselves man can put them to bad uses and bad purposes; while in so far as man uses wisdom . . . he can only use it for good purposes.

The paleontologist does not step out of his sphere when he establishes the hypothesis of evolution and applies it to the origin of the human being. But the philosopher must warn him that he is out of his field when he tries to deny for that reason that the human soul is a spiritual soul which cannot emanate from matter, so that if once upon a time the human organism was produced by a mutation of an animal organism, it was because of the infusion of a soul created by God.[5]

Although criticism of a position is futile when those who hold it make a virtue of its mysteries and when they regard themselves as superior to the usual canons of scientific intelligibility, those who are not so fortunately placed may find the following observations not irrelevant. In the first place, there is a perfectly clear sense in which science does supply answers as to "why" things happen and are what they are. Thus, if we ask why the moon becomes eclipsed at certain times, the answer is that at those times the moon moves into the earth's shadow; if we ask why the moon behaves in this way, the answer is given in part by the theory of gravitation; if we ask why bodies behave in the manner predicated by this theory, the answer is supplied by the general theory of relativity. On the other hand, if we repeat this question concerning relativity theory, no further answer is at present forthcoming, so that for the present at least this theory is an "ultimate" or "brute" fact. Furthermore, if some day relativity theory should become absorbed into a unified field-theory embracing both macroscopic and microscopic phenomena, the unified field-theory would explain why the equations of relativity theory hold, but at the same time it would become the (perhaps only temporary) "ultimate" structural fact. In science the answer to the question "why" is therefore always a theory, from which the specific fact at issue may be deduced when suitable initial conditions are introduced. The point of these familiar remarks is that no matter how far the question "why" is pressed—and it may be pressed indefinitely—it must terminate in a theory which is itself not logically demonstrable. For no theory which explains why things happen as they do and not otherwise can be a logically necessary truth. It follows that those who seek to discern the laws of nature to be necessary, as well as those who "hope to see that it is necessary that there should be an order of nature," are violating an elementary canon of discursive thought.

In the second place, it is obvious that anyone who invokes an "absolute cause" (or God) to explain "why" the world exists, merely postpones settling his accounts with the logic of his question: for the Being who has been postulated as the Creator of the world is simply one more being into the reasons of whose existence it is possible to inquire. If those who invoke such a Being declare that such questions about His existence are not legitimate, they surmount a difficulty only by dogmatically cutting short a discussion when the intellectual current runs against them. If, on the other hand, the question is answered with the assertion that God is his own cause, the question is resolved only by falling back upon another mystery; and at best, such a "reason" is simply an unclear statement of the grounds upon which scientists regard as unintelligible the *initial* "why" as to the world's existence. But a mystery is no answer if the question to which it is a reply has a definite meaning; and in the end, nothing is gained in the way of intellectual illumination when the discussion terminates in such a manner.

In the third place, the postulation of an "absolute cause" or an "ultimate reason" for the world and its structure provides no answer to any *specific* question which may be asked concerning any particular objects or events in the world. On the contrary, no matter what the world were like, no matter what the course of events might be, the same Ultimate Cause is offered as an "explanation." This is admitted in so many words by Professor Gilson: "The existence or non-existence of God . . . is a proposition whose negation or affirmation determines no change whatever in the structure of our scientific explanation of the world and is wholly independent of the contents of science as such. Supposing, for instance, there be design in the world, the existence of God cannot be posited as a *scientific* explanation for the presence of design in the world; it is a *metaphysical* one."[6]

But just what does an "explanation" explain when it explains nothing in particular? What understanding of our world does a metaphysics provide which is compatible both with a design in the processes of nature as well as with its absence, with the existence of specific goods as well as with their nonexistence, with one pervasive pattern of causal interactions as well as with another? A high price in unintelligibility must be paid when the canons of scientific discourse and inquiry are abandoned.

And finally, the assumption that there is a superior and more direct way of grasping the secrets of the universe than the painfully slow road of science has been so repeatedly shown to be a romantic illusion, that only those who are unable to profit from the history of the human intellect can seriously maintain it. Certainly, whatever enlightenment we possess about ourselves and the world has been achieved only after the illusion of a "metaphysical wisdom" superior to "mere science" had been abandoned. The methods of science do not guarantee that its conclusions are final and incorrigible by further inquiry; but it is by dropping the pretense of a spurious finality and recognizing the fallibility of its self-corrective procedures that science has won its victories. It may be a comfort to some to learn that in so far as man uses "wisdom" he can aim only at the good; since the most diverse kinds of action—kindly as well as brutal, beneficent as well as costly in human life—are undertaken in the name of wisdom, such a testimonial will doubtless enable everyone engaged in such an undertaking to redouble his zeal without counting the costs. But it is not wisdom but a mark of immaturity to recommend that we simply examine our hearts if we wish to discover the good life; for it is just because men rely so completely and unreflectively on their intuitive insights and passionate impulses that needless sufferings and conflicts occur among them. The point is clear: claims as to what is required by wisdom need to be adjudicated if such claims are to be warranted; and accordingly, objective methods must be instituted, on the basis of which the conditions, the consequences, and the mutual compatibility of different courses of action may be established. But if such methods are introduced, we leave the misasmal swamps of supra-scientific wisdom, and are brought back again to the firm soil of scientific knowledge.

4

The final variety of current criticism of science to be considered rests its case on the alleged facts of history. The development of science, it is admitted, has brought with it an increase in material power, a broadening of the average span of human life, and a wider distribution of innumerable goods than was possible in earlier days. Nevertheless, so the criticism runs, human happiness has not increased and the quality of life has not improved. On the contrary, increased power over material nature has generated a deadening monotony and uniformity in men's lives, has produced ghastly brutalities, cataclysmic wars, and fierce superstitions, and has undermined personal and social security. Science deals with instrumentalities and is incapable of determining values; and with the spread of secular naturalism and the consequent decline of religious influences, men have grown insensitive to the distinction between good and evil, and have identified material success with ethical excellence. Intellectual historians join hands with preachers and publicists in placing the blame for contemporary Fascism upon the demoralizing effects of positivistic philosophy. And in language solemn and threatening Professor Maritain warns his readers of the dreadful consequences which allegedly flow from scientific naturalism: "Let us not delude ourselves; an education in which the sciences of phenomena and the corresponding techniques take precedence over philosophical and theological knowledge is already, potentially, a Fascist education; an education in which biology, hygiene and eugenics provide the supreme criteria of morality is already, potentially, a Fascist education." [7]

Whatever may be the validity of the causal imputations contained in such criticism, it cannot be denied, unfortunately, that many of its characterizations of modern society are well founded; it is certainly not the intent of the following comments to dispute them. It must nevertheless be noted that the implied judgment, according to which the quality of modern life is inferior to that of earlier societies unburdened by an institutionalized natural science, is based on a definite set of preferences or values in terms of which human history is surveyed. But while it is clear that there is nothing reprehensible in employing definite standards of valuation (for example, such as are involved in Catholic Christianity), such standards need to be made explicit and should not be assumed as self-evident and above criticism. For it is sheer dogmatism to assume that only one conception of spiritual excellence is valid; and it is the height of discourtesy and parochialism to damn a society as immoral simply because its standards of excellence differ from one's own. Moreover, comparative judgments as to the happiness of men are notoriously untrustworthy, unless they are based upon objective measures of well-being. And if the material conditions of life are discounted as indications of "true" happiness, the critic's evaluations of different cultures are a better guide to his own preferences and loyalties than to the ostensible subject matter of his judgment.

Let us turn to the causal imputations contained in the criticism under consideration. Almost no argument is required to show that if the growth of science may validly be held responsible for the ills of modern society, then the fact that men marry may no less validly be declared the cause of the evils of divorce. For surely, divorce would be impossible unless men first married, just as our present social distresses would not exist unless the advance of scientific knowledge had first made possible our present institutional structures. But to convert marriage into the cause of divorce, and the advance of secular knowledge into the cause of social ills, is to convert the *context* in which problems arise into an *agent* responsible for our inability to master them. As well argue that in order to eliminate the evils of divorce men must stop getting married, as recommend the de-secularization of modern society as a solution for its difficulties; in either case the conversion of context into cause is an unintelligent performance. The development of science has brought with it new opportunities for the exercise of human energies, and has helped set the stage for the emergence of new problems. How many of these problems have remained unsolved because vested interests and the cake of custom have prevented the application to them of the methods of controlled inquiry which the natural sciences use so successfully, it is difficult to judge. But in any event, the indictment of scientific intelligence as solely responsible for our present difficulties not only involves an arbitrary selection of one factor from a complex of others distinguishable in the social scene; it arbitrarily rejects the one instrument from which a resolution of these difficulties may reasonably be expected.

Consider, finally, the charge that science "cannot determine values," and that therefore the apprehension of the elements of a good life must be obtained through some form of emotional experience. Now whatever be one's views as to the nature of values—whether they are regarded as relative or absolute, dependent on human preferences or not—it must be admitted that a science (such as astronomy) which does not concern itself with values and which does not contain value-terms in its vocabulary, is incompetent to establish value judgments. The thesis that *some* sciences cannot determine values is thus trivially true. On the other hand, every rational appraisal of values must take cognizance of the findings of the natural and social sciences; for if the existential conditions and consequences of the realization of values are not noted, acceptance of a scheme of values is a species of undisciplined romanticism. Accordingly, unless values are to be affirmed on the basis of uncontrolled intuition and impulse, all the elements of scientific analysis—observation, imaginative reconstruction, dialectic elaboration of hypotheses, and experimental verification—must be employed. Knowledge of biology and hygiene are indeed not sufficient for an adequate conception of the moral life; but if one may judge from the historical functions of some philosophic and theologic ideas in perpetuating economic inequality and human slavery, and in sanctioning the brutal shedding of human blood, neither is a knowledge of philosophy and theology.

It is often urged that what is good for man lies outside the province of scientific method, because the determination of human goods requires a sympathetic understanding of the human heart and a sensitive, individualized perception of the qualities of human personality; and the exercise of such powers, it is maintained, has no place in the procedures of science. But this objection rests, at bottom, on a failure to distinguish between the psychological and sociological conditions under which ideas originate, and the validity of those ideas. Thus, it is reported of Schiller that he used to place a rotting apple on his desk for the stimulus the odor of the fruit provided to his writing; but while this is an interesting item about the conditions under which Schiller obtained his inspirations, it has no bearing on the issue as to quality of his poetry. Similarly, the unusual circumstances —whether personal or social—under which many seers and religious prophets obtained their visions are not relevant in a consideration of the soundness of their moral exhortations. More generally, the psychology and the sociology of research are not identical with its logic. Those who disparage the application of scientific methods to the evaluation of human goods, on the ground that those methods exclude the exercise of a sympathetic imagination, are not only mistaken in their factual allegations; they are also well on the road to identifying the sheer vividness and the emotional overtones of ideas with their validity.

NOTES

1. Two citations from recent writers will help convey the flavor of the alternative methods which have been proposed.

"Imagination is more adequate to reality than reason, for reality is not rational; therefore poetry and religion are better adapted to the real than the sciences. The real is not abstract and general. It is always concrete and individual; that is the reason why imagination alone can grasp it, whereas the intellect cannot fully conceive it. A theory of imagination . . . is urgently needed as a foundation for ethics, esthetics, philosophy of history and of religion, and even for metaphysics." (Richard Kroner, in a paper read before the Third Conference on Science, Philosophy and Religion, as quoted in *The New York Times,* August 29, 1942.)

"It is an axiom of sound method that any experience is, in some manner and to some degree, *intrinsically* cognitive. An experience of love . . . is at the same time an insight into the loveable nature of what is loved; an experience of moral urgency . . . is an insight into the rightness of the action to be performed; an experience of reverence . . . is an insight into the divinity of what is reverenced. Every such experience is a growth in wisdom and the wisdom is not testable by scientific techniques. . . . " (Philip Wheelwright, "Religion and Social Grammar," *The Kenyon Review,* vol. 4 [1942], pp. 203-4.)

2. Arthur J. Balfour, in an essay contributed to *Science, Religion and Reality* (ed. by Joseph Needham), pp. 15-17.

3. Brand Blanshard, "Fact, Value, and Science," in *Science and Man* (edited by Ruth Nanda Anshen), pp. 189, 203.

4. Etienne Gilson, *God and Philosophy,* pp. 72, 140. Although Whitehead's manner of arriving at his speculative cosmology is radically different from that cultivated by neo-Thomists, his evaluations of the limitations of natural science are frequently not dissimilar. He comments as follows on "the grand doctrine of Nature as a self-sufficient, meaningless complex of facts": "Newton left for empirical investigation the determination of the particular stresses now existing. In this determination he made a magnificent beginning by isolating the stresses indicated by his law of gravitation. But he left no hint, *why in the nature of things there should be any stresses at all.* The arbitrary motion of the bodies were thus explained by the arbitrary stresses between material bodies, conjoined with their spatiality, their mass, and their initial states of motion. By introducing stresses—in particular the law of gravitation—instead of the welter of detailed transformations of motion, he greatly increased the systematic aspect of nature. But he left all the factors of the system—more particularly, mass and stress—in the position of detached facts *devoid of reason* for their compresence. He thus illuminated a great philosophic truth, that a dead nature can give no reasons. All the ultimate reasons are in terms of aim at value. A dead nature aims at nothing." A. N. Whitehead, *Modes of Thought,* pp. 183-84, italics not in the text.

5. The first paragraph is taken from the essay "Science and Wisdom," contained in *Science and Man,* pp. 66-7, 72, 94. The second paragraph is from the essay "Science, Philosophy and Faith," contained in the volume *Science, Philosophy and Religion,* the proceedings of the First Conference on Science, Philosophy and Religion, p. 181.

6. Gilson, *God and Philosophy,* p. 141.

7. In the essay "Science, Philosophy and Faith," *op. cit.,* p. 182. Neo-Thomists have no monopoly in the making of such casual imputations. Thus, in his essay "Fact and Value in Social Science," Professor Frank Knight writes as follows: "In the field of social policy, the pernicious notion of instrumentalism, resting on the claim or assumption of a parallelism between social and natural science is actually

one of the most serious of the sources of danger which threaten destruction to the values of what we have called civilization. . . . It is a serious reflection that the unsatisfactory state of affairs in social science has largely resulted from the very progress of science. . . . " *Science and Man* (ed. by Ruth Nanda Anshen), pp. 325-26.

Bibliography

Angeles, Peter A. *The Problem of God: A Short Introduction.* Columbus, Ohio: Charles E. Merrill Publishing Company, 1974. Paperback.

Ayer, A. J. *Language, Truth and Logic.* 2d ed. New York: Dover Publications, Inc., 1946. Paperback.

Baier, Kurt. *The Meaning of Life.* Inaugural lecture delivered at the Canberra University College on October 15, 1957. Canberra: Government Printer, 1957.

Blackham, H. J., ed. *Objections to Humanism.* Philadelphia: Lippincott, 1963.

Blanshard, Paul. *Classics of Free Thought.* Buffalo, N.Y.: Prometheus Books, 1976. Paperback.

Bradlaugh, Charles. *Charles Bradlaugh—Champion of Liberty.* London: Watts & Co., 1933.

Cohen, Morris R. *A Dreamer's Journey.* Boston: Beacon Press, 1949.

Darrow, Clarence. *The Story of My Life.* New York: Charles Scribner's Sons, 1932.

———. *Verdicts out of Court.* Edited by Arthur and Lila Weinberg. New York: Quadrangle Books, 1963.

Dewey, John. *A Common Faith.* New Haven: Yale University Press, 1960. Paperback.

Ducasse, C. J. *A Philosophical Scrutiny of Religion.* New York: The Ronald Press Company, 1953.

Flew, Antony. *A New Approach to Psychical Research.* London: C. A. Watts & Co., Ltd., 1953. Paperback.

———. *God and Philosophy*. New York: Dell Publishing Co., Inc., 1966. Paperback.

Flew, Antony, and MacIntyre, Alasdair, eds. *New Essays in Philosophical Theology*. London: Student Christian Movement Press. New York: Macmillan, 1955. Paperback.

Freud, Sigmund. *The Future of an Illusion*. Translated by W. D. Robson-Scott. Garden City, N.Y.: Doubleday Anchor Books, 1957. Paperback.

———. *Moses and Monotheism*. Translated by Katherine Jones. London: Hogarth Press, 1939. Paperback.

———. *Totem and Taboo*. London: Hogarth Press, 1955. Paperback.

Fromm, Eric. *Psychoanalysis and Religion*. New Haven: Yale University Press, 1959. Paperback.

Hawton, Hector. *Controversy: The Humanist-Christian Encounter*. Buffalo, N.Y.: Prometheus Books, 1975. Paperback.

Hepburn, Ronald. *Christianity and Paradox*. New York: Humanities Press, 1958.

Hook, Sidney. *The Quest for Being*. New York: St. Martin's Press, 1961.

———, ed. *Religious Experience and Truth*. New York: New York University Press, 1961. Paperback.

Huxley, Julian. *Religion Without Revelation*. Revised edition. New York: New American Library, 1958. Paperback.

Huxley, T. H. *Science and the Christian Tradition*. New York: Appleton & Company, 1894.

Ingersoll, Robert G. *The Gods, and Other Lectures*. Washington, D.C.: C. P. Farrell, 1882.

———. *Lectures and Essays*. London: Watts, 1904-1905.

———. *The Philosophy of Ingersoll*. Edited by V. Goldthwaite. New York: P. Elder, 1906.

Kaufmann, Walter. *Critique of Religion and Philosophy*. New York: Harper & Row, 1958. Paperback.

———. *The Faith of a Heretic*. Garden City, N.Y.: Doubleday, 1961. Paperback.

Knight, Margaret. *Honest to Man: Christian Ethics Re-examined*. Buffalo, N.Y.: Prometheus Books, 1976.

Kolenda, Konstantin. *Religion Without God*. Buffalo, N.Y.: Prometheus Books, 1976.

Kurtz, Paul, and Dondeyne, Albert, eds. *A Catholic/Humanist Dialogue*. Buffalo, N.Y.: Prometheus Books, 1975. Paperback.

Lamont, Corliss. *The Illusion of Immortality*. New York: Frederick Ungar Publishing Co., 1965.

———. *The Philosophy of Humanism*. New York: Frederick Ungar Publishing Co., Inc., 1965.

MacIntyre, Alasdair. *Difficulties in Christian Belief*. London: Student Christian Movement Press, 1959.

———. *Metaphysical Beliefs*. London: Student Christian Movement Press, 1957.

Macy, Christopher, ed. *Science, Reason, and Religion*. Buffalo, N.Y.: Prometheus Books, 1975.

Madden, Edward H., with Hare, P. H. *Evil and the Concept of God*. Springfield,

Ill.: American Lecture Series, 1968. A monograph in the Bannerstone Division of American Lectures in Philosophy.

Martin, C. B. *Religious Belief.* Ithaca, N.Y.: Cornell University Press, 1959.

Maslow, Abraham. *Religions, Values and Peak Experiences.* New York: Viking Press, 1975. Paperback.

Matson, Wallace I. *The Existence of God.* Ithaca, N.Y.: Cornell University Press, 1965. Paperback.

McCloskey, H. J. *God and Evil.* The Hague, The Netherlands: Martinus Nijhoff, 1974.

McPherson, Thomas. *The Philosophy of Religion.* London: D. Van Nostrand Co., Ltd., 1965. Paperback.

Mencken, H. L. *Treatise on the Gods.* New York: Vintage Books, 1958.

Mitchell, Basil, ed. *Faith and Logic.* Boston: Beacon Press, 1957.

Nagel, Ernest. *Sovereign Reason.* Glencoe, Ill.: The Free Press, 1954.

Nielsen, Kai. *Contemporary Critiques of Religion.* New York: Herder and Herder, Inc., 1971.

———. *Scepticism.* New York: St. Martin's Press, 1973.

———. *Ethics Without God.* Buffalo, N.Y.: Prometheus Books, 1973. Paperback.

———. "In Defense of Atheism," In *Perspectives in Education, Religion, and the Arts,* edited by Howard E. Kiefer and Milton Munitz. Albany: State University of New York Press, 1970, pp. 127-56.

———. "Religion and Commitment," In *Religious Language and Knowledge,* edited by Robert Hyman Ayers and William T. Blackstone. Athens: University of Georgia Press, 1972.

Otto, Max. *The Human Enterprise.* New York: F. S. Crofts & Co., 1940.

Robinson, Richard. *An Atheist's Values.* London: Oxford University Press, 1964.

Russell, Bertrand, *Mysticism and Logic:* London: G. Allen and Unwin, 1949. Paperback.

———. *Religion and Science.* London: Oxford University Press, 1935. Paperback.

———. *The Scientific Outlook.* Glencoe, Ill.: The Free Press, 1940. Paperback.

———. *Why I Am Not a Christian.* Edited with an appendix on the Bertrand Russell case by Paul Edwards. London: George Allen and Unwin, Ltd., 1957.

Scriven, Michael. *Primary Philosophy.* New York: McGraw-Hill Book Co., 1966.

Sellars, Roy Wood. *The Next Step in Religion.* New York: The Macmillan Co., 1918.

Stace, Walter T. *Religion and the Modern Mind.* Philadelphia: J. P. Lippincott Co., 1960. Paperback.

Thrower, James. *A Short History of Western Atheism.* Buffalo, N.Y.: Prometheus Books, 1975.

Twain, Mark. *Letters from the Earth.* Edited by Bernard De Voto. Greenwich, Conn.: Fawcett Publications, Inc., 1962.